Heaven Is Empty

SUNY series in Chinese Philosophy and Culture
Roger T. Ames, editor

Heaven Is Empty

A CROSS-CULTURAL APPROACH TO "RELIGION" AND EMPIRE IN ANCIENT CHINA

FILIPPO MARSILI

Cover image of the Chinese Terracotta Warriors from iStockphoto.

Published by State University of New York Press, Albany

© 2018 State University of New York

All rights reserved

No part of this book may be used or reproduced in any manner whatsoever without written permission. No part of this book may be stored in a retrieval system or transmitted in any form or by any means including electronic, electrostatic, magnetic tape, mechanical, photocopying, recording, or otherwise without the prior permission in writing of the publisher.

For information, contact State University of New York Press, Albany, NY
www.sunypress.edu

Library of Congress Cataloging-in-Publication Data

Names: Marsili, Filippo, author.
Title: Heaven is empty : a cross-cultural approach to "religion" and empire in ancient China / Filippo Marsili.
Description: Albany : State University of New York Press, [2018] | Series: SUNY series in Chinese philosophy and culture | Includes bibliographical references and index.
Identifiers: LCCN 2017059913 | ISBN 9781438472010 (hardcover : alk. paper) | ISBN 9781438472027 (pbk. : alk. paper) | ISBN 9781438472034 (ebook)
Subjects: LCSH: China—Religion—History. | China—Religious life and customs. | China—History—221 B.C.–960 A.D. | Han Wudi, Emperor of China, 156 B.C.–87 B.C. | China—Kings and rulers—Religious aspects—History.
Classification: LCC BL1825 .M37 2018 | DDC 299.5/1—dc23
LC record available at https://lccn.loc.gov/2017059913

10 9 8 7 6 5 4 3 2 1

Do you have Chinese ghosts? Millions. Said Lee.
We have more ghosts than anything else.
I guess nothing in China ever dies. It's very crowded.

                                    —John Steinbeck, *East of Eden**

See, in these silences when things let themselves go and seem almost
to reveal their final secret, we sometimes expect to discover a flaw in
    Nature,
the world's dead point, the link that doesn't hold, the thread that,
disentangled, might at last lead us to the center of a truth . . .
These are the silences where we see in each departing human shade
some disturbed Divinity.

                        —Eugenio Montale, "The Lemon Trees"**

---

*John Steinbeck, *East of Eden* (New York: The Viking Press, 1952), 261.
**Eugenio Montale, "The Lemon Trees," in *Cuttlefish Bones*, trans. William Arrowsmith (New York, W. W. Norton, 1992), 7; the original Italian poem is in Eugenio Montale, "I Limoni," in *Ossi di seppia* (Milano: Mondadori, 1948), 10.

Contents

Acknowledgments	ix
Author's Note	xi
Introduction: An Empire without a "Religion"	1
1. Readings of the "Sacred": Chinese Religion, Chinese Religions, and Religions in China	23
2. Writing the Empire: *Ex Pluribus Plurima*	59
3. Narrating the Empire: Metaphysics without God, "Religions" without Identity	101
4. Time, Myth, and Memory: Of Water, Metal, and Cinnabar	135
5. Place and Ritual: From *Templum* to Text	173
Conclusions: The Importance of Getting Lost	209
Notes	217
Bibliography	289
Index	321

Acknowledgments

This book has been conceived and written throughout a long process and in different places. Innumerable teachers, colleagues, and friends made it possible with their help, encouragement, and example, and I hope I can at least duly acknowledge some of them here. Of course, the shortcomings, mistakes, and oversights are all mine.

The advice and support I received at Saint Louis University's Department of history in the past few years from Phil Gavitt, Charles (Hal) Parker, Damian Smith, Torrie Hester, Mark Ruff, Silvana Siddali, Jennifer Popiel, Lorri Glover, Flannery Burke, Douglas Boin, Luke Yarbrough, Claire Gilbert, and Fabien Montcher have been both fundamental and heartwarming. I also am particularly grateful to Thomas Madden, Michal Rozbicki, and David Borgmeyer, whose contributions, respectively as heads of the Centers for Medieval and Renaissance Studies, Intercultural Studies, and International Studies went beyond their individual generosity. Fellow Sinologist Pauline Lee of the Department of Theology has been crucial in helping me refine themes and arguments in my manuscript and for getting me acquainted with the latest developments of American scholarship on history of religions.

Christopher Ahn and Diane Ganeles of SUNY Press followed me with professionalism and patience making my first editorial experience with a monograph both instructive and pleasant. I am also grateful to the three anonymous readers for their precious comments and advice.

Among all the friends and colleagues who accompanied me during different phases of my project, I thank Rebecca Wanzo, Colin Burnett, Tobias Zürn, Jacqui Shine, Srdjan Smajic, Nicole Eaton, Victoria Smolkin, Wenshing Chou and Margaret Tillman for making the arguments, structure, and prose of the book much more effective (and tolerable) than they might have been otherwise.

Special words of gratitude are due to Miranda Brown, without whose thoughtful advice and graciousness *Heaven is Empty* would not have been possible, and David Spafford, who, as a mentor, colleague and friend, has inspired and helped me in so many ways over two decades that it would be impossible to provide an exhaustive account here.

I shall never be grateful enough to Professor Michael Loewe, who after a long day of conferences was so kind to spend his dinner time casting light on many questions I had on Emperor Wu of the Han.

As for my time as a graduate student at University of California, Berkeley, many are the teachers to whom I am intellectually and personally indebted. Michael Nylan painstakingly guided me from the confusion on my early days in the U.S. through the early phases of an academic profession in Han studies. David Johnson, in addition to introducing me to the richness of Chinese popular culture, provided invaluable feedback on my final manuscript. By pointing out structural analogies between Chinese and Greco-Roman historiography, Carlos Noreña was the first to encourage me on the path of comparative history. Erich Gruen, Mary Elizabeth Berry, and Patricia Berger still represent models of intellectual rigor and compassion that one day I hope to emulate as a teacher and scholar. I am also thankful the Department of History, the Center for East Asian Studies, the Haas and Quinn foundations, and to Jennifer Nelson of the Robbins Collection at UC Berkeley for supporting me at different stages of my project.

Among the teachers I had in Italy, I am especially grateful to Paola Nardella, Claudia Santi, Corrado Pensa, Arcangela Santoro, as well as the late Piero Corradini, Daniela Tozzi Giuli, and Paolo Daffinà who, in different roles and at different institutions, passionately introduced me to historical and cultural aspects of the ancient civilizations of the Mediterranean and of Inner and East Asia. A special mention goes to Chiara Peri of the Jesuit Refugee Service in Rome, where, as a volunteer, I started to grapple with the many aspects of the thorny question of interculturality.

I finally thank my families in Italy and Taiwan and my wife Lidan for the unconditioned love and support showed throughout this long process.

Filippo Marsili
Taipei, July 2018

Author's Note

Heaven is Empty addresses theoretical questions that are of interest to the broader readership of world history and history of religions. I have therefore decided to depart from customary practice in Sinological studies and move the original Chinese passages that form the basis of my arguments from the body of the text. The interested reader will find the passages, along with their related philological questions, in the endnotes.

Introduction

An Empire without a "Religion"

> I heard a saying that "he who knows the "heaven" of Heaven may make himself a king, but he who does not have this knowledge may not. To the king the people are Heaven, whereas to the people food is Heaven.
>
> —Li Yiji, "The Mad Scholar"[1]

Monotheisms and Globalizations

In the past few decades, discussions on the role of religion in shaping the interconnections of politics, society, and culture have acquired a particular urgency. Since the end of the Cold War, after 9/11, and even more so with the surge of IS, religion has come to occupy a central position in discourses on the most sensitive aspects of globalization.[2] Popular media, public intellectuals, and academics regularly address religion either as the main cause of conflict or as the potential basis for a harmonious intercultural dialogue. In either case, most analyses tend to reify religion as if it were an independent historical subject endowed with agency, and—more or less explicitly—regard it as the foundation stone of collective cultural identities. In other words, once it is redefined more broadly as an essential component of "culture," religion constitutes a pivotal factor in the study of group attitudes toward politics and institutions, social distinctions, economic behaviors, gender relations, and sexuality. These ideas are so ingrained in Mediterranean and Euro-American worldviews that even openly secular or atheist authors tend to articulate their arguments within ethical and epistemological parameters that reflect the unitary and totalizing bias of monotheism.[3]

Turning to the comparative study of ancient civilizations, the recent surge of China as a world power has prompted a new generation of scholars of antiquities to juxtapose Augustan Rome (27 BCE–14 CE) and Qin-Han China (221 BCE–220 CE) as two crucial phases in the trajectories of Western and Eastern civilizations.[4] Their projects have demonstrated that institutional and economic analyses based on quantitative data allow for a deeper understanding of political and economic centralization across the globe.[5] However, the empirical orientation that traditionally characterizes philological and historical scholarship has so far prevented these studies from engaging the postmodern and postcolonial critique of the validity of "religion" as a cross-cultural heuristic category.[6] Such an oversight, together with the adoption of Augustan Rome as a universal template for the examination of ancient empires, perpetuates the conceit that political unification must be based on a shared religion or unitary conception of the sacred. As a result, specialists and the general public alike still tend to assume the systemic, identitary, and moralistic interpretation of world religions that characterize modernity as timeless and intrinsic to the very notion of the divine.

Heaven Is Empty argues that unified rule is possible without cultural unification, and that cultural unification is possible without a shared religion. By offering a radical reinterpretation of the meaning of the "sacred" in Early China, I propose a novel approach to the study of the role of "religious" beliefs and practices in forging institutions and identities in the ancient and contemporary world. My research engages the fields of history of religion, world and intellectual history, sinology, and classics. In reconstructing the crucial political and cultural battles that shaped China in the period of unification under the Qin and Han empires (221 BCE–220 CE), it questions the teleological, unitary, and identitary preoccupations that have driven indigenous and foreign scholarly theorizations of religion in ancient China since the end of the nineteenth century.[7] More specifically, this study challenges the indiscriminate application to the Qin and Han periods of conceptual categories developed in the study of Greco-Roman and organized religions and suggests that such applications often cloud our understanding of Qin-Han China and present a serious obstacle in comparative studies.

In the past few years, specialists of more recent periods of Chinese history have begun to deconstruct the introduction in Sinological scholarship of the very concept of a unitary religion, which occurred as a consequence of a partly voluntary adoption of foreign ideas following the dramatic clash with Western colonial interests at the end of the nineteenth century.

Early China scholars, on the other hand, because of a series of factors that we will explore in detail below, traditionally tend to operate within intellectual concerns and frameworks established by Euro-American academics. Especially in the case of the phenomena customarily studied under the category of religion, most Sinologists still seem informed by the teleological and systemic preoccupations typical of Christian historiography and that more or less openly reflect the cultural legacy of Hegelianism, both in the approaches indebted to German sociology and in Chinese state-sponsored Marxist readings.[8]

In the particular case of the study of empire formation, the application to the Han Dynasty of the Augustan model of a "state religion" based on "divine rulership" justifies inferences about the question of the sacred in early China that downplay the specificity and richness of indigenous worldviews.[9] Unless we assume the universality of a Western conception of "religion," even in handling measurable data, we should consider that cross-cultural inquiries into the past are based on culture-specific categories and criteria of inclusion and exclusion that are hardly relevant for the subjects under study.[10] As Douglas Northrop remarks, "[S]cholars are of course situated culturally and historically, with predispositions and theoretical frameworks shaped by positions in a modern, especially Anglophone and capitalist West . . . [W]orld history studies a 'globe' that has been conceived through Euro-American historicist epistemologies . . . It is therefore neither objective nor value-neutral—and far from truly global."[11] In support of Northrop's observation, it should suffice to note that while no one would question the legitimacy of an academic pursuit of an "early Chinese religion," studying Roman civilizations in terms of *yin* 陰 and *yang* 陽, *qi* 氣, or *dao* 道 would be deemed absurd both by Western and Chinese scholars. Clearly, the processes of intellectual borrowing seem to work only in one direction.

Reacting to these tendencies, I tackle the question of "religion" with a dialectic and reflexive methodology and a special attention to the intellectual attitude Reinhart Koselleck defines as "consciously admitted positionality."[12] My work provides a study of early China that accounts for indigenous contexts and concerns while historicizing and problematizing the motivations and methods that inform our scholarly approaches and intellectual paradigms.[13] As quipped by the ancient Chinese thinker Zhuangzi (c. 369–286 BCE), the knowledge of the Other and of the Self proceeds through interdependent heuristic processes—"Without the Other there is no Self."[14] Thus, *Heaven Is Empty* does not aim at countering or confirming the refutation of the knowability of the Other of some of postmodern scholars. It instead strives to acknowledge the inevitable subjectivity of all intellectual approaches as an integral part of its empirical analysis.

The Argument: Metaphysics in Historical Narratives

Among Sinologists, only Robert F. Campany has systematically questioned the applicability of Euro-American approaches to ancient Chinese religions.[15] He has convincingly challenged the tendency to conceive traditions such as "Buddhism" or "Daoism" in terms of theoretical coherence, collective agency, "faith," or "belief."[16] Taking my cue from his "fluid" approach to the performative aspects of ritual in the Chinese early middle period (c. 100–600 CE), I focus on the formative years of the empire, before the introduction of Buddhism set in motion a series of cultural transformations that I consider crucial in our understanding (and misunderstanding) of Chinese ancient religions.[17]

My approach hinges on the observation that the diffusion of new South-Asian beliefs and practices in the first century CE (at the earliest) coincided with the introduction of a universalistic notion of religion that caused notable changes in the way the Chinese envisioned their relationship with "the sacred."[18] The moralizing potential of the "divine" as a vehicle for personal development provided new modalities for interactions within and among communities (real and imagined) and for the formalization of individual and group identities, which, as Erich Gruen points out in his study of Mediterranean civilizations, "in antiquity did not possess a pure and unadulterated character."[19] The impact of Buddhism thus prompted the Chinese to formalize the theoretical foundations of indigenous traditions according to new paradigms. The social function of the sacred was profoundly transformed through the guidance of an organized clergy, the adoption of a scriptural corpus, and the new territorial dynamics produced by the construction of stupas and temples. From an epistemological point of view, these elements made Chinese, Greco-Roman, and Judeo-Christian experiences more easily comparable, while fueling the scholarly tendency to conceive ancient civilizations indiscriminately in unitary, systemic, and identitary terms—after all, Buddhism arose in an Indo-European context.[20]

One of the most dangerous conceits regarding the interdependence of religion and collective identities revolves around the question of China's inclusion among the "great world civilizations." It has become customary to imply that the moral foundations of a complex society must derive from an organic conception of the "sacred." Debates on whether the origins of China were quintessentially "secular" or "religious" inevitably appropriate traditionally Euro-American philosophical preoccupations while implicitly subsuming the universality of Abrahamic models. For example, while some scholars extol the civilization of the Yellow River as one of the earliest instances of secular society, others, by referring to the supposed "spirituality" of Confucianism[21] or the monotheistic nature of the Chinese notion of Heaven, argue that ancient China was endowed with an indigenous ethical tradition comparable to Christianity.[22] On the other side of the spectrum, positivistic and Marxist analyses tend to treat popular religious traditions as evidence for the superstitious mentality of the earlier periods of Chinese civilization, one that must be overcome by a more "rational" and "modern" attitude.

Heaven Is Empty holds that these tendencies still underlie cultural complexes that can be traced back to the fateful clash with foreign powers, when late nineteenth-century Chinese elites felt compelled to rethink the early history of their country in non-native terms. Although these sentiments and ideas are culturally legitimate and represent an integral part of the current Chinese intellectual universe, once applied to the study of ancient societies, they can engender insidious anachronisms.

In order to formulate culture-specific notions, *Heaven Is Empty* looks at the scholarship on the sacred in the ancient Mediterranean world and tests the applicability of its heuristic tools to early Chinese contexts. It concentrates on historical, literary, and material sources dealing with the imperial propaganda produced to justify the dominion of Rome over the ancient Western world and of the Qin and Han dynasties over the Central States. The comparison of the Augustan age with the dynasty of the Western Han (206 BCE–9 CE) serves as the starting point for a broader critique of the ways the hegemony of Abrahamic models produces views of the past that are still instrumental in the persistence of Eurocentric approaches to current intercultural debates on political and cultural identities.

Elusive Rulers, Lacunose Accounts, Inadequate Models

The main protagonists of this book are Emperor Wu 武 of the Han (r. 141–87 BCE), his court archivist Sima Qian 司馬遷 (c. 145 or 135–86 BCE) (who was in charge of recording both human and astronomical events), and the first history of China from its origins, the *Records of the*

Grand Historian (*Shiji* 史記, hereafter *Records*), which Sima Qian completed by integrating and finishing the work begun by his father Sima Tan 譚 (c. 165–110 BCE).[23] However, studying Emperor Wu's period through the accounts of his official historians represents a much less straightforward endeavor than it may appear. The two chief problems in the study of the *Records* are the well-known falling out between Emperor Wu and Sima Qian (which led to the castration of the latter), and the complicated issue of the *Records*' authorship and transmission.[24] *Heaven Is Empty* highlights the fact that, although recent scholarship has demonstrated that a syncretic form of "Confucianism" was established as a state doctrine only after the death of Emperor Wu, most readers of the *Records* anachronistically attribute to its authors a mature and self-conscious understanding of "Confucianism" as a coherent moral-philosophical doctrine, although it had not yet been formalized as such at the time. Furthermore, most scholars have routinely overlooked the fact that neither of the Simas was allowed to witness the most important phases of the historic ceremonies carried out by their sovereign. It is equally striking that despite the length of his reign (fifty-four years) and the sheer magnitude of his achievements, Emperor Wu always occupied a very ambiguous position in Chinese and Western historiography. The *Records* describes this sovereign as superstitious, inconsistent, and hopelessly under the sway of the untrustworthy *fangshi* 方士 (experts in esoteric practices and bodily practices, especially hailing from the coastal areas of the former states of Qi and Yan). The *History of the Former Han* (*Han Shu* 漢書), by Ban Gu 班固 (32–92 CE) praises him as the emperor who, after the bemoaned period of persecutions and ostracism against the Classicists (in Chinese *ru* 儒, traditionally translated as "Confucians") began to appoint them to important positions at court. In contrast, the poetry and popular or "apocryphal" literature of the Tang period (618–907) expressed longing for the marvelous times of Wu's reign, a lost golden age when the Son of Heaven leisurely consorted with female deities in his private rooms.

Tellingly, the prolific British sinologist Michael Loewe, widely recognized as the most authoritative and influential Han studies scholar, routinely attributes the most impactful military campaigns and policies carried out in this period to Wu's generals, ministers, and advisors, thereby implicitly suggesting that the emperor himself lacked leadership skills, political savvy, and agency. Although he never explicitly makes the point, Loewe treats Wu as a puppet in the hands of court factions or charlatans—a viewpoint he happens to share with Sima Qian.[25]

There is no question that Emperor Wu had the opportunity of benefiting from the service of several exceptionally talented statesmen. However, it cannot be ignored that almost all of his influential ministers and courtiers eventually fell out of grace or died after a very brief—albeit successful—period in office. There is, however, one interesting exception to this rule: the minister Sang Hongyang 桑弘羊 (152–80 BCE), who enjoyed Wu's confidence until the end of his reign. Sang is remembered as the staunch promoter of radical economic centralization and state monopolies, which eventually turned several aristocratic and wealthy families against Emperor Wu. Richard von Glahn has aptly branded this political model as "*mercantilist* fiscal state," which "aspired to supplanting private commerce with state-run institutions managed by enterprising merchants recruited to government service."[26] Sang also features in the *Discourses on Salt and Iron* (*Yantielun* 鹽鐵論), the partially fictionalized account of a court debate on the pros and cons of economic centralization that took place after Wu's death.[27] In the diatribe against the supporters of devolutionary measures and relative autonomy of regional elites, Sang is the champion of the court faction that envisioned a big government directly in charge of all the fundamental productive and administrative activities. The importance of Sang's political longevity supports my thesis that despite the accusations of incoherence and superstition directed against Emperor Wu's ritual reforms, they in fact constituted an integral part of the legitimization of radical economic centralization—the first priority of his government.

In the *Discourses*, in contrast with our current understanding of economics as an independent field, discussions on the viability of state monopolies also explore the themes of ritual and historical memory, while including elements that we would define philosophical or mythological.[28] In the *Records* and other Han Dynasty texts, whose declared focus is not the implementation of specific politics, narratives about myths, rituals, and the legitimization of hereditary monarchy intermingle with economic questions rather frequently. I argue that if we ignore the traditional boundaries between academic disciplines and textual traditions and look at these sources while framing specific "religious" debates in their historical contexts, mythological disquisitions about ancient cultural heroes and sages acquire a much more concrete background. In the case of the *Records*, if we complement its reading with contemporary documents such as the *Huainanzi* or excavated manuscripts from Mawangdui, it becomes clear that the rivalry between Classicists and *fangshi* also overshadows radically different positions about Emperor Wu's centralizing reforms.[29]

Wu's long reign, according to Michael Loewe, was characterized by a struggle between *Modernists*, those officials who envisioned a government based on radical and administrative centralization, and *Reformists*, those who opposed it.³⁰ Marianne Bujard, by concentrating on the cultural aspects of these tensions, has highlighted the rivalry at court between the Classicists, who propounded a form imperial authority thoroughly informed by the "Confucian" textual tradition, and the *fangshi*, on whose expertise Wu would rely in his quest for physical immortality.³¹ As mentioned above, Sima Qian's attribution of his sovereign's inconsistencies and flimsiness to the influence of these magicians is well known. Surprisingly enough, Han scholars seem to overlook that Sima Qian disapproved of the contemporary Classicists as well. My point is that since his attacks are seldom straightforward, Sima Qian's overt admiration for Confucius and familiarity with the texts associated with his teachings can be easily mistaken for an endorsement of the various contemporaries that claimed the Master as their inspiration. In fact, I argue that Sima Qian's own strong background in the *Classics* allowed him to weave an informed and subtle—albeit indirect—critique of the superficiality, hypocrisy, and opportunism of most of the Han Classicists. Conversely, since he could not be as well versed in the cultural traditions of the peripheral regions from which the *fangshi* hailed, he limits his sarcasm to their continuous references to spirits, ghosts, extraordinary phenomena, and immortality, without engaging the possible import of the ceremonies Emperor Wu inaugurated under their advice. I demonstrate that the *fangshi*'s contribution to Wu's ritual activities, which the *Records* describes as an incoherent congeries of badly understood esoteric regional traditions, was often consistent with the political agenda of the Modernists, for it aimed at legitimizing a charismatic, all-powerful, and autocratic conception of rulership.

Recently, Tamara T. Chin has detailed how Han literary genres reflected the dramatic impact of Sang's program on Han perceptions about the economic relations between China and foreigners, and between center and periphery.³² For example, she analyzes the development of the rhapsody *fu* 賦 as the "primary scene of ideological contestation" against Wu's aggressive economic politics and lavishness. Chin argues that the eventual reduction the in the size and ornamentality of this poetic form echoed the increasing popularity of positions that advocated for a return to the frugal ways of the Western Zhou.³³ Paralleling Chin's work, *Heaven Is Empty* focuses on Han discourses on economic models by concentrating on rituals and mythological narratives. It reconstructs substantial components of Wu's ideological strategies by integrating the fragmentary accounts provided by the *Records* with contemporary material evidence, court poetry, and received and excavated documents conventionally associated with the Huang-Lao tradition.³⁴

As eloquently summarized by Chin, Eastern Han historiography engaged in the erasure of the *Records*' "arresting, unsettling, reflexive and yet internally inconsistent treatment of the very terms and conditions of discourse on frontier and market."[35] As for the issue of state ceremonies and propaganda, I illustrate how the model of kingship pursued by Emperor Wu did not survive his death. Attuned to Confucius's "secular" dislike of direct involvement with spirits and ghosts, new generations of intellectuals would misunderstand or misrepresent the sovereign's ritual reforms. Disconnected from a specific strategy for the cultural legitimization of centralization, their memory would survive as testament of Wu's extravagance and superstition.

Overlapping Historical and Cultural Contexts

Ideological interpretations of the Western Han, celebrated as the first "Confucian" dynasty, have inevitably produced several misunderstandings and interconnected anachronisms that are still influential in contemporary scholarship. For centuries Chinese and Western scholars alike, despite contrasting views on his political contribution, have praised Emperor Wu for allowing the Classicists to regain a central position in the political and cultural life of the realm. According to the narrative validated in Han historiography, the Qin (221–206 BCE), the first unifiers of China, had ruthlessly vanquished their rivals and imposed a regime of violence and intimidation. It was only with the adoption of so-called "Han Confucianism" as a state doctrine under Wu that, dynastic histories claim, the unified empire received full moral legitimation and won popular support. "Han Confucianism" was supposedly based on the holistic and metaphysical reading of Confucius's *Spring and Autumn Annals* (*Chunqiu* 春秋) exposed by the Classicist Dong Zhongshu 董仲舒 (179–104 BCE) in the *Luxuriant Gems of the Spring and Autumn* (*Chunqiu fanlu* 春秋繁露).[36] His syncretic intellectual system complemented the theory of the Mandate of Heaven (*tianming* 天命) with "heterodox" cosmological speculations developed in the former state of Qi (Dong's birthplace) during the pre-imperial period, such as those revolving around yin and yang or the Five Phases/Elements. Dong's elaboration explained the violence that had led to the establishment and consolidation of political unity as an integral part of the moral principles underlying cosmic changes and cycles. In short, this doctrine allowed propagandistic historiography to credit the Han with the inauguration of a moral imperial line, which reframed preexisting theories about cosmic rulership within the ethical standards of the legendary Sage Kings of yore celebrated by Confucius. According to the Master, the ancient sovereigns conformed their rule to Heaven without becoming directly involved with the spirits and ghosts worshipped in popular cults. Chinese officials and intellectuals cultivated Confucius's secular attitude for centuries, until the beginning of the Republican era in 1912.

Only recently have philological and historical inquiries demonstrated that the Classicists (or "Confucians") were still barely relevant at Wu's court, and that the text in which Dong Zhongshu elaborates his theories gained cultural preeminence, or was actually composed, in a later period.[37] It was *Han Shu*, completed at the beginning of the first century CE, which pushed back the "triumph of Confucianism" to the prosperous age of Emperor Wu, prompting generations of later historians to adopt Mediterranean models of "divine rulership" and overlook the uniqueness of his ritual vision.

Complicating matters further, in the crucial moment of the "opening" of China, late Qing 清 (1644–1911) intellectuals chose the conceit of a Wu-promoted "Han Confucianism" as the model for the creation of a modern Western-like state religion. Vincent Goossaert and David Palmer have meticulously traced the introduction of a Western notion of religion into China back to this dramatic period.[38] Before the unprecedented defeat suffered in the First Sino-Japanese War (1894–95), China lacked both a single term that could translate the English "religion" and the very notion that this concept could become an instrument for the construction of a national identity. It was in the aftermath of this unprecedented and humiliating defeat that the Qing reformers decided to follow the example of the victor, Meiji Japan (1868–1912). It seemed to them that their neighbors had swiftly entered "the modern age" thanks to the ideological fervor spurred by the West-inspired cult of the emperor. His divinity and association with the origins of the country had inspired all Japanese, regardless of class and status, to sacrifice themselves for the common good, overcome the history of humiliations imposed on Japan by foreign countries, and become a feared power in their own right.

The hesitant and ineffective responses of the Qing Dynasty to the Opium Wars (1839–1860), the Taiping Rebellion (1850–1864), and other political and economic catastrophes of the nineteenth century had already deeply compromised the allegiance of the Chinese people to their government. After the unforgivable debacle of 1895, the Qing reformers believed that only a Meiji-like state religion could reestablish cohesion and trust between the rulers and the ruled in China. In looking at the past for legitimizing precedents, these officials and intellectuals became particularly interested in the level of administrative efficiency and international reputation enjoyed by the Chinese empire under Emperor Wu. In this period, following almost a century of instability, the Han finally prevailed over internal and external enemies. Wu's officials established a firmer grip on the periphery and bolstered the treasury with the enforcement of state monopolies on salt, iron, and alcohol. These measures fostered an unprecedented period of prosperity and confidence, which Emperor Wu endeavored to celebrate with the performance of the solemn rituals for the legitimation of the dynasty, which his predecessors had preferred to postpone. Even if subsequent historians bemoaned Wu's aggressive and expensive policies as the principal cause of the economic crisis that would haunt his successors, his legacy was salvaged by his purported sponsorship of Confucian scholars. Starting with the Eastern Han, generation after generation of Classicists (or Confucians) would credit Emperor Wu with ending the ostracism they suffered under the Qin and reintegrating them at court.

Looking back to the tumultuous years following the defeat of the first Sino-Japanese war, in a political and cultural context heavily conditioned by the foreign menace, a group of Qing reformers resorted to interpreting "Han Confucianism" as an indigenous "state religion" to be revived for nation building purposes. In doing so, they engendered a long series of intertwined anachronisms and misunderstandings that have never been systematically deconstructed.

In addition to deconstructing these cultural processes, *Heaven Is Empty* reconstructs the political and cultural struggles that eventually led to the hegemony of a "Confucian" view of state and society a few decades after Emperor Wu's death. As importantly, it offers the first detailed interpretation of Emperor Wu's private and public rituals as integral to his imperial vision. If the Classicists opposed it, it is because it was incompatible with the hierarchical understanding of social and political relations that reflected the interests of the landed elites, a group to which they likely belonged. They embraced Confucius's condemnation of popular cults as a direct attack against Emperor Wu's attitude toward spirits and ghosts, and an implicit one against his "Modernist" agenda. In other words, I interpret early Han "Confucian" criticisms concerning popular religion as a reaction to the Emperor's attempt to impose a centralizing, autocratic, independent, active, and extremely mobile conception of monarchy. Wu's plan to strip local aristocracies of political and economic privileges was paralleled by his attempt to bypass their mediating function and opposition by reaching out to his subjects directly, through appropriation of or participation in local ritual traditions. As we will see in more detail below, during this phase, the Classicists often contrasted these policies through literary references to alternative ritual and mythological models. In response to the *fangshi*'s spreading of allegorical stories celebrating all-powerful legendary monarchs of the past who did not need ministers to communicate with the common people, the Classicists offered a contrasting narrative about founding fathers who succeeded only because of moderation, collegial rule, and decentralization.

It is important to remember that the Qin's administrative reorganization of China in commanderies and counties had greatly reduced the political and economic prerogatives of local aristocracies. It had been through the exploitation of the discontent—and military resources—of these elites that the founder of the Han, Liu Bang, was able to overthrow the unifiers of China. However, once in power, he had no choice but yield to their demands. While maintaining part of the Qin's bureaucratic structure, Liu Bang was compelled to bestow on his aristocratic allies extremely large estates that they could rule autonomously from the court. His successors, being still economically and militarily dependent on the periphery, continued to comply with this arrangement until Emperor Wu succeeded in bringing these territories back under the political and fiscal control of the central government. The opposition he faced was both political and cultural.

Finally, from a theoretical point of view, *Heaven Is Empty* relies on a comparative approach to test the applicability of the traditional notions of "religion," "myth," "ritual," and "polytheism" to the Qin-Han contexts. In reconstructing the historiographical phases that led to the establishment of "Confucian" interpretations of this period, it proposes categories based on indigenous concerns. Emperor Wu's efforts toward capillary bureaucratic and economic centralization did not—and could not—imply the creation of an imperial religion because unitary, systemic, identitary, and moral interpretations of the divine were not hegemonic in early imperial China.

Grappling with the Issue of "Religion" in Chinese History and Society

This book closely examines the development of the question of "an early Chinese "religion" in chapter 1. Here I want to provide a brief synthesis of what I consider to be the main features of notions of religion that are based on the hegemonic role of monotheist models vis-à-vis conceptions of the divine throughout Chinese history. Of course, avoiding simplifications and generalizations is impossible in such an enterprise, and the outline I offer should be taken as a list of provisional comparative signposts that will help the reader establish some preliminary criteria for the study of "religion" in early imperial China. Throughout *Heaven Is Empty*, the concepts described in this section will progressively be replaced by notions gleaned from specific textual and cultural contexts.

First of all, monotheistic/Abrahamic notions of religion rely on ideas about the "sacred" and the "divine" that, despite evident etymological connections with the Latin terms *sacer* and *divinus*, have evolved differently over time in different parts of the world. By generalizing, we can say that these attributes now characterize the superhuman realm as ontologically separate from the human, as well as absolute, eternal, complete in itself, devoid of any negative connotation (i.e., perfect), and knowable through Revelation. Such features, once translated into social structures, inform a notion of religion that is supposed to define one's ethical and intellectual attitude about all aspects of reality. This form of allegiance is expected to be exclusionary (professing allegiance to one creed excludes the possibility of acknowledging the truthfulness of any other) and characterized by the same degree of structural coherence that we value in philosophical and legal systems.

Even a cursory look at Chinese civilization shows that most of these criteria do not apply. The semantic range of the Chinese character *shen* 神, which usually translates the English "sacred" or "divine," is far broader than that of its Western counterparts and varies depending on textual and cultural contexts. It is etymologically linked to *shen* 伸, to extend, and refers to everything that is more than human or extraordinary. Importantly, it does not necessarily imply the moral connotation of "holy." Furthermore, if we are inclined to interpret *shen* in light of the classic Chinese notion that every element of the cosmos is made of different concentrations of *qi* 氣 (breath/energy/matter), it would be erroneous to define the Chinese "divine" in terms of ontological separation and absolutes. For these reasons, and in keeping with Poo Mouchou's and Roger Ames's work, I prefer to use "extra-human," (meaning "more than human") instead of "superhuman" or "supernatural," which imply the existence of distinct realms.[39]

As for Chinese organized religions, as is well known, the Three Traditions (*sanjiao* 三教, i.e., Daoism, Confucianism, and Buddhism) do not require exclusive commitment. Their various practices and systems of beliefs, which at times overlap, can be followed universally regardless of one's allegiance to one or more of them. They can be instrumental in addressing specific critical phases of life such as birth, death, marriage, procreation, illness, success, loss, and so on, but do not necessarily subsume a holistic vision that can indiscriminately be applied to all human and extra-human phenomena. As for their social usage, references to transcendence—under the rule of the Chinese Communist Party (1949–) as well as during the imperial period (3rd century BCE–1911)—do not have a primary role in legitimizing political power, defining shared morals, or establishing specific public identities. Of course, Marxism's proverbial rejection of religion as "the opiate of the people" relegates the sacred to the private sphere. Yet we should not underestimate the impact that Confucius's (551–479 BCE) prejudice against direct interaction with non-human entities exerted on Chinese institutions and culture. Chinese intellectual and political elites, who were selected through a system of examinations based on the "Confucian" canon, maintained that rituals were less important for the connection they provided with ancestral spirits than for the sense of respect and harmony they fostered among the living. They believed that a revival of the ritual tradition associated with the exemplary Western Zhou 周 Dynasty (1046–771 BCE) which Confucius had promoted, was crucial to the stabilization and perpetuation of the hierarchical structure of society, as it required participants to follow ceremonial protocols determined by age and status. On the other hand, these elites considered the various forms of devotion to local deities useless at best, and at worst a threat to the moral fabric of society. It is important to emphasize that the prevalence of this "anti-religious" attitude did not automatically translate into the suppression of popular cults, nor did it prevent them from prospering. It simply relegated their treatment to popular, unofficial, or less respectable literature, some of which would be collected, starting with the 3rd century CE, under the genre aptly named "accounts of anomalies" (*zhiguai* 志怪).[40]

The apparent "vagueness" or "ambiguity" of Chinese attitudes toward the divine are more easily understandable if we consider that early China lacked an institution that held undisputed authority over questions regarding the relation between spirits and ghosts, the sociopolitical order, and the common people, as the Catholic Church did in Europe and elsewhere. In other words, Chinese elites did not conceive of ritual propriety in terms of dogma versus heresy, orthodoxy versus heterodoxy, or as a theological speculation on the true nature of the divine. The realm of the divine, including ancestral spirits and ghosts, did not constitute an indisputable source of moral authority. On the contrary, the elites tended to fear spirits and ghosts as agents of chaos and uncertainty. People who were interested in regulating political and social institutions according to sound moral principle were supposed avoid invoking ghosts and spirits at all cost.

I argue that such an attitude became dominant only after Emperor Wu's death, when the "Confucian" Classics were definitively installed as the only legitimate source of ritual propriety, by which even the Son of Heaven had to abide. When in the second half of the first century BCE officials at court promoted the "revival" of the emperor's sacrifices to Heaven described in the literary canon, they were *de facto* tethering the ruler to their exclusive philological expertise and possibly political interests. Even though this move practically elevated the *Classics* to the status of scripture, the systems of values they illustrated, at least in theory, did not underlie revealed and absolute truths. The Classicists simply celebrated the wisdom and authority deriving from a superior literary education focused on the study of an exemplary past.

Another often overlooked factor concerning the study of religion and power during the Qin and Han is the novelty of the empire as a form of unified government. When the Central States were united in 221 BCE, the polities that we now call China had been divided for more than five centuries. The Qin and early Han rulers were pressed to contain the armies of local aristocratic lords who resented the loss of independence. In addition, their political priorities consisted of administrative, economic, and fiscal centralization; the establishment a common script; the standardization of legal codes, coinage, and systems of measurement; and the repair of roads and canals to facilitate the movement of people and goods. In these conditions, structuring the realm on a shared conception of the divine would have been unfeasible, if not altogether unthinkable.

Of course, prior to and in addition to the institution of the ceremonies mentioned above, the Qin and early Han rulers did conduct sacrifices, but these had nothing to do with the establishment of a state religion (i.e., for all the subjects of the empire) but rather with ensuring the military and economic success of the government. At the same time, as we will see, early emperors as individuals seemed interested in practices that focused on personal well-being, and these acts of worship took place in the presence of a few courtiers or in private. The fact that extant Qin and Han monumental architecture seems conceived more for the spirits of the dead than for a living public further supports the point that the Qin and the Han did not develop a religious cult of the emperor for propagandistic reasons comparable to that of the Romans. The available evidence can justify hypotheses about the existence of a *religion for the emperor* but not of an *imperial religion* of the Western kind.

Time and Space: The Structure of *Heaven Is Empty*

Following contemporary trends in religious and ritual studies, I organize my analysis of Emperor Wu's ceremonies around the "Kantian absolutes" of time and space.[41] However, mindful of the specific concerns expressed in the Chinese sources, I interpret *time* more narrowly as the intellectual justification of hereditary monarchy in terms of mythical or historical narratives, and of continuity and rupture with the past. By *space* I mean the conceptual and ritual reconfigurations of the extension of territorial control that took place under Emperor Wu's rule. In my examination of *religion*, I include dynamics, systems, and phenomena (human, natural, or cosmic) such as fate, fortune, and elaborate theories of historical causation, that the documents consider as having an impact on human lives regardless of contingency (i.e., metahistorical factors).

Since this book's reconstruction of Emperor Wu's ritual activities proceeds from a historicization and deconstruction of Western paradigms, its conceptual vocabulary undergoes the continuous scrutiny and readjustments implied in the work of cultural translation. At times in keeping, at times in contrast with the *Records'* vantage point, *Heaven Is Empty* interprets Emperor Wu's "religion" as discrete clusters of rituals that never consolidated into a unitary understanding of the cosmos. Some of these rituals represented a response to personal or familial crises and were aimed at seeking immediate relief in alchemic practices or the intervention of spirits and ghosts. Some satirized specific familial, aristocratic, and paternalistic conceptions of the state and family expressed in the *Classics*, while promoting an autocratic and non-collegial conception of power. Still others constituted an escamotage to elude the opposition of court factions and justify controversial decisions as divinely inspired. The most complex and dispendious ceremonies of Emperor Wu's reign were part of a far-reaching program of political propaganda aimed at the elites. To the paternalistic and collaborative rule embodied by the Western Zhou, which Li Feng has efficaciously labeled *delegatory kin-ordered settlement state*, they opposed a centralizing, autocratic, "Huang-Lao" or "Daoist" model of cosmic rulership that was still popular in the early decades following the unification.[42] The rituals inaugurated or recovered by Emperor Wu—in open contradiction to the exemplary, passive, moral, father-like rulership of the Sage Kings of the Confucian tradition—portrayed the Son of Heaven as a formidable warrior capable of harnessing the forces of the cosmos, leading his armies against human and non-human enemies, pacifying the world, and ensuring the productivity of the land, while redistributing its fruits without relying on aristocratic intermediaries. After Emperor Wu's death, this paradigm, not uncommon in ancient African and Eurasian civilizations, succumbed to the "devolutionary" model propounded by the Classicists, whose "secularism" would prompt generations of intellectuals to dismiss the import of regional ritual traditions.

In terms of methodology, *Heaven Is Empty* draws research hypotheses from cross-cultural comparisons, verifies working categories against specific historical and cultural Han contexts, and engages in the recovery of native priorities and concepts. Chapter 1, "Readings of the 'Sacred': Chinese Religion, Chinese Religions, and Religions in China," establishes the epistemological foundation of the book's arguments and provides a critical reasessment of the application of Western paradigms to the study of the divine in early China. The chapter engages in a critique of the implicit ethnocentrism of discourses on the inclusion of China into the pantheon of the "great world religions," and on whether its most influential cultural traditions were "religious" or "philosophical." The inevitable circularity of these abstract questions reveals more about the concerns of Western scholarship than about the actual preoccupations of ancient Chinese. This chapter offers a cultural history of the application of classic and Abrahamic ideas of tradition, knowledge, and morals to early Chinese realities. Finally, it proposes revised, expanded, or alternative interpretations of notions such as "religion," "divine," "myth," and "ritual" that overcome traditional essentialist, phenomenological, or structuralist approaches and that better fit the study of the Han Dynasty.

Chapter 2, "Writing the Empire: *Ex Pluribus Plurima*" concentrates on the historiographical strategies of the *Records* and subsequent literature in addressing the question of the relationship between political power and "religion." It reconstructs the epistemological criteria of the *Records* as well as its conceptions of the relationship between ritual, text, and historical memory, especially in terms of the text's conversation with the past and contemporary historiographical traditions. In looking at the section of the *Records* chronologically closer to Emperor Wu's period, this chapter explores the development of Sima Qian's interactions with his sovereign (who notoriously condemned the historian to castration) as well as the historian's complex attitude toward the legitimacy of the Han Dynasty. It analyzes Sima Qian's treatment of Confucius's cultural legacy, his portraits of contemporary Classicists at court, and his ideas about the relationship between intellectuals and power.

Following on Michael Puett's reading of Sima Qian's historiographical approach, I further elaborate on the *Records*' pessimist outlook.[43] I argue that its acknowledgment of the disjunction between the cosmic, political, and moral realms was both the cause and the result of what may appear to a contemporary readership as a multi-vocal literary approach. In other words, I interpret Sima Qian's skeptical attitude towards the linearity of human and especially divine agency (or "secular" sensibility) once compared with that of his Greco-Roman counterparts, more as the result of his inductive empirical approach than a conscious rejection of religion akin to contemporary secularism or atheism.

In analyzing Sima Qian's heuristic criteria, this chapter documents the progressive formalization of the domains of *li* 禮 and *si* 祀, which scholarship in English customarily lumps together under the category of "ritual." According to my reconstruction, *li* and *si* respectively referred to rituals that did not involve direct contact with the divine and to cults that focused on deities connected to specific communities and areas. In other words, they epitomize the non-universalistic, hierarchical conception of the divine in early China, as individual ceremonial duties and objects of worship varied according to rank, status, and locality.

Chapter 3, "Narrating the Empire: Metaphysics without God, 'Religions' without Identity" expands the theme of the legitimization of unified rule by examining the purported teleological structure of the *Records* and its treatment of Heaven as a meta-historical factor in the formation of the Han empire. It takes into consideration the broader context of the close and seldom explored relationship between narratives about empire formation, universalism, and teleological trajectories. More specifically, this chapter historicizes what I call the "hegemony of monotheism" in Abrahamic and non-Abrahamic historiographical traditions. In tracing the development of the conceit about the superiority of unitary narratives in the ancient Mediterranean, I compare the role of Heaven in the *Records* and of Fortune in Polybius in the creation of the Han and Roman empires. Although Sima Qian's analytical approach can more easily be compared to that of Livy or Tacitus, I focus on Polybius because his attitude toward Rome's history would eventually serve to justify both secular and confessional unitary historiographical attitudes. In addition, Polybius was arguably the first historian who identified Roman cults as having a mere political end, while his search for a unitary imperial trajectory enabled confessional historians to recognize an implicit sense of the divine even in "pagan" narratives, insofar as they acknowledged the ultimate unity of the world.

By considering the impact of Polybius's and Sima Qian's personal experiences and unique cultural contexts on their work, I show the extent to which the two authors associated unified rule with the triumph of universal values or the establishment of divine justice. At the same time, I investigate how (if at all) the two authors complemented their unitary narratives about empire formation by accounting for other factors, such as geography, political structures, individual agency, ethnicity, and gender. In the end, the Greek Polybius recognized the causes of Rome's triumph in the superiority of its mixed constitution, which combined institutional models previously implemented in Greece. He invoked Fortune only when the unpredictable military successes of the less-civilized Romans would otherwise be inexplicable, to compensate for his less than impeccable sense of causality. As for Sima Qian, according to traditional readings, Heaven seemed to favor the re-unification of the Central States despite the immorality, lack of intellectual sophistication, and dearth of political experience of the founder of the Han Dynasty. According to my interpretation, the Chinese historian instead treated the theme of Heaven rather ironically, as the residue of a rhetorical tradition—the Classicist one—that wanted to believe in the intrinsic morality of the cosmos. In the end, even if both authors considered the possibility that a single factor or being could have a direct role in the success of a given leader or lineage, neither of them conceived of the divine in the systemic, identitary, and exclusionary terms typical of the Abrahamic religions.

Chapter 4, "Time, Myth, and Memory: Of Water, Metal, and Cinnabar" deals with Emperor Wu's justification of empire in terms of past traditions by contrasting this rhetoric with the diversified forms of propaganda devised by Octavian in Rome. The chapter focuses on the debates concerning different ideals of rulership that took place under Emperor Wu in the form of philological or mythological disquisitions on the Yellow Emperor, Yu the Great, and the interactions of monarchs with spirits and ghosts. I pay particular attention to Wu's involvement with alchemists and experts of esoteric practices (*fangshi* 方士) as recounted by Sima Qian. The historian openly denounced these magicians as charlatans who flocked to court from the Northeast, eager to exploit the emperor's gullibility with stories about the Yellow Emperor's quest for immortality. I contend that the historian was also trying to suggest that Emperor Wu would have chosen the "wrong" model of rulership even without the *fangshi*'s tricks. I show how, through a complex system of geographical and biographical references, Sima Qian wove a subtext that indicted Emperor Wu for rejecting the moral paragons of the Sage Kings of the Zhou Dynasty. According to the historian, his sovereign was too focused on becoming a "Hegemon King" (*bawang* 霸王), a title once held by the rulers of the ancient state of Qi. These dynasts had briefly prevailed over the other warring states thanks to the shrewd management of economic resources and exploitation of popular superstitions, and Sima Qian saw Wu as making an effort to model himself after them.

In addition, by taking into account information derived from newly excavated manuscripts, this chapter recovers three different interpretations of the import of the Yellow Emperor as a model of rulership. I make the case that these mythological interpretations respectively supported three distinct conceptions of monarchy: individualistic, collegial/delegatory, and interventionist. Through a close study of the language used in Han economic texts, I show how philological diatribes on the myths surrounding the Yellow Emperor, Yu the Great, and the Nine Tripods documented in the *Records* and other contemporary texts functioned as a proxy for more practical debates on fiscal centralization and state monopolies on iron and minting. Finally, I demonstrate how, despite Sima Qian's possible misgivings and oversights, some aspects of Emperor Wu's quest for immortality were likely formulated as an indirect criticism of the "Confucian" aristocratic conception of the state conceived as a family, which in turn reflected and served the values and interests of local landed elites. Unlike Octavian in establishing the Principate, the Chinese ruler could not appeal (not even instrumentally) to the unchallenged authority of values such as those of the Roman Republic or *mos maiorum*. Wu's approach to rituals and beliefs was a peculiar blend of the tendency to use religion as an *instrumentum regni* and as a privileged form of individual escapism. In ancient Rome, regardless of one's personal beliefs, openly showing allegiance to the gods that protected the city amounted to an acknowledgment of civic values and a display of patriotism. Emperor Wu had instead to deal with the absence of cults whose worship surpassed local communities, while facing the growing opposition of a faction that condemned all involvement with extra-human forces as a source of political chaos and moral uncertainty.

Chapter 5, "Place and Ritual: From *Templum* to Text," addresses the issue of the legitimization of the Han in terms of territorial rituals and metaphors. It redefines the notion of "sacred space" in Chinese contexts through comparisons with Greco-Roman notions of *templum*, Octavian's "transformation" into Augustus, and debates on rituals of place in Han sources. In my reading, with the institution of the Principate, the Roman emperor (and his army) became invested by the community with the authority of defining the physical extent of Rome's political and cultural domain. This vision was not dissimilar from the role pursued by Emperor Wu. My analysis of the *Records*' fragmentary accounts of the sacrifices to Taiyi and Houtu against the data provided by contemporary received and excavated manuscripts and material evidence, suggests that Wu meant to refute ritual conceptions that supported the devolutionary political paradigm embodied by the Zhou Dynasty. In its place he envisioned a more active model of sovereignty according to which the Son of Heaven constituted the active engine of the empire and was the key factor in its expansion, preservation, and prosperity.

However, after Wu's death, the Classicists imposed a cultural model that attributed the specific function of sacralizing traditions, practices, and notions of physical space to those texts whose exegesis they monopolized. In other words, the *Classics* became a fundamental instrument for protecting discrete ideas and policies from empirical scrutiny, as they were considered the hallowed product of exemplary figures of a Chinese Golden Age. What in many Mediterranean civilizations was achieved by means of scriptures, temples, and religious specialists became in China the realm of the Classicists and their books.

Wu's ritual model envisioned the ruler as the sole creator of political and cultural boundaries. The new set of state ceremonies devised by the Classicists at the end of the first century BCE instead tied the actions of the sovereign to the putatively preordained script represented by the *Classics*, while limiting his ritual actions to Chang'an and its surroundings. From this point on, the capital city was supposed to represent the whole realm. Functioning as a microcosm, sacrifices held in the capital would extend to the rest of the empire. I make the case that the set of state rituals customarily known as "Han imperial religion," which implied the sovereign's exclusive worship of Heaven and Earth, was devised to turn the royal function into a symbolic, more passive one. Hence, it is more apt to think of it as a "religion for the emperor" rather than an "imperial religion."

I end this study with the exploration of a further, more elusive dimension of "Han religion" that, I argue, represents a form of resistance against the Classicists' (eventually successful) attempt to establish an abstract, more passive conception of rulership. This dimension concerns the emperor's interest in spirit possession and shamans operating in and around the capital. The *Records* tends to dismiss this inclination as a further symptom of the ruler's gullibility and lack of moral mettle. I suggest a different interpretation. Emperor Wu's documented approach to the sacred, as well as the contemporary survival around the former Han capital of popular legends concerning the personal magic or thaumaturgic power of Han rulers, point toward the possibility that, at least in part, these encounters with the spirits belonged to a specific political strategy. The emperor's forays to visit possessed individuals might have constituted a means to reach out to the common people by showing a form of devotion despised by educated elites, while eluding the control of specific court factions. This kind of interaction further attests to the fact that an abstract conception of the empire, which could be worshipped in effigy or metonymically through the Son of Heaven, was not yet imaginable or functional, or that at least it needed to be complemented with recourse to popular or "un-orthodox" traditions. It is possible, in other words, that Emperor Wu had tried to take advantage of cultural channels with which his own historians did not, or could not, have any familiarity in order to establish a form of political and economic control dreaded by contemporary intellectual elites.

A few final words about the intentionally anachronistic title of this book. *Heaven Is empty* because, in ontological (or Buddhist) terms, it was devoid of any essential, distinctive, independent, or objective characteristics, let alone an individual will. Sima Qian's conception of Heaven did not imply a personal god, as it did in Christianity, nor did it represent the ultimate and eternal abode of the souls of the blessed. But, if we prefer to rely on definitions that are perhaps more consistent with the existential and cultural concerns of the Qin-Han Chinese, Heaven was *empty* because it did not host spirits or ghosts, or any other super-, extra-, or non-human beings. Rather, fearsome or venerable extraordinary beings were all thought to inhabit the same earthly realm as the living. If non-human factors could affect society, it was not because of their superior or transcendental nature, but because people allowed them to come close enough to bring disorder and unpredictability into human affairs.

1

Readings of the "Sacred"

Chinese Religion, Chinese Religions, and Religions in China

> The subjects on which the Master did not talk were—extraordinary things, feats of strength, disorder, and spirits.
>
> —*Analects* 7, 20

> Ji Kang asked: "What kind of man is Confucius?" Ran Qiu, [one of Confucius's students] replied: "In acting, he is principled; in reaching out to the common people, he tries to value spirits and ghosts so that he would have no regrets. In carrying out his plans, even if he accumulated the wealth of one thousand villages, he would not regard it as a gain."
>
> —*Shiji* 47, 1934

The Hegemony of Monotheism, Founding Fathers, and the Necessity of a Chinese Religion

From a methodological point of view, a crucial advance in recent scholarship on the history of religions has been a reappraisal of the influence of unitary and essentialist historiographical biases on analyses of pre-Christian realities and non-Christian religions. Among its most noteworthy contributions, this new direction has led researchers to reconsider the Christian/pagan dichotomy as an anachronistic retrojection, while highlighting the pluralism and fluidity of the ancient Roman cultural world.[1] According to Clifford Ando, for example, the flexibility and adaptability of ancient Roman religion was a consequence of its reliance on orthopraxy, which was in turn based on "empiricist epistemology."[2] This means that instead of founding their rituals on a scriptural, mythological corpus, ancient Romans privileged direct observations of phenomena purportedly produced by the gods, which could obviously vary. A further insight provided by Ando's historicization is an interpretation of the Roman religion in pluralistic terms. In his analysis of popular English translations of the Latin *religio*, he points out that usage of this word in ancient Roman contexts referred to "the sum total of current cult practice." Namely, among ancient Romans, the word did not refer to an essentialist understanding of religion but rather implied that there existed different *religiones*—that is, different forms of connection with and commitment to different gods.[3] Consistently, the current study of Roman religion pays particular attention to the tension between prescribed and proscribed, public and private cults as vehicles for the negotiation of identities and hierarchies within and among specific communities of the ancient world.[4] As James Rives observes:

> [T]he mainstream Greco-Roman religious tradition, the tradition of the Roman Empire's social, economic, and political elite . . . did not conform to the expectations that many people would have of "a religion": there was no unified and coherent set of beliefs and principles, no sacred scriptures, no priestly class, and no associated moral code. Instead of "a religion" we can more usefully think of it as a group of loosely related but largely distinct ways of thinking about the interacting with the divine world.[5]

The question of religion becomes even more complex when we consider imperial or state religions, where references to the "sacred" are instrumental in justifying institutional changes in terms of continuity with past traditions. Claims about the privileged connection of a particular lineage with the "divine" served the purpose of de-historicizing the origins of the lineage's political authority. Through association with absolute, transcendental factors or immortal beings that played a crucial role in the foundational phases of a given civilization, the political privileges of certain families and groups become impervious to contingency, despite the possible incompetence, eventual fallibility, and inevitable mortality of their members.

In monotheistic systems, the theoretical coincidence of the "divine of the rulers" with the "divine of the ruled" facilitates propagandistic efforts required for the "sacralization" of specific institutions. For example, the Catholic Church in Italy exploited the resilience of "polytheism" among the common people by formally embracing the countless saints worshipped throughout the peninsula as discrete emanations of the same, unique, and indivisible divine substance.[6] In non-monotheistic systems the de-historicization of power requires more socially nuanced approaches. For example, Octavian Augustus (r. 27 BCE–14 CE) succeeded in legitimizing the establishment of hereditary monarchy by successfully catering to different social groups. Through different media, he famously managed to satisfy different attitudes towards the notion of "divine rulership"—from the openly hostile senators in the capital to commoners and slaves in the western and eastern portions of the empire.

Octavian's strategy benefited from the relative cultural integration of the Mediterranean world. In those times, save a few exceptions, "religion" did not determine cultural identity and political allegiance in an exclusionary way.[7] In addition, the similitudes among the gods worshipped among Indo-European and non-Indo-European peoples, thanks to millennia of intense contacts and migrations, allowed for the so-called *interpretatio romana*—the practice of accepting the deities of conquered peoples as simply different versions of those worshipped by the Romans.[8]

As for the Han Empire, at least until Emperor Wu's death, the extant sources do not attest to the existence of public rituals in which rulers and subjects could participate together. The ceremonies and practices described in the "Confucian" Classics, in which the divine had basically no active function, would become fundamental in defining elite roles and identities only in a later period. At least during the early Han, the coexistence of different regional ritual traditions had not yet given way (and would not for centuries) to a unitary, identitary, or exclusionary conception of the sacred that could be considered "orthodox."[9] The bureaucratic centralization that progressively brought local ritual activities under the aegis of the government was mainly aimed at fiscal and political control of regional centers of power. Despite the adoption of a common vocabulary for administrative purposes, the process of bureaucratization did not correspond to the creation of a "common religion." Han documents show that local ritual traditions were not necessarily mutually intelligible.[10]

The identification of China's political unification with the establishment of shared morals and a coherent vision of the cosmos probably took place in the decades between the Western and Eastern Han. The notion that the elaboration of a "Han state doctrine" corresponded to the formalization of a state religion was the invention of late nineteenth-century Qing reformers.[11] However, betraying a "unitary bias," scholars have regularly ignored or misinterpreted available evidence. The Sinologist Derk Bodde, for example, author of a seminal work on Han festivals, relied more on later Eastern Han accounts than on the *Records*' closer (and in some cases firsthand) descriptions.[12] Lester Bilsky, in his study of state religion in ancient China, admits that "[g]overnment policies during the reign of Emperor Wu were not predicated on a single, coherent philosophical system." Yet by applying an arbitrary distinction between philosophy and religion, Bilsky interprets Han cults in light of the synthetic approach to "Han Confucianism" that would prevail only later on.[13] Similarly, the temptation of favoring unitary models despite a lack of historical evidence is still conspicuous in otherwise theoretically sophisticated contemporary analyses.[14]

It seems that for professional Sinologists abandoning the construct of a "Chineseness" founded on the cultural preeminence of a holistic cosmology, the integration of moral and political spheres, or the correspondence of macrocosm and microcosm, is tantamount to admitting the subalternity of Chinese civilization.[15] Recently, as the foreign and modern origins of a unitary conception of religion have entered mainstream academic conversations, scholars of China have begun to exercise special caution around the notion of the sacred.[16] Nonetheless, their recourse to "subcategories" such as myth and ritual, secular and sacred, or the distinction between philosophy and religion does not necessarily yield a less problematic approach.

For example, K. E. Brashier, in the most erudite and insightful study to date of the cognitive and social aspects ritual in early China, observes:

> The people of early China had no ready word for "religion" as a sui generis discourse, but that of course does not mean that they had no religion. They had many of the components that we may consider "religious"—spirits, prayers, sacrifices, afterlife and so forth—but they simply did not draw a circle around those components and then label the circle as we do.[17]

The problem with this reasoning is that although it seems to relativize the category of "religion" as a non-Chinese creation, it uncritically accepts its traditional attributes, or those elements that we customarily include in the same sphere as religion, i.e. "spirits, prayers, sacrifices, afterlife and so forth."[18] If we imagined the Abrahamic notion of religion as a jar in which we arbitrarily collect disparate elements of Chinese civilization, we could consider Brashier's approach as simply removing the label without breaking the glass. Even if we were willing to hold on to the conceit of religion as a meta-cultural and meta-historical notion, should we not prioritize instead the categories and practices that explicitly concerned the ancient Chinese? For example, if, we replaced "religion," as Brashier does, with the equally foreign notion of "the sacred" (understood as the superior realm of the paradigmatic and superhuman) why should we not also include in the same category all those speculative instruments to which the ancient Chinese would resort to explore their relationship with the cosmos, such as the calendar, music, astronomy, or the art of reading facial features?

Also, if we adopt the phenomenological dichotomy between the spheres of the sacred and of the profane, how ought we to categorize Chinese ghosts and spirits, since their non-human, or more-than-human unruly nature seems to partake of both realms?[19] Finally, should we not feel as uncomfortable in conceptualizing an "early Chinese religion" as we would if we were called to tackle the issue of an early Roman Confucianism since, after all, ancient Romans had *patria potestas* (i.e., moral and legal authority of fathers) and *pietas* (i.e., devotion to all kinds of recognized authorities).

My point is that the biggest problems in the more or less implicit application of Abrahamic notions to the study of Early China lie in the (1) old conceit about the preeminence of theological knowledge over all other speculative doctrines; (2) the assumption that the divine or invisible must occupy an ontologically superior realm in early China as well; (3) the idea that the sacred-profane dichotomy can be unproblematically assumed as a cross-cultural category; (4) the fundamental role of religion in defining individual and collective identities in an exclusionary way; (5) the extra-human origin of foundational shared values; (6) and finally the expectation that all societies must conceptualize non-human phenomena as all parts of one integrated system, or coherent universe.

Chinese Religions and Comparative Approaches

In the last three decades, the impact of postmodernism and postcolonialism has prompted the most preeminent American scholars in the field to reconsider the foundational methodology of the comparative study of religion. Postmodernism has discredited universalistic approaches, both phenomenological and diffusionist, as well as the search for meta-narratives, while radically challenging the epistemological premises of the knowability of the Other. Postcolonialism, on the other hand, has deconstructed traditional Western scholarly attitudes toward non-European civilizations, denouncing their foundations as ethnocentric and driven by more or less overt cultural and political imperialism.[20] Under the severe scrutiny of these intellectual movements, the comparative study of religions suddenly appeared inadequate, arbitrary, or illegitimate. In short, it was clearly in need of a radical overhaul.

A Magic Still Dwells, a collection of papers given at the American Academy of Religion in 1995 and 1996, provided a compelling defense of cross-cultural approaches. By building on the work of Jonathan Z. Smith, the authors proposed a new framework that is more focused on historical processes and the specificity of contexts, while programmatically aware of the biases and agendas conditioning the research process. As Smith observes:

> [T]here is nothing 'natural' about the enterprise of comparison . . . In the case of the study of religion, as in any disciplined inquiry, comparison, in its strongest form, brings differences together within the space of the scholar's mind, for the scholar's own intellectual reasons. It is the scholar who makes their cohabitation—their "sameness"—possible, not 'natural' affinities or processes of history.[21]

Such vision produces an intellectual approach that is ethically inspired by reflexivity and a dialogical perspective. "Reflexivity" refers to the educated attention to the explicit and implicit dynamics of the subjectivity of the comparative act. The "dialogical perspective," according to Diana L. Eck, involves

> taking seriously the fact that there are people on both sides, all sides of the process of understanding. Not only are the religious lives, texts, or phenomena, we study situated in particular historical, geographical, intellectual and cultural contexts, but so are we who attempt to understand them . . . [T]he study of religion is itself a form of dialogue involving not only encounter with our subjects of study, but continue reflection on personal, religious or intellectual presuppositions that shape the intention and direction of our own study.[22]

From an epistemological point of view, the authors of *A Magic Still Dwells* overcame the nihilist excesses of postmodernism by agreeing on one irreducible universal. In their opinion, it is possible and necessary to engage in comparison because of the natural human inclination to both recognize and create patterns for heuristic and explanatory purposes.[23] Yet patterns do not constitute inflexible and impermeable conceptual boundaries. As William E. Paden remarks, patterns can be problematized and enlarged by distinguishing between *comparativist* and *insider* domains of meaning.[24] In addition to bringing into focus differences, what Paden calls "the bilateral nature of comparative perspective" can also help unveil otherwise unrecognized connections.[25] This kind of reflexivity defines the new comparative approach as morally committed to the development of compassion and solidarity while striving to historicize and overcome the negative and critical scrutiny of postmodernism and early postcolonialism.[26] The authors of *A Magic Still Dwells* redefined the comparative study of religion as a reflexive and heuristic effort, one entailing a methodology based on *description, comparison, redescription,* and *rectification*.[27] Though it no longer aspires to the realization of ontological truths, the ethical inspiration behind the comparativist project had been rekindled by the pursuit of new dynamic bases for cross-cultural dialogue. Some authors still cling to this moral focus, as though they hope to recover a semblance of the "original" concern with unity that defined the study of religion before it became the object of relentless historicization and contextualization. In other words, despite the fact that the field has made considerable advances, the general reliance on monotheistic/systemic frameworks has remained oddly resilient. Once outside its confessional or social dimension, the emotional and ethical investment at the core of the so-called Great Religions can induce even the most scrupulous specialists to project (more or less consciously) Judeo-Christian sensibilities onto non-Western contexts.

The Meaning and End of Religion by Wilfred Cantwell Smith can be taken as an example of how attachment to the Abrahamic notion of religion can create further compensatory reifications.[28] After tracing the development of ideas surrounding "religion" in the West, Cantwell Smith's groundbreaking work proposes discarding the essentialist notion of religion in favor of focusing on "transcendence, traditions, and faith," as though especially "transcendence" and "faith" were universal categories that do not need historicization.[29] Cantwell Smith's emphasis on transcendence, traditions, and faith, is ultimately of little use when studying ancient sources that lack analogous concerns.[30]

Timothy Fitzgerald suggests that even the purportedly scientific study of religion, as in Cantwell Smith's case, can disguise an "ecumenical liberal theology" which structurally constitutes a "godless" version of traditional teleological approaches.[31] As Fitzgerald bluntly states, religion as a universal cross-cultural category "does not pick out any distinctive cross-cultural aspect of human life," while it is always inevitably charged with ideological extra-academic purposes.³² In light of these considerations, scholars of non-European premodern traditions, regardless of confessional, cultural, or political agendas, should be encouraged to adopt programmatic self-consciousness in order to deal with the intrinsic and inevitable analytical biases specific to their own motivations and methodologies.

One of the few thorough reflections on the applicability of Western concepts and approaches to China is Robert Ford Campany's essay "On the Very Idea of Religions (In the Modern West and in Early Medieval China)."³³ Campany takes his cue from Cantwell Smith's historicization and J. Z. Smith's analytical rigor in order to scrutinize several metaphors and rhetorical constructs customarily used to reify Chinese traditions as though they were independent entities endowed with autonomous historical agency.³⁴ Concentrating on early medieval Chinese texts, Campany notes that theoretical concerns surrounding notions such as "faith" and "belief" were alien to contemporary worshippers, who rather focused on practical, performative aspects of rituals:

> So pervasive is the habit of reification that we do well to remind ourselves that "religions" do not exist as things in the world. The pertinent res [from Latin: things, objects] include texts, images, and other artifacts; structures such as temples and tombs; and the people who made, used, or otherwise came into contact with these. Anything else is an idea. So, if "Daoism" or "Buddhism" are unitary, perduring things, they are so because we, possibly along with cultural others (though certainly not early medieval "Daoists" or "Buddhists," since the English language in which it is possible to form the word "Daoism" did not yet exist), imagine and construct them as such in the ways we speak, not because they are natural existents we find in the world alongside the res we characterize as "belonging to" them.³⁵

In advocating for a more nuanced approach, as much attuned to similarity as to diversity, Campany rejects the tendency, exemplified by the work of Émile Durkheim (1858–1917) and Clifford Geertz, to think of religions as coherent symbolic systems.³⁶ To overcome the teleological reification of "religion" and the recourse to "belief" and "isms" as categorizing devices, Campany endorses the framework of Benedict Anderson's "imagined communities" and Ann Swidler's "repertoires of resources" (which she in turn derived from Michel Foucault's vocabulary).³⁷ Campany invites us to think of the coherence of such imagined communities as something repeatedly claimed, constructed, portrayed, or posited in texts, rituals, and other artifacts and activities, rather than as simply given. Much of this claiming concerns the past: the importance of retrospective selection, organization, and classification by latecomers as they tell the stories of communities they are in the process of imagining, highlighting certain aspects of the past and creatively forgetting others, cannot be overstated. Processes of the (again often retrospective) construction of lineages and the selection and arranging of scriptural canons are places where the process of community-imagining can be observed especially clearly. As we observe such processes at work, we will notice common touchstones, things referred to again and again—certain words, figures, stories, or texts—but how these are portrayed, used, and interpreted may vary so dramatically that the mere notation of references to them gains us very little.[38]

Nonetheless, if we move to the study of the early Chinese empires, Campany's theoretical and methodological insights need further elaboration. During the Eastern Han (25–220 CE), through the merchant routes of Central and South Asia, Chinese civilization encountered (and eventually appropriated or recreated) Buddhism.[39] Texts predating this period do not seem to envision, even implicitly, a conception of "religion" comparable to our current unitary framework. It is yet unclear whether the impact of foreign ideas and practices stimulated some ancient Chinese to rethink local teachings—such as those associated with Huang-Lao 黃老, alchemy, or the search for immorality in a more self-conscious and structured fashion—or whether these ideas and practices simply compelled preexisting traditions to come to the fore.[40] However, even though it is not yet possible to reconstruct the circumstances and modalities of such changes, we can acknowledge the rising popularity of some ideas, absent from earlier sources but appearing around the first century CE: the notion that the bases of social and individual fulfillment could ultimately reside in revealed meta-historical truths; more organic conceptions of afterlife; and a focus on institutionalization and moralization of the relations among practitioners through shared rituals and beliefs. More importantly, the assumption that such rituals could be broadly understood and adopted beyond geographical, ethnic, social, and cultural boundaries gained relevance. It cannot be overlooked, for example, that the acknowledgment of the importance of scripture, temple, and clergy in identifying Buddhism as an "organized religion" coincided with the appearance of early forms of organized "Daoism."[41]

During the Han, however, we see that intellectual elites between the first century BCE and the second century CE, in assembling a legitimizing literary canon (a loose repertoire of rules, models, and examples) did not regard direct contact with deities fundamental to the creation of an ideal community. In fact, they feared that extra-human forces might undermine the morality of the secular rituals that were supposed to be at the heart of the ideal Confucian society. As for Sima Qian, in his narration of the unification of China, he did not conceive the extra-human realm as either ontologically separated or, as Western religious tradition might, transcendent, but as one of several aspects of reality that could be experienced during one's life. The chapter of the *Records* devoted to the biographies of Sima Qian and his father Tan states that although the world is one, it can be understood and acted upon in different ways, all of which have their advantages and shortcomings.[42] The authors of the *Records* believed that the most urgent task in the early decades of the Han Dynasty was to provide the recently formed unified polity with administrative efficiency and social stability. Accordingly, they identified those communities that developed around Yin and Yang, Dao, the Ru, the School of Names, Mozi's followers, and the Legalists through their practical preoccupation with politics, not their beliefs and practices concerning the metaphysics of personal development.[43]

Once we establish that a unitary interpretation of religion is not a universal concept that can be applied to all realities, we realize than even discerning what aspects of early Chinese life should be studied *sub specie religionis* becomes an arbitrary exercise.[44] It seems obvious that, as Jonathan Z. Smith suggests, "religion" should be used only heuristically as a research tool and systematically historicized as a specific cultural creation.[45] The implicit response of recent scholarship on early China to these concerns seems to consist in the retention of the popular category of religion as a loose container to be filled with philological, archaeological, or historical inquiries that in various ways touch upon subjects pertaining to the "religious sphere." Projects such as the collective multi-volume *Early Chinese Religion*, for instance, still offer original and insightful contributions, but when it comes to the unifying theme of the project, in most on the contributions "religion" lurks about like an ancient ghost: almost no one dares to face it directly, some allude to it without actually mentioning its name, and most feel free to depict it in artful ways.[46]

An Ethnocentric Conundrum: Civilization without Religion

Scholars such as Daniel Dubuisson and, more recently, Tomoko Masuzawa, have framed the establishment of the universality of the concept of "religion" as a specific European cultural product.[47] According to their analyses, the "construction" and "invention" of world religions took place as a result of the intensification of contacts between modern Europeans and the Other outside the Mediterranean world, when redefining old identities in a global context became a priority. The projection of familiar models and approaches onto more or less alien realities served immediate classificatory needs, while also establishing new hierarchies that reinforced the sense of Western superiority. Due to mutated political and cultural circumstances, theology lost its undisputed place as the "queen of the sciences."[48] Nonetheless, other fields, although generally rejecting the discipline's explicit confessional goal (and, in so doing, complying with the new concern with reason and science) continued to pursue unity and systemic coherence—both of which were an important part of the legacy of Greek and Roman intellectual traditions that early modern Europeans were rediscovering (and recreating) as models.

Despite the deconstructive and critical efforts of the past two decades, several recent comparative endeavors remain more or less overtly committed to the specific objects of theology, which are visible in their enduring emphasis on teleological trajectories and systemic biases. It is still popular to claim that the linear progress of humankind can be appraised independently of geographical, cultural, and historical boundaries, through a dialogue between Reason and Revelation. The reason for the resilience of these methodological and ideological tendencies is that even current scholarly discussions on religion(s) have to come to terms with the sensitive role of the sacred in contemporary political questions. Current intellectual approaches in the field of political science are inclined to reify identitary interpretations of religion and refer to them deductively as source of both collective identity and agency. In advocating the need to establish the conceptual basis for a cross-cultural dialogue, influential debates on the anticipated "clash of civilizations," for example, tend to identify religion as a meta-cultural element that simultaneously represents the cause of and the solution for ethnic, cultural, and political conflicts.[49]

In the field of sociology of religions, Robert Bellah's magnum opus, *Religion in Human Evolution*, attests to the undying popularity of "religion" as a universal metaphor for social structures and interactions independent of the contingencies of history and geography. Bellah posits religion as "a system of beliefs and practices relative to the sacred that unite those who adhere to them in a moral community."[50] While this interpretation may be useful in studying modern and contemporary contexts, it is not easily applicable to early Chinese realities.

Roy Rappaport's influential *Ritual and Religion in the Making of Humanity* is another example of the projection of Durkheim's intellectual legacy into contemporary debates on the developmental trajectory of humankind. It propounds a new concept of religion founded on postmodern science as a remedy to the contemporary hiatus between society and nature.[51] This illustrates how the hope for a harmonious world founded on universally shared values can also guide comparative works that do not have religion at the foreground. Such a propensity often results in the surprising adoption of phenomenological assumptions that specialists of religions have abandoned decades ago. The all-powerful deity of Judaism, Christianity, and Islam becomes, despite the absence of any supporting textual evidence, the more or less implicit protagonist even of early Chinese historical narratives. This attitude underlies the popular conception of the sacred as a trans-cultural subject that transcends the empirical methods of historical research—as if different religions of the world constituted discrete epiphanies of the same supernatural truths, or as if they were psycho-linguistic archetypes to which everyone can refer regardless of their field of expertise.[52] For instance, in a recent and otherwise compelling comparative project carried out by Georg Iggers and Edward Wang, we can find the following statement, presented as unproblematic: "in the works of Confucius and Sima Qian there were frequent references to the *tian* (Heaven), or the Chinese notion of God."[53]

Understandably, students of early China have to cope with even more theoretical and methodological obstacles. Both the conceptual repertories and the very disciplines applied to the study of the past (history, archaeology, anthropology, sociology, and so on) originated in Europe to investigate specifically European questions. Since the mid-nineteenth century, Chinese scholarship developed alongside or as an answer to foreign political and academic approaches. Even though current research tends to concentrate on native themes and priorities, the intellectual "challenges" and "reactions" from both sides are mostly still formalized by means of non-Chinese hermeneutical traditions.[54] In the study of the extra-human, for example, several scholars seem prone to unproblematically accept conventional boundaries between fields such as religion, alchemy, magic, and superstition that are clearly derived from European experiences.[55]

Furthermore, we cannot overlook the complex bearing that the recent prodigious "Western-style" economic development in China exerts on reformulations of individual and collective identities in a nation which still officially defines itself Communist.

The tension between religion and secularism characterizes discourses on foundational and shared values in almost all countries with an Abrahamic heritage. The implied interdependence of faith, morality, and identity affects both scholars who were formed in contexts deeply indebted to the three main monotheistic creeds and those who reject these paradigms. The assumption that religion universally determines the social and institutional structures of communities (an assumption largely due to the continuing influence of Karl Marx and Max Weber) makes even the study of the past susceptible to cultural, ideological, and political agendas.[56] In the case of China, for example, recognizing in early periods the existence or the absence of a unitary religion inevitably impinges on broader debates concerning comparability and exceptionality. Assessing the Abrahamic-like moralizing influence of "the sacred" in crucial formative moments of Chinese civilizations can easily turn into an essentialist discussion about ethnic and national identity, which in turn has an obvious bearing on the perception of China's current and future role in global politics and economy.[57] For these reasons, while there already exists a sound comparative approach that analyzes institutions, economic structures, and practices across ancient Chinese and Mediterranean civilizations, the study of cultural factors, especially "religion," seems much more problematic.[58]

The reasons for the methodological vagueness that marks the study of the extra-human sphere in China, however, are not all connected to Euro-American ethnocentrism. For example, among the most influential is Confucius's alleged "aversion" to those manifestations of popular religiosity that were not validated by the hallowed textual tradition. Such a bias, through the Ming and Qing governing elites and via the Jesuit fathers who portrayed Confucius as a secular humanist, would deeply influence European views of the Central States.[59] The privileged relationship of European diplomats and missionaries with Confucian elites and the literary focus of the Chinese imperial examination system also reinforced the role of textual analysis as the key to cultural and political authority. Ever since Confucius's times and throughout the imperial era, arguments on political questions customarily required educated references to legitimizing textual and historical precedents, which resulted in the overt politicization of philology. Not surprisingly, the study of the Chinese past has often turned into a proxy for ideological battles that still reverberate in contemporary scholarship, as discussions on the interpretation of ancient civilizations tend to conflate the sensitive issues of academic objectivity, ethnic, and cultural identities for polemic purposes.[60]

Among the effects of China's "opening to the West" is the persistence of a peculiar blend of positivistic and Marxist prejudice against religion as a factor that hinders scientific and social progress.[61] In stark opposition to this trend, many hold that defining China as "secular" or "atheist" corresponds to implicitly denying its full inclusion among the world's great civilizations and spiritual traditions. Some aspects of the recent "Confucian revival," are openly oriented toward the recovery of purportedly religious or spiritual aspects of Confucianism an indigenous alternative to the diffusion of Western-style materialism originated by the economic growth of the 2000s.[62]

It should not be forgotten that beginning with the earliest intercultural exchanges the Western search for a distinctive Chinese religion has served specifically European preoccupations. The Jesuits treated the Chinese as enlightened heathens capable of ethical concerns but lacking knowledge of the one true God. Enlightenment thinkers for their part looked to China as a model of a strong state without an established church. German idealists, on the other hand, bemoaned the "lack of transcendental drive" in Chinese civilization and argued that this absence prevented Chinese subjects from realizing the freedom of the individual spirit within a modern nation state.[63]

The search for a quintessential "Chineseness" can be interpreted as an alternative to the transcendental absolutes of western cultures. Although it has produced original and effective interpretive models, such a concern still tends to defy the specific aim of the historical research—the study of change in context.[64] For example, even if it were methodologically sound to study the Shang 商 (ca. 1600–1046 BCE), the Zhou (1046–256 BCE), and the subsequent periods under the assumption that each represented a discrete moment in the teleology of a unitary civilization, continuity between different notions and practices concerning the extra-human cannot be inferred in the absence of historical evidence. From a methodological point of view, the difficulty of reconstructing the writing and editing processes of the received textual tradition in a strictly chronological order should make researchers wary of implying historical connections between these sources, the "religious" materials they present, and the cultural and political contexts to which they are conventionally related.[65] Early historical sources, however, defy such a linear conceit. Even a cursory glance suggests that the relationship between the human and extra-human realms presented in the *Records*, for example, is not patterned in ways that match the holistic and totalizing nature of the Abrahamic religions, nor the high level of integration within social and institutional structures that characterizes the classic Mediterranean world.⁶⁶

The existence of a Chinese state religion does not predate the nineteenth century and, in fact, is associated most closely with the Hundred Days reform movement of 1898. After suffering a humiliating defeat at the hands of Meiji Japan (1868–1912) and negotiating the Treaty of Shimonoseki in 1895, Chinese politicians thought that the introduction of Western concepts and technologies could strengthen the empire of the Qing 清 (1644–1911) and protect it from future foreign threats. It is in this context that the Western model of an organic relation between political authority and the extra-human entered the agenda of late Qing reformers. Adopting from Japan the Western ideas of "divine right" or "divine power" (*shenquan* 神權) and the conceptual dichotomy between religion (*zongjiao* 宗教) and superstition (*mixin* 迷信), Qing reformers attempted to enforce a more systematic institutional control over education at the expenses of popular cults. To this end they implemented the "Build education with temple property" policy (*miaochan xingxue* 廟產興學). ⁶⁷

Clearly, the politicization of religious beliefs and practices that characterized the Mediterranean world since the fourth century CE and that also interested the Chinese reformers of the late imperial age is not applicable to early imperial China.⁶⁸ In the West, this process developed alongside a specific conception of civic identity based on the Christian creed and the legal expression of the exclusivist relationship of "orthodoxy" and "heterodoxy." Fundamental in this transformation was the increasing discretionary power of the bishops, ecumenical councils, and the Catholic Church.⁶⁹ Also important is the fact that the definition of orthodoxy became instrumental in determining which religious communities would be exempted from imperial taxation.⁷⁰ When Theodosius I (r. 379–395) made Christianity the official religion of the Roman Empire, outlawing all other cults in 380, orthodoxy came to coincide with full citizenship and civil rights.⁷¹ A century earlier, in the transition between *principate* and *dominate* between the third and the fourth century, the divine investiture of the ruler was invoked to justify the Senate's progressive loss of power, an institution that, until the end of the Severan Dynasty (193–235 CE), was expected—at least formally—to produce the collegial appointment of the Roman emperor.⁷² The adoption of a state doctrine that instituted a universalistic and monotheistic religion allowed the Empire to advertise its unified rule as sacred and necessary while allowing it to claim more pervasive control over political and social institutions.

In the Middle Ages, the sacraments, whose authority derived from the Vicar of Christ in Rome, were instrumental in defining and regulating social interactions at the local level. During the Reformation and the Counter-Reformation periods, between the fifteenth and sixteenth centuries, local struggles around religion and political authority reflected the conflict between the dominance of the Roman Church and the assertion of new socioeconomic realities and cultural identities all over Europe.[73]

By contrast, the social, political, and institutional aspects of beliefs and practices in early imperial China are far less clearly delineated, while their meaning has often to be sought at the local or individual level. Accordingly, the Taiwanese scholar Mu-chou Poo has characterized the relationship of the early Chinese with the extra-human realm by emphasizing their focus on personal welfare.[74] Still, it might be useful to establish—from a methodological point of view—whether the prevalently individual nature of Chinese relationships with non-human forces should be regarded as the defining element of an organic system of beliefs and practices, or as just one of many diverging aspects in the comparative study of early China and the ancient Mediterranean world.

The Axial Age: History Becomes Philosophy, and Philosophy Reverts to Religion

In order to cope with the methodological difficulties of studying the realm of the invisible in early China, some scholars have established more or less arbitrary conceptual boundaries between religion and philosophy. The peculiar concern with recognizing this distinction in Chinese civilization too arguably coincides with the arrival of Jesuit missionaries in the sixteenth and seventeenth centuries. As the first Westerners to engage in fruitful dialogue with Chinese intellectual and political elites, their representations of the host civilization had a profound impact on European perceptions of China.[75] The translations and accounts produced by the missionaries tended to portray the indigenous mainstream tradition associated with the hegemonic Classicist/*ru* ideology (known in the West as "Confucianism") as a secular humanistic doctrine, in no small part because religious rivals within the Catholic Church were eager to indict the Jesuits' involvement in Chinese rituals as a form of nativist idolatry.[76]

And while the purported "secularism" of Chinese society has served as an example for European rationalistic or anti-clerical movements, to emphasize the "religious nature" of Confucianism or other traditions of the Central

States today amounts to re-introducing China into a global (but actually Abrahamic-centered) discourse on "great world religions and civilizations."[77]

In similar fashion, historians of philosophy tend to view the cultural liveliness of China's Warring States period (475–221 BCE) through comparisons with the achievements of the Greeks in the sixth and fifth centuries BCE. In addition to Confucianism, several scholars have re-conceptualized the cultural traditions of the Mohists, Legalists, Taoists, and adherents of the Yin-Yang tradition with the intent of recognizing in them a degree of theoretical consistency in some way comparable to the one acknowledged in the philosophical schools of the ancient Mediterranean.[78]

It is especially due to the work of Fung Yu-lan (1895–1990) that these traditions have been elevated to the Chinese counterpart of the Western philosophical heritage. Fung, a student of the pragmatist philosopher John Dewey (1859–1952), founded a non-Marxist approach to Chinese intellectual history by separating a "philosophical" tradition from a "religious" one. He did so by excluding "non-rational" elements—even though such a conceptual distinction is not formalized in the early Chinese sources. Fung justified the perceived lack of systemic coherence of Chinese traditions by emphasizing their concentration on practice and individual development rather than on doctrinal speculation.[79] At the same time he was interested in historicizing the formation of the schools by tracing their origins back to the professional advisors employed by Warring States lords and tasked with finding solutions to issues concerning political relations, economic administration, ritual, and warfare.[80]

Fung's apologetic and reductionist stance remains popular among scholars. Angus C. Graham, for example, suggests that those who are willing to engage Chinese thought from a philosophical point of view should "not scruple" to come to terms with the imperfection of Chinese syllogisms and accept the impossibility of fully disengaging analytic from correlative thinking.[81] As Graham states:

> Taking Chinese thought seriously is not simply a matter of acknowledging the rationality of some of it (and perhaps denying the name 'philosophy' to the rest), nor of discovering something valuable to oneself in the poetry of Lao-tzu or the diagrams of the Yi. Its study constantly involves one in important contemporary issues in moral philosophy, the philosophy and history of science, the deconstruction of established intellectual schemes, the problems of relating thought to linguistic structures, and correlative thinking of logic.[82]

As this passage suggests, even scholars who are willing to "take Chinese thought seriously" still often do so from the vantage point of western hermeneutical tendencies and conceptual categories.

Revivals of the "religious and philosophical" Axial Age theory, associated with the German philosopher and psychologist Karl Jaspers (1883–1969), have often succored sinologists like Graham who are concerned with the "fuzziness" of the cultural traditions of China and its inclusion among the "great world civilizations." Jaspers's thesis reflects the tendency to reach beyond the boundaries of historical inquiry to find a grounding for an intercultural analysis, as he postulates the involvement of all humankind in a religious and philosophical journey toward universal truths. In light of the "spiritual" aim of the Axial Age, the moral focus usually acknowledged at the core of mainstream Chinese traditions seems to overshadow the "imperfection" of its intellectual systems. As Jaspers writes: "In the years centering around 500 BC—from 800 to 200—the spiritual foundations of humanity were laid, simultaneously and independently, in China, India, Persia, Palestine, and Greece."[83] According to Jaspers, Taoism and Confucianism, the Upanishad and Buddhism, Zoroastrianism, Judaism, Platonism, and other religions and philosophies of the classic and Hellenistic ages represented the "simultaneous" and polycentric epiphany of the same revelation. He suggests, in short, that discrete cultural achievements by people in different cultural and material circumstances served the same (basically Western) ideas of progress and civilization. Drawing from German idealism, Jungian psychology, and Weberian sociological analysis, such a theory more or less implicitly offers a philosophical justification for a universalism typical of Christianity.

In addition, the Axial Age theory presents some major methodological problems. This is especially evident when one tries to identify traditional religious models within specific historical contexts. Axial Age theorists tend to edit out those aspects of the relationship between human beings and the extra-human that they do not see as contributing to the rational development of the individual within society. Jaspers and his cohort overlook the function of those practices and beliefs that occupy an important position in the fabric of any community. Therefore, they take "metaphysics" into consideration only insofar as it can be analyzed consistently by means of a systemic philosophical approach. Jaspers also assumes that a notion of spirituality informed by a theoretical synthesis based on the cultural heritage of the Mediterranean world lies at the origins of all civilizations. Thus, he exempts the Abrahamic concept of religion historical scrutiny and posits it as an a priori descriptive category, or—in Hegelian terms—as the metaphysical foundation of history.⁸⁴ A further consequence of Jaspers's approach is that universalism no longer represents only an ethical and political attitude but becomes an epistemological axiom that can seriously hamper a strictly historical approach.

Such a tendency has prompted scholars to analyze Chinese thought largely to ascertain whether it complies with or diverges from the imagined common journey of humankind from the "one single origin" to the "common goal." More specifically, when applied to the Han era, the Axial Age theory has led scholars to concentrate on the negative role exerted by the unified rule of the Han. Heiner Roetz, for example, has argued that the "rise of Confucianism to state orthodoxy," its "ossification," and the "monopoly on opinions" extinguished the cultural liveliness, richness, and variety of the (axial) Spring and Autumn (770–476 BCE) and Warring States (475–221 BCE) periods.⁸⁵

However, Roetz's claims, which are based on elite sources, are flatly contradicted by both historical and archaeological evidence. As we will see more in detail throughout the following chapters, during the first decades of the Han dynasty, and at least until the end of Emperor Wu's reign in 87 BCE, no literary, doctrinal, or cultural orthodoxy—let alone religious and philosophical schools founded on well-defined and canonical texts, ideas, and practices—even existed.⁸⁶ Moreover, it is impossible to read Emperor Wu's private and public ritual activity in the *Records* as an attempt to establish religious or Confucian orthodoxy; rather, it appears there were very few principles and behaviors that all Classicists featured in the *Records* would have approved.⁸⁷ Even when the Emperor did employ Classicists, he preferred the advice of masters of esoteric techniques of immortality (*fangshi* 方士), such as those from the coastal regions of Qi 齊 and Yan 燕.⁸⁸ It is under the sway of these *fangshi*, according to Sima Qian, that Emperor Wu performed new state cults, such as those to Houtu 后土 and Taiyi 太一.⁸⁹ Textual and archeological evidence concerning elite burials from all over the country confirm the cultural richness that the *Records* describes.⁹⁰ Although Emperor Wu and his advisers were especially interested in enforcing administrative and economic uniformity, he nonetheless tolerated and even exploited cultural and religious diversity in order to forestall opposition to his centralizing policies.⁹¹ Early China lacked not only a state-imposed religion and ideology, but also a cultural tradition of systemic approaches to the extra-human.

I suggest that the emphasis on the correspondence between macrocosm and microcosm, apparent through an inferential reading of some

Chinese philosophical texts, could in fact represent an intellectual reaction to perceived cultural fragmentation and political instability. Historians of philosophy Roger Ames and David Hall have argued that

> [t]he 'organismic' metaphysics which explicates the relationship between part and whole and constitutes the common ground on which the Confucian and the Taoist traditions have been erected, when fully appreciated, can be extended to virtually all areas of Chinese culture and used as a basis for understanding why the Chinese have traditionally chosen to construe human experience in the way they do.[92]

This argument, which is mostly based on the analysis of speculative texts, compellingly reflects the view of several Chinese thinkers, but starkly contrasts with the approach of the first Chinese universal history. The *Records* describes people's actions in the world as a continuous struggle to understand the different principles that animate coexisting—but not coinciding—moral codes, political realms, and existential levels. According to the *Records*, everyone—rulers and subjects, leaders of different states, human beings and spirits—abides by different rules and is moved by different necessities. Although it seems that the authors of the *Records* hoped at first that the political unification under the Han would finally facilitate the return to a mythical Golden Age, they did not equate the Han rule with the reestablishment of the morals of yore. In fact, the *Records* remarks that from the Zhou to the Han, too many changes and losses had occurred to consider the restoration of a common cultural tradition feasible or even conceivable.[93]

After all, it could be argued that the tendency to emphasize variation and inconsistency represents one of the distinctive features of the "historicist" (as opposed to the "philosophical") approach. As for the relationship between the human and the extra-human spheres, although the *Records* profusely describes beliefs and practices concerning the invisible, it limits its inquiry to empirically observable phenomena. In general, the *Records* concentrates on the effects that beliefs and practices about the extra-human exert on human lives, rather than on the nature of the extra-human realm.

Xu Fuguan 徐復觀 (1903–1982) famously remarked that Sima Qian's analytical acumen makes readers feel disappointment that the *Records* ultimately lacks an explicit or overarching philosophical view.[94] But, as I will show below, Sima Qian's exceptionality lies in echoing a plurality of voices and views while recounting a process of political unification. His comprehensive history does not succumb to the temptation of bending the interpretation of causality to a known end—the Han Empire. The Grand Historian concentrated more on cultural lineages, geographical origins, and specific competences of important figures than on their intellectual views. Whether the experts to whom the *Records* refers were interested in merely human or in extra-human factors, none of them exhibit the preoccupations that characterize Western philosophical and religious traditions. If several current notions of religion in China are expressed in precise philosophical and juridical language and predominantly informed by the ontological dualism of noumenon and phenomenon and the principles of identity and non-contradiction, it is because they reflect some of the political and cultural features of the modern world that produced them. Plato's (428/427–348/347 BCE) dialectic thought, Aristotle's (384–322 BCE) systemic approach and categories, and, eventually, the Judaic notion of a monotheistic God are some of the elements that contributed to the formalization of modern notions of religion. The idea of systemic unity acquired a special emphasis as a consequence of a Christian reading of the Roman Empire. The dialectic of monotheism versus polytheism (the system of the heathens), oneness versus multiplicity, orthodoxy versus heterodoxy, absolute versus relative, and secular versus sacred still variously inform the ways in which we argue about the moral foundations of contemporary nation states. Before they can be applied to Chinese thought, the epistemological validity of these categories needs to be checked against the historiographical, cultural, and political contexts in which the authors and protagonists of the *Records* were operating.

Philology as Mythology

Given the methodological, conceptual, and ideological obstacles to applying a unitary notion of religion to early China, it seems obvious that reducing the topic to smaller or disarticulated unities, such as myth or ritual, should simplify our enterprise. But non-Chinese priorities have also shaped scholarly approaches to Chinese antiquities that concentrate on myth and ritual, especially insofar as these have been understood as the foundational and performative components of European religions and societies.

Whether European scholars conceive myth and ritual as coextensive or independent, their work has evolved alongside and been influenced by cultural and political debates.[95] Ever since Plato's criticism of the irrationality of popular and oral culture, myth has featured negatively against logos in conversations about modalities of knowledge, shared values, and political consensus.[96] Because of its rich literary and symbolic dimensions, the category of myth is usually reserved for the (often condescending) analysis of pre-Christian civilizations, usually in a context where primitive "fables and superstitions" are pitted against the "truths" embodied by scriptures and sacraments on the one hand, or reason and science on the other.[97] Beginning in the early modern period, when the Renaissance and the Reformation were shaking Europe to its foundations, a rekindled interest in local languages, folklore, and myths coincided with new claims about collective identities as a political and cultural challenge to the hegemony of Catholic Rome. Eventually, criticisms of myths complemented the struggle of Enlightenment thinkers against religious obscurantism. Subsequently, the Romantics reached for these "fables" in their longing to connect with a heroic past. It was in this context that the German intellectual Johann Gottfried von Herder (1744–1803) reevaluated myth as "primordial and authentic" as the truest expressions of a people's spirit and identity.[98]

In the second half of the nineteenth century, while the comparative study of religion was attaining academic autonomy, the study of ancient myths became central to the philological search for the roots of Western languages and civilizations. Adalbert Kuhn (1812–1881) in Germany, Friedrich Max Müller (1823–1900) in Britain, and later Georges Dumézil (1898–1986) in France built on the assumption that cultures belonging to same linguistic family (such as the Indo-European) shared the same psychological, cultural, and social structures, and that these structures could be accessed and reconstructed through myths.[99] The scholarship of these pioneers of comparativism privileged the literary heritage produced by educated elites. Their approach tended to posit religions as well-structured linguistic systems: it emphasized the internal coherence of specific narratives while neglecting elements dubbed "idiosyncratic." Since the aim of early comparative efforts was to investigate the origins of European civilizations, the etymological, formal, and genealogical relations among Indo-European languages were translated into disquisitions about cultural origins and derivations through the analysis of the rich mythological heritages of ancient India, Greece, and Rome.[100] Among the intellectual products of this tendency were the fateful conceptualization of the fundamental separation between Aryan and Semitic groups and the conceit that varying levels of relationships with the supernatural defined social and racial hierarchies.[101] At the same time, some philologists, by appropriating Carl G. Jung's (1875–1961) notion of archetypes, interpreted religious symbols and behaviors as evidence for universal psychological paradigms.[102]

In the wake of Charles Darwin's (1809–1882) and Herbert Spencer's (1820–1903) trailblazing theories, comparative scholars strove to adjust their methodology to cultural evolutionism.[103] At a moment when many intellectuals believed that humankind could finally do away with religion, the new scientific sensibility offered specialists of ancient mythology the possibility of presenting their philological efforts as non-confessional, academic, and "rational" approaches to the question of the sacred.[104] In keeping with this secular inclination, the sociologist Émile Durkheim (1857–1917) and the anthropologist and ethnographer Claude Lévi-Strauss (1908–2009) pioneered extremely productive academic traditions that, rather than concentrating only on texts and mythological narratives, expanded the scope of the research to explain and order all facets of past and living cultures (e.g., environment, material culture, and interpersonal relations) regardless of their levels of literacy. Durkheim famously read mythological and ritual traditions as projections of social structures and dynamics. Lévi-Strauss recognized in the synchronic (as opposed to historical) study of myths throughout the world elementary structures of the human mind and their relation to material conditions. This insight led him to the production of enormously influential interpretive and classificatory paradigms, such as the basic opposition of communities of hunter/gatherers and farmers, the definition of primitive mentality as prone either to adaptation or systematic planning, and the roles of totems and taboos in the formalization of group interactions and identities.[105]

Finally, in the past few decades, the impact of postmodern and postcolonial radical critiques of traditionally Western heuristic approaches has prompted leading researchers to reconsider the universality of the categories of myth and ritual. Bruce Lincoln's definition of myth as "ideology in narrative form" exemplifies the acknowledgment of the need for a more critical and reflexive attitude.[106] According to Lincoln, a scholarly text "is not discourse of free invention" but results "from a dialectic encounter between an interested inquirer, a body of evidence, and a community of other competent and interested researchers, past, present, and future. All who participate are committed to a sustained engagement with the data and also with one another, their engagements being mediated by shared principles of theory and method, which—like the evidence and its interpretation—are subject to renegotiation in the space of their texts and conversations."[107]

If we translate this approach to the study of "Chinese myths," we note that the phase of renegotiation is further complicated by the non-Chinese methods and theories to which scholars are bound to resort. Moreover, as a further obstacle toward a reflexive approach to Chinese antiquities, we may find a peculiar blend of modernist, evolutionary biases (also intrinsic to Marxist approaches), together with the spirit of competition spurred by the perceived necessity to explain the original features of Chinese civilization in terms of difference from Western paradigms.

But before delving into the methodological and theoretical aspects of the issue, let us return to the origins of intercultural contacts. As we have seen above, Europe was introduced to the heritage of Chinese civilization through the translations of highly educated Jesuit missionaries who began to settle in the country between the end of the sixteenth and the beginning of the seventeenth centuries. Their understanding of Chinese culture was largely the result of their interaction with local intellectuals and officials. The acceptance of Jesuits among Chinese elites was also a consequence of these Europeans' extraordinary efforts to acquire philological mastery of texts that constituted the core curriculum for the selection of functionaries at all levels of the imperial administration.[108] All Chinese who occupied a respectable social position cherished these *Classics* as the heritage of the Zhou dynasty and the fruit of Confucius's editing and compiling efforts.[109] At the center of the ethical world of the *Classics* and their commentaries lay the notion of *li*, which consisted of highly formalized norms and behaviors about etiquette and propriety that were held to be the foundation of social hierarchies and interactions. Given that the *Classics* were regarded as the ultimate source of political authority and moral legitimacy, it was not difficult for European observers to recognize their "quasi-scriptural" function. Distinguishing the purported central message of the *Classics* from Abrahamic religions was the non-supernatural origin of the cardinal values and rituals identified with *li*. Ancient texts did not attribute these ideas and practices to the will of a divine entity, but to the teachings of sage rulers of the past.

However, if the extra-human realm did not seem to play an important role in Chinese society, it mainly depended on the fact that Westerners would more likely make contact with cultural elites, who tended to despise local ritual traditions as the result of ignorance and superstition. Western observers noted that Chinese elites regarded the study of select texts as both an indispensable means for recovering the founding values of Chinese civilization and an exclusive path to political authority. The intellectual attitudes of those foreigners who mastered literary analysis profoundly conditioned the development of Western approaches to Chinese mythological and ritual traditions.[110] Thus the text-based conceit of China as a secular empire served as a foil in European post-Reformation debates on the relationship between authority and the sacred, as well as in modern debates about the origin and destiny of western civilization.

It was the non-conformist Christian minister, missionary, and Sinologist James Legge (1815–1897) who laid the foundation for the integration of China in academic comparative discourses on world religions. When he contributed to Max Müller's monumental *Sacred Books of the East* with his translation of the *Classics*, this newly accessible corpus of "scriptures and founding mythology" finally made it seem possible to investigate China with the same interpretive tools and frameworks that had been applied to other global civilizations.[111] However, probably because of his isolation from mainstream intellectual life and because his own faith, Legge did not take into account contemporary theories on the study of ancient mythology, a field that was just acquiring methodological independence in the mid-nineteenth century.[112] As Anne Birrell notes, Legge's enormously influential translations treated Chinese myths either as imperfect renditions of biblical truths or as fictionalized (or simply faulty) historical accounts.[113] The same ambivalence that permeates Legge's work characterizes the major twentieth-century trends in the study of Chinese myths. Scholars who heavily rely on philology tend to assess the basic features of ancient Chinese civilization by perusing the received and excavated textual traditions without referring to ongoing methodological debates or systematically scrutinizing the recourse to foreign conceptual and methodological traditions. Programmatic comparative projects usually lean, more or less explicitly, toward either phenomenological assumptions or structural explanations. Furthermore, the adoption of foreign paradigms often makes them vulnerable to ideological or non-academic concerns.

The reactions to Gu Jiegang's 顧頡剛 (1893–1980) scholarly legacy exemplify some of the intellectual tensions surrounding the study of Chinese history. Gu's groundbreaking work focused on the connection between philology, mythology, and national identity.[114] Consistent with the preoccupations of the scholars associated with the Hundred Days reform movement, such as Kang Youwei 康有為 (1858–1927) and Gu's teacher Hu Shih 胡適 (1891–1961), Gu was interested in the reasons for China's "failure to modernize," as well as in reevaluating the cultural value of folk traditions.[115] The monumental multivolume oeuvre he edited, *Critiques of Ancient History* (*Gu shi bian* 古史辯), took issue with the traditional role of Chinese educated elites. In Gu's opinion, Chinese literati, instead of pursuing historical truth, had served the conservative interests of the ruling house by fabricating a myth of a golden age that reinforced the idea of Han cultural uniformity.[116]

According to Gu, the more the classic texts described myths as remote, the more likely it was that these myths represented the propagandistic creation of recent times. Of course, the very mention of Han cultural uniformity and reliability of traditional sources inevitably touches upon sensitive issues such as Chinese political unity, identity, and nationalism. Hence, when "history and nationalism as an imagined community" became united, in the years of the Nanjing Decade (1927–1937), Gu's challenge to traditional interpretations of the Chinese past turned into ideological debates about the very legacy and fate of Chinese civilization.[117]

Concurrently, European scholars inaugurated an intellectual trend that strove to go beyond the text, refute a top-down approach, and account for and reconstruct the contribution of popular and oral culture to the formation of Chinese mainstream literary tradition. Such a methodology, which arguably laid the foundations of the most productive and original approaches to Chinese religions, is deeply indebted to classic French sociology, a discipline that echoed contemporary European concerns with modernity and its discontents. The most influential representative of this tradition was the French Sinologist Marcel Granet (1884–1940), a student of Émile Durkheim and a collaborator of Marcel Mauss (1872–1950).[118] On the basis of his ethnographic research, Granet argued that the myths described in Chinese literary tradition derived from folk festivals and reflected social dynamics and commoners' rituals.[119] Ever since Granet's groundbreaking work, the relationship between elite and popular culture has been a central concern in sociological, anthropological, and historical studies of Chinese religion and mythology.[120] Scholars who have adopted this approach, especially in researching extant practices in China and Taiwan or to more recent or better-documented historical periods, have efficaciously described the performative aspects of rituals and unraveled the interaction of elite and popular mythological traditions in the negotiation of local identities across different cultural, social, and economic conditions.[121] Formulations such as the triad of "Gods, Ghosts, and Ancestors" and the "Bureaucratic" or "Imperial Metaphor" as models for the analysis of popular preoccupations with extra-human beings and heaven and hell likely represent the earliest effective theoretical advances based on the empirical observation of Chinese realities.[122]

Obviously, students of early China only have access to fragmentary evidence that cannot be supported by ethnographic inquiries or fieldwork. One consequence of this set of objective obstacles is the continued reliance on a philological approach. From a theoretical point of view the philology field tends to resort, more or less overtly, to structuralist or phenomenological frameworks that often present Chinese culture in "apologetic" terms.[123] For example, according to Anne Birrell's still valuable *Chinese Mythology: An Introduction*, the impossibility of addressing Chinese myths with the analytical rigor usually reserved for the classic Mediterranean tradition is due to the fact that "China lacked a Homer, or a Hesiod, a Herodotus or an Ovid, who recounted myth and shaped its content and style," as a consequence of which "early Chinese myth existed as an amorphous, untidy, congeries of archaic expression."[124] Instead of analyzing the conditions and contexts that produced different narratives, Birrell proposes to compensate for the inadequacy of Chinese literary traditions through an interdisciplinary (or composite) method rooted in Bronisław Malinowski's (1884–1942) functional approach, and in Otto Rank's and Lord Raglan's studies of Indo-European and Semitic heroic models, which were in turn influenced by Jungian archetypes.[125]

Since Birrell holds that the concept of myth does not have any substantive character, she organizes her subject matter through structural categories. Although her work acknowledges typically Chinese cultural products such as "Myths of Yu the Great" and "Immortality," it heavily relies on structuralist themes such as "Origins," "Culture Bearers," "Saviors," and "Destroyers." The problem with these paradigms is that they mainly stem from investigations of Indo-European and biblical sources and therefore do not necessarily resonate with early Chinese cultural concerns.[126] In prioritizing cosmogonic and foundation myths, Birrell does not account for their marginality in the cultural and ritual worlds of early China.[127] Even if her adoption of structural categories proves fruitful in constructing consistent sorting criteria for the study of literary sources, her insistence on methodological consistency often leads to unjustified assumptions about systemic models. *Chinese Mythology* carefully analyzes the connection between mythological themes and texts, but in explaining them within dominant Chinese cultural traditions (which she characterizes as Taoist, Confucian, and Buddhist), Birrell posits cultural boundaries and allegiances that were not thoroughly formalized in early China. It is likely due to this preference for systemic unities that *Chinese Mythology* favors explanations based on uniformity and standardization when discussing the long process of the establishment of the Han, despite the richness and variety of contemporary evidence.[128]

As for the Qin and Han periods, Birrell anchors her mythological analysis to Rémi Mathieu's thesis that "[O]ne direct result of the unification of feudal states into one empire during the Ch'in and early Han eras was that a process of homogenization of local mythological traditions occurred."[129]

However, historical sources suggest that, while Emperor Wu's politics were undoubtedly aimed at imposing economic and bureaucratic centralization, from a cultural and ritual point of view they were characterized by the acceptance and exploitation of local diversity rather than an attempt to enforce homogeneity. For instance, in Birrell's analysis, the *Records'* mention of a "pentad of gods" serves as evidence of the Han establishment of a "new pantheon" that was supposed to differ "fundamentally from the older pantheons."[130] Yet the section in question in the *Records* mentions the "pentad of gods" only in passing—and without ever suggesting that it replaced existing cults. The *Records* emphasizes the connection of the pentad with the unpopular Qin Dynasty, in the context of the description of rituals under the Han as a congeries of multifarious and often obscure traditions.[131] In brief, there is no proof that China had an organic polytheistic system that was widely acknowledged and embraced or that reflected the nation's political, social, and cultural stratification in the same way that ancient Greek and Roman religions did.[132]

Among the most cogent surveys on the subject so far is Mark Lewis's "The Mythology of Early China." This essay caps the author's original research on the myths of the Yellow Emperor (Huangdi 黃帝), Chi You 蚩尤 and political violence, and myths about the flood.[133] The thematic organization of the article reflects the author's acknowledgment of the complex relevance of Chinese mythological traditions in different sources and for different social groups.[134] Thus Lewis defines the main object of his essay as the collective and anonymous expression of the values at the basis of a given social group over time.[135] Lewis presents this definition as a response to deconstructivist readings of myths:

> To argue that the category "myth" has no substantive character but is determined by the concerns of the culture that produces a given story or stories, entails certain consequences for any application of comparative methods, an approach which is advocated by Anne Birrell . . . If there is nothing inherent in the structure or content of a story that marks it as a myth, then any resemblance in such contents or structures across cultures is not necessarily of any significance, and the tracing of such resemblances without first analyzing the place(s) and meaning(s) of a story within its own culture will not produce useful insights.[136]

Although Lewis's work undoubtedly enriches our knowledge of the specific myths with which he engages, his theoretical assumptions are not exactly a breakthrough in the field: most contemporary scholars of myth would agree with his argument about the foundational function of specific narratives within specific social and cultural contexts. Moreover, even in the wake of postmodern and postcolonial critiques to classical and modernist interpretations, historians of religions are for the most part not invested in rejecting the category of "mythology" *tout court*. Their methodologies do not rely on dismissing myths as "illusion" or "invention," but instead on the programmatic problematization of the supposed universality of influential assumptions that continue to undergird phenomenological and structural intercultural analyses. Today's specialists tend to prioritize the scrutiny of meta-historical conceits according to which the study of myths would help unveil universal psychological archetypes concerning social dynamics or collective and individual interactions with the (universally understood) divine. What leaves Lewis's theorizations open to critique is not his interest in myth, but rather his inclination to combine structuralist paradigms with Abrahamic notions about the sacred. For example, Lewis begins his section on the "sage kings" in this way:

> [A]lthough modern scholars state that the early Chinese treated the sage kings as human beings, this was not entirely true. During the Warring States and early empires the idea became widespread, if not universal, that the sage kings and dynastic founders—including the Han founder, about whom even the moderately skeptical Sima Qian recorded that he was sired by a dragon—were in fact the offspring of powerful spirits, dragons or forces of nature sired on human women. This assumption shows that the sage kings were not in any sense simply human. They were rather semi-divine beings, who marked the interface between the human world and the spirits.[137]

It is not clear which interpretation of the divine underpins the author's analysis: a monotheistic conception of the divine as an ontologically superior dimension that legitimizes specific values by sheltering them from contingency, or, in keeping with the ancient Greeks and Romans, the divine as a morally ambiguous and composite realm, which is nonetheless fundamental in defining social order and individual allegiance to the polity.

As for the Chinese context, ancient texts are largely uninterested in ascertaining in which ontological dimensions ghosts and spirits dwell and more invested in assessing the extent to which the involvement of divine beings in human affairs could be beneficial or detrimental to the establishment of a harmonious and prosperous society.[138] But whereas Chinese myths (i.e., exemplary and foundational narratives) were surely important in discourses about the dynamics and principles of communal life, in early imperial China we find no attempts to create a unitary vision of the divine, a polytheistic system, or a pantheon that could represent and legitimize the different strata of society.

Going back to, Lewis's focus on Sage Kings, he aptly defines these ancient sovereigns as the embodiment of tensions between nature and culture at the basis of the creation of distinct societies, which they customarily resolve by harmonizing human institutions with cosmic cycles. However, the creation of a unitary vision of imperial power, at least until the last decades of the Western Han, did not imply a reorganization of the various narrative traditions of the former warring states. Innumerable versions of tales about founding figures featured in various political and cultural debates during the early Han. Yet the possibility that they could have extra-human connotations or qualities was never the crucial point of the mythological narratives.[139] In the specific case of the *Records*, it is clear enough that its authors envisioned a model of rulership that was not based on direct contact with extra-human elements. As for the non-human origin of the founder of the Han, mentioned by Lewis as evidentiary in the passage cited above, my reading suggests that that Sima Qian reported rumors about a dragon in order to mock people's gullibility, which he believed Liu Bang 劉邦 (256–195 BCE) had successfully exploited.

As for my approach, I adopt Lincoln's definition of "ideology in narrative form," and analyze myths (or foundational and exemplary stories) insofar as it is possible to reconstruct the literary, cultural, and historical context in which they were told; to borrow Wendy Doniger's words, I analyze them "as classics." [140] We shall see how in the confrontation between Classicists and their intellectual opponents, a vision of foundational myths as separate or independent from the intervention of extra-human forces progressively prevailed among politicians and intellectuals connected to the court. In this process of separation of the human from the "divine," the legitimizing function shifted from the mythological narratives to the texts that contained them.[141] The act of reading or evoking the *Classics* became functionally "ritual," while the texts themselves came to represent the sacred, inviolable space of meaningful performance, the "templum."

Rituals for the Living and for the Dead

While inquiries into the religions of the Other have traditionally addressed myth in terms of meaning, narrative, and belief (albeit presumptively fallacious belief), ritual has routinely been relegated to the putatively less sophisticated sphere of action. More recently, trailblazing scholars such as Jonathan Z. Smith and Catherine Bell have elevated the study of rituals to an autonomous and extremely lively field. They have elaborated a conception of ritual independent of notions of religion, transcendence, and the sacred. Bell has richly redefined ritual within a broader cultural and social context as *formalized activities that establish links and hierarchies between individuals and groups.*[142] J. Z. Smith argues that "[r]itual is not an expression of or a response to the 'Sacred'; rather, something or someone is made sacred by ritual."[143] Smith employs "sacred" in its etymological, pre-Christian Latin meaning of *sacer*, that which is "made special" or "set apart," either because it is exceptionally beneficial or exceptionally accursed. Moving away from the Protestant insistence on the "emptiness of ritual as a blind and thoughtless habit," Smith redefines ritual as "a process for marking interest," "a mode of paying attention," especially through the specification of place. For him, "[t]here is nothing that is inherently sacred or profane. These are not substantive categories, but rather situational ones."[144]

For scholars of early China, it has been somewhat more difficult to cash in on the theoretical advances of ritual studies. While most sinologists still hesitate to move beyond a phenomenological and substantial interpretation of "the Sacred," a second problem arises from the fact that the English term "ritual," when applied to early China, can ambiguously refer to a confusingly wide range of ideas and practices. It can translate the specifically "Confucian" *Li* 禮, which stands for social customs, norms of propriety, courtesy, and etiquette that involve human interactions and ancestral sacrifices, but it can also describe any number of practices concerning spirits, ghosts, elemental transformations, and the quest for immortality.[145] While the values associated with *Li* would become an integral part of the official imperial ideology, the second group of concerns was routinely chastised in the literary canonical tradition.[146] The *li* of the *Five Classics*, and in particular of texts such as the *Liji* 禮記 (*Records of Rites*), the *Zhouli* 周禮 (*Rites of Zhou*), and the *Yili* 儀禮 (*Etiquette and Rites*), originally referred to the specific actions, clothing, implements, and timing of elite conduct, especially in state ceremonies, ancestral sacrifices, weddings, funerals, and mourning.[147] It is unclear whether these works reflected aspects of the culture of the exemplary Zhou, or whether they address concerns more specific to the ages of their later compilers and editors. Whether they served originally as descriptive or prescriptive texts, they provided ideas and practices that have come to be considered as foundational to the formalization of a

Chinese cultural identity. As Yuri Pines writes, "*li* was a hallmark of Chinese civilization, a dividing line between Chinese and aliens, and often between elite and commoner."[148] The evident centrality of *li* in Chinese hegemonic intellectual life has provided scholars in China and the West with models for positing a quintessential and ahistorical "Chineseness" that extends from the Neolithic period to more recent times.[149] On the other hand, because of its specificity, the study of *li* has developed independently of some of the non-Chinese paradigms that dominate other areas of study.

If we examine the mainstream interpretations of *li* against the analytical benchmarks proposed by Catherine Bell for the study of ritual activities, this concept appears to align consistently with the categories of "formalism," "traditionalism," and "invariance," while it also perfectly describes, in David Kertzer's terms, "behavior that is socially standardized and repetitive."[150] Differentiating *li* from conventional rituals is the interpretive class of "Sacral Symbolism," for its relationship with the extra-human realm cannot be easily translated into traditional Western religious concepts. It seems that originally *li* mainly consisted in food offerings to the ancestors. But with the ascendancy of the Classicists in the last decades of the Western Han, the focus on invisible ancestors shifted towards formalized interactions among the living. By favoring Confucius's and especially Xunzi's (312–230 BCE) interpretations, Chinese elites extolled *li* on account of the harmonious (and hierarchical) social relations that its practice would foster—not because of the supposed superior nature of its objects of worship.[151] In other words, at least until the Song dynasty, *li*'s cultivation was not aimed at the pursuit of superior metaphysical knowledge or a more intimate relationship with the divine, but at promoting and consolidating social practices and values.[152]

From a comparative perspective, *li*'s relative independence from extra-human factors, once it was appraised against Abrahamic traditions, prompted Western observers to articulate influential formulations that emphasized the secular origin of the Chinese sense of morality.[153] And at the beginning of the twentieth century, when Western-style reforms seemed finally inevitable, Qing-Dynasty (1644–1911) intellectuals and officials recognized in *li* the basis for a Chinese way to modernity that was compatible with reason, scientific progress, and traditional social values.[154]

However, as Michael Puett notes, the putative efficaciousness of elite rituals was not limited to the regulation of human relations, but extended to nature and the sphere of the dead as well.[155] As his analysis of the *Liji* demonstrates, between the Warring States period and the first decades after the unification there existed different competing views of rituals that reflected tensions and transformations in the political and cultural realms. According to a specific foundational myth in the *Liji*, it was the Sage Kings of yore who introduced sacrificial practices. Through food offerings, they hoped to tame those unruly forces that could threaten human life after a state of primeval harmony was interrupted. These potentially dangerous powers were either emanations of "mountains, forests, rivers, valleys, and hills that could sent out clouds, make wind and rain, and cause to appear strange phenomena," or spirits of the ancestors that would come back and haunt those relatives who had not properly fed them.[156] Only the sages could recognize these manifestations as "spirits" (*shen* 神) or ghosts (*gui* 鬼) and decide how members of the elite class should appease them, in accordance with their position in the polity, within the family, and on the basis of the extra-human entities present in the land under his control.[157] The *Liji* offers different accounts of the nature of these extra-human beings, but it is clear that its authors conceived these spirits and ghosts as made of the same substance as human beings and natural elements—*qi* 氣 at different concentrations.[158] However, as Puett points out, the ancient Chinese did not seem interested in theoretical or theological questions, and were rather concerned with orthopraxis.[159] In conclusion, he considers sacrifice, as defined in the *Liji*, the foundation of civilization. By means of sacrifice,

> ghosts are transformed into ancestors, capricious spirits and natural forces are transformed into hierarchically proper spirits, disparate biological families are transformed into a single created family. Similarly, the sacrificer is then transformed by his new relationship to these transformed recipients of the sacrifice: he gains a proper reverence for the ancestors, familial feelings, toward biologically unrelated people, and the like. If the sacrificer is the ruler, his position of power is greatly enhanced, as he comes to be situated in the crucial position between humanity and the world of ancestral and divine powers—he comes to be seen as the father and mother of the people as well as the Son of Heaven.[160]

It is impossible to ascertain whether the *Liji* describe situations that correspond to historical reality or whether they propound ideal, fictional scenarios. Either way, the conception of *li* that ultimately became dominant concentrated particularly on its human aspects. During the final decades of the Western Han, educated elites would privilege a more indirect form of contact with their biological and cultural ancestors through the cultivation of intellectual legacies and literary memory.¹⁶¹ At the same time, regardless of their private behavior, they began to denounce local cults as unrefined and dangerous.

Polarized views on civilization and nature, artifice and spontaneity, and social constraints and individual freedom hinged on the metaphorical or metonymic power of *li*. In the prevailing official rhetoric, *li* coincided with the very civilization of the Central States. In the *Zhuangzi* 莊子, however, *li* arises when human beings lose contact with the cosmos and its rhythms. In the "Wisdom Travels North" ("Zhi bei you" 知北遊) section, which mocks and reverses typical *ru* reasoning, society and its moral underpinnings are presented as the result of human inability to comprehend the Way and live in harmony with the cosmos:

> Those who know [the Way] do not speak [of it], those who speak [of the Way] do not know [it]. Hence, the wise man practices the doctrine of silence. The Way cannot be conveyed, [perfect] virtue cannot be achieved, [whereas] benevolence can be practiced, and righteousness can be partially attained, as li consists in deceiving one another. For these reasons, it is said that "Once the Way is lost, then virtue arises; once virtue is lost, then benevolence arises; once benevolence is lost, then righteousness (*yi* 義) arises: once righteousness is lost, then *li* arises. *Li* is the domestication of the Way and the beginning of disorder."¹⁶²

Even if, as Puett points out, it is difficult to relate these intellectual debates to specific historical circumstances, it is clear that an emphasis on the social and hierarchical aspects of sacrifice coincided with the passage from a "feudal" and aristocratic organization of the territory to the more centralized, bureaucratic, and meritocratic rule of the Qin and Han. The ascendancy of ideas about the superiority of *li*, in other words, may be understood as a form of cultural resistance put up by waning cultural elites in the wake of the disintegration of the Zhou system.

Building on these considerations, through a close reading of the *Records* against more or less contemporary texts such as the *Guanzi* 管子, the *Huainanzi* 淮南子, and the Mawangdui excavated corpus, the following chapters will historicize different views of ritual in the context of debates on specific political and economic issues. We will see how between the complex and elusive cultural universe of the *Classics* and the triumph of "Confucian" rhetoric of the late Western Han, the *Records* attests to an original historical sensibility reflecting a phase of transition, uncertainty, and disappointment. In the world of Sima Qian and his father, *li* has lost its ties with its original ritual context and circumstances. It upstages discrete ritual actions and becomes the epitome of a perfect society that is no longer possible to revive.[163]

Conclusions: Comparativism, Ambiguity, and Intercultural Dialogue

Since my approach is not programmatically bound to the discovery or production of models, I am not opposed to what Adam Seligman and Robert Weller describe as "embracing ambiguity," especially as I am aware of the problematic aspects of inter-cultural translations.[164] Hence, more than offering new definitions, *Heaven Is Empty* seeks to establish new bases for a fluid intercultural dialogue in which specific aspects of a given phenomenon are unveiled through the juxtapositions of putatively comparable realities. My approach follows Jonathan Z. Smith's heuristic steps of "description," "comparison," "redescription," and "rectification." A major premise underlying *Heaven Is Empty* is that the investigation of the Other in time and space does not prescind from the analysis of the self—a need for "reflexivity" informs its speculative attitude.

Arguably, Chinese educated elites did not embrace a cultural attitude that integrated the individual, the political, and the extra-human realms until the impact of Buddhism and Zhu Xi's 朱熹 (1130–1200) "metaphysical" reinterpretation of the *Classics*.[165] We shall see how the process of legitimation of unified rule attempted under Emperor Wu was aimed at safeguarding the dynasty both in space and time. Specific rituals (i.e., formalized performances) and myths (i.e., propagandistic narratives) were meant to shelter fundamental aspects of the Han rulership, such as territorial expansion and hereditary succession, from contingency through a process that we could call, by borrowing from the traditional "religious" vocabulary, "sacralization."[166] Therefore I consider the treatment of historiographical approaches and criteria of reliability a methodological priority. Since the ancient Mediterranean world still constitutes the source of influential interpretative models for the study of antiquities, this project gleans its working hypotheses and questions from Greco-Roman historiographical accounts about empire formation.

In any case, the impossibility of associating the "seminal" period of the Western Han with the establishment of a holistic and synthetic mentality should not imply that the study of early Chinese materials is therefore less worthwhile or rewarding. The treatment of Emperor Wu's reign in the *Records* can represent a fascinating case study to challenge non-Chinese hermeneutical paradigms.[167] Whether the emperor conceived his attitude toward the extra-human as *instrumentum regni*, aimed at achieving a *pax deorum* on behalf of the empire, or whether he was simply concerned about preparing for his personal salvation, we have to focus on the fact that he prevented his official historians, who might have had a different cultural background or agenda, from witnessing some of the most important state sacrifices. The following chapter looks at the elusiveness of Emperor Wu's sacrifices while reconstructing Sima Qian's historiographical approach, his interpretation of *li*, and its relationship with previous cultural models.

2

Writing the Empire

Ex Pluribus Plurima

Heaven wanted my death . . . My life's work is over . . . No one knows me.
[Yet] I am not angry at Heaven, I do not blame men.
I studied what is below and reached what is above.
Only Heaven knows me!

—Confucius[1]

The greatest directness seems roundabout, people say.
Even the Way itself twists and turns.
Is this perhaps what they mean?

—Sima Qian[2]

One who knows the mandate does not blame Heaven.
One who knows himself does not blame men.

—*Huainanzi*, Liu Xiang[3]

Empires, Historiography, and Cultural Unification

The idea that political centralization goes hand in hand with cultural homogenization is so rooted in the way we study the formation of empires that it is more often implicitly assumed than demonstrated. Raising questions about the cultural unity of a civilization is in some instances even regarded as tantamount to doubting its degree of "development and maturity."

The idea that the homogenization of diverse religious perspectives into one unified religion is a fundamental step toward the organization of extensive and integrated political systems also affects projects that focus on pre-Christian or non-Western civilizations. Implicitly, monotheistic models of religion are generally adopted as the gold standard for religions everywhere. Non-Abrahamic religions are tacitly assumed to be lacking some crucial feature that prevents them from being a vehicle of moral unity. In this chapter, I make the case that not only does "religious diversity" not necessarily constitute an obstacle toward political centralization, but in certain circumstances, as in Qin-Han China, can positively favor it.

I argue that in Han China—as well as in Augustan Rome—the formalization of an official state doctrine did not imply the disappearance of other approaches to the divine. In fact, the efficaciousness of propaganda for unified rule often lies in its flexibility, as this quality allows for the coexistence of different and seemingly contradictory practices and beliefs. In other words, ambiguous justifications for political authority can accommodate a multitude of interpretations that reflect disparate cultural and social backgrounds.

Recent scholarship has demonstrated that the Qin and Han dynasties extended their program of bureaucratic centralization to the rituals that were carried out locally throughout the country. However, an implicit unitary bias can still lead to the assumption that early imperial authorities were concerned with the more abstract, theoretical aspects of popular practices, such as the nature of the divine or the consequences of the humans' allegiance to it. For example, the Sinologist Yang Hua 楊華, through an analysis of both received and excavated documents, has offered a convincing reconstruction of the new regulations about ritual activities implemented during the early imperial period.[4] Yet Yang overlooks the need to address the problem of whether and to what degree it is possible to compare the bureaucratization of sacrifices carried out under the Qin and the Han, with the establishment of an imperial cult (of the Augustan kind, for example). Furthermore, it is unclear whether his analysis hinges on a unitary notion of religion of the Abrahamic kind, or on a phenomenological understanding of the sacred as a universal psychological paradigm. Yang cautiously defines the process of administrative centralization carried out during the early imperial period as "unification of religious authority" (*shenquan tongyi* 神權統一). He aptly describes Emperor Wu's eccentric combination of different ritual traditions as a process of "amalgamation" (*hunyi* 混一) rather than "unification" (*tongyi* 統一).[5] However, his unproblematic usage of the loan word "religion" (*zongjiao* 宗教) can lead readers to assume that "religious unity" is an original/primeval condition that needs to be recovered or, alternately, a goal to strive for.

As Yang shows, the Qin were preoccupied with imposing political control over various forms of communal rituals that had existed before imperial unification at the level of the village (*li* 里), the smallest administrative unit below the district or county (*xian* 縣). The Western Han took over the Qin's capillary bureaucratization of the various local activities and extended it to the cults practiced in the South, home of the ruling Liu family. Finally, Emperor Wu enlarged the customary ritual circuits of the Son of Heaven to include the area of Mount Tai 泰, in the East, which was traditionally regarded as the abode of the most powerful spirits. Yang interprets the Qin and Han reforms as primarily aimed at regulating the frequency of local ritual activities, the entities that could be worshipped, and the nature of the offerings. As for the possible theoretical underpinning of these provisions, Yang notes that excavated Qin legal documents attest to the formalization of the concepts of licit (*zheng* 正) and illicit (*yin* 淫) sacrifices (*si* 祀).[6] Illicit sacrifices were those that were not included in the official regulations and were not believed to yield a favorable outcome. Illicit sacrifices were sacrifices to spirits with whom the worshippers did not have a direct blood relation or that resided outside the worshippers' home area.[7]

However, the fact that early imperial governments sought direct control over local sacrifices should not give us license to assume that they were trying to impose a kind of religious unity comparable to the theological orthodoxy of post-Nicaean Christianity. In fact, it is clear enough that Qin and Han officials were preoccupied with more practical questions, such as the extension of the fiscal basis and the prevention of organized dissent at the periphery. For centuries, ritual events at the village level had accompanied seasonal changes, defined the different phases of farming activities, and explained the relationship of local communities with their environment, which included both ancestral and natural spirits. Sacrifices played a crucial role in fostering social cohesion through the legitimization of local hierarchies, shared values, and identities. Therefore, it is not surprising that the central government attempted to extend its aegis over all activities at the core of village life. This priority notwithstanding, because of the lack of a shared conception of the divine, Qin and Han officials could only enforce a kind of case-by-case "orthopraxy," as forms and objects of worship varied widely from region to region and from village to village. It seems that the meaningfulness of a given ritual tradition depended largely on its unique links to regional landmarks or social realities.

In brief, there is no evidence that the relative standardization of a non-alphabetic script that started with the Qin made different local traditions mutually intelligible. On the contrary, I argue that labeling a variety of practices by using a limited set of characters that did not provide univocal phonetic information could not but widen the epistemological gap between elite and popular culture, eventually preventing the "center" from being privy to the nature of rituals at the "periphery." Similarly, we should carefully consider the actual extent of political unity attained by the early empires. The Qin's centralizing plans, which entailed prohibiting the private possession of weapons, could hardly be called completely successful given that, after only fourteen years of reign, they succumbed to armed rebellions originating from the former southern state of Chu 楚. As for the Western Han, their founder never held direct administrative control of more than one third of the empire; he was compelled to distribute the rest of the country among his powerful allies, who ruled over their large estates or kingdoms (*guo* 國) as economically and politically independent vassals. Emperor Wu was the first sovereign who seemed capable of extending the authority of the court to the periphery, yet he faced relentless opposition during his lifetime, and his policies were almost all reverted after his death. In other words, given the lack of political unity in the country, it was extremely unlikely that the court would be able to impose uniformity in the elusive realm of spirits and ghosts. From a practical point of view, the variety and idiosyncrasy of local deities could hardly serve ideological propaganda for unified rule. Even if religious unity was thinkable, it was surely not feasible. This chapter shows how, despite centuries of unitary readings, the *Records* was actually extremely accurate in assessing the degree of political and cultural integration—or lack thereof—of the early Chinese empires.

The Points of Views of the First History of China

While contemporary scholarship (especially in the West) seems focused on a radical reassessment of the nature and extent of the unity of the early Chinese empires, the ideological implications of a deconstruction of the foundational phases of the creation of a Chinese identity still make essentialist tendencies difficult to overcome. Since specialists began ascribing to Eastern Han historians' formalization of a propagandistic and teleological interpretation of the early imperial period, Sima Qian's treatment of the Qin and Han dynasties has become a crucial element in the reappraisal of the origins of a Chinese cultural identity (today, "Han" also means ethnically Chinese).

Readers have customarily approached the *Records* with the expectation that, despite Sima Qian's grudges against Wu, the document provides a complimentary account of the Han dynasty. But the closer we scrutinize his historiographical approach, the more his relationship with the Han dynasty appears complicated. In addition to attending to the well-known questions of the authorship and transmission of the *Records*, specialists have typically focused on Sima Qian's direct involvement with Han court politics.[8] Stephen Durrant, in *The Cloudy Mirror*, has interpreted the *Records* in light Sima Qian's personal vicissitudes, making the case that it should be read more as a literary autobiography than an objective historical work.[9] Michael Nylan has pointed out that the complexity of Sima Qian's emotional investment in the *Records* owes much to the fact that castration made the historian ritually unfit to carry out ancestral sacrifices, thus prompting him to use his historiographical work to celebrate the name of his family for future generations.[10] Michael Puett has interpreted Sima Qian's relationship with the task of narrating the unification of China in terms of a tragic disconnect with the past as well as with the age in which he was living.[11]

Traditionally, analyses of Sima Qian's personal contribution to the *Records* have relied more on *The Letter to Ren An* 任安 than on his autobiographical and less reflexive chapter in the *Records* itself.[12] In this famous missive to an unjustly incarcerated old acquaintance, Sima Qian vividly recalls the circumstances of his own political and personal disgrace, linking his experience to the classic trope of the honest politician who would rather face tragedy than renounce his principles. His memoir offers an eloquent reflection on the consolation he derives from his dedication to the masterpiece started by his father, and expresses hope that future generations will be able to appreciate his contribution.[13] Recently, in the *Letter to Ren An and Sima Qian's Legacy*, a group of European and US-based experts on the *Records* have proposed a comprehensive reassessment of the questions surrounding the authenticity and enormous cultural import of this missive.[14] Whether they regard the letter as penned by Sima Qian himself, a posthumous elaboration based on some of his notes, or an exquisite example of literary impersonation produced by disciples or descendants, the authors of the volume agree that the letter attests to the paradigmatic status the *Records* had achieved by the beginning of the Eastern Han (the *terminus ante-quem* for the composition of the letter).[15] By that point, the vicissitudes of Sima Qian's life and the tortuous process of the creation of his masterwork were indissolubly interconnected, so much so it has become impossible to consider the text of the *Records* apart from questions of authorial intent, the various political perspectives coursing through the document (some complementary, some conflicting), and the paradigmatic status of the *Records* in Sinology. Mindful of the inextricability of these factors, Esther Kim has adapted Michel Foucault's concept of "author-function," to the study of the *Records*, proposing to handle the text as the sum of different readings have over time shaped the ways in which we approach it.[16]

Building on these contributions, I regard the *Records* both as a composite work and as the expression of a single individual's ideas and experiences. But whereas traditional approaches tend to explain the (often only apparently) idiosyncratic aspects of the *Records* either as a result of the intricate history of the text's compilation and transmission, or in light of Sima Qian's personal predicaments, I additionally consider the irreducibility of early Chinese cultural priorities and concerns to Western paradigms. For example, the *Records* does not conceptualize *history* as a flux, stream, or unitary trajectory, as Western historians customarily do. Aware that an exhaustive recovery of Zhou rituals—and therefore moral continuity with the past—is impossible, Sima Qian instead selects discrete episodes from history to serve as a warning or inspiration to contemporary elites. However, the "lessons" Sima Qian provides are not (and could hardly be) straightforward.[17] Both the structure and the style of the *Records* make the study of historical agency particularly challenging and fascinating. Proverbially, Sima Qian conveys his personal opinions through subtle or veiled terms: *weiyan* (微言). Also, according to the principle of "mutual illumination" (*hujian fa* 互見法), he tends implicitly to suggest similitudes and contrasts, parallels and divergences, by juxtaposing comparable biographies and events. The *Records*, as readers know, consists of 130 chapters subdivided into five sections: the Basic Annals (*Benji* 本紀); the Hereditary Houses (*Shijia* 世家); the Linked Biographies (*Liezhuan* 列傳); the thematic monographs of the Treatises (*Shu* 書) on ritual, music, pitch pipes, the calendar, astronomy, sacrifices, rivers and waterways, and financial administration; and the Chronological Tables (*Biao* 表).[18] References to a single individual are often scattered across several sections and chapters, which express different and sometimes contrasting perspectives on the same person by detailing his or her interactions with other historical figures and involvement with various political institutions. Similarly, information on an ethnic group, a period, or a cultural tradition is customarily distributed throughout the text.

Sima Qian seems to be writing for a public eager to approach the *Records* not only as an invaluable source of historical knowledge but also as an educational experience. The ideal readers of the *Records* learn to navigate the text in all directions, reading some passages multiple times and weaving a network of nonlinear connections between them.[19] In my case, I often complement fragmentary accounts of debates in the *Records* with both older and contemporary sources that give expression to cultural and political traditions with which Sima Qian could not have been familiar, or with which he would not directly have engaged. Hence, since I believe that the interpretive itineraries with which we approach the *Records* inevitably tend to be subjective, it is necessary to be as transparent as possible about our intellectual choices and goals.

Considering the unavailability in early China of an identitary and systemic notion of the sacred, this chapter reconstructs the criteria informing the *Records*' treatment of the question of the legitimacy of the Han empire in terms of continuity with the past and control over different peoples and territories. I argue that Sima Qian regarded social rituals (*li* 禮) as the fundamental means to nurture ancestral memory and sacrifices (*si* 祀) aimed at getting in touch with various spirits and entities inhabiting the different regions of China. As we will see, Sima Qian was of the opinion that neither *li* nor *si* could serve as a moralizing influence during the Han era. He considered contemporary Classicists not competent or honest enough to recover the moral and ritual legacy of the Zhou. As for the possibility of interacting with spirits and ghosts, Sima Qian either chastised this notion as an infantile delusion or disparaged it as cunning way to take advantage of people's gullibility. In general, he considered any interest in the realm of the invisible as a potential source of chaos and uncertainty. Eventually, mentioning "ghosts and spirits" (*gui shen*) became a formulaic and at times condescending way to refer to a multitude of popular beliefs and practices. Especially for these reasons, Sima Qian preferred to concentrate on human dispositions, political structures, and material circumstances. Hence, because of the unique multivocal narrative style of the *Records*, readers and historians are best advised to seek agency in the interrelation and indissolubility of these three factors.

Ritual and Memory in Early Imperial China

Whatever the nature of the *li* of the Zhou dynasty might have been, its interpretation in the *Records* is related to a deep feeling of loss, disconnectedness from the past, and displacement.[20] In a passage that initially seems to emphasize a line of ritual continuity in Chinese imperial dynasties, the *Records* actually foreground the contingency of official ceremonies:

After the Qin ruler assumed the title of emperor (*di* 帝) and established the capital in Xianyang 咸陽, the Five Peaks and the Four Rivers were all situated in the East. From the Five Sovereigns (*wudi* 五帝) to the Qin, periods of glory and decay alternated incessantly and the Illustrious Mountains and the Great Rivers fell either under the control of the feudal lords or the Son of Heaven. Since the ways to sacrifice to them underwent changes over several generations, it is not possible to recount them. When the First Emperor unified the world, he instructed the officials in charge of sacrifices to regulate the ways Heaven, Earth, the Illustrious Mountains, the Great Rivers, and ghosts and spirits were customarily worshipped.[21]

The passage remarks that the Qin ruled from an area not included in the traditional ritual circuits of the previous Xia, Shang, and Zhou dynasties. The Han, under whom Sima Tan and Qian were writing, could be considered even more "off-center," for their lineage, the Liu, hailed from the "exotic" kingdom of Chu in the south and established their capital, Chang'an, just a few miles southwest of Xianyang, the Qin capital. Instead of celebrating the Qin and the Han as the dynasties that finally reestablished the loftier ritual standards of the Zhou, the *Records* tends to sketch the situation following the unification as a confusing congeries of competing regional political powers and cultural traditions which early imperial governments did not seem willing or able to sort out. According to the *Records*, the unity of the empire, at least until Emperor Wu's times, was exclusively political.

This is not surprising. Since the fall of the Western Zhou in 771 BCE, China had ploughed through five centuries of instability and internecine conflicts. Despite the perduring and pervasive rhetoric of the continuity of Chinese civilization from the Neolithic to the present, to Han elites it was not at all obvious which cultural models their dynasty should adopt. Sima Qian was distressed that political unification did not represent an outgrowth of the triumph of Confucius's ideals but was instead the reward for political shrewdness and cunning. He often turned the biographies of exemplary men of the past in the *Records* into a pretext for voicing longing for a lost golden age whose return seemed anything but imminent.

It was only after Emperor Wu's death in 87 BCE that official historiography would produce an unambiguously apologetic view of the empire. The Eastern Han historian Ban Gu 班固 (32–92 CE), in his *History of the Former Han* (*Han Shu* 漢書, hereafter *Han Shu*), decided to celebrate

Wu's reign—probably because it was remembered as the longest and most prosperous at the time—as the moment in which the Classicists were finally called to play a major political and cultural role at court as a consequence of the imperial appointment of Dong Zhongshu 董仲舒 (?179–?104 BCE).[22] The *Han Shu* posthumously anointed him as the progenitor of the new generation of Classicists and the creator of the Han state doctrine, known in English as "Han Confucianism." Consequently, interpretations of "Han Confucianism" have for centuries relied on the *Luxuriant Gems of the Spring and Autumn* (*Chunqiu fanlu* 春秋繁露), which historians have customarily treated as a coherent expression Dong's thought.[23] This text, based on the Gongyang 公羊 commentary to the original *Spring and Autumn Annals*, complements Confucius's moral principles with cosmological factors such as yin and yang and the Five Phases, which had gained preeminence during the Warring States.[24] According to the *Luxuriant Gems*, the Mandate of the monarch consisted in maintaining harmony between man and nature by heeding the warnings sent by Heaven in the form of omens.

But such a reading of Emperor Wu's rulership, which probably owes to the resilient appeal of unitary and organic theories, does not find any support in the *Records*.[25] Sima Qian, a contemporary and at least an acquaintance of Dong's, does not provide any evidence confirming that this specialist of the *Spring and Autumns Annals* elaborated a complex moral-cosmic system of thought that influenced Wu's imperial ideology and politics. Recently, the foremost experts of the *Luxuriant Gems* have questioned the traditional attribution of this text. Sarah Queen and John Major have redefined it as a "work of an anonymous compiler living between the fourth and the sixth centuries CE who brought together a number of writings associated with Dong Zhongshu and other masters and disciples of the Gongyang Learning."[26]

I argue that these anachronisms served specific cultural and political purposes. Eventually, with the claim that the *Luxuriant Gems* ought to encapsulate the functions of the Son of Heaven, post-Wu classicists meant to subordinate royal actions to their expertise, which would extend from textual analysis, ritual protocols, and political advice to the field of cosmological speculations, which had traditionally been the monopoly of "less respectable" masters, such as the *fangshi* coming from the northeastern regions. In brief, with the exaltation of Dong Zhongshu's role, Ban Gu created a foundational myth that linked the Classicists' ascendancy to the political high point of the Han.

Another problematic historical construct that had been instrumental in justifying the preeminence of the Classicists at court had been an emphasis on their moralizing influence on the establishment of the Han vis-à-vis the dynasty they overthrew. The extant version of the *Records* includes at the end of the "Basic Annals of the First Emperor of Qin" ("Qin Shihuang Benji" 秦始皇本紀) the famous "Discussion of the Faults of the Qin," ("Guo Qin lun" 過秦論) by the Classicist Jia Yi 賈誼 (ca. 200–168 BCE), who condemned the Qin in terms that would become idiomatic.[27] According to his narrative, the First Emperor unified China only because of the superiority of his armies. He did not rule as a benevolent sovereign but as ruthless tyrant. He did not follow the example of the legendary Sage Kings of the past, but rather despised all forms of non-practical learning, killed Classicists, and burned their books. Predictably, the regime of terror he had established did not survive his death and ultimately gave way to the virtuous reign of Han.[28] Although the *Records* complicates and contradicts this interpretation implicitly and explicitly in several instances, the inclusion of Jia Yi's treatise (probably an interpolation) has justified the attribution to the first history of China of an idealistic and laudatory interpretation of the rise of the Han. This conceit, together with the anachronisms engendered by Eastern Han historiography, begat a series of misunderstandings, often ideologically driven, that still strongly influence current searches for an early Han religion in the purported recovery of an updated form of Confucianism.

Fortunately, a recovery of the *Records*' rather impartial and nonteleological treatment of contemporary events allows for the contextualization and reconstruction of the debates on the evolution of *li*, which cannot be separated from its treatment of political events. Once analyzed against Han debates on centralization, discussions on ritual in the *Records* acquire a much more concrete dimension and provide a new insight into the possible allegiance of Classicists, whose concerns seem consistent with those of landed elites. The majority of the discussions on ritual prerogatives in Han received and excavated sources as well as on the sections of the *Luxuriant Gems* written in the same period all reflect concerns about the consequences of the extension of the political prerogatives of the central government over the periphery.[29] But let us first summarize the relevant political changes brought about by the unification.[30]

The most impactful measure the Qin undertook upon unifying China was the enforcement of the *junxian* 郡縣 system against the "feudal" power structure traditionally associated with the Zhou.[31] This innovation implied the replacement of old territorial hierarchies based on decentralization and enfeoffment with the new administrative unities of the commanderies (*jun*) and counties (*xian*). By appointing to them functionaries who purportedly had no ties with local hereditary elites, the court hoped to reorganize the country under a more efficient regime of bureaucratic and fiscal centralization.[32]

It was the statesman Shang Yang 商鞅 (390–338 BCE, also known as the Lord of Shang) who had initially introduced the *junxian* system in pre-imperial Qin.[33] With the intent of tightening the state's grip on human and economic resources, Yang had relied on these reforms to trump aristocratic privileges and gain direct control of taxation. The promulgation of written laws allowed him to push for a meritocratic revolution by making everyone accountable. He began to select functionaries no longer on the basis of birth, but of their administrative, entrepreneurial, and military competences. Now successes on the battlefield and wealth deriving from trade could open the path to a political career as much as the revenue connected to land ownership. As a consequence of these transformations, the Qin soon acquired an unprecedented level of administrative economic efficiency and swiftly rose as the paramount military power of the Warring States period. After the unification of China, the prime minister of the First Emperor, Li Si 李斯 (280–208 BCE), extended the *junxian* system to all the conquered territories without showing any respect for preexisting political arrangements and hierarchies.[34]

Members of the old landed nobility who had suffered dispossession and political marginalization under the Qin played a major role in the revolt that overthrew their dynasty after only fifteen years of reign. The contribution of these elites proved fundamental in the victory of the commoner Liu Bang over competing rebel coalitions. After being proclaimed Son of Heaven of the Han in 202 BCE, Liu Bang kept the *junxian* system, but wisely left most of his aristocratic and powerful allies in charge of large estates (*guo* 國), which were ruled, *de facto,* as independent hereditary kingdoms.[35] It was probably the appeasement of regional elites that allowed the Han to succeed where the uncompromising Qin had failed.

Going back to Emperor Wu's extremely long reign, most of the measures undertaken in his time pursued both political and economic centralization. Wu directed his efforts at the extension of the *junxian* system over areas his predecessors had purposely overlooked and eventually managed to bring all of the *guo* under the aegis of the central administration. With the establishment of monopolies on salt, iron, liquors, and the construction and renovation of roads, canals, and bridges Wu's government strove to superimpose a state or emperor-run economy over the interests of local markets and elites.[36] As I show below, the struggle between the factions of the Modernists (the supporters of centralization) and Reformists (the opponents of centralization) was often fought in the rhetorical arena of discussions on rituals, myths, cosmologies, and "the divine," as in early imperial China the "cultural" and the "political" were not necessarily separated.

The Solitude of the Sages: The Elusiveness of *Li* and the Unification of China

Two-thirds of the *Records*' "Book on *Li*" (the "Li shu" 禮書), in its extant form, reproduce passages from the *Xunzi* 荀子, the text whose "secular" reformulation of *li* and Heaven Sima Qian embraces in his treatment of the Qin and Han dynasties. Probably because of its composite nature, no major scholarly work on the early Han has concentrated on the actual contents of the "Book on *Li*" as though, being a copy, it could offer no original insights. However, its initial paragraphs do not reproduce the volume attributed to Master Xun (ca. 310–220 BCE) but instead spin an interesting synthesis of the years spanning the period from the unification of China to Emperor Wu's reign. This section seems consistent with Sima Qian's historiographical sensibility, treats the questions *li* and politics as deeply connected, and offers an unusually direct assessment of the merits of the Han.[37]

From a structural point of view, the inclusion of the "Book on *Li*" among the *Records*' eight thematic monographs (on the history of music, pitch pipes, the calendar, astronomy, sacrifices, rivers and waterways, and financial administration) helps clarify Sima Qian's categorizing criteria and cultural priorities. First of all, if compared with the "Book of *Feng* and *Shan*," the monograph on *li* contributes to the disambiguation of the usage of the term "ritual" in early Chinese contexts. The "Book on *Li*" exclusively includes practices that were first documented in the *Classics* and did not imply direct contact with spirits and ghosts—the very practices Confucius and Master Xun had celebrated as the foundation of an orderly, hierarchically structured, moral, and prosperous society. The "Book on the *Feng* and *Shan* Sacrifices," by contrast, offers a sampling of all those cults performed by Chinese rulers whose origins, nature, and proper performance were not attested in the *Classics*, involved direct contact with extra-human entities, and had destabilizing or uncontrollable effects on the practitioners and their community. The "Treatise on *Li*" thus begins:

> The Grand Historian remarks: How vast and beautiful Virtue (*De* 德) is! It oversees all phenomena, and serves all beings. Is that

not a human faculty? I visited the Master of Ceremonies and examined what has been emended and added during the Three Dynasties. I apprehended that it is by refining human feelings that *Li* is created, it is by relying on human nature that Decorum (*Yi* 儀) is established. And the origin of this is so remote!³⁸

Following Mark Csikszentmihalyi, I interpret the Virtue cited here as an active—not only moral—energy or charismatic power through which one can positively affect the lives of other people.³⁹ This passage describes *de* 德 as the force that enables men to be in charge of all phenomena and living beings. It also plays a fundamental role in the establishment of ethical standards such as *li* and *yi* (decorum). However, according to the paragraph above, this kind of Virtue does not operate beyond contingency. It implies gradual improvement through education and refinement. It defines civilization as an ongoing process predicated on a critical analysis of the past. From our point of view, this characterization of *De* defines the *Records'* outlook on the development of humankind as relatable to modern Western "historicistic" and "humanistic" sensibilities. But after this introduction, the text surprisingly proceeds to straddle a conceptual realm that is traditionally considered at odds with a typically Confucian worldview:

> The way of men is the warp and the woof of all things, there are no rules that it does not penetrate; it is kept close through Benevolence (*Ren* 仁) and Righteousness (*Yi* 義), it is controlled through Penalties (*Xing* 刑) and Punishments (*Fa* 罰). Therefore those of profound virtue gain position and respect, while those with a large fortune gain favor and glory. And this is what keeps everything together within the four seas and governs and gives balance to the people.⁴⁰

After stating that man is the measure of all things and that only human faculties can be trusted for the maintenance of social order, the text unexpectedly recognizes the positive function of the rule by laws (i.e., punishments and rewards) conventionally considered at the core of Qin's political practice. But such an acknowledgment is only surprising if we give credit to the "official" interpretation established with Eastern Han historiography, according to which the Western Han flourished on account of a wholehearted adoption of Confucian moral values. If in the *Discourses on Salt and Iron* Dong Zhongshu's thought is reported correctly, he believed that a Sage promotes moral growth without relying on penalties.[41] Also, we find an intermediate position on the opportunity of institutionalized violence in a passage from a work by Dong Zhongshu cited in the *Han Shu* and in a section of the *Luxuriant Gems* Allan and Major date to Emperor Wu's period.[42] These texts, in identifying punishments with the cooling function of yin, consider them as an integral part of the moral/cosmic whole. Importantly, they clearly subordinate the role of punishments to that of moral education, which corresponds to the warming power of yang.[43] Warming produces birth and cooling maturation, but, admonishes the *Luxuriant Gems*, the role of the yang element is hundred times more important than that of yin; since: "moral education compares to penalties in a similar way, the Sage increases his love and decreases his sternness. He extends his generosity and limits his penalties."[44]

Going back to the passage in the *Records*, in mentioning punishments and penal codes, it does not include them in a broader discussion on nature and cosmology. It simply reports the historical fact that early Han did not reject the practical ways of their predecessors but continued to rely on the deterring power of institutional violence. Furthermore, on the same note of compromise with the more materialistic concerns associated with the Qin, along with the role of the virtue, this passage praises the contribution of the wealthy to state and society.

The following paragraphs in the "Book on *Li*" directly quote Confucius and return to the civilizing function of *li*, more or less by paraphrasing the interpretation provided by Master Xun.[45] According to the passages, *Li* is fundamental in curbing human excesses and establishing and consolidating social hierarchies. It is instrumental in displaying, justifying, and creating status and its distinctions:

> When men go around in chariots, they gild their seats and adorn their harness in order to make their appearance more sophisticated. The eye loves the five colors and so men make them vibrant and nuanced in order to manifest their power. The ear enjoys bells and musical stones and men harmonize them with the eight instruments in order to excite their feelings. The mouth finds pleasure in the five flavors and men enrich them with condiments and spices in order to develop men's taste. The sentiments are attracted to precious and valuable things, and men carve and polish jade objects in order to accord them with their own senses.

For these reasons the ceremonial carriage with grass mats, the leather caps with cotton cloths, the red strings with the hollow guitar, the Great Supper with simple water are used by men to curb their excesses and extravagances and try to correct their shortcomings. All this determines the order between ruler and minister in the affairs of the court, between the honorable and the lowly, the noble and the poor, and reaches down to the common people in the distinction of different carriages, clothing, residences, drinking and eating, marriage rules for men and women, funerals and sacrifices so that all actions can be proper and suitable, all things controlled and refined. Confucius said: "In the imperial ancestral sacrifice, I do not want to know anything that happens after the libation."[46]

The concluding quotation of a well-known saying by Confucius confines the scope of *li* to the visible, human elements of ritual without mentioning ancestral spirits (i.e., the original objects of the ceremonies). But again, the *Records*, with the following passage, offers an interpretation of the Han dynasty that sharply contrasts with the one that would become mainstream. The leaders of the Han did not conform to *li* of the Zhou, the set of rituals and etiquette norms extolled by Confucius. The text suggests that even though *li* could still orient the behavior of some well-educated individuals, its memory was no longer fully recoverable and current generations were not virtuous enough to place such a lofty standard at the center of their lives:

When the Zhou fell, *li* was abandoned, music corrupted, and the important and the petty became all mixed up. Master Guan had three wives in his house. Those who abide by the law and heed what is correct suffer the insult of their contemporaries. The extravagant and licentious and unworthy usurpers are regarded as famous and glorious. From Zixia, one of the most important disciples of Confucius, there was already this saying: "When I go out and I see refined elegance and abundant beauty I take pleasure; when I stay inside and listen to the teaching of the Master, I rejoice. My heart is conflicted between these two goods, and I am not able to decide." And could men of more middling and lower virtue not gradually be drawn toward the loss of the doctrine and the adoption of current customs? . . . After Confucius passed away, the disciples who received his doctrine scattered, disappeared, and did not flourish. Some went to Qi and Chu, some crossed rivers and seas; is this not a disgrace?[47]

Fundamental for my analysis is the reference in this passage to Master Guan (Guanzi 官子, 725–645 BCE), a political adviser at the court of Duke Huan 桓 of Qi in the Spring and Autumn period.[48] A man of low origins, Master Guan did not distinguish himself for following the moral path of the sages admired by the Classicists. The collection of essays on statecraft named after him formulates a political doctrine based on the concept of *bawang* 霸王 (ruler-hegemon), who would lead a prosperous and powerful state while ignoring *li* and relying instead on pragmatism, administrative efficiency, written laws, economic planning, and military organization.[49]

Tellingly, in its typical "dialectic" fashion, the *Records* narrates his life immediately after the famous parable of the noble Bo Yi 伯夷 and Shu Qi 叔齊, which opens the section of the "Linked Biographies" (*Liezhuan* 列傳). The chapter on Bo Yi and Shu Qi illustrates models of coherence and honesty that can be the exact opposite of Master Guan's practical approach. The two noble brothers Bo Yi and Shuqi were so stubborn in maintaining their virtue that they not only shunned the riches and honors attached to their status, but also rejected their father's throne and their political duties. Their absolutely idealistic conception of authority almost brought them to prevent the legendary King Wu (r. 1046–1043 BCE) from conducting his army against the last corrupt sovereign of the Shang and eventually founding the Zhou dynasty, the golden age of Chinese civilization that the Han purportedly endeavored to imitate.[50] In implicitly suggesting that even this still unparalleled paragon of virtuous rulership was built on violence and bloodshed, the *Records* betrays its ultimately pessimistic, tragic conception of political power. At the same time, the juxtaposition of this story with Confucius's critique of Master Guan, who had no moral compass and overcame his humble birth by making the best of the circumstances in which he found himself, alludes to the values on which the Han had been founded.[51] As we will see in detail in chapter 4, it is also to Master Guan and the ancient state of Qi that the *Records* traces back the majority of the rituals carried out under Emperor Wu, so as to hint that the current Son of Heaven wished to conform his rule to that of a hegemon, and govern by virtue of his military power, not by pursuing impractical moral standards.

The passage also illuminates the rather aristocratic view of virtue held by his author. Sima Qian regarded the rigid boundaries between the noble and the lowly, which *li* was supposed to maintain and reinforce, as the foundation of a harmonious society. From this vantage point, the reference to the "the mixing of the grandiose and the petty" (*da xiao xiang yu* 大小相踰), which according to the lines cited above was a consequence of the loss of the cultural legacy of the Zhou, represents a further indictment of the current dynasty. As everyone knew the Han's royal lineage, the Liu 劉, had non-elite origins. But did nobility in all its interpretations really matter in those troubled and turbulent years? The *Records* openly laments that conforming to Confucius's standards was beyond reasonable expectations at the time. That the Han would succeed thanks to timeliness, expediency, occasional shrewdness, chance or mere luck, according to the *Records*, was after all acceptable, or at least understandable.

As though at this point continuing the discussion on *li* and the Master's legacy were no longer useful, the political elements of "Book on *Li*" become even more explicit. If the Han ruled successfully while relying on the institutional apparatus set up by their predecessors, historians—in contrast with Jia Yi's influential judgment—could not portray the Qin dynasty in exclusively negative terms.[52]

> When the Qin gained control of the world, of all the social norms and customs of the Six Kingdoms they chose what they thought to be best. Although this did not conform to the rules established by the sages, they honored the previous political leaders and controlled the ministers, while the different offices of the court worked together as it was done in the past. When the reign passed to Gaozu 高祖 [posthumous title of Liu Bang 劉邦, who founded the Han], and his power shone over everything within the four seas, Shusun Tong made additions and subtractions that basically conformed to what the Qin had previously established. From the appropriate title of the Son of Heaven down to the official denominations of the various functionaries and offices, he made just a few changes.[53]

If this reference to the continuity of the Qin and Han rule were not clear enough, the *Records* also offers portrayals of Emperors Wen 文 (r. 180–157 BCE) and Jing 景 (r. 157–141 BCE), Wu's grandfather and father, that are incompatible with the Golden Era characterized by political wisdom and "Confucian values":

> When Emperor Wen took power, officials advanced some proposals concerning customs and rituals (*li*). Emperor Wen was fond of the practices of the Dao, and since he considered *li* too complicated

and the formalities of etiquette too ornate to be of any benefit for the government, he did not have anything to say about bodily appearance and dismissed the question. At the time of Emperor Jing, the Imperial Counselor Chao Cuo 晁錯 made his name because of the matter of punishments and *li*. Several times he intervened to admonish the emperor. He said: "The vassal states have to defend and assist; this rule was valid in the past as it is today. Now the big kingdoms have individual governments and different institutions. They do not report to the functionary of the capital. I am afraid that they will not be able to establish a line of legitimate power." Emperor Jing followed this plan. The six states opposed it and revolted. They demanded Chao Cuo's position and head, so the emperor executed him in order to get rid of the trouble. . . . Afterwards, officials began to take special care only in establishing good connections and in enjoying their posts peacefully. No one dared again to raise criticism.[54]

Here the *Records* provides a rare and extremely meaningful synthesis of the establishment and consolidation of the Qin and Han empires, whose treatment is otherwise scattered throughout its complex structure and chapters. In addition, this paragraph epitomizes a further distinctive feature of the *Records*' historiographical approach: While its explicit and conclusive assessments tend to focus on positive aspects of the Han rule, it is in the treatment of details that the narrative deftly leads the reader's attention to more problematic elements in a more prudent fashion. The passage above describes the ritual reforms by the Classicist Shusun Tong in laudatory terms, which are contradicted in much more detailed sections of the *Records*. In light of the "Book on *Feng* and *Shan*," (as we will see in detail later in this chapter) for example, it is evident that the sentence "Shusun Tong made additions and subtractions that basically conformed to what the Qin had previously established" implies that Shusun in fact concocted a haphazard patchwork of mainly misunderstood regional traditions. With regard to Shusun's moral qualities, Sima Qian characterizes him in the chapter on Han Classicists rather explicitly as a manipulative opportunist.

In recounting the consequences of the rebellion of the Seven Kingdoms, the text is making the case that the Han Empire could survive as long as the Son of Heaven was willing to coexist with nearly independent local polities. As Chao Cuo (ca. 200–154 BCE) feared, the plan to establish a common and transmissible cultural tradition all over China was ultimately deluded. Contrary to what Han scholarship customarily holds, the passage quoted above does not equate the eventual repression of the rebellion in 154 BCE with a definitive victory of the center over the periphery.[55] Chao Cuo's tragic demise looms as a somber admonishment for those advisers who promoted radical centralization.[56]

The final paragraphs of the section of the "Book on *Li*" sound like an explanation of (or rather an apology for) the political directives by which Sima Qian was compelled to abide. Moral and cultural relativism, which in the passage above are embodied by Master Guan, are the price that must be paid for political stability. The Han ruled as a new dynasty. Like the Qin, the text seems to suggest, they are not claiming a privileged bond with the celebrated tradition of the Zhou. Consequently they are free to establish and hand down a new standard.

> After the current emperor took charge, he summoned experts in the *Classics* and arts and ordered them to decide about ceremonies, but in more than ten years they produced no results. Then someone said that in the ancient age of the Great Peace the people were in harmony and happiness, good omens appeared everywhere, so that rules and actions were established on the basis of popular mores. The emperor heard this and through the Imperial Secretary issued this decree: "I am ruling by mandate.[57] Every sovereign flourishes on different bases, there are different ways to a common goal. To act by following the people is to study customs and then make rules. Those who criticize [the present situation] all exalt the ancient past, but what should the common people look up to? The Han dynasty is the enterprise of just one family, if standards and rules cannot be passed down, how can we talk about posterity? Those who perform grand deeds are eminent and exert great influence. Those who govern in a shallow pond are petty and narrow minded. How could we not try?" Hence Emperor Wu replaced the first day of the first month of the lunar year with the beginning of the Taichu age; he changed the colors of clothes, performed the *feng* sacrifice on Mount Tai, re-organized the ceremonial apparatus for ancestral shrines, sacrificial places, and public offices. By doing so he established a constant standard to be transmitted to posterity.[58]

Here the *Records* casts doubt on Wu Emperor's rule in an idiomatically subtle way. The text explicates the doctrine that came to inform the court's ceremonial activities after the Classicists and other masters failed to provide new viable protocols. One of the rhetorical devices the *Records* uses to discredit a particular theory as unsubstantiated is to emphasize the obscurity of its origin. "Someone said" (*huo yan* 或言) usually introduces pieces of information that the text wants to stigmatize as preposterous or fraudulent. In this case, the anonymous reference to the Great Peace, the utopian time when everyone lived in harmony with nature and did not need a moral guidance (a trope popular in several non-canonical cultural traditions of early imperial China), sharply contrasts with the golden age of the austere Zhou, whose lofty model Sima Qian had already indicated as completely out of reach for the Han. In the imperial decree cited in this passage, the *Records* synthesizes an approach to rituals that is mercilessly scrutinized but never openly criticized in the "Book on the *Feng and Shan*." By dismissing those who look to the past for guidance, Emperor Wu immodestly declares the uniqueness of his rule and the customs of common people as the model for his government. When the *Records* follows this declaration by reporting that Emperor Wu thereupon proceeded to establish "constant" ceremonial standards (*yi wei dian chang* 以爲典常) for posterity, it is difficult not to suspect an ironic intent. In fact, the only constant in Emperor Wu's ritual activities, according to the "Book on the *Feng* and *Shan*," is his cluelessness and incoherence. But considering Sima Qian's personal grudges and biases from a different angle, it is likewise possible that his otherwise extremely resourceful emperor tried to impose a vision with which the historian could not be familiar.

If we look at the ritual innovations mentioned at the end of the passage above, we notice that, together with the proclamation of the Grand Beginning (*Taichu* 太初) in 104 BCE, Emperor Wu introduced the practice of naming different political phases on the basis of the registration of purported prodigies (Reign's Marker *Nianhao* 年號), which would last, albeit with some changes from the Ming (1368–1644) on, until the fall of the Qing in 1911. Could this be interpreted as an attempt to create a form of legitimization of different political phases that was rooted in the empirical observation of nature? If so, the emperor's cluelessness and incoherence, so lamented by Sima Qian, might be understood as the ritualization of adaptability and expediency.

The Recovery and Re-creation of *Li* after Emperor Wu

A fundamental text for the historicization of the epistemological shift between the pessimism of the *Records* and the triumphalism of later historical works is *The Discourses on Salt and Iron* (*Yantielun* 鹽鐵論), the literary account or re-elaboration of a court debate ordered by Emperor Zhao 昭 (r. 87–74 BCE) in 81 BCE, when he was only thirteen.[59] Scholars have customarily looked at this text as an important source of information about early ideas about economics. However, if we do not impose conventional (and arbitrary) disciplinary boundaries, as I show, we cannot but further note that early Chinese sources considered politics in "holistic" terms, and that what would appear to us as a "fusion of horizons" was rather the norm than an exception.

The *Discourses*, as well as the *Records*' "Book on *Li*," reports exchanges on ritual practices and cultural models in the same context as debates on administrative and economic centralization. In this case, though, the association of specific cultural traditions with clearly identifiable political approaches is more explicit.[60] The *Discourses* presents the Classicists successfully arguing against some of the Han officials who had played an important role in shaping Emperor Wu's policies—policies that would be progressively abandoned after the sovereign's death.[61]

Opposed to government monopolies, the development of trade and commercial routes, the harsh enforcement of collective justice, and expansive military campaigns, the Classicists proposed a less active form of government. They envisioned a benevolent and paternalistic rule based instead on agriculture that relinquished political and economic duties to local elites. The Classicists held that an ideal leadership would maintain peace among the people of the Han and foreigners alike simply by moral example, without directly intervening in regional matters.[62]

Conversely, the government representatives accused the Classicists of ineffectiveness and parochialism, in a way that seems to conflate cultural and political stances. After all, according to the officials, while all respected masters (*zhusheng* 諸生) had been merely concerned with their petty land possessions and local affairs, it was the Qin who defeated the enemies of civilization and unified the warring states.[63] The officials held that public ceremonies and ritual practices had no educational function. If they mattered at all, it was only insofar as their extravagance and lavishness could impress and intimidate neighbors and foreigners. In the officials' opinion, abstract theories concerning past models, as well as the relationship among men, institutions, and cosmic forces—particularly if compared with practical and expedient strategies—had all ultimately proved useless to the government. The Classicists replied that the approaches that had been hitherto adopted by Han rulers had thrown the country and its rulers into confusion. As for the militaristic Qin, while they had been able to achieve swift territorial gains thanks to shrewd conduct, it should have been evident that they lost everything within two generations because of the lack of a superior moral vision.[64]

It was in discussing ritual matters that the Classicists introduced that moral/cosmological synthesis that would eventually be adopted as official ideology by the Han and the subsequent dynasties. The Classicists traced their stance back to Duke of Zhou and Confucius's promotion of frugality and a vision of rituals that excluded direct contact with ghosts and spirits.[65] Then, they acknowledged Dong Zhongshu, a specialist of the Gong Yang tradition of the *Spring and Autumn Annals* classic, who had integrated Warring States theories about natural and cosmic changes with the moral teachings of *li*, as their more direct forefather:[66]

> It was first the ceremonial officer from Jiangdu 江都,[67] Master Dong, who explained yin and yang and the succession of the four seasons by saying that what is generated by the father is nourished by the son, what is perfected by the mother is treasured by the son. For this reason, spring generates humanness (*ren* 仁); summer develops charismatic virtue (*de* 德); autumn perfects righteousness (*yi* 義); and winter treasures *li* 禮. This is the order of the four seasons, which the Sage takes as a model. He does not rely on punishments in order to promote improvements. Hence he develops and expands the teaching of virtues (*de* 德).[68]

The *Discourses* sanctions the end of the aggressive centralizing phase that characterized Emperor Wu's age. Emblematically, Sang Hongyang 桑弘羊 (152–80 BCE), the Imperial Counselor (*Yushi Dafu* 御史大夫), who in the *Discourses* championed interventionist politics and a pragmatic conception of sovereignty, was executed (together with the members of his family) in the aftermath of a complicated palace plot just one year after the debate took place, in 80 BCE.[69] Then, as reconstructed by Michael Loewe, under emperors Xuan 宣 (r. 74–49 BCE) and Yuan 元 (r. 49–33 BCE) the relevance of *li* increased steadily together with the influence of the Classicists, while officials began to take formal steps for the establishment of a state worship for the house of Zhou.[70]

Finally, in 31 BCE, during the reign of Emperor Cheng 成 (r. 33–7 BCE), the reforms proposed by the minister Kuang Heng 匡衡 reshaped imperial ceremonies in a way that ritually contradicted Wu's active model and would characterize Chinese imperial authority for centuries.[71] The new plan seemed aimed at eliminating practices that were too extravagant, those that were conducted away from the capital or associated with peripheral Warring States traditions, and those not sanctioned in the *Classics*. Tellingly, the new regulations abolished the imperial "ritualized hunts" or "patrolling expeditions" (*xunshou* 巡狩), which were traditionally carried throughout the realm; notably reduced the number of shrine activities patronized by the court; discontinued the sacrifices of Taiyi and Houtu inaugurated under Emperor Wu; and established the periodic worship of Heaven and Earth by the Son of Heaven in the southern and northern suburbs of the Chang'an.[72] In this way, the emperor could ritually maintain harmony in the empire without leaving the capital, as it now epitomized the ceremonial pivot of the whole realm. Such a synecdochic representation of unified rule coincided with the adoption of the theories attributed to Dong Zhongshu as state doctrine and implied that the complex relationship of men and nature would be understood in terms of microcosm and macrocosm and through philological exegesis. In practice, Kuang Heng's reforms were meant to subordinate the activities of the Son of Heaven to the *Classics* and their experts, while preventing him from checking on regional elites under the pretext of participating in local rituals. The devolutionary conception of rulership with which, in the *Discourses on Salt and Iron*, the "Reformists" had challenged the "Modernists" had finally triumphed.

Everything Comes Together:
Ban Gu and "The Treatise on the Five Phases"

If we solely rely on the *Records*, we have to conclude that Dong's cultural influence was minimal during his lifetime.[73] After the early mention of him in the *Discourses of Salt and Iron*, it was the Eastern Han historian Ban Gu 班固 (32–92 CE) who sanctioned Dong's thought as the official doctrine of the Han.[74] "The Treatise on the Five Phases" ("*Wuxing zhi*" 五行志), in Ban Gu's *History of the Former Han* (*Han Shu* 漢書), opens by celebrating the bridging of the epistemological gap between the present and the past that Confucius and Sima Qian had both decried. Ban Gu invokes the theory of the Five Phases as the definitive explanation of the interpenetration of human and natural rhythms.[75] From different mythological traditions, he weaves a unitary narrative that traces back the origins of political authority to those Sage Men (*shengren* 聖人) of antiquity (i.e., culture bearers and paradigmatic sovereigns) who created (or received) systems to interpret the natural world and that legitimized political authority.[76]

According to the "Treatise on the Five Phases," Fu Xi 伏羲, the predynastic ruler often mentioned as the initiator of Chinese civilization, learned to read the cosmos thanks to the Eight Trigrams that the Yellow River had yielded. The future founder of the Xia 夏, the first mythical dynasty, Yu the Great, upon controlling the Flood, was able to retrieve from the Luo River the several sets of instructions, including those concerning the Five Phases, which came to constitute the *Great Plan* (*Hong Fan* 洪範), the supreme "ruler's handbook."[77] The first sovereign of the Zhou dynasty, King Wu, obtained the *Great Plan* from Jizi 箕子 (or Master Ji), a sage of the Shang who had opposed in vain the last corrupt ruler of his dynasty. As the *Hong Fan* became obsolete, King Wen of the Zhou updated and expanded the *Classic of Changes* (the *Yijing* 易經, based on the Eight Trigrams retrieved by Fuxi). When the Zhou decline began, Confucius wrote the *Spring and Autumns Annals* (*Chunqiu* 春秋), implemented the concepts of Yin and Yang in his commentary to the *Classic of Changes*, perfected the *Great Plan*, and showed with clarity the "Way of Heaven and Man" (*Tianren dao* 天人道).[78]

At this point, the "Treatise of the Five Phases" documents the interruption of this line of legitimate sovereigns and epistemological systems by mentioning the notorious, and likely greatly inflated, burning of the *Classics* and killing of the Classicists, perpetrated by the Qin.[79] The description of this dark age sets the scene for the appearance of Dong Zhongshu, the hero who, at the time of Emperor Wu, allegedly vindicated and rekindled the intellectual lineage of the Classicists.

The author of "Treatise on the Five Phases" is clearly interested in attributing to Classicists a critical role in the legitimization of the Han. According to the genealogy outlined above, the Classicists' exclusive mastery of ancient texts allowed the current sovereigns to attune their kingdom to cosmic rhythms and coherently perpetuate an ancient tradition of moral rulers. It is noteworthy that Eastern Han texts customarily refer to the Son of Heaven as Sage Man (*shengren* 聖人) and equate him to the extraordinary individuals that set the bases of Chinese civilization. And it was only the Classicists who, thanks to their specific knowledge and skills, could validate such an analogy and equate the Han rule to the cyclical return to the Golden Age. Of course, the teleological linearity and uniformity of the Classicists' tradition woven in the *History of the Former Han* is mostly a literary idealization and sharply contrasts with the accounts of the *Records*. Both Sima Tan and Qian, who benefited from a much more direct experience of the circumstances and events that characterized the early imperial period, from the Qin to Wu's era, tended to portray the Classicists mostly as contentious and self-serving individuals who often lacked a common understanding of and even a basic commitment to the values they advertised. Likewise, the reforms of the sacrifices promoted by the Classicists under Emperor Cheng in 31 BCE could not represent the return to a legitimate form of imperial rituals established under the Zhou. Even though the symbolic meaning of the ceremonies to Heaven and Earth would eventually be "universally" accepted, what recent scholarship defines as "Han official religion" did not subsume discrete forms of "local religion" within a new and "universal" conception of "the sacred." It rather represented "a religion for the emperor."

Further evidence of the composite nature of rituals in China is provided by the Eastern Han thinker Wang Chong 王充 (ca. 27–100) in the *Lun Heng* 論衡 (*Disquisitions*). Before engaging in his famous criticism of misguided beliefs concerning non-human phenomena in the chapter "On Sacrifices" ("Jiyi" 祭意), "the first Chinese materialist" or the "Chinese Lucretius"[80] synthesizes the mainstream or official understanding of ritual in his time:

> According to the *Liji* 禮記, the sovereign offers sacrifices to Heaven and Earth, the feudal princes to the Mountains and Rivers, the ministers and high dignitaries to the Five Genii,[81] the scholars and the common people to their ancestors. The sacrifices in the ancestral hall and those to the spirits of the Soil and Grain, from the Son of Heaven reach down to the common people.[82]

This passage attests to the "return" to the feudal and hierarchical (and absolutely non-unitary) ritual conception associated with the Zhou dynasty and the *Liji*, which was now firmly established as a source of authoritative models. The conclusion of this passage leaves no doubt that all these constant or fixed dispositions (*chang zhi* 常制) regulated the clearly distinct realms of the "sacrifices" (*si* 祀)—which according to the *Records* implied direct contact with extra-human entities—and ritual propriety," (*li* 禮). However the "rationalizing criticism" of these conceptions Wang provides in the same chapter implicitly confirms that the very possibility of a common understanding of rituals under the Eastern Han was still hindered by the resilience of geographic and social differences:

> The mountain forests, the valleys of the rivers, the hills and cliffs can emit clouds and produce winds and rain. These curious

phenomena are all regarded as spirits (*shen* 神). The ruler of the world sacrifices to the numerous spirits, the princes offer sacrifices as long as they are in their territory of origin, but not when they lose it.[83]

Spirits (or misconceptions about them) are deeply rooted in the territory; they would surely be ineffective (or meaningless) if eradicated. As for the Son of Heaven, after tending to the rituals specific to his position (those recreated by the Classicists in the late first century BCE), he would take charge of some the local ones simply because his authority trumped the privileges of any other lord. It is unthinkable that the ruler could personally tend to the myriad of cults performed throughout the empire. And there is no evidence that he did so. Bureaucratic control over regional ritual activities could not correspond to the creation of a "state religion." The possible participation of the emperor in specific local traditions did not necessarily imply a process of synthesis or homogenization, nor the realization of an anachronistic "religious unity."

The Classicists and "the People"

The paramount role of Confucius's cultural legacy in shaping Chinese historiography and civilization during the imperial era makes it difficult for scholars not to overemphasize the role of the Classicists during the early Han. However, after five centuries of political disunion and violence, the *Records*, as the first comprehensive history of China, does not seem willing to acknowledge any specific cultural tradition on which the Han could rebuild the moral foundations of an empire that was more the fruit of utopian models than of historical memory.

We have seen above how the *Records* questioned the effectiveness and honesty of most of the Han Classicists, while admonishing that a return to the moral rule of the Zhou would have been anachronistic anyway.[84] But it should not be surprising that Sima Qian himself considered a classic education fundamental and Confucius the greatest master who ever lived. As his upbringing demonstrates, it was not at all uncommon for a scholar of the former Han to study under different masters or appreciate contrasting philological or intellectual approaches.[85] Probably because Qian spent almost all his life in the capital city of Chang'an, he developed an attitude that was immune to the regional factionalism that characterized some of the cultural battles of the period.⁸⁶ As for the rivalry between *fangshi* and Classicists at Wu's court, Sima Qian seemed committed to denouncing the shortcomings and intrigues of individuals on either side.⁸⁷ Qian did respect some of the Classicists for their expertise in specific texts, but he doubted that their knowledge could have any practical application. After all, misgivings and contempt against this category of people seemed rather widespread until Sima Qian's time.

The *Records* chapter on Confucius, for example, recounts an episode in which the Master's career as a political advisor was hindered by the fact that he could himself be considered a Classicist (*ru* 儒) in a period in which more practical approaches to politics seemed to dominate the market for advisers.⁸⁸ According to the *Records*, the Master's fame had reached such a level that it was about to earn him an appointment in the retinue of no less than the powerful Duke Jing 景 (r. 547–489 BCE) of Qi (the state of the *bawang*). Duke Jing had been so impressed with the famous statement about the correspondence of political and familial relations ("Indeed, if a gentleman does not act as a gentleman, a minister does not act as a minister, a father does not act as a father, and a son does not act as a son, how could I eat food, even if I had it?") that he had promptly summoned the Master to court to question him about statecraft.⁸⁹ The development of what might have been a sort of job interview satisfied Duke Jing. However, when he was in the act of rewarding Confucius with an estate, Prime Minister Yan Ying 晏嬰 (or Master Yan, Yanzi 晏子, 589? –500 BCE) interrupted with a tirade against the Classicists' reputation that eventually persuaded Duke to stay away from Confucius and his ilk:⁹⁰

> The Classicists arguments are so deceptive that cannot be taken as a model. Haughty and arrogant, they follow only their own opinions; it's not possible to use them to lead the people. They attach enormous importance to funerals, abandon themselves to grief and break the bank for expensive burials; they cannot be used to regulate customs. They go from place to place talking about loans; they cannot be used to manage the government. Since the great saviors died and the court of Zhou fell into ruin, the rites and the music have been discontinued for a long time. Now Confucius is emphasizing appearance and embellishments, complicating the rites for ascending and for descending. . . . The following generations have not been able to completely comprehend his teachings; a whole life is not enough to master his rites.

If the lord wants to employ him to reform the customs of Qi, it would not be possible to use him to lead the common people.[91]

The argument against the Classicists's expensive and impractical interpretation of mourning rituals had already been made in similar terms in the *Mozi* 墨子.[92] In an another Warring States collection of texts on statecraft, *The Annals of Master Yan* (the *Yanzi Chunqiu* 晏子春秋), we read of the same Yan Ying as he points out to Confucius that the Classicists are unable to adapt to different circumstances or understand that different people might have different needs.[93] Sima Qian seemed perfectly in tune with this polemic, but he engaged it sideways in order to refine his indictment of Wu's political management, while more broadly casting a severe judgment on his own times and society. We have seen above that Yan Ying's biography is narrated in the "Guan Yan Liejuan" 管晏列傳, together with that of Guan Zhong, his predecessor among Qi prime ministers and the champion of the pragmatic model of kingship embodied by the ruler-hegemon that Emperor Wu, according to the *Records*, was trying to emulate.[94] Considering Sima Qian's rhetorical strategy of defining recent personalities by comparing them with similar characters of the past, his political targets and the analogies with the situation in the Han capital seem rather obvious. Was the historian actually lamenting that, in a court that was run often in a practical and at times ruthless way by a hegemon-like sovereign such as Wu, wise advisers (like Confucius) were being unjustly marginalized because of the (deservedly) bad reputation of individuals with whom they could be associated? Furthermore, whereas accusing Confucius of being unable to "reform the customs of Qi," and "lead the common people (*ximin* 細民)" was perfectly coherent with the worldview of a pragmatist such as Yan Ying, the text leads us to suspect that Sima Qian was in fact more inclined to accept the Master's aristocratic aloofness, or unpopularity, as a sign of intellectual superiority—a consideration on which our historian might have lingered to console himself.

However, conjectures about Sima Qian's motivations aside, the theme of the connection between social upbringing, relational competence, and timeliness plays an important role in his narration of Guan Zhong and Yan Ying's personal vicissitudes. Guan's biography in the *Records* emphasizes that he became an esteemed minister after overcoming a childhood of hardship and poverty and that he eventually made a name for himself in administering the finances of his state with great profit. Yan, on the other hand, was born the son of state minister. Perhaps because of his familiarity with exceptional personalities, he rarely followed etiquette around his superiors, but proved himself intelligent and flexible enough to become a successful and esteemed politician.⁹⁵ As we have seen, the passage cited above historicizes the moral shift ensuing the fall of the Zhou and the subsequent "mixing of the high and low," which corresponded with the moment in which new circumstances made Confucius's political vision obsolete or unpractical. In more contemporary terms, Sima Qian appears to interpret social mobility as an alarming sign of political, cultural, or even cosmic crisis. According to his reconstruction, it seems that the house of Zhou, in its inexorable fall, had also dragged down its allies and rivals, who, in a comparable way—but starting from an inferior standard—entered their own decline. In such an optic, Master Guan and Master Yan had to cope with different stages of Qi's involution, which in practice meant serving lords endowed with different skills and attitudes. Sima Qian concludes the chapter with their biographies in this way:

> Although Master Guan was known as an excellent minister of his generation, Confucius looked down on him. Is it because, when the rule of Zhou was in decline and Duke Huan 桓 [r. 685–643 BCE] was an example of virtue [Master Guan] did not encourage him to take the throne but only to claim the title of *hegemon* (*ba* 霸)? There is a saying that goes: "Support his virtues, correct his shortcomings so that high and low can be close in harmony." Is this not about Guan Zhong? As for Master Yan, when he was holding the dead body of [his lord] Duke Zhuang 莊 [r, 553–548 BCE],⁹⁶ he could cry [in front of the enemies of his lord] then leave [unharmed] after taking care of the rituals. Is this what people say "once you see what is right and do not act, you lack courage?" Also, as for Yan's straightforward eloquence and way to deal with his lord's authority, does not the saying: "when you enter the court display complete loyalty, when you leave it, focus on correcting mistakes" apply? If Master Yan were still alive today, I would be so delighted to serve him even if in the position of whip-wielding lackey on his carriage!⁹⁷

While the first part of this passage is rather self-explanatory, the second one needs to be complemented with pieces of information that, once recovered from other chapters of the *Records*, emphasize the ironic subtlety of Sima Qian's final comments. Duke Zhuang, whose demise Master Yan bemoaned conspicuously, had been Duke Jing's predecessor. According to the *Records*' chapter the "The Hereditary House of Duke Tai of Qi" ("Qi Tai Gong Shijia" 齊太公世家) Duke Zhuang, during his short reign, did not shine for political acumen or morality. In the short account on his tenure, we learn that against Yan's advice, he had unsuccessfully backed a rebellious faction in the neighboring state of Jin 晉 and that he was eventually struck down by the henchmen of the powerful minister Cui Zhu 崔杼, who had helped him secure the throne of Qi and with whose wife he was having an affair.[98] Surprisingly, Master Yan was not afraid of making a public display of grief in front of his lord's enemies. If they did not kill him on the spot, the *Records* reports, it was only because Yan benefited from wide popular support and Cui Zhu, especially in such a sensitive moment, needed the subjects of Qi on his side.[99]

The mention of the "whip-wielding lackey" instead refers to a more humorous episode narrated in Yan's biography and involving the ambitious wife of his charioteer. When the young woman happened to come across her husband taking around his master for the first time, she went home, waited for him and then asked for a divorce, for she could not accept that her tall, handsome, and elegant spouse could be the servant of a man as short and ugly as Yan Ying. But when Yang Yin heard the sad story, with no hesitation he promoted the forlorn man from charioteer to Senior Official (Daifu 大夫).[100]

Sima Qian's accounts of the lives of Guan Zhong and Yang Yin seem to make the point that in assessing the career of political advisers it is fundamental to consider the rulers they served and the reception of their actions among those below them as though they were inseparable factors. When the text mentions "the people" (*min* 民), it is not clear if we can safely interpret it in abstract terms, as the totality of the non-aristocratic subjects of the state of Qi, or more narrowly as those individuals or groups who, although they did not hold any top hierarchical position, had the possibility of affecting the tenure of a given sovereign or official concretely. The anecdote of the charioteer and his wife suggests that for Sima Qian it was not at all negligible that Yan Ying's "popularity" potentially reached to all the men and the women who had direct contact with the court. Innumerable are the stories in Chinese early sources referring to sovereigns or ministers whose lives were dramatically saved by guards or servants going beyond their usual duties—often at the risk of their own safety—because of an act of generosity received in the past that the noble benefactors had completely forgotten. So, when Cui Zhu says that he has "to let Yan Ying go because he needs the people on his side" he might mean individuals like the charioteer/now Senior Official mentioned by the *Records*, who owed everything—his status, income, and domestic harmony—to the minister's benevolence. From this point of view, criticizing the Classicists for not being able to gain a good reputation might amount to accusing them of being so self-involved and insincere that none among their lords, colleagues, and court personnel would trust them, let alone take an arrow in their stead. If the Master, Confucius, was delusional in advocating the universal applicability of his moral standards (i.e., *li*) to all people and circumstances, Sima Qian seems rather frustrated that the Classicists, individuals with whom he shared intellectual models, so often failed to elicit positive influences on political authority due to their self-serving pettiness and detachment from reality.

One example of his misgivings about these textual specialists is his unflattering portrait of the so-called "father of the Han Classicists" (*Han jia ru zong* 漢家儒宗), the controversial Shusun Tong 叔孫通 we have seen mentioned in apparently laudatory terms in the "Book on *Li*." Through his portrayal, the *Records* offers further support for its implicit and explicit arguments about the continuity of the Qin and Han rules. Thanks to his sycophantic and opportunistic ways, the *Records* narrates, Shusun had managed to gain favor at the Qin court in the early years of the empire, and, later, with the founder of the Han Liu Bang/Gaozu 高祖 (206–195 BCE), although he was notorious for not missing any chance to ridicule the Classicists and their hallowed texts.[101] "All I possess I have won on horseback," the Han founder was reported saying, "[. . .] Why should I care about the *Documents* and the *Odes*?"[102] According to an anonymous cavalryman cited in the *Records*, this emperor would routinely curse the Classicists, and whenever a visitor came to see him wearing one of their typical hats, he would promptly snatch the headdress and urinate in it.[103]

However, Liu Bang conceded that the Classicists might prove useful as the battles against his rival Xiang Yu 項羽 (232–202 BCE) were drawing to an end. Since the dynasty needed some form of cultural legitimization, he summoned the most popular Classicist of the time, Shusun Tong, and asked him to create new ceremonial protocols for the imperial court. As the *Records* reports, Shusun Tong wooed Gaozu's enthusiasm not by recovering Zhou protocols as one would have expected from a Classicist, but through a fanciful concoction of preexisting regional rituals, including those of Qin. The emperor was so impressed that he suddenly seemed aware of his royal prerogatives: "Today for the first time I realize how exalted a thing it is to be an emperor!"[104]

The *Records*, although always in subtle ways, never conceals its contempt for Liu Bang/Gaozu's poor judgment and morals.[105] However, it seems not to condone the way he was approached by Shusun's behavior, who not only lacked the proverbial haughty inflexibility of most Classicists, but also that sincere concern with his ruler or at least his people that characterized Yan Ying. More broadly, in Shusun Tong's biography, Qian shows how, especially in the case of less than competent sovereigns, the rhetoric of power is often the ambiguous product of hypocrisy and gullibility. Cunning advisors—even if of Shusun's dubious kind—have the potential to impose their views on unsophisticated or oblivious rulers whose authority is often the result of mere intrigue and violence.[106]

In the *Records*, even a sovereign customarily praised for his wisdom, such as Emperor Jing 景 (156–141 BCE), seems positively wary of any debate on the prerogatives of dynastic power. He appears to be not completely aware of the nature of his exceptional power and responsibilities, which confirms that a Zhou/Confucian conception of rulership was not yet established. In an episode described in "Biographies of Ru Scholars" ("Ru lin liezhuan"), two court advisors, the Erudite (*boshi* 博士) Yuan Gu 轅固 from Qi 齊, and Huang Sheng 黃生, presumably a Huang-Lao expert, engage in a passionate discussion on the legitimacy of the use of violence against tyrannical rulers.[107] Were founders of dynasties actually assassins, or did the fact that they eventually won popular support and achieved success mean that they had actually received the Mandate? In other words, could their actions be judged according to different moral standards? When Huang Sheng provocatively suggests that even the Han founder, Liu Bang, might have been at fault in replacing the Qin ruler, Emperor Jing, instead of defending the legitimacy of his own dynasty, simply invites the two debaters to move away from such a risky subject. From that episode on, Sima Qian remarks, the topic of dynastic change and violence was no longer discussed at court, as though he had ultimately become persuaded that political power and moral behavior were tragically irreconcilable.[108]

Of Omens, Emperors, and Men

As we have seen, according to the Gongyang tradition, all phenomena were theoretically explainable as elements of a cosmic-political whole. The universal balance toward which the cycles of yin and yang and the Five Phases gravitated was informed by the moral principles of harmonious hierarchical interrelations and filial piety. In this scheme, historiography was an indispensable tool for deciphering the messages of Heaven to his Son (the emperor) and humankind, while justifying the Han settlement of China as intrinsic to the natural order. Consequently, the interpretation of omens served as an instrument for assessing whether the sovereign was ruling according to the Mandate and fulfilling his duties.[109] A famous passage in the *Luxuriant Gems of Spring and Autumn* thus reads:

> Disasters are Heaven's warnings; anomalies are Heaven's threats. If Heaven warns [the ruler] and he does not understand, then Heaven sends anomalies to awe him . . . In all cases, the sources of all disasters and anomalies originate entirely from the state's shortcomings. When shortcomings have just begun to germinate, Heaven sends fearful disasters to warn and inform the ruler. If, after being warned and informed, the ruler still has not mended [his ways], then [heaven] displays strange anomalies to frighten him. If, after being frightened, he still has no fear, then misfortunes and calamities occur.[110]

As we have seen, however, Sima Qian was not keen on identifying any clear pattern in the unfolding of historical events. The treatment of prodigies in the *Records* seems to point to a tragic disjunction between Heaven and human affairs. Yet Sima Qian does not make clear whether he considered such a breach to have been caused by the moral unworthiness of the men of his time, or whether he regarded it instead as an epistemological conundrum resulting from an unbridgeable ontological separation. What the *Records* clearly suggests, though, is that the rhetoric of omens could be exploited for political advantage: rulers and ruled alike were sensitive to the possibility that disasters and portents should be tied to the mishandling of monarchic power. The ambiguous space between society and nature, Heaven and Earth, the living and the dead, light and darkness, offered too many opportunities for mystification, without offering any solid basis for logical arguments or the cultivation of moral qualities. For this reason, Confucius warned against paying attention to any phenomena that transcended ordinary social interactions.

The *Records* regularly casts doubt on anyone who claimed to have the ability to translate natural phenomena or prodigies into political lessons—obviously not any less so in the case of Classicists. Furthermore, at least during the realm of Emperor Wu, advertising competence in the science of prognostication was risky business. If we focus on the "Ru lin" chapter, which collects the biographies of the most famous Classicists, we learn that Dong Zhongshu's effort to record and study disasters and prodigies nearly cost him his life at the hand of Emperor Wu.[111] After a mysterious fire destroyed the mortuary altar to Gaozu in Liaodong 遼東 in 139 BCE, an envious colleague of Dong's, one Zhufu Yan 主父偃,[112] managed to present a copy of Dong's treatise on omens to the Son of Heaven. Since the book might have provided arguments for interpreting the accident, which occurred at the altar of the founder of the Han, as an indictment of the conduct of the current ruler, the young Wu immediately summoned all the court advisors for an opinion. The *Records* reports only the words of Lü Bushu 呂步舒, a disciple of Dong, who apparently did not recognize the work as his master's and judged it stupid and worthless.[113] Since Wu abhorred the very idea of such a potentially dangerous manual, he impulsively condemned Dong to death, but then, fortunately for the scholar, changed his mind and pardoned him. After the incident, the historian remarks, Dong Zhongshu no longer dared to express his theories about disasters and portents.

This passage not only attests once more to the irrelevance of Dong under Wu's reign, but also to the vulnerability of the very notion of imperial legitimacy throughout the Western Han. As in the anecdote (which appears in the same chapter of the *Records*) about Emperor Jing and the dispute over the morality of rulers who come to power by murdering their predecessors, this episode represents another instance in which the *Records* describes a Han sovereign lacking the confidence conventionally attributed to moral and just rulers. As Martin Kern shows, Emperor Wu would eventually use the interpretation of portents to his own advantage in a way unsurpassed by other Han emperors.[114] However, in this circumstance, Wu, still an adolescent, appears understandably insecure. Following in the footsteps of his proverbially wise father, he prefers to quash a debate that could not only have ended in an indictment of his and his father's mandate to rule, but also cast a shadow on the legitimacy of the entire Han dynasty. As for the supernatural aspects of the event, Sima Qian does not provide the reader with any information to ascertain whether the fire was a portent, a deliberate fraud, or a mere accident. By reporting the omen and the fear elicited by political authority, the historian offers his disenchanted view on the hypocrisy and cynicism characterizing contemporary court politics. Whatever Sima Qian might have thought of the attribution of Dong's treatise, the account of Lü Bushu's intervention may speak to the relative isolation of court advisors, as they did not seem to constitute a like-minded group of intellectuals. If instead Lü had denied Dong's authorship of the treatise because he wished to protect his master, we would have further evidence to conclude that the *Records* does not regard Han Classicists as wholesome scholars and advisers who would stoically stand by their ideas and principles.

In any case, under such circumstances, how was it possible to establish any solid line of doctrinal transmission and moral unity? Provided that the cosmos was readable as an organic whole, was there a universally accepted theory to rely on, with trustworthy and unbiased interpreters? Finally, if we trace back the biography of the lesser known protagonists of this episode (as we always should in the case of the *Records*), we learn that Zhufu Yan, Dong Zhongshu's enemy, is mainly remembered as a vocal supporter of the government's politics of centralization against the autonomy of the kingdoms (*guo*), whose leaders would eventually have him executed.[115] At this point, we should not exclude that at stake in the promotion of "Han Confucianism" were only cultural issues. Members of the educated elites must have been sensitive to the emperor's intent to attack the economic independence of regional aristocracies. And the wealth deriving from landowning was traditionally strictly connected to the very possibility of devoting time and energies to the study of the *Classics*.

Historiography as an Educational Journey

The chapter devoted to Confucius in the *Records* ends on a tone of distress and despair, as the Sage realizes that all his hopes to exert a positive influence on his contemporaries are lost.[116] The Master interprets the famous capture of the *lin* 麟 unicorn in 481 BCE, the fourteenth year of duke Ai 哀 of Lu 魯, narrated in the *Spring and Autumn Annals*, as an epoch-changing sign.[117] But what seems to afflict Confucius the most is not just the close of an age and the approach of his own demise, but the lack of any interpretive system for reading the new cosmic order and the interruption of his cultural lineage. Right after he acknowledges the omen, the Master laments that the Yellow and the Luo 雒 Rivers had not, as in the past, yielded any miraculous tools like the Eight Trigram system and the Great Plan (*Hong Fan* 洪範), with which men had once read the cosmos.[118] The *Records* immediately connects this passage with the death of Confucius's favorite disciple Yan Hui 顏回, which provoked the Master's complete despair: "Heaven wanted my death . . . my career is over . . . No one knows me. [But] I am not angry with Heaven, I do not blame men. I studied what is below and reached what is above; who knows me is Heaven indeed!"[119]

The mention of Heaven, far from being a reference to any personal deity, does not celebrate the investiture of Confucius as a new king.[120] Rather, it underscores Confucius's exceptionality and isolation both from his contemporaries and the sages of the past. Tellingly in the same text, the Master praises Bo Yi and Shu Qi as the only ancient sages who did not surrender their will nor dishonor their bodies, having rejected power and deliberately lived in seclusion.[121] As we have seen above, their case represents a crucial conundrum. Convinced that it was never legitimate to rebel against one's ruler, regardless of his corruption and unworthiness, they tried to dissuade King Wu from attacking the last sovereign of the Shang. Had Bo Yi and Shu Qi succeeded, the Zhou Dynasty, the absolute paragon of moral government and society, would not have existed. However, unlike them, Confucius states that he did not even follow a fixed set of rules and principles, letting the reader assume that he would have been able to grasp the exceptionality and expediency of King Wu's treason.[122] Therefore, going back to his favorite student's death and concern with his legacy, if there was no one who could codify his teachings for the sake of future generations, if different circumstances required different decisions, Confucius had no choice but to embark upon the writing of the *Spring and Autumn* annals, in which, case by case, he would reveal or conceal a ruler's deeds and misdeeds. The Master confided that it would be up to posterity to examine case by case and single out whose conduct was exemplary or misguided:

> Therefore [the Master], by using historical records, composed the *Spring and Autumn Annals*, which starts with duke Yin and goes until the fourteenth year of duke Ai [481 BCE], through the reign of twelve dukes. Having as a basis Lu, which was connected to Zhou, in turn preceded by Yin [Shang], he moved through three dynasties. He simplified his style but broadened the meaning. For this reason when the princes of Chu and Wu proclaimed themselves "kings," the *Spring and Autumn* annals devalued them by using the term "viscount." When at the time of the meeting of Jiantu, the Son of Heaven of Zhou was summoned, the *Spring and Autumn* annals dissimulated the fact by stating instead that the sovereign went "hunting at Heyang." It

is going back to those examples that we find a lesson for the present times. The principles of devaluation and dissimulation will be raised and explained at the appearing of true sovereigns. If the principles of the *Spring and Autumn* annals are carried out, all the unruly ministers and criminals of the world will be scared.[123]

Thus, if the *Annals* was Sima Qian's model, his approach to history writing is consistent with Confucius's emphasis on the Rectification of Names *zheng ming* 正名. Recording events does not constitute an instrument for reading the past, but rather for comprehending the political, social, and cultural circumstances of proper linguistic and moral choices. But these were choices that might bear fruits only in the future, since, after all, the Master's exceptional existence had been the most untimely of all.

At stake in the linguistic decisions that historiography entails is the determination of proper human interactions and hierarchies. Again, we know that "the Book on *Li*" conceives *li* in terms of highly formalized but contingent cultural and social relations. Unlike "Han Confucianism," the *Records* does not interpret *li* as resonating with cosmic and natural rhythms. According to the *Records*, the main task of the historian does not consist in disclosing universal laws or presenting the past through detailed argumentations in order to make specific points, but rather in revealing the subtle rhetoric of annalistic language. Sadly, political necessity and ethical coherence could not be reconciled in any intellectual endeavor.

Sima Qian seems especially interested in allowing the reader to establish an emotional connection with the protagonists of its stories and the circumstances of their lives, the complexity of which is rather evoked, represented, and accepted as such rather than interpreted.[124] The theme harmonizing with exemplary men of the past (or the Other in general) instinctively through the universality of human feelings is also enunciated in the incipit of the "Book on Music" ("Yueshu" 樂書) in the *Records*, which is in turn consistent with *Xunzi*'s consideration of the ethical role of music in fostering solidarity.[125]

A further level of complexity of the *Records* is represented by the contrast between its structure, which, as noted by Mark E. Lewis, suggests a "comprehensive, hierarchical order of space," and the interconnection of the existential trajectories of its human protagonists.[126] The exemplary personalities in the *Records* are not treated as complete, separate psychological universes; instead, we see them through the interaction of various factors and accidents. This work defies any attempts at a conventional biographical reading, since the information on any given character or subject is scattered throughout different chapters and sections. The *Records* multiplies points of view and angles to such an extent that it is extremely difficult to single out any epistemic structures. Its narrative style employs neither a holistic approach to human experience, nor, as the historian Xu Fuguan lamented, an original and coherent "philosophical" vision.[127] In Foucauldian terms we can say that the *Records*, instead of taking into consideration the "point of view of the rules," or the "positive unconscious of knowledge" over time, focuses on the point of view of all the subjectivities involved in all sides of the process of writing history. This perspective defies any attempt to reduce the variety and fluidity of the material presented in the *Records* to structural paradigms.[128]

Considering the current debates on received and excavated texts and on the controversial issues concerning the chronology, transmission, and editing processes of textual traditions during the Han, we cannot know whether, or to what extent, the *Records*' approach was innovative or, instead, whether it was more or less in keeping with the different cultural trends and intellectual attitudes of his times.[129] In a fashion echoing the *Zhuangzi* chapter entitled "Enjoyment in Untroubled Ease" (*Xiao Yao You* 逍遙遊), the *Records* does not engage in a reading of reality premised on the acknowledgment of a modular correspondence between microcosm and macrocosm. It does not attempt to interpret specific cases as coherent manifestations of an "organicistic" cosmic/moral system, in which every aspect of reality is connected or coordinated to the whole.[130] In other words, the *Records* does not follow a comprehensive approach to human experience in the world. Wherever the extra-human is mentioned in the *Records*, it does not have the traits of a coherent, not to mention moral, system. Rather, it partakes of the same fluidity, complexity, and ambiguity as the human sphere.[131]

Conclusions: "Every Structure Is a Hidden God"

"Any structure," remarked Benedetto Croce (1866–1952), "is the ingenuous re-proposition of a hidden god; any systemic approach might actually constitute a crypto-theology."[132] In his attempt at formalizing a purely philosophical historicism that could emancipate the Hegelian idealistic tradition from any form of transcendence, Croce meant to attack Marxist materialism in general and its Italian interpretation called *philosophy of praxis* in particular.[133] In the *Prison Notebooks,* Antonio Gramsci (1891–1937), in a passionate defense of such an intellectual approach, argues that the concept of structure produces metaphysics only if it is approached theoretically, whereas in his own interpretation structure has to be seen historically as the whole of the social relations that constitute the living and working environment of real men.[134] In Gramsci's view, a structure refers also to those objective conditions that can and must be studied with the instrument of philology (i.e., language in context) and not of philosophical speculation. As Gramsci sees it, subjective conceptions of reality produced by a given social group, once explained historically, could be treated as real facts, concrete acts instrumental to the processes by which communities provide for themselves a moral unity.[135]

In its treatment of extra-human factors, Sima Qian seems likewise more interested in acknowledging the role subjective beliefs had in the traditions that constituted the multifarious cultural/ethical world in which he was living than in analyzing and understanding them *per se*. Events that happened in the remote past, or that were unverifiable because connected to the "divine sphere," clearly interest the *Records* as social-political forces, especially to the extent to which they stand as a model or a source of legitimacy for the influential intellectual traditions (or factions) of Qian's own times, or as a moral paragon for a present crisis.[136] On the other hand, in analyzing more recent events, some of which Sima Qian or his father had likely directly witnessed, the *Records* tends to frame the occurrence of "miraculous events" as attempts at exploiting human gullibility or evidence of the moral bankruptcy of the Han age. Ethical choices are what really matters to the Grand Historian. His main interest consists in isolating human factors and defining the limits of human actions. Consequently, the *Records* reads as a multifaceted literary enterprise, in which the treatment of discrete cases, instead of leading through an inductive process to the formulation of broader narrative patterns, seems rather aimed at refuting any generalizing and abstracting analytical tendency.[137] Going back to the issue of the role of the "divine," unlike the conventional conception a pantheon entails in the ancient Greco-Roman world, the whole of "spirits and ghosts" in the *Records* does not constitute an organic cosmos, a system of deities that preside over different sectors of reality and whose interactions could help to explain natural and historical events.[138] Moreover, the "deities" of the *Records* do not yet inhabit Heaven, nor is their gaze felt as a ubiquitous witness and judge of human actions—their "moral jurisdiction" usually does not cross regional or village boundaries.[139] Rather, the *Records* evokes spirits and ghosts to expose the vulnerability of the human condition and the fragmentary nature of human experience. It is especially preoccupied with the very possibility of producing an accurate record of alleged encounters with the extra-human. Spirits and ghosts, in the chapters of the *Records* that deal with recent events, almost never have a major impact on humans' lives. If they ultimately affect what men feel, think, and do, it is indirectly through the suasive, threatening, or apotropaic power of the stories told about these beings. By juxtaposing fantastical tales narrated by magicians, charlatans, and alchemists and occultists associated with *fangshi*, with Sima Qian's visits to the relics connected to the cults or tombs of deities, the *Records* suggests that what really matters are the extant traditions and social practices related to the putative intervention of the divine. In other words, it seems that the space and the dialectic between the visible and the invisible provided the authors of the *Records* with the possibility of positing unpredictability at the center of its narrative, emancipating the question of success and failure from any deterministic schemes, and finally concentrating on the verifiable circumstances of human actions, especially agency and timeliness, even though such questions as agency and timeliness in the *Records* must be deliberately left open to debate and negotiation.[140] As we saw in the early sections of this chapter, the question will be definitely closed by Eastern Han historiography, with the assumption that the Han Empire sanctioned the correspondence of cosmic and political orders.

The perceived lack of a "philosophical" concern in the *Records*' historiographical approach is nothing more than the projection of the systemic frame of mind which is typical of European cultural history regarding Han China. Nonetheless, the establishment of unified and centralized rule under the Han Dynasty might conceivably have produced a teleological trajectory in the all-embracing and "universal" narratives of the *Records*.[141] While ideal and idealized rule, according to the cultural expectations of the elites of Sima Qian's times, entailed the integration of the political and moral realms, the Grand Historian did not equate his own age with a new golden age. Not only did his contemporaries fail to live up to the best examples in the hallowed tradition, but in times of turbulent change and uncertainty, human beings could not conceive and rely on a caring and omniscient deity, or even on the comforting notion of a consistent and intelligible metaphysical system. As we will see in the following chapter, the various references to Heaven/Tian in the *Records* do not clarify the boundaries of human agency, leaving the issues of historical causality and necessity open.

3

Narrating the Empire

Metaphysics without God, "Religions" without Identity[1]

> All profound changes in consciousness, by their very nature, bring with them characteristic amnesias. Out of such oblivions, in specific historical circumstances, spring narratives.
> —Benedict Anderson[2]

> High Heaven does its business without sound, without smell.
> —*The Odes*[3]

> Any structure is the ingenuous re-proposition of a hidden god; any systemic approach might actually constitute a crypto-theology.
> —Benedetto Croce[4]

Heaven, Fortune, and Universalism in Early Chinese and Greco-Roman Historiography

In the post 9/11 world, the specter of a "clash of civilizations" and the urge to establish the basis for fruitful intercultural dialogues have prompted researchers to look for comprehensive views (i.e., *Weltanschauungen*) that treat civilizations as moral and ideological unities. Such approaches—especially when the comparison is cultural—tend to treat mankind's relationship with the purported supernatural as a crucial element that explains collective agency and defines identity.[5] However, these conversations on religion rarely cross the conceptual boundaries of the Abrahamic traditions with the consequence that contemporary debates on universalism, secularism, and neoatheism tend to conceive of the relationships between religion, identity, and agency in unitary terms, reflecting what I call the "hegemony of monotheism."[6]

In chapter 1, I argued that the preeminence of Abrahamic conceptions of the sacred in the West is in part a consequence of Christian apologetic interpretations of the dominion of Rome over the Mediterranean. I reconstructed the *Records*' analytical approach to ritual and historical memory, political unity and cultural continuity, contingency and subjectivity, in order to show that a unitary conception of religion did not exist that could be unproblematically used to foster cultural integration. In this chapter, I focus on ascertaining whether the first history of China subsumes these elements under a "big picture," or if, in recounting the unification of the country under the Qin and the Han, it implies or refers to the existence of any meta-historical factor, such as Fate or the will of an all-powerful deity. I argue that the *Records* offers no such unifying element; instead, the text emphasizes that references to extra-human intervention often represent a ploy to disguise the "heteronomy of ends" of the protagonists of history.

Part of my task in this chapter will be to show that the common tendency to use the monotheistic models to approach the notion of Tian (Heaven) in early China is misguided and deleterious to our understanding of early Chinese relationships with the divine, as is the (somewhat less common) tendency to explain Tian in terms of "the Chinese notion of God,"[7] "supreme authority," or "sky-god."[8]

From a cross-cultural point of view, I consider the possibility that it is the very structure of teleological narratives about empire formation that necessarily produces monotheistic, systemic, universalistic, moralistic, or identitary conceptions of the "sacred." To this purpose, I compare the treatment of Heaven in the *Records* to the role of Fortune in the political unification of the ancient Mediterranean under Rome, as narrated in Polybius's (200–118 BCE) *Histories*. These authors produced their masterworks before Buddhism and Christianity popularized a universalistic and relatively institutionalized conception of the sacred in East Asia and in the Mediterranean. The joint study of the *Histories* and the *Records* thus allows me to concentrate on two unrelated conceptualizations of universal rule, as it extended over different civilizations and cultural traditions.[9] In more practical terms, I here explore the different personal backgrounds and cultural contexts that shaped the *Records* and the *Histories* and the extent to which, in explaining unified rule, they accounted for the intervention of non-human or universal elements in relation with individual choices, material factors, specific institutions, ethnicity, social structures, or morals.[10]

The comparison of the *Records* with Polybius's work becomes extremely relevant especially in light of the Greek writer's influence on Western historiography. With the recovery of the classic traditions in Europe, educated elites became particularly fascinated with Fortune in the *Histories*, as it steered Rome's destiny toward imperial glory. Considering his concern with narrative and political unity, they would praise Polybius's approach—although that of a pagan—as intrinsically compatible with the teleological (and theological) message of Christianity.[11] At the same time, in influencing Machiavelli (through Livy), Polybius's cynical interpretation of Roman cults also provided European non-confessional historiography with an argument for defining religion as *instrumentun regni* (i.e., "instrumental to political power.")

In addition to offering a new conceptual framework for the study of Sima Qian's treatment of metaphysics, this chapter brings contemporary theories of religion, universality, and identity to bear on the study of ancient civilizations. As we shall see, the notion of a universalistic, super-ethnic religion that propounds the unity of the metaphysical, moral, and empirical realms, was alien to both Sima Qian and Polybius. Their worldviews, formed before the advent of monotheism in China and Rome, can enlarge our conceptual repertoire and make it better suited to the study of the originality and complexity of non-Abrahamic, or non-monotheistic understandings of the divine.

The Records, Universalism, and the Extension of Civilization

Sima Qian and Polybius shared the dual privilege of observing and explaining the exceptional convergence of events and personalities that had enabled the establishment of a single hegemonic power over the world as they knew it. Setting them apart from each other were differing ideas regarding the relative position of each one's own civilization vis-à-vis foreign cultures and sociopolitical traditions. While in the Central States, the discourse on civilization had traditionally been self-referential, Greco-Roman historians tended to approach their subjects in comparative terms. In other words, the ways in which they did or did not formalize cultural identity and otherness were hardly similar.

Around and across the Mediterranean Sea, peoples, goods, practices, and ideas traveled through trade, diplomacy, migration, colonization, and warfare from time immemorial.[12] Identities had developed in the awareness of the coexistence of different civilizations that represented not only a challenge but also an example. The proximity and the relevance of the "Other," the foreign, the strange, and the hostile, had been fundamental in the formalization of both group and individual consciousness.[13] It would be impossible, for instance, to follow the history of ancient Mesopotamia, Egypt, and Israel without considering their composite natures and mutual connections, not forgetting the importance of cultural diffusion, and the violent impact of external forces. If we look closely at classical historiography, we see that it was fear and admiration of the Persian Empire that prompted the Greek city-states to formalize and embrace a pan-Hellenic identity.[14] In turn, the ancient Romans constructed the idea of a distinctive national character against the cultures of Greece and the Greek colonies in southern Italy, as well as the Etruscans and the other peoples of the Peninsula.[15] The analytic approach of the historians writing in and about the ancient Mediterranean tended to be comparative both in methodology and in purpose, since they had to acknowledge the commensurable political and cultural relevance of other past and contemporary ethnic, cultural, and political realities.

By contrast, early imperial China elites regarded their culture as the epitome of civilization, or as the only conceivable one. Ancient Chinese sources held that illiterate and savage neighbors could always be "emancipated" through Sinicization.[16] Few today would overlook the import of non-autochthonous elements in Chinese culture throughout history, yet the received textual tradition represents the "Other" as an alternative to "Civilization" only in a dialectical and paradoxical way.[17] Although the *Records* addresses the negative trope of the uncivilized barbarian in critical terms, its relatively unprejudiced treatment of the Other seems more instrumental to Sima Qian's preoccupation with the employment of competent officials in foreign politics than indicative of a genuine interest in the Other itself, as the civilization of the Central States seemed to have no conceivable alternatives.[18] As Tamara Chin has pointed out, Sima Qian "avoids anthropological rhetoric." Unlike Ban Gu in the *Han Shu*, and Fan Ye 范曄 (398–445 CE) in the *History of the Later Han* (*Hou Han Shu* 後漢書) the Grand Historian does not include his account of Han frontier campaigns in "a narrative of cultural and moral superiority."[19]

Sima Qian, born by the Yellow River, just a few miles north of the Han capital Chang'an, had always been close to the geographic and cultural center of the empire, and spent his life in the shadows of the imperial court.[20] As he recollects in the autobiographical chapter of the *Records*, members of his family had served as official historians (*shi* 史) ever since the semi-mythical first Chinese dynasty of the Xia (2100–1600 BCE). For centuries, the Sima family had faithfully recorded human, natural, and astrological events, as all phenomena were traditionally considered intertwined with the lives of the ancient Chinese and their ruling dynasties. According to tradition, over time, royal power had shifted from the Xia to the Shang (1600–1046 BCE), and then to the Zhou (1046–256 BCE), who eventually lost direct political control over the Central Plains in 771 BCE during a "barbaric" invasion that forced them eastward. The ensuing centuries of fragmentation and violence culminated with the Qin reunifying China in 221 BCE. Their seemingly unpopular empire ended when Liu Bang 劉邦 (?256–195 BCE, posthumously known with his temple name of Gaozu 高祖), a commoner from the region of the former state of Chu, defeated his aristocratic rivals and established the Han (206 BCE–220 CE), the dynasty under which Sima Qian was born and raised.

Liu Bang and his immediate successors were hesitant to legitimize their supremacy through triumphalist state propaganda. As we have seen in the previous chapter, semi-independent kingdoms continued to challenge the authority of the Han for decades after the dynasty's foundation, compelling its leaders to respond with measures that, in their ruthlessness, closely resembled those used by the despised Qin.[21] When Emperor Wu embarked on the ceremonial glorification of the Han Empire, its historical trajectory was celebrated by the court archivists Sima Tan and his son Sima Qian. But after five centuries of political and cultural disunion—provided that an "original unity" was anything more than a literary creation—weaving the histories of the Central States into a single narrative was not an easy task. Complicating matters was the fact that the ruling lineage of the Han did not originate from the Central Plain, the region at the core of the three traditional dynasties of the Xia, Shang, and Zhou,[22] but from the southern state of Chu. Furthermore, the two Simas' historiographical approach was inevitably conditioned by their problematic relationship with the ruler whose triumph they were expected to celebrate. In addition to Tan's exclusion of the *feng* and *shan* sacrifices and consequent death, Sima Qian's view must have been severely conditioned by the "Li Ling 李陵 Affair" of 99 BCE. That year the historian tried to defend the conduct of a general who chose to save himself and his remaining troops instead of leading them on a suicide mission against the onslaught of an overwhelming enemy. Emperor Wu became so angry at Sima Qian for the apology that he imposed on him a cruel choice: death or castration.[23] Although extremely humiliating, the historian chose mutilation, for it would still allow him to perpetuate the glory of his family through his literary enterprise.

It should come as no surprise that Sima Qian did not believe that the unification of China meant the necessary culmination of a "divine" plan or the realization of a just order. The Grand Historian was too aware that the triumph of the Han represented the realization of selfish interests through violence and conspiracy, rather than the victory of a superior moralizing will. By traveling the empire to verify historical and geographical circumstances, Sima Qian became acquainted with the multifarious cultures and customs of the different areas of China. He accepted multiplicity and seemed to comprehend cultural and ethnic diversity as a quantitative (not qualitative) deviation from the known standard. As we have seen in the previous chapter, through individual and collective biographies, annals, chronological tables, and monographic essays, the 130 chapters of the *Records* account for multiple subjectivities in a multifaceted narrative that complicates the recognition of seemingly straightforward historical causation. Further, Sima Qian's accounts of the Other seem self-referential in that they are mainly inspired by the didactic purpose of advising the court about pressing situations.

The *Records* treats the most formidable enemy of the fledging Han dynasty, the nomadic Xiongnu 匈奴, as a by-product of the Central States, for it traces their origins back to the royal family of the Xia dynasty.[24] What we call "religion" had a small role in defining their identity as a distinctive group. According to the text, these nomads were related to the same extra-human forces worshipped by the Chinese. Like the Chinese, the Xiongnu sacrificed to Heaven and Earth, as well as ghosts (*gui*) and spirits (*shen*), albeit in their own ways.[25] More importantly, Xiongnu society represented a diametric opposite of the Confucian ideal, for it lacked literacy, agriculture, care for the elderly, *li*, and righteousness (*yi*).[26] On the positive side, according to the *Records*, these nomads seemed emancipated from some of the exaggerations of a more sophisticated set of social rituals and etiquette. The first history of China informs us that the overly elaborate and strict norms of propriety (*li*) did not constrain the royal lineage of the Xiongnu. It was in fact, fairly stable and durable, as elite men could marry the widows of relatives in violation of basic Chinese incest taboos.[27]

As for the Otherness of the people of Chu, homeland of the founder of the Han, the *Records* traces their origins back to the mythical sovereign Zhuan Xu 顓頊, a nephew of the ancestor to all Chinese people, the pre-dynastic Yellow Emperor. Zhuan Xu certainly did not establish a reign based on the secular social rituals and exemplary filial piety that would become Confucius's model. He "followed Heaven by according himself to its rhythms, prescribed norms that complied with spirits and ghosts, [and] transformed the people by controlling the Five Qi."[28] Since the Warring

States period, Chu, in spite of, or because of its relative exoticism, had become an integral part of discourses concerning the cultural traditions of the Central Plain.[29] And unsurprisingly, the *Records* does not hold—at least directly—that the foreign and non-aristocratic origins of Liu Bang might constitute an obstacle to his claims to leadership over all China. After all, political unity was possible even without *li*, while, as we have seen above, different styles of rule might fit different periods and circumstances.

In the *Records*, China, albeit characterized by several cultural and political traditions, seems the only conceivable civilization. Neighboring peoples and foes are depicted not in terms of absolute Otherness or diversity, but inclusively as gradual digressions (due to behavior more than birth) from the established norm and of the known world, since their genealogical origin is always sought within the cosmos of the Central States. And it should be noted that because of the millenary history of contacts and interdependence between Eastern and Central Asia, no peoples who clashed with the polities of the Central Plains could be considered completely alien.

Universalism in Polybius

For Polybius, who lived under the hegemony of foreign forces, the world had many possible centers, and civilization many possible forms. As Frank W. Walbank points out, both Polybius's life and oeuvre were deeply affected by "the impact of the outside world upon Greece."[30] Son of the eminent statesman Lycortas, Polybius was born in 203 BCE in the Arcadian city of Megalopolis, which was a member of the Achaean League—a confederation of Hellenic *poleis* whose aim was to protect Greek autonomy, especially against the intrusions of the Macedonian power.[31] The League had to confront first Sparta's resurgence, and then the rising power of Rome.[32] Under such threats, many had hoped that the Antigonid King Perseus of Macedon (212–166 BCE), one of the political heirs of Alexander the Great (356–323 BCE), could safeguard Hellenic independence. But the Third Macedonian War (171–168 BCE) against Rome ended with Perseus's total defeat. After the fatal battle of Pydna in 168, the last Antigonid ruler was deported as a hostage, along with his entourage and the members of the Hellenic political groups who had supported him directly or indirectly. Among them was the historian Polybius.[33]

At the time of his exile, Polybius had already spent more than thirty years at the center of the Hellenic political scene as an active member of the Achaean League. In the footsteps of his father and elder brother, who both participated in diplomatic missions to Rome, he seemed destined for an even more illustrious political career. Around the age of twenty, Polybius was chosen to accompany the urn of the beloved leader of the Achaean League, Philopoemen (253–183 BCE), during his funeral. In 170/69 BCE, at the age of thirty—the youngest age of eligibility—Polybius was selected as Military Commander (*hipparchos*) of the Achaean League. The position of Supreme Commander (*stratêgos*) seemed likely to be his next prestigious appointment.[34]

Yet the historian's exile in Italy did not mean isolation from the center of political activity. Whereas his fellow countrymen and hostages were usually not allowed in the capital city, Polybius—thanks either to his influential acquaintances or because the host government wanted to keep an eye on him—was permitted to spend his exile in Rome. Here Polybius was welcomed in the preeminent cultural and political circles of the time. He enjoyed a relative degree of freedom, which enabled him to travel within and outside Italy and to take part in hunting expeditions. Most importantly, Polybius became a tutor and friend of P. Cornelius Scipio Aemilianus (185–129 BCE), the military and political leader who would later be associated with the siege and destruction of Carthage in 146 BCE (to which the historian would be a direct witness) and the subsequent establishment of Rome as the paramount imperial power of the Mediterranean.[35]

After promoting a policy of "cautious Achaean independence in international affairs," and witnessing the disbanding of the Achaean League with the destruction of Corinth by the Romans in 146 BCE, Polybius, repatriated in 150 BCE, became involved in the reconstruction of Greece and in the political mediation between Greece and Rome, which would gain him durable fame and praise among his countrymen.[36] In terms of allegiance and identification, these experiences determined the complexity of Polybius's historiographical approach. Through the long process of composing and publishing the *Histories*, the historian's analytic attitude was shaped by different political and cultural realities.[37] The "last writer of a free Greece and the historian of its conquest" lived in a period characterized by strong intercultural connections.[38] In writing the *Histories* for both Roman and Hellenic audiences, Polybius offered a Greek perspective on Rome's triumphal advance in the Mediterranean.[39] Simultaneously, the historian had to justify for his fellow countrymen the legitimacy of foreign hegemony over the Hellenic world, while also helping them cope with a new administrative reality. The emphasis on contemporary and "pragmatic history,"[40] namely the specific attention to military strategy, politics, and institutional structures, was not just a stylistic and intellectual choice, but allowed Polybius to connect ethnicity and history in a more complex way.[41] For the Achaean historian, who represented the voice of the vanquished, political dominance did not inevitably result in cultural superiority.[42]

It is well known that Polybius recognized Rome's "mixed" constitution as one of the principal factors in its surge to power.[43] He interpreted the interplay of consuls, senate, and people in Roman politics as the balanced coexistence of monarchy, aristocracy, and democracy—forms of government that had already been implemented in the Hellenic world with varying degrees of success.[44] Yet Polybius's explanation of Rome's extraordinary rise necessarily required an assessment of the lapse, however momentary, of Greek supremacy.[45] It is not surprising that, as Craige Champion points out, the historian's attitude toward the cultural identity of his hosts seems equivocal.[46] Whether the Romans were members of the civilized Hellenic world or barbarians was, according to Polybius, "historically contingent upon the health of the institutional structures of the polity" and determined by the alternating cycles of "reason" and "unbridled passion."[47] Institutions and politics could influence the fate of civilizations. Ethnicity (or culture) did not determine the outcome of historical events in an absolute way.

Yet the dramatic shift of the cultural and political axis of the Mediterranean world must have had a very deep impact on Polybius. Roman dominion seemed to overshadow the achievements of the Persian, Spartan, and Macedonian empires, the most formidable the historian had ever observed and studied.[48] The unprecedented convergence of events and peoples of the known world that had determined Rome's supremacy also made possible, for the first time, the writing of a synoptic and universal history.[49] And, as we shall see, Fortune would have an interesting role to play in Polybius's narrative endeavor.

A Brief Cultural History of Heaven

The notions of "Heaven" and "Mandate of Heaven" have traditionally been at the basis of studies concerning religion, metaphysics, and the relationship between cosmic and human orders in early China.[50] Throughout the imperial age, Heaven had been evoked in connection with dynastic legitimacy, both in public state ceremonies and in discourses concerning the extra-human origin of political power.[51] In current cross-cultural analyses, the notion of "Heaven" allows for the comparative analysis of Chinese civilization. Heaven can epitomize the supposed integration of the natural, political, and moral orders that purportedly characterizes Chinese civilization, or be equated to the personal Creator God of Judaism, Christianity, and Islam.[52] In the former case, Heaven (read as "Nature") still occupies a preeminent position in theoretical models that emphasize the distinctive "organicistic" nature of Chinese early thought, which also belies a cultural complex toward the systemic bias of Western philosophical traditions. In the latter case, Heaven explicitly becomes either the "Chinese version of the Christian God,"[53] or the historical manifestation of the psychological archetype of patriarchal authority.[54]

However, as archeological evidence demonstrates, Heaven was far from representing the unity of Chinese civilization during the first decades of reunification, for it was conceived, depicted, and worshipped in different ways depending on cultural and geographical contexts.[55] But even in earlier periods it was hardly comparable to a monotheistic being of the Abrahamic traditions. Ancient texts, for example, mention Heaven in the same universe as Shangdi 上帝 (Supreme Tearch [Sovereign], or Supreme Ancestor/s), without clarifying the respective functions or the hierarchical relationship of these entities.[56] In the "Great Announcement" ("Dagao" 大誥), one of the earliest texts of the *Documents* (*Shangshu* 尚書), a rebellion in the western territories prompts the young King Cheng 成 (r. 1042–1021 BCE?) of the Zhou to address vassals and senior officials at court and ask for support for a punitive expedition. In the speech, Cheng connects the mandate (*ming*) not only to Heaven, but also to dynastic ancestors (*shangdi*) and to his father Wu 武 (called in this instance Ningwang 寧王, the Tranquillizing King):

> Yes, I who am but a little child am in the position of one who has to cross deep water. It must be mine to go and seek how to cross over. I must diffuse the elegant institutions of my predecessor and augment the Mandate which he received from Heaven. So shall I not be forgetful of his great work, nor shall I dare to restrain the majesty of Heaven seen in the inflictions it sends down. The Tranquillizing King left me the great precious tortoise to bring into connection with me the intelligence of Heaven. I consulted it and it told me that there would be great trouble in the region of the west . . . I, the little one, dare not disregard the Mandate of the *shangdi* (上帝命). Heaven, favorable to the Tranquillizing King, gave such prosperity to our small state of Zhou. The Tranquillizing King divined and acted accordingly, and

so he calmly received his Mandate . . . The king says: "You who are the old ministers are fully able to examine the long-distant affairs. You know how great was the toil of the Tranquillizing King. Now where Heaven shuts up and distresses us it is the place where I must accomplish my work. I dare not but do my utmost. [. . .] Heaven moreover is thus toiling and distressing my people, so that it is as if they were suffering from disease. How dare I allow the Mandate, which the Tranquillizer my predecessor received, to be without its happy fulfillment?"[57]

If *shangdi* refers here to royal ancestors of the Shang, it is not surprising that the new rulers of the Zhou, while careful not to appear disrespectful and impious, would rather connect their dynastic claims to the relatively more impersonal Heaven than to the forefathers of the Shang.[58] But Heaven's command did not amount to unavoidable fate. A good ruler could prove himself worthy by promptly reacting to the Heaven-sent disasters and challenges that were meant to choose and test deserving sovereigns.

In the section of the *Documents*, called the "Great Plan" (likely a work of the fourth century BCE), we find a version of the myth of cultural transmission that sheds further light on *shangdi* and Heaven.[59] According to this text, they clearly played different roles in legitimating and supporting specific ruling houses.[60] The Zhou seemed interested in emphasizing appointment by virtue rather than through mere lineage and bloodline, which they considered a lamentable custom of the Shang. Still, their knowledge about the new cosmic order occurs thanks to the betrayal of a former member of the Shang aristocracy, Jizi (Master Ji), who transmitted the wisdom of Heaven's plans to the founder of the Zhou, King Wu.[61] Jizi had faithfully served the Shang for years, but when their last sovereign Zhou 紂 showed signs of immorality and recklessness, he forsook them in disgust. So according to the "Great Plan" he spoke to King Wu:

> I have heard that of old time Gun 鯀 [the mythical father of Yu the Great] dammed up the inundating waters and thereby threw into disorder the arrangement of the Five Phases. The *di* (帝) were roused to anger and did not give him the Great Plan with the Nine Divisions (*jiu chou* 九疇) whereby the proper virtues of the various relations were left to go to ruin. Gun was then kept prisoner till his death, and Yu [Gun's son and founder of the first dynasty of the Xia] rose up to continue his

undertaking. To him Heaven gave the Great Plan with its Nine Divisions and thereby the proper virtues of the various relations were brought forth in their order.[62]

This passage associates Heaven with the cosmic order the Zhou vowed to maintain. Jizi mentions water control to allude to Yu the Great's rescue of the Central States from the great flood. This founder of the Xia and of Chinese civilization famously managed to channel the violence of nature by letting the flood freely flow in the canals he had built, rather than "hubristically" constraining it. Therefore, Heaven rewarded him with organized knowledge concerning the working of the cosmos, the correct practice of government and justice, and the moral and physical norms aimed at the pursuit of individual happiness.[63] The harmony between the cosmic and human orders seemed thus established.

In the "Great Oath" ("Taishi" 泰誓), as well contained in the *Documents*, we see Heaven "evolving" in a way that makes it more compatible with Dong Zhongshu's synthesis. In the passage below, King Wu pairs Heaven with Earth and depicts them as the parents of the people. The ruler is, of course, Heaven's favorite son, while the villain, the ruler of the Shang, is described in terms that would customarily be used to condemn the hubristic Qin (this being one of the many elements that prompts philologists to suggest a later date for this text):[64]

> Heaven and Earth are the father and the mother of all creatures; and of all creatures man is the most highly endowed. The sincere, intelligent, and perspicacious among men becomes the great sovereign and the great sovereign is the parent of the people. But now Zhou, the king of Shang, does not reverence Heaven above and inflicts calamities on the people below. He has been abandoned to drunkenness and reckless in lust. He has dared to exercise cruel oppression. Along with criminals he has punished all their relatives. He has put men into office on the hereditary principle . . . he neglects the ancestral temples and does not sacrifice in them. The victims and the vessels for the millet all become prey of wicked robbers, and still he says: "The people are mine, the mandate is mine," never trying to correct his contemptuous attitude. Now Heaven to protect the inferior people made for them rulers and made for them instruc-

tors, which might be able to help the *Shangdi* and secure the tranquility of the four quarters.⁶⁵

The role of the ruler in safeguarding what Heaven generates is also described in the *Annals of Master Lü* (*Lüshi Chunqiu* 呂氏春秋). This encyclopedic work is attributed to Lü Buwei 呂不韋 (291?–235 BCE), a cunning merchant who eventually managed to become the Great Chancellor (*Chengxiang* 丞相) of the Qin and who, according to the *Records*, might have been the natural father of none other than the founder of the dynasty, Ying Zheng 嬴政 (259–210 BCE), the First Emperor.⁶⁶ So reads the *Lüshi Chunqiu*:

> Heaven is what engenders life in things; man is what fulfills that life by nurturing it. The person who is capable of nurturing the life that Heaven created without doing violence to it is called the Son of Heaven. The purpose of the Son of Heaven's activity is to keep intact the life Heaven originally engendered. This is the origin of the offices of government. The purpose of establishing them was to keep life intact.⁶⁷

In the same work we also find a very clear statement defining the boundaries of Heaven's power, human agency, and success. In the following passage, Yu the Flood Controller represents the exemplary sovereign who receives the investiture to rule from the sage Shun 舜 because of his virtue and accomplishments and despite hereditary lines. As for Heaven, it seems to indicate everything that according to the author is beyond human control: preconditions and set circumstances—perhaps more "chance" than "fate," once we consider the importance the text attributes to human agency:

> That one's accomplishments and name are established as greatness is attributable to Heaven. This is why it is wrong not to be mindful of what is attributable to human effort. . . . That Yu encountered Shun was attributable to Heaven. Yu's making a circuit of the world searching for worthies whose service would benefit the black haired people [the common people], and his dredging and diking of rivers, ponds, streams and marshes so that they would be passable—these Yu did completely on his own and are the result of human effort.⁶⁸

By contrast, one of the Mawangdui silk manuscripts describes the relationship between Heaven and man in far more conflicting terms. Scholars have attributed these texts, which are dated to the second century BCE and connected to the provincial aristocracy of the Han, to the so-called Huang-Lao 黃老 tradition.[69] Huang-Lao constituted an original blend of the "Daoistic" concern with yin, yang, and cosmic rhythms, with the "Machiavellian" shrewdness of the political doctrine of the Legalists (*fajia* 法家). We can see how Heaven in this passage, as in the *Records*, shows no sympathy for men:

> Heaven and Earth are not partial. The four seasons do not cease. Heaven and Earth are positioned, and so the sage performs his tasks. Should he exceed the limit and fail to make [the correspondence between his actions and Heaven and Earth] Heaven will send down calamity. Should man conquer Heaven by force, take care to avoid and not face him. Should Heaven in turn conquer Man, follow and march with it.[70]

In the tradition of Confucius's purported disinterest in extra-human factors, Master Xun's views are the closest to the ideas expressed in the *Records*. In his essay on Heaven ("Tian lun" 天論), Master Xun famously separates cosmic rhythms and historical events. For him the scope of human action lies on non-transcendental, ethical bases:

> Heaven's action is constant. It is not preserved because of a [sage ruler such as] Yao 堯, it does not perish because of a [tyrant such as] Jie 桀. If one responds to the constancy of Heaven's action with good rule, good fortune will ensue. If one responds to the constancy of Heaven with disorder, misfortune will ensue.[71]
> ... Thus, the gentleman cherishes what lies within his power and does not long for what lies within Heaven. The petty man forsakes what lies within his power and cherishes what lies within Heaven.[72]

Even though Sima Qian did not formulate his ideas about the disconnection between Heaven and men in such explicit terms, his "secular" approach to the issues of historical causality and fate can be more easily detected in the narration of more recent events. Given his direct involvement in the court politics of the time, he could not allow his contemporaries to interpret his disenchantment with Wu and imperial politics as a personal attack or an indictment to the legitimacy of the Han. Astutely, Sima Qian limited himself to presenting evidence without systematically providing explicit judgements. It would be up to his more patient and assiduous readers to pay attention to the complex game of cross-references and parallels whereby he discredits the reliability of sources or chastises specific behaviors. By means of irony and rhetorical questions concerning Heaven and its role in human affairs, Sima Qian would invite his public to read between and across the lines.

Gaozu, Empress Lü, Heaven and Yin and Yang's Anomalies

As we have seen in chapter 2, despite Eastern Han re-elaborations, Emperor Wu's conception of sovereignty had little to do with the symbolic function formulated in the *Luxuriant Gems of the Spring and Autumn* and attributed to Dong Zhongshu. Wu never worshipped Heaven in the filial terms of Confucius's conception of *li*. He never seemed content with merely ruling by example as a moral paragon. As for Sima Qian, although he mentions Dong as one of his many teachers, his historiographical approach is not consistent with the belief in the mutual influence of Heaven and men (*Tian ren xiang guan* 天人相關), in the readability of the world through the correspondence of microcosmic and macrocosmic phenomena, or in the providential, regulatory function of Heaven. The awareness of a disjunction between morality and success, as well as the inadequacy of the traditional literary heritage for the interpretation of present events would often surface in his work. In the *Records*, events do not unfold as a superior design, while the various meanings of Heaven—from fate or chance to a mere astronomical or natural element—are not synthesized in a unitary view.

First of all, the *Records* seldom mentions the Mandate of Heaven in connection with the Han.[73] Unless the text is referring to the Zhou Dynasty, we more often find the expression "receiving the mandate" (*shou ming* 受命), which does not imply the extra-human investiture of a ruler, but that his sovereignty was generally acknowledged and accepted. The *Records*, especially in the chapters dealing with events that occurred during the Qin and the Han, which were closer to the time of the authors,[74] does not interpret omens and portents as manifestations of a superior design directly connected to Heaven; in fact, in most cases it openly suggests that they were just a fabrication.[75] On the relationship between Heaven and the destiny of imperial houses, the *Records* is intentionally ambiguous and, in the case of the founder of the Han, Liu Bang, it connects his successes with the controversial (and notoriously vicious) Empress Lü 呂.

The collective chapter on imperial consorts, the "Houses of the External Relatives" ("Waiqi shijia" 外戚世家), clearly questions the possibility of understanding or controlling the fates of men (and rulers), while stating that, no matter how skilled rulers may be, their eventual success will also be owed to the support of an exceptional spouse.[76] Given the necessity of producing and grooming a male heir in a patrilineal aristocratic system, conjugal love was definitely the most relevant among the Five Relations (*Wu Lun* 五倫) cherished by the Classicists. Of note is that the *Records* explains gender relations in terms of complementarity, but does not explicitly and systematically refer to yin-yang dualism, as would become customary after Ban Zhao's 班昭 (45–ca. 116 CE) *Instructions for Women (Nüjie* 女誡*)*.[77] In fact, the *Records* introduces Lü's role in the creation of the empire by emphasizing the impossibility of discerning the interplay of factors contributing to a joyous marriage.[78] Despite the ambiguity of Sima Qian's treatment of Gaozu's consort (and the disapproval of later commentators), the *Records* devotes one of the basic annals to Lü, a woman who ruled on behalf of her son, the weakling Emperor Hui 惠 (194–188 BCE).[79] This chapter depicts Lü as shrewd and manipulative, ready to resort to torture and murder, while unsuccessfully attempting to replace the ruling Liu lineage with members of her own family. According to the *Records*, she plays a fundamental role in holding the reins of the fledging empire in a tumultuous age.[80] Her practical sense both complements and emphasizes the volatile temper and self-absorption of her husband.

First of all, the *Records* does not describe the successes of the future Gaozu as the result of a clear plan or steadfast will. The outcomes of his impulsive actions usually exceed his intentions, and he regularly encounters people who are ready to correct his mistakes or repurpose his shortsighted schemes. It was not even Liu Bang's own decision to ask for Lü's hand in marriage. According to the *Records*, Liu Bang met his future wife only because of his bloated self-esteem and unwillingness to abide by the norms appropriate to his non-aristocratic rank.[81] The text reports that, one day, early in his career, Liu Bang learned that an eminent gentleman was holding a reception for the most important persons in town. Anxious to obtain an invitation, the penniless Liu Bang submitted a fake document attesting to his impressive wealth. At the banquet, no one seemed to fall for the trick, but the host—Liu Bang's future father-in-law—seemed pleased with the young man's carefree manners and gregariousness and spent all evening drinking and chatting with him. Master Lü had a talented and unwedded daughter, whom he had raised to expect that she could one day marry someone of high status. Claiming that he had recognized in the young man's face the marks of future success, he overcame his wife's opposition and on the spot betrothed the future empress of China to Liu Bang. The *Records* implies that if the founder of the Han had any agency in this episode, it was limited to making false claims about his wealth and status, and being good at partying.

Another famous passage, traditionally interpreted as suggesting that Liu Bang was destined to greatness, offers an example of how a different take on some apparently minor details in the *Records* can completely change our interpretation of a seemingly unproblematic anecdote. The episode takes place a few years into the couple's marriage. The *Records* introduces the story with a description of a young Lü working in the fields with her children (the future Emperor Hui and Princess Lü Yuan). Suddenly, a mysterious wanderer appears out of nowhere. He looks at their faces and see in them a destiny as worldwide illustrious people (*tianxia guiren* 天下貴人), which, of course, the reader cannot but interpret as a consequence of the future achievements of their momentarily absent husband and father. But when Liu Bang arrives on the scene, the stranger has vanished. Not content with a secondhand account of the prophecy, he reaches the old man and receives the announcement of unspeakable glory: "If what you said will come true," he saluted the man, "I will not forget the favor." But according to the *Records*, after Liu Bang's achieved fame, no one was able to locate the old man.[82]

One would expect such an anecdote to provide straightforward evidence of Liu Bang's predestined greatness and the important role that Heaven will play in his career as a politician and ruler. Instead, Gaozu's biography in the *Records* is scattered with seemingly irrelevant bits of information that, once pieced together, give us a clear sense of Sima Qian's opinion of the husband and wife. First, we should note that the principal witness of the portentous encounter is Lü, who would have clearly benefited from fueling her husband's delusions of grandeur. As for Liu Bang, the *Records* informs us that he was able to arrive at the scene of the prophecy only at a later time, as he had been busy in what seems to be described as an outhouse (*pangshe* 旁舍).[83] Ambiguous details of this kind are customarily excluded from official biographies of rulers, saints, and saviors, and they do not represent a defining feature of Sima Qian's historiographical style, either. Their inclusion in the history of the founder of the Han could only serve to remind the reader of Liu Bang's lowly nature—and to implicitly ridicule allusions to the Mandate of Heaven. One is hardly inspired to contemplate heavenly matters within smelling distance of the toilet. Yet, if we instead focus on the theme of "popularity" already explored in the previous chapter in the case of Sima Qian's account of Yan Ying's career, we cannot fail to note that, in the *Records*, "folksiness" often characterizes successful politicians and their willingness to appear generous with the common people.

Going back to the unification of China, years after this episode, when winds of rebellion had begun to shake the Qin Empire, the appearance of a peculiarly shaped cluster of clouds convinces the already paranoid First Emperor that the rise of a new Son of Heaven might be imminent. The uncanny vapors (called "Son-of-Heaven *qi*," *tianzi qi* 天子氣) are reported hovering above Liu Bang's whereabouts. Contrary to the expectations most readers would have had, however, the *Records* does not describe Liu Bang's excitement at the opportunity to challenge the Emperor for the throne. The author instead notes that the future Han ruler is not overly keen on embracing the heavenly anointment. Afraid that he might soon be called to face the Qin army, he decides to make himself scarce and disappears. Fortunately for him, his wife's practical sense overrides his reluctance (and possibly his cowardice). By following the itinerary of the clouds, Lü discovers her husband's hiding place and sets him again on his journey toward his destiny.[84] While this anecdote once more emphasizes Lü's role in the founding of the Han, it offers nothing to reassure the reader about Liu Bang's mettle as a leader. In the end, the entire extent of Heaven's involvement in earthly affairs is limited to the appearance of strange clouds that ambiguously point to an individual who proves clueless about their import as an omen and reacts by cowering in fear.

Only when Gaozu fatally falls, does he finally seem ready to embrace the implications of his extra-human investiture. But again, the emperor's overconfident statement reported in the *Records* makes him sound delusional rather than solemn or wise. We learn that, upon being visited by the realm's best doctors, whom his wife had summoned to his deathbed, Gaozu stubbornly refuses any treatment. His rationale is that "the Son of Heaven cannot be cured by human remedies."[85] Before drily reporting on the emperor's subsequent demise, the *Records* focuses on Lü's reaction: she shows concern about the imminent replacement of the old Xiao He 蕭何 (d. 193 BCE), the skillful minister to whom Sima Qian clearly ascribes the military and political successes of the Han.[86] She had no doubts about on whom the stability of the dynasty depended.

In sharp contrast to the standard rhetoric of wife-husband yin-yang dynamics, the *Records* inverts the passive and active roles associated, respectively, with women and men. As for the accounts reporting the intervention of Heaven, regardless of what Sima Qian actually believed, they seem aimed at emphasizing Gaozu's shortcomings. The portrayal of Liu Bang offered by the *Records* does not highlight the character traits that, according to traditional accounts, make a leader worthy of receiving the Mandate. On the contrary, it seems to further attest to Sima Qian's bemoaned "mixing of the noble and the lowly" that he saw as the quintessential quality of his age.

Liu Bang, a Snake, and Heaven's Involvement in the Fall of the Qin

At this point our reader should not be surprised to learn that even the famous episode regarding the appearance of a dragon above Liu Bang is much more problematic than traditionally held. Once we pay attention to some pieces of information skillfully placed by Sima Qian at the margins of the main narrative, we are compelled to realize that the author's intention might have been substantially different from the celebration of Liu Bang's predestination. First of all, the *Records* implies that the future Son of Heaven is not aware of the prodigy or of its import. When the miraculous beast, the symbol of imperial power, manifests itself above Liu Bang's body, he is lying sprawled in his favorite brothel, passed out after one of his drinking binges. As if the lack of gravitas of the setting were not enough, the text also informs us that the only witnesses of the extraordinary event are Old Woman Wang and Madame Wu, apparently the managers of the very businesses of which Liu Bang was such an assiduous and generous customer that he was often granted an extension of credit.[87]

It is plausible that the story of the omen was spread after the founding of the dynasty, when Gaozu's subjects would have had reasons to recall anecdotes that, ex post facto, legitimized his investment as Son of Heaven. As for the two businesswomen, like many individuals who crossed paths with Liu Bang when he was a commoner, the *Records* imply that they were trying to turn their acquaintance with him to their own advantage.

From a historiographical point of view, Sima Qian seems particularly interested in the readiness of people from all walks of life to exploit the popular fascination with spirits, ghosts, and uncanny events for economic or political ends. Regardless of the skepticism of its author, the *Records* regards omens and beliefs about them as factors that can shape communities at all levels and trigger historic social or institutional transformations. This element is even more evident in the way the *Records* treats the prodigies that played a crucial role in shaping various events, from the revolts against the Qin to Liu Bang's triumph as Emperor. Omens play a crucial role in the initial spark of the revolt that would eventually lead to the fall of the Qin in 206 BCE.[88] The protagonists of this episode are Chen She 陳涉 and Wu Guang 吳廣, two humble hired laborers hailing from the former state of Chu in the South. Famously, in 209 BCE, in the second month of the second year of the reign of Huhai 胡亥 (229–207 BCE), also known as Second Emperor of Qin, they are ordered to conduct a group of 900 conscripts to garrison a village in the North, near present-day Beijing, against possible Xiongnu attacks. As a heavy rain begins to fall, Chen She realizes that his group has no chance of reaching destination on time. Under the Qin, the punishment for being late at an imperial appointment could even include decapitation. Aware of their meager chances of survival and having very little to lose at this point, Chen She and Wu Guang decide to revolt. Even if they were destined to fail, they console themselves, at least they would die while fighting for the honor of their homeland, Chu, which the Qin had defeated and conquered more than ten years earlier.[89]

At the time, everyone seemed to know that the sovereign of China, Huhai, the son of the First Emperor, had infamously taken the throne from the legitimate heir, his brother Fu Su 扶蘇 (d. 210 BCE) thanks to a conspiracy plotted by the eunuch Zhao Gao 趙高 (d. 207) and Chancellor Li Si 李斯 (c. 280–208 BCE).[90] The two high officials, after forging the First Emperor's will in favor of Huhai, compelled Fusu to commit suicide. But since no one had seen his corpse, some believed that the legitimate heir was simply hiding while awaiting an opportunity to revenge himself.[91] Thus, taking advantage of this rumor, Chen She convinced Wu Guang to stir and lead a rebellion disguised, respectively, as Fusu and the beloved Chu general Xiang Yan 項燕 (the grandfather of Xiang Yu 項羽, Liu Bang's future rival), who had bravely fought the Qin as well, before mysteriously vanishing. Upon embarking on their military enterprise, Chen and Wu decide to consult a diviner. The response sounds positive but ends with an ominous note: "You will accomplish all your plans and achieve success. But then, would you seek responses with ghosts?"[92]

At the time the passage was written, everyone knew that Chen and Wu would both perish (and be in the ghosts' number) before the establishment of the Han. The *Records* is probably satirizing their naïve optimism in hindsight. According to the text, the two rebels reacted enthusiastically at the divination and felt encouraged to make up their own omens. Chen and Wu swiftly wrote "Chen shall be a king" on a piece of white silk and stuffed it in the belly of a fish to the astonishment and awe of the soldiers who were going to savor it during the common meal.[93] Chen also sent Wu to hide behind a shrine in a grove by the camp. When night fell, Wu produced light effects by concealing a torch underneath a basket while imitating the cry of a fox (an animal believed to belong to the realm of spirits), howling: "The great Chu will rise, Chen She will be king!"[94]

This proved to be enough to convince the laborers to rebel, fight, and eventually die at Chen and Wu's orders. The *Records* emphasizes Wu Guang's good relationship with the troops, even going so far as to suggest that they would have done anything for him.[95] Charisma and leadership qualities also characterized the founder of the Han; according to the *Records*, regular soldiers easily related to the unsophisticated, sluggish, and frequently inebriated Liu Bang. If we compare the three rebels, we see that Liu Bang succeeded where Chen and Wu had failed, because, in addition to his popularity among commoners, he also benefitted from the support of aristocratic leaders, who represented an element of continuity with the elite traditions of the Central States.

Sima Qian acknowledges that people's beliefs about omens and other heaven-related matters can be exploited by crafty politicians and military leaders. For example, we see Chen and Wu actively manipulating the popular fascination with stories about semi-divine leaders and crafting (albeit rather clumsily) omens that win them the favor of the rebels. Liu Bang instead simply acknowledges and eventually takes advantage of prodigies witnessed and interpreted by other people, as in the case of his grateful soldiers.

In narrating Chen's revolt, Sima Qian, in addition to the enthusiasm the soldiers derive from the fabricated omens, considers a range of other factors to be equally important: the climatic conditions, the fear of a dreadful punishment, Chen's almost mindless ambition, the soldiers' attachment to Wu Guang, and the perceived illegitimacy of the Second Emperor's succession. In reporting these circumstances, Sima Qian also makes sure the reader does not overlook the subjectivity of all points of view. For example, the chapter about Chen She does not end with the customary remarks by the Grand Historian but with an essay by the famous erudite Jia Yi 賈誼 (c. 200–168 BCE), who, instead of referring to the illegitimacy and unworthiness of the son of the First Emperor, provides a general assessment of the rule of the Qin and of the moral reasons for their collapse. He defines them as exceptionally ruthless and an aberration in the millenary political tradition of Central States, which was founded on filial piety.[96] Provided that these remarks are not the result of interpolation, if we consider that the *Records* makes the point several times that the Han followed the political approach of the Qin even up to Emperor Wu, in concluding with Jia Yi's treatise, Sima Qian was either simply avoiding exposing his discontent more directly or providing his more careful readers with a subtle and ironic assessment of the inadequacy of the dynasty.[97]

Returning to Liu Bang's biography, the circumstances of his act of insubordination and rebellion parallel very closely those of Chen She's revolt, as though Sima Qian wanted the different personalities to stand out more clearly. The *Records* narrates that when the future Gaozu was still just a village head, he received the order to conduct a group of convicted laborers from his hometown in the south to the site where the First Emperor of Qin was building his mausoleum. Along the way, the laborers began defecting and disappeared in such numbers that Liu Bang feared he might reach his destination alone. Surprisingly, instead of reacting with authority, Liu Bang stopped his march, got drunk, and then decided to return home after releasing all the men under his command.[98]

The action is set to reach the center of the empire and the locations of the fundamental struggle for the unification that would be the main topic of the *Records*. Yet Sima Qian describes Liu Bang as merely concerned with his petty habits and his obscure hometown—at the time, not only did he not harbor any revolutionary dreams, but even held the Qin in awe.[99] A group of about ten men decided to accompany him back home. While crossing the swampy area, a scout rushed back and suggested that they all retreat, as a big snake was blocking the path. Liu Bang, still drunk, boasting of brave soldiers' fearlessness, advanced, pulled out his sword, and beheaded the reptile. He continued on his way for a while before falling asleep under the effect of all the alcohol he had consumed. Meanwhile, a man who was lagging behind reached the spot of Liu Bang's heroics, where he found an old woman weeping. According to her story, she was grieving for her son, the son of the White Emperor (Baidi 白帝), who, after assuming the semblance of a snake, had been slaughtered by the son of the Red Emperor (Chidi 赤帝).[100] The man was incredulous. He wished to enquire further to ascertain her sincerity, but she suddenly disappeared. When Liu Bang finally woke up, he was delighted to hear the man's extraordinary account. And it seems that from that day on Liu had his self-confidence dramatically bolstered while his followers looked up to him with increasing awe.[101]

The *Records* relates the miraculous events that purportedly sanctioned the extra-human investiture of the Han to the accounts of convicted laborers who must have been grateful for their release from a feared corvée that might have meant death (the men who worked at the mausoleum of the First Emperor were routinely killed at the end of their duty) and to their magnanimous, sometimes sluggish, and often intoxicated leader. If portents were to manifest Heaven's will about the fate of dynasties, the *Records*' narrative surely casts some shadows of doubt on their reliability. If there is a superior design concerning the fall of the Qin and the rise of the Han, both Chen She and Liu Bang's goals seem selfish and shortsighted. By contrast, the element that becomes more evident is the text's focus on personalities, behaviors, and interactions.

Thus, if we compare Chen She and Liu Bang's stories, the almost reckless resoluteness of the former contrasts with the heedlessness and indolence of the latter. In many instances, despite his bad judgment or cowardice, Liu Bang (and the future of the Han Dynasty) was saved by the prompt advice and intervention of his aides. According to the *Records*, Liu Bang lacked two fundamental Confucian qualities: respect for tradition and filial piety. Famously, after his successful march, Liu Bang was ready to destroy the buildings and archives of the old capital city, even at the risk of compromising administrative continuity; he did not show special concern that his father was held hostage and, while being chased by his enemies, was prepared to dump his son and heir and elder daughter from his carriage in order to accelerate his flight.[102]

The *Records* portrays Liu Bang as scarcely aware of the importance of the historic events in which he played the role of protagonist. He would ask his more articulate officials to explain why he managed to defeat the braver and more competent Xiang Yu. However, even though Liu Bang did not seem to grasp the value of effective propaganda, he left the most sophisticated and shrewd of his followers to connect his rule to glorious ages of the past through literary citations. His famous dialogue with the Classicist Lu Jia 陸賈 (d. 170 BCE) clarifies the *Records*' take on the creation of the rhetoric about the triumph of the Han. Lu Jia tries repeatedly to persuade the emperor of the value of the *Classics*, but what he obtains is a scornful reply:

"All I possess I have won on horseback!" said the emperor. "Why should I bother with the *Odes* and *Documents*?" "Your Majesty might have won it on horseback, but can you rule it on horseback?" asked Master Lu. ". . . Qin entrusted its future solely to punishments and laws, without changing with the times and thus eventually brought about the destruction of its ruling family. If after it had united the world under its rule, Qin had practiced benevolence and righteousness and modeled its ways upon the sages of antiquity, how would Your Majesty ever have been able to win possession of the empire?" The emperor grew embarrassed and uneasy and finally said to Master Lu, "Try writing something for me on the reasons why Qin lost the empire and I won it, and on the failures of the states of ancient times."[103]

Liu Bang would eventually take credit for recognizing and exploiting the talent of his officials, as though letting them save him from his own inconsiderate behaviors and shortsighted decisions was part of his conscious plan:

> When it comes to sitting within the tents of command and devising strategies that will assure us victory a thousand miles away, I am no match for Zhang Liang 張良. In ordering the state and caring for the people, in providing rations for the troops and seeing to it that lines of supplies are not cut off, I cannot compare to Xiao He. In leading an army of a million men, achieving success with every battle, and victory with every attack, I cannot come up to Han Xin 韓信. These three are all men of extraordinary ability, and it is because I was able to make use of them that I gained possession of the world.[104]

Finally, it is clear that when the *Records* mentions Heaven and its positive role in determining human affairs, the text is merely reporting ideas and beliefs, cultural factors that, in the opinion of its authors, played a fundamental role in shaping historical events. When Sima Qian directly refers to Heaven in his personal remarks, the ambiguous and even tautological tone of his statements is likely meant to admonish the readers that historical causes are to be sought beyond grandiose proclamations and official truths. After the narration of the struggles between the Qin emperor and the feudal lords, to whom he refused to grant estates that in dimensions befitted aristocratic ranks, the fourth Chronologic Table (*biao* 表) on the states of Qin and Chu reads thus:

> Yet from the lanes of the common people there arose the signs of a man of kingly stature whose alliances and military cam-

paigns surpassed those of the Three Dynasties [the Xia, Shang and Zhou]. Qin's earlier prohibitions served only the noble and the wealthy [of Qin] and helped them remove the obstacles they had to face. Therefore [Gaozu] manifested his indignation and became the leader of the world. Why do people say that no one can become a king unless he possesses land? Is such a man not to be considered a "True Sage" (Dasheng 大聖)? Is this not the work of Heaven? Is this not the work of Heaven? The man who is able to receive the mandate and become emperor, is he not a True Sage?[105]

Is the *Records* stating that Heaven is the power that allowed a commoner to reestablish the privileges of a group of dispossessed landowners? Is the historian referring here to the momentous convergence of exceptional personalities around Liu Bang? Did he prevail because those aristocrats, generals, and politicians whom Sima Qian ultimately credits with his success chose Liu Bang as a leader simply on account of his charisma and popularity with the troops as they thought that the future Gaozu, being a landless outsider, could not interfere with their specific interests? Is the text suggesting that a legitimate ruler is just the one who, ex post facto, can be acknowledged as having real power?

Sima Qian's answers seldom follow his rhetorical questions directly. The "Annals of Xiang Yu," Liu Bang's formidable foe, together with the accounts of the most egregious shortcomings of the future emperor, offers a more explicit insight into Sima Qian's understanding of Heaven. Ever since his childhood, Xiang Yu showed extraordinary strength, ambition, and courage, qualities that were countered by his impatience, rashness, and no inclination to wasting time on details or compromising with allies and enemies. When, despite his superior military skills and bravery, Xiang Yu finds himself in a cul-de-sac with just a few horsemen, having to face thousands of Liu Bang's troops, he understands that his time has come. So he justifies his imminent defeat to his soldiers:

> It has been eight years since I led my army forth. In that time I have fought over seventy battles. Every enemy I faced was destroyed, everyone I attacked submitted. Never once did I suffer defeat, until at last I became dictator of the world. But now suddenly I am driven to this desperate position! It is because

> Heaven would destroy me, not because I have committed any fault in battle. I have resolved to die today. But before I die, I beg to fight bravely and win for you three victories.[106]

But Sima Qian, in the final remarks of the "Annals of Xiang Yu," does not hesitate to flatly contradict the general and his self-serving interpretation of the power of Heaven:

> [I]t was hardly surprising that the feudal lords revolted against him. He boasted and made a show of his own achievements. He was obstinate in his own opinion and did not abide by established ways. He thought to make himself a dictator, hoping to attack and rule the empire by force. Yet within five years he was dead and his kingdom lost. He met death at Dongcheng, but even at that time he did not wake to or accept responsibility for his errors. "It is Heaven," he declared, "which has destroyed me, and no fault of mine in the use of arms!" Was he not indeed deluded?[107]

The *Records*' rhetorical and ironic way of referring to Heaven is even more evident in the recollection of a statement by Master Li (Li Sheng 酈生), "the Mad Scholar," an outspoken wise man of humble origins who would end up being boiled alive and whose biography—very interestingly—is paired in the *Records* with that of the wise Classicist Lu Jia. Here Master Li is advising about possible military strategies against Liu Bang's fiercest rival, and advocating the necessity of controlling the granaries.

> I heard a saying that "he who knows the 'heaven' of Heaven may make himself a king, but he who has not this knowledge may not. To the king the people are Heaven, whereas to the people food is Heaven"[108]

Heaven here clearly refers to the specific knowledge required to get the best out of specific circumstances or social conditions. It does not present any extra-human connotation. It is an empty word that can be used to glorify one's contingent aims or justify unexpected failures. It is connected to adaptability and receptiveness, rather than to constants and absolutes. And in this respect, Liu Bang acted, almost unconsciously, as an empty center around which different interests and agencies could converge.

Polybius and Fortune between the Hellenic World and Rome

As for the role of Fortune (*Tychê*, Τύχη in Greek, *Fortuna* in Latin) in the Greco-Roman world, it epitomized neither the extra-human investiture of ruling lineages nor the organic connection of the human and natural realms. Yet, as J. J. Pollitt points out, in the social and political uncertainty that characterized the Hellenistic period, Fortune positively turned into an obsession.[109] Customarily personified as a female deity, Tyche was often chosen as the patron of newly founded colonies, as their future could not be entrusted to a preexistent, cultic tradition.[110] Between the rise of the Macedonian empire and the consolidation of Rome's power over the Mediterranean, the known world seemed to be undergoing continuous and unforeseeable transformations.[111] Whether life was subject to unpredictable chance, as the Epicureans held, or ruled by unchangeable destiny, as the Stoics believed, Fortune could be invoked to support the precarious existence of individuals or communities throughout the Mediterranean and the ancient Middle East.[112]

According to literary and legendary tradition, it was the sixth king, Servius Tullius (578–535 BCE), who introduced the cult of Fortune to Rome by building the temples of Fortuna Primigenia and Fortuna Obsequens on the Capitoline.[113] Either the son of a slave or the heir of an enemy chief killed by the Romans, Servius, surrounded by signs of supernatural predestination, was raised at court among the servants. Queen Tanaquil, the wife of Lucius Tarquinius Priscus (616–579 BCE), the first Etruscan ruler of Rome, perceived her lineage as extremely vulnerable. She arranged for Servius to marry her daughter as she hoped that he would be the savior of her husband's dynasty.[114]

Thus, upon the violent death of her husband Tarquinius Priscus, Tanaquil solicited Servius to take over the throne. As he showed clear signs of an extra-human investiture, Tanaquil argued that Servius's lowly lineage should not count against him. She admonished Servius that in accomplishing his royal mission, he should consider who he was and not from whence he came.[115] Servius reigned for forty-four years, until his murder in 535 BCE by his son-in-law, Lucius Tarquinius Superbus, Tarquinius Priscus's son and the seventh and last king of Rome. His proverbially violent and corrupt reign led to the revolt of 509 BCE and to establishment of the Republic.

Servius Tullius's relationship with Fortune has been connected to the "anomaly" of his kingship, which he achieved, despite his non-Roman and probably non-aristocratic origins, thanks to the influence and scheming of a foreign woman.[116] In the words of Plutarch (46–120 CE), Fortune epitomizes the exceptional character of Servius's reign:

> This was a token of his birth from fire and an excellent sign pointing to his unexpected accession to the kingship, which he gained after the death of Tarquinius, with the zealous assistance of Tanaquil. Inasmuch as he of all kings is thought to have been naturally the least suited to monarchy and the least desirous of it, he who was minded to resign the kingship, but was prevented from doing so; for it appears that Tanaquil on her death-bed made him swear that he would remain in power and would ever set before him the ancestral Roman form of government. Thus to Fortune wholly belongs the kingship of Servius, which he received contrary to his expectations and retained against his will.[117]

The role that Fortune plays in the *Histories* does not seem to coincide with the fulfillment of Polybius's hopes and expectations, either. Unlike Christian Providence, it does not constitute the manifestation in history of an unambiguous supernatural plan or the victory of rightful forces. In the Fortune of the *Histories*, the historiographical and the moral levels are only connected to the extent to which Tyche's unexpected turns test men's wills and skills, just as Rome's triumphs must have challenged the Hellenic pride of Polybius. As clearly stated in the proem of the *Histories*, Fortune represents the factor that allows events to converge toward one end. Unlike the *Records*' treatment of Heaven, Polybius programmatically sets Tyche at the center of the theoretical model that should inform his *Histories*:

> For what gives my work its peculiar quality, and what is most remarkable in the present age is this. Fortune has guided almost all the affairs of the world in one direction and has forced them to incline towards one and the same end; a historian should likewise bring before his readers under one view the operations by which she has accomplished her general purpose. Indeed it was chiefly this that invited and encouraged me to undertake my task; and secondarily the fact that none of my contemporaries have undertaken to write a general history, in which case I should have been much less eager to take this in hand.[118]

It is in the universality of his approach, Polybius claims, that his oeuvre is superior to previous historiographical enterprises.[119] Other authors, such as Ephorus and Herodotus, had already included remote lands and civilizations in their narrations, but the unprecedented scope of Rome's conquests made it possible to entwine the unitary, teleological narrative that would characterize the *Histories* as a groundbreaking work:

> Now up to this time the world's history had been, so to speak, a series of disconnected transactions, as widely separated in their origin and results as in their localities. But from this time forth History becomes a connected whole: the affairs of Italy and Libya are involved with those of Asia and Greece, and the tendency of all is to unity. This is why I have fixed upon this era as the starting-point of my work.[120]

It is to this unitary end, as Momigliano has noted, that Polybius's persistent popularity up until the modern age is due.[121] Although Polybius did not share Herodotus's narrative talent and richness or Thucydides's analytical rigor, critics could still praise the quasi-Christian universality of the *Histories*.[122] But unlike Providence, Polybius's Fortune does not embody the moralizing will of a conscious deity. The only instance in which the Greek historian qualifies Fortune's agency in determining Rome's success as a non-arbitrary, quasi-ethical act is in reference to the work *On Fortune* (*Peri Tyches*) by the Aristotelian philosopher Demetrius of Phalerum (ca. 350–280 BCE).[123] Just as Demetrius was able to foresee Tyche punishing the hubristic Persians at the hand of the Macedonians, so too does Polybius acknowledge the punishment of hubris in the defeat of Perseus at Pydna by the Romans in 168 BCE. The initial fault lay in the scheme devised in 203 BCE by Perseus's father Philip V of Macedon, together with Antiochus III of Syria, to attack and divide the kingdom of the infant Ptolemy V of Egypt.[124]

Polybius considered Fortune's direct moralizing function only occasionally, and hardly as an element of a conscious plan. Its main role was to test human behavior and exemplify the didactic purpose of history writing:

> All historians . . . have impressed on us that the soundest education and training for a life of active politics is the study of History, and the surest and indeed the only method of learning how to bear bravely the vicissitudes of Fortune.[125]

Despite the theoretical statements that open the *Histories*, scholars deemed Polybius's connection of Fortune and empirical facts as one of the most problematic and inconsistent features of his writing. According to Walbank, both linguistic ambiguity and philosophical naiveté characterize Polybius's narrative recourse to Fortune. As the British scholar notes, in the *Histories*, the word "*tyche*" is sometimes employed loosely as a tense of the verb τυγχάνω, "to happen." This usage is consistent with the mention of Tyche in casual conversations during Polybius's times, when it referred to agents considered completely outside human control, or was simply uttered as an interjection—much like "Heaven," or "God" in contemporary English speech.[126]

As for Polybius's philosophical inconsistency, in Walbank's opinion, the Greek historian often mentioned Tyche in order to compensate for his unsophisticated application of the principle of causality in the *Histories*.[127] Whenever Polybius could not account adequately for the "interactions of events and the dynamic and dialectical character of almost any train of causation," Fortune would intervene, almost as a *deus ex machina* of the Greek tragic literary tradition.[128] In other instances, Tyche coincided with the unpredictability of meteorological and natural forces. As Polybius states in one of the surviving fragments of Book 36, which deals with the Macedonian Wars, 215–148 BCE:

> In finding fault with those who ascribe public events and incidents to Fate and Chance, I now wish to state my opinion on this subject as far as it is admissible to do so in a strictly historical work. Now indeed as regards things the causes of which it is impossible or difficult for a mere man to understand, we may perhaps be justified in getting out of the difficulty by setting them down to the action of a god or of chance, I mean such things as exceptionally heavy and continuous rain or snow, or on the other hand the destruction of crops by severe drought or frost, or a persistent outbreak of plague or other similar things of which it is not easy to detect the cause. So in regard to such matters we naturally bow to public opinion, as we cannot make out why they happen, and attempting by prayer and sacrifice to appease the heavenly powers, we send to ask the gods what we must do and say, to set things right and cause the evil that afflicts us to cease. But as for matters the efficient and final cause

of which it is possible to discover we should not, I think, put them down to divine action.[129]

The last sentences of this passage clarify Polybius's concern with direct divine intervention, which he strives to exclude from the explanation of causal connections. In the narration of Hannibal's heroic march through the Alps, for example, he chastises the bad habits of previous authors who embellished the simple history of facts by mentioning the intervention of supernatural forces.[130] However, somewhat like Sima Qian, Polybius recognizes that beliefs in Fortune or any other meta-historical factor deeply condition humans' behavior and can therefore be exploited politically. In the case of Rome he acknowledges the value of religious beliefs in restraining the behavior of Rome's masses. In his opinion, the political exploitation of the sacred and of people's irrational fears makes Rome superior to its contemporary rivals:

> But the most important difference for the better which the Roman commonwealth appears to me to display is in their religious beliefs. For I conceive that what in other nations is looked upon as a reproach, I mean a scrupulous fear of the gods, is the very thing which keeps the Roman commonwealth together. To such an extraordinary height is this carried among them, both in private and public business, that nothing could exceed it. Many people might think this unaccountable; but in my opinion their object is to use it as a check upon the common people. If it were possible to form a state wholly of philosophers, such a custom would perhaps be unnecessary. But seeing that every multitude is fickle, and full of lawless desires, unreasoning anger, and violent passion, the only resource is to keep them in check by mysterious terrors and scenic effects of this sort. Wherefore, to my mind, the ancients were not acting without purpose or at random, when they brought in among the vulgar those opinions about the gods, and the belief in the punishments in Hades: much rather do I think that men nowadays are acting rashly and foolishly in rejecting them.[131]

And it is perhaps Polybius's view of religion as *instrumentum regni* that, through Livy (59 BCE–17 CE), would inspire Niccolò Machiavelli's

(1469–1527) influential analysis of the political use of religion throughout Western history.[132]

Conclusion: The Rhetoric of Empires

Here begins our tale. The empire, long divided, must unite, long united must divide. Thus it has ever been. In the closing years of the Zhou dynasty, seven kingdoms warred among themselves until the kingdom of Qin prevailed and absorbed the other six. But Qin soon fell, and on its ruins two opposing kingdoms, Chu and Han, fought for mastery until the kingdom of Han prevailed and absorbed its rival, as Qin had done before. The Han court's rise to power began when the Supreme Ancestor [i.e., Gaozu] slew a white serpent, inspiring an uprising that ended with Han's ruling a unified empire.[133]

This is how the unglamorous and partly fortuitous events that had led an often-intoxicated womanizer like Liu Bang to re-found the empire were celebrated in the *Romance of the Three Kingdoms*, which represented the written version of popular tales narrated over the centuries throughout China during the Ming dynasty (1368–1644). Over the years, founding fathers, no matter how base and trivial their motives and practices might have been, often acquire an aura of paradigmatic nobility that tend to discourage critical inquiries and inhibit intellectual curiosity. It happens that historians have to bend to necessity or powerful patrons, but in some way, their deeper grasp of the interplay of personalities and events often surfaces behind more or less spontaneous propagandistic goals.

Polybius's seemingly contradictory treatment of Fortune clearly stems from his complex relationship with the rise of Rome, which he had to accept and explain despite his possibly different emotional attachments. The traditional association of Tyche in the ancient Mediterranean world with new political realities provided Polybius with an evocative unifying element that could resemble a conventional god. Also, it constituted an intermediate stage toward a rationalistic refutation of the role of the divine in history. Fortune, according to Polybius, acted to a certain extent as a traditional force in that it seemed to punish and reward specific ruling lineages by following a hereditary principle. Simultaneously, as the fates of different civilizations and polities were coming together in a new world, in the *Histories*, Fortune replaced the rivaling orders represented by the myriad of Mediterranean gods, even though it could not embody specific universal values yet.

By contrast, the *Records* challenges traditional beliefs and expectations about the unity of the universe and the correspondence of the political and moral orders by unraveling the complexity of human factors and their interactions. For these reasons, while Polybius's discourse on Fortune engages in comparative, cross-cultural analyses, the very notion of Heaven in the *Records* brings into question the importance and readability of precedents and the continuity of the civilization of the Central States between past and present. Heaven and Fortune are both associated with the possibility of change, the unpredictable, and the mysterious. But while Tyche's female connotation characterizes fate as fickle and ultimately unreliable, in the *Records*, even the traits of elusiveness associated with Heaven are, in a way, part of the shared tradition, neither external nor foreign.

Both the *Histories* and the *Records* stress the function of beliefs concerning the divine in shaping the fate of civilizations. However, whereas the institutionalization of irrational fears, as Polybius remarks, reinforced the identity and cohesion of Roman society against external threats, the multifarious world of popular religion depicted in the *Records* had no echo in the establishment of the official dynastic doctrine at the end of the Western Han, as references to an active relationship with the extra-human realm would famously disappear from official discourses on statecraft and morality until the end of the nineteenth century.[134] Heaven, which would be at the center of theories about the interconnection of the natural and human realms, is treated in the *Records* as an obsolete linguistic residue, as the text shows the inadequacy of traditional knowledge in understanding the present.

Ultimately, neither Polybius nor the authors of the *Records* believed that political unification necessarily coincided with the establishment of superior justice or, in other words, with a kind of order they might have actually welcomed. Their historical sensibility did not lead them to expect that the world must make sense as a whole. For them, extra-human forces—to the extent to which their intervention could be proven—were not clearly acting in accordance with a precise design that entailed the manifestation of universal, super-ethnic values. In those times and circumstances, the *Records* and *Polybius* did not conceive the extra-human realm, "the divine," as intrinsically fair or coherent—or as One.

4

Time, Myth, and Memory

Of Water, Metal, and Cinnabar

Alas! I sincerely wish I could be like the Yellow Emperor!
Then, for me, leaving behind my wives and children would be as easy as taking my slippers off!

—Emperor Wu[1]

The Immortals do not seek for the ruler of men. It is the ruler who must seek for them.
And unless one sets about the task with an open-minded attitude, the immortals do not come.

—Gongsun Qing (a magician from Qi)[2]

Now the last age by Cumae's Sibyl sung, has come and gone, and the majestic roll
Of circling centuries begins anew: Astraea returns, Returns old Saturn's reign,
With a new breed of men sent down from heaven

—Virgil[3]

Divine Kings, Their Audiences, and Their Descendants

Studies on divine kingship in different geographical and historical contexts have produced a vast array of analytical methodologies and paradigms. Briefly outlined, the shared conclusion (or assumption) of most approaches is that the association of rulership with extra-human, transcendent, immutable, or eternal elements can serve to legitimize both political continuity and change.⁴ Claims about divine origins or anointments can make political succession within discrete lineages appear hereditary, despite historical contingency and human fallibility and mortality. The acknowledgment of rulers as descendants of gods or demi-gods who featured in the foundational tales of ancient polities represented a forceful justification of exclusive power and aristocratic privileges. Establishing a genealogical connection with the divine agents who originated specific political and cultural traditions allowed ruling families and clans to advertise their values and interests as absolute or timeless, while strongly connecting their own history and identity with that of the communities they led.

For these reasons, the idea that political leadership must be rooted in a special relationship with the sacred and the metahistorical—and, therefore, with absolute moral laws—is so ingrained in Western thought that it still is more or less openly advocated even in the legitimization of contemporary secular political and social institutions. Despite the nearly universal acknowledgment of the centrality of the principle of "separation of powers," for example, in contemporary America the majority of voters expects candidates for relevant political offices to be open about their personal relationship with the sacred. And such an expectation is based on the resilience of the idea that the country's prosperity and successes might depend on a privileged rapport between political leaders and the divine.

After all, even current understanding of the nation constitutes a by-product of European early modern reactions to the dominion of the Catholic Church. Since the monopoly on religious exegesis constituted the basis of Rome's political claims, the challenge of the Reformation gave way to a series of alternative unitary interpretations of Christianity. Different communities would express demands about administrative autonomy on the basis of distinctive linguistic and cultural identities that were in turn linked to distinctive interpretations of the sacred. And it is especially for this reason that it is so difficult to disentangle the questions of religion, identity, politics, interculturality, and universalism in a contemporary world that is still largely explained in terms of the tension between nation-states and collective, exclusionary attitudes to "religion."

In the study of ancient civilizations, the resilience of models and approaches deriving from the "Christianization" of the Roman Empire is evident in the popularity of the assumption that political, cultural, and moral unity must be predicated on the purported unity of the divine⁵—a conceit that through the dominance of Western human sciences now also informs the scholarship on early China. In the case of the Qin and Han Empires, this tendency is reinforced by the comparisons with Rome under Octavian Augustus (r. 27 BCE–14 CE), when the introduction of the divine cult of the emperor became instrumental in justifying hereditary monarchy and universal rule. But we find similarities only to the extent to which we are willing to understand early China deductively, by assuming the universality of Western experiences. Once we ground our inquiry in an inductive analysis of specific historical circumstances, it is evident that Augustus did not succeed because his reforms resonated with his contemporaries' innate need for a cohesive experience with the divine. It was by catering to different coexisting attitudes toward the sacred and the astute use of different media that he overcame senatorial opposition and won the support of different strata of society.

Ever since the exile of the last king in 509 BCE, Roman elites tended to equate hereditary monarchy with tyranny. The Senators had lived in fear that particularly gifted leaders could stand upon the common people's penchant for god-like kings and elevate themselves above the authority of Republican assemblies and institutions. They were especially afraid that kings, in light of the purported autonomy and timelessness of their divine prerogatives, could overrule the crucial principles of collegiality and temporality on which Roman public offices were based. Tellingly, the fact that, according to popular myths, Romulus had to kill his twin Remus in order to establish a royal line sounded like a warning against the intervention of the divine in political matters, as though it would inevitably lead to the division and destruction of aristocratic families. As for the conspiracy that resulted in Julius Caesar's assassination in 44 BCE (which, for including his adoptive son Brutus, was technically a parricide), it seemed to confirm the inevitable tragedy that would befall those who ventured to exploit their god-like charisma to become absolute rulers.

But this did not mean that devotion (*religio*) to the various official gods had no role in Republican Rome. The elites upheld public cults and sacrifices as an instrument for the survival of the *mos maiorum*, the unwritten values and practices of the ancestors on which the community and its hierarchies were purportedly founded.[6] Openly taking part in religious celebrations therefore corresponded to a patriotic act, as the gods were thought to have an active role in the city's safety and prosperity.[7] If Octavian succeeded where his uncle and adoptive father had failed—in *de facto* ending the Republican era and introducing hereditary monarchy—this was in part due to his careful handling of his association with the sacred.

As we will see in detail below, Emperor Wu's intention to exploit foundational narratives and ritual traditions in order to explain and reinforce the politics of his government was not too dissimilar from that of Octavian. However, it is difficult to ignore that the two rulers operated in cultural contexts in which the reference to previous institutional models and their popularity among different social groups was radically different. During Emperor Wu's reign, a common basic vocabulary for the discussion of the relationship between humans, political institutions, and the cosmos did not exist that could serve a starting to impose a "state religion." Octavian instead was able to deify himself by relying on a well-known palette of ideas and concepts relating to the divine as the source of timeless values, cultural continuity between past and present, and social harmony. He had the possibility of drawing on a popular repertoire of myths and narratives whose message could be grasped and appreciated across different areas and social strata.

The cultural legacy of Rome's Republic compelled political leaders to not underestimate structured forms of dissent and organized opposition. In the case of the reestablishment of monarchy, historical, epigraphic, and archaeological evidence indeed show the ways in which Octavian succeeded in tailoring propaganda strategies to different social groups and communities within Rome and in the provinces.[8] In addresses to the Senate and in official documents, Octavian simply presented himself as a *primus inter pares*, a first among equals, or a consul with enhanced powers, who was invested with the special task of restoring Republican values after decades of violence and civil wars.[9] Despite the elusiveness and frugality of his persona, the humble tone of his public statements, and the fact that he did not use his name to inaugurate the impressive buildings that characterized his ambitious plan of urban renewal for Rome,[10] the divine cult of the emperor allowed Augustus (and even more so his successors) to link Rome's dominion to the god-like person of the ruler throughout the Mediterranean and across all social classes. Even though he always formally rejected his own divinity, by posthumously acknowledging that of Caesar, his uncle and adoptive father, Augustus (more safely) defined himself as the son of a god, and only implicitly and indirectly as a god himself.[11] Building on Caesars's failed plan, references to the intervention of gods in Rome's foundation stories allowed Octavian to present himself as in keeping with the historical trajectory of the City, while at the same time stressing the timelessness of the institutional changes he had brought about.[12]

Golden Age poetry, temples, statues, portraits on coins, and precious objects sanctioned him as a god on earth while common citizens, slaves, and freedmen in the capital revered him as one of the household deities.[13]

In addition, the official nature of the provincial cult of the emperor, often in association with a divinized and anthropomorphized Rome, represented for the local elites in charge of it an efficient strategy to maintain and manifest their connection with the center of power.[14] In brief, because of the Roman successful precedent, the divinity of the emperor transferred to the empire as an institution. And it was on its unity and sacredness the Catholic Church eventually elaborated its apologetics.

Returning to our comparative perspective, it is evident at this point that Han rulers could not as easily exploit Chinese conceptions of the divine (i.e., spirits and ghosts) for political, community-building purposes, nor rely on any well-established, widely recognizable cultural or mythological tradition. As we saw in the previous chapter, the history of Rome's rise to power is the story of an unprecedented expansion of a single city over the entire territory of the known world. Even though the legacy of Hellenic civilizations was constantly acknowledged as fundamental to Rome's self-image, the political and ideological center of the empire was never in doubt. Things took a very different turn in China. After five centuries of uncertainty and strife following the fall of the Zhou Dynasty in 771 BCE, the Qin and Han Dynasties—whose clans originated beyond the borders of the area considered to be the cradle of Chinese civilization—had to claim the geographical center of China and redefine it culturally. Even though, by Emperor Wu's time, few would contest the administrative and economic authority of the central government, its relationship to Chinese cultural traditions was still in the process of being defined.

I mentioned above that new regimes customarily seek legitimization through the promotion of rituals that emphasize, regardless of evidence, their continuity vis-à-vis a hallowed past. But whereas Augustus's cultural and institutional model was obvious and recent—namely the Republic—the five centuries of political experienced by China did not facilitate the acknowledgment of universally accepted archetypes. Emperor Wu was therefore able to draw from the very ample repertoire represented by the multifarious traditions developed throughout China just before the Classicists established a cultural standard through which this age would be reinterpreted and reinvented for centuries. But, for these very reasons, his contribution set him apart both from his predecessors and his successors.

Going back to Rome, Caesar's historical legacy would probably have been very different had Octavian not honored his memory, successfully introduced hereditary monarchy, and fatefully established the bases for interpreting the trajectory of the Roman Empire as a foundational moment in the creation of a European and Western identity. Even though Emperor Wu did not succumb to any assassination plot and on his throne sat one of his sons, he had no political heir who carried out or celebrated his political vision, like Octavian did with his adoptive father. Wu's plans died with him.

Paradoxically, it cannot be said that Emperor Wu has been forgotten. The fifty-four years of rule (from 141 to 87 BCE), which include battles, court intrigues, betrayals, affairs, scandals, a tragic falling out with his official historian, and involvement in magic and witchcraft, make Wu of the Han one of the most well-known sovereigns of ancient China. He has been the subject of non-academic biographies and award-winning TV shows. Even the most synthetic world history surveys never fail to mention his reign in association with the definitive establishment of the Han Dynasty as a military and economic power and with the adoption of Confucianism as a state doctrine. Yet, unlike the First Emperor of the Qin, whose ruthlessness has become idiomatic, the historiography on Emperor Wu never settled on an easily recognizable portrayal.

His own archivist, Sima Qian, in a more or less veiled fashion, criticized this sovereign for his inconsistency, flimsiness, and obsession with alchemy and immortality, which allegedly made him extremely vulnerable to charlatans and bad choices; Eastern Han standard histories glossed over his eccentricity and dislike for the Classicists at court and posthumously hailed him as the patron of "Han Confucianism"; Tang Dynasty poets and unofficial biographies celebrated him as the champion of more fortunate times in which even the Son of Heaven was not afraid to consort with the spirits.[15]

Michael Loewe, the foremost Western scholar of the Han, in his encyclopedic work on the dynasty, has seldom credited this sovereign with a leading role in the many military, political, cultural, and economic achievements of his age. In appraising the institutional and social structures and the various individualities of Wu's long and eventful reign, Loewe has almost regularly attributed the exploits of his government to exceptionally competent ministers and officials. According to his research, the most intricate circumstances and events of this period can often be explained through a minute analysis of the interplay of groups of interest such as those connected to Wu's grandmother and her allies in the early years of reign, and the families of the imperial consorts, court cliques, and various magicians and impostors in his adult and old age.

Loewe's sophisticated conception of historical agency of course hardly befits a traditional "great-personalities approach." His oeuvre has unraveled the complexities of Emperor Wu's age in a way that makes it impossible to reduce this fascinating period to the will of a single sovereign. However, there are some elements of continuity that cannot be ignored. First of all, Emperor Wu maintained the throne for an extremely long period in an age characterized by violence, secret plots, and betrayals. Although it is undeniable that he repeatedly benefited from the services of brilliant politicians and generals, over the fifty-four years of his reign most of them fell out of grace with their sovereign and were replaced by colleagues whose tenure was often as brief. Interestingly enough, one influential personality who accompanied Wu since the early years of reign to the ruler's death was that Sang Hongyang 桑弘羊 (152–80 BCE), whom we have already encountered in chapter 2 as the champion of the Modernists in the *Discourses on Salt and Iron*. We have enough evidence to hold that if Emperor Wu eventually allowed Sang to exert so much power, he must have considered his contribution crucial. Although Sang was a self-taught official, with no important intellectual affiliations, he spent his political career focusing on the creation of a centralized economy that included the enforcement of the famous monopolies on iron, salt, and alcohol.

Reformists clearly opposed these politics. Their arguments relied on the *Classics* to demand the return to the purported laissez-faire approach of the Sage Kings of the past. In the Reformists' opinion, an ideal ruler should trust local administrators, abstain from interfering with their decisions, respect preexisting social hierarchies, while supporting thrifty landowners and farmers instead of adventurous merchants and businessmen. Hence, it makes perfect sense that Emperor Wu was particularly interested in mythological and ritual traditions that envisioned an all-powerful and independent sovereign. The model of rulership he privileged was based on the notion of a superior warrior who ruled his peoples directly, without the mediating role of the nobility, and who travelled constantly throughout the empire in order to muster its economic and human resources. The opposition, by contrast, was partial to the more passive kind of rulership praised in the *Classics*. The legendary Sage Kings ruled by example without leaving the capital, while devout ministers, belonging to the most important families of the realm, took care of all the rest.

It cannot be considered a coincidence that in the years following Emperor Wu's death and Sang Hongyang's execution (because of charges made by members of the former opposition), the abolition of their centralizing policies went hand-in-hand with the establishment of a set of protocols that reduced the Son of Heaven's ritual functions to the perimeter of the capital city. From Chang'an, the Son of Heaven could maintain order in the universe without having to embark on expensive ceremonial expeditions across vast stretches of the empire.

It is on account of being compiled during these turbulent years that the *Records*, as an official history, represents a unique contribution. It provides readers with the opportunity to observe debates on possible models for imperial rulership and their regional variations that took place before the formalization of a cultural orthodoxy and as they were being carried out by means of discussions on foundational myths. However, because of the absence of a complete "Basic Annals of Emperor Wu," historians have traditionally focused on the chapter "Book on the *Feng* and *Shan*" to garner information about Sima Qian's own age and his relationship with the Son of Heaven.[16] Read as a stand-alone chapter, it at first appears to solemnize Wu's celebration of the *feng* and *shan* sacrifices as the beginning of a new golden age.[17] Upon further analysis, however, it becomes evident that positive statements about the announced successes of the Son of Heaven are contradicted by the very structure of the chapter, which seems to emphasize the lack of coherence of Wu's ritual plan, and by the history of the state ceremonies performed before his reign since the Shang dynasty.[18]

Instead of positing these sacrifices as an element of the formalization of a "state religion" and comparing them to analogous ceremonies carried out by other ancient sovereigns in different areas of the globe, I first analyze the narration of Wu's performance of the *feng* and *shan*, vis-à-vis the position Sima Qian attributes to them in the history of Chinese ritual traditions.[19] Then, in reconstructing Emperor Wu's ritual program, I complement the fragmentary accounts sketched in the *Records* with data provided by other Han Dynasty received and excavated texts, as well as available material evidence. The image that emerges is that of an era of uncertainty in which it was not obvious yet which social and political models would most benefit the dynasty. The cosmological, ritual, and alchemic traditions of the former state of Qi still played an important role at the Qin and Han courts. In the absence of an institutional space for political debates, supporters of laissez-fare and of the centralizing measures of Wu's government sparred by promoting alternative readings of the Yellow Emperor as an ideal ruler, while re-elaborating myths concerning floods, bronzes, and immortals.[20]

From a methodological point of view, the study and reconstruction of Emperor Wu's ritual activities requires a broader reassessment of current conceptualization about an "early Chinese religion." For example, the assumption that "divinity" represents a self-explanatory universal category, in addition to "familiarizing" and "essentializing" specific traits of ancient Chinese societies, does not allow us to appraise the richness of elite and popular attitudes toward spirits and ghosts.[21] Likewise, the conceit that the adoption of a state religion represents an indispensable step toward the creation of a shared cultural identity subordinates the study of the early Chinese empires to the misleading systemic and teleological paradigms typical of Abrahamic traditions. At the same time, the application of models deriving from analyses of ancient Mediterranean polytheistic systems produces the tendency to interpret textual variations of a given myth (e.g., on the Yellow Emperor) as different versions of an "original" story, rather than as coexisting, discrete elaborations of elements belonging to a loosely shared repertoire of themes and symbols. In other words, in approaching the complex world of the *Records* we should consider as a research hypothesis the possibility of having myths without a mythology and rites without a religion.

Political adversaries perceived Emperor Wu's ritual activities as aimed at legitimizing specific aspects of the centralizing politics of his government. From a cultural point of view, the emperor rebuked the devolutionary rhetoric (and maybe vested interests) of the Classicists at court by favoring the inclusion of elements from "non-canonical" traditions in state ceremonies and foundational myths. As for Sima Qian, he does not seem willing to take part in the debate and acts almost as a neutral chronicler. His admiration for Confucius's teachings made him wary of lingering on non-empirical, non-human topics, while his intellectual upbringing likely prevented him from developing familiarity with some aspects of the regional cults that Wu was trying to coopt. As for his dislike for contemporary self-declared followers of the Master, it was balanced by his misgivings about his ruler's character and politics.

Gods, Saints, Sages, Ancestors, and Immortals

By refashioning stories featuring traditional gods and heroes, political leaders could rhetorically reconcile continuity and change, the noble and the humble, the familiar and the foreign, the civilized and the savage. Julius Caesar's propaganda strategies, for example, share several elements with the ancient Middle Eastern/Mediterranean trope of revolutionary rulers (including different kinds of saviors, from Sargon of Akkad to Jesus of Nazareth) who, by claiming at the same time royal/divine origins and a special connection with the common people, sought to undermine the authority of the groups currently in power. Specifically, Caesar tried to "write" a narrative that exploited references to the divine in order to depict his actions as aimed at the reinforcement of a timeless, essential Roman identity.

When he inaugurated the temple of Venus Genitrix in 46 BCE, in characterizing the goddess as the ancestor of his clan and mother of the Trojan Homeric hero Aeneas, Caesar was linking his lineage to the purported Hellenic origins of Rome, while underscoring the values proudly cherished by its citizens.[22] As narrated by Livy, a Republican who eventually acquiesced to Augustus's monarchic rule, in fleeing from a burning Troy, Aeneas showed exemplary compassion and filial piety as he carried on his shoulders his father Anchises—who was completely human—to safety.[23] The intercourse of one of Aeneas's female descendants with the Roman god of war, Mars, reinforced the divine element of his lineage, while infusing it with otherworldly military prowess. One of the fruits of this union would be Romulus, the founder and first king of Rome. In his veins run divine and therefore aristocratic blood, but the fact that according to the myth he was rescued and fed by a she-wolf and raised among shepherds pointed to the importance of the connection of his lineage with the communities inhabiting the wilder areas outside the city.[24]

In carrying out his plan, Caesar clearly benefited from the cooperation of several influential members of the elites who seemed willing to bestow on him the official symbols of divinity. After the battle of Thapsus in 46 BCE, the Senate honored him with a chariot and erected a statue in his likeness, which bore the inscription "demigod." The following year, after the battle of Munda, the Senate moved the statue and chariot from the Capitol to the temple of Quirinus, an important god in the political and religious cosmology of early Rome, and gave the statue a new inscription that declared Caesar an unconquered god (*Deus Invictus*). Finally, in the last months of his life, Caesar received from the Senate the paraphernalia associated with the major Roman gods: he was decreed a state divinity (*divus*), which led to the establishment of an official cult (*Divus Iulius*) to which a state priest (*flamen*) was assigned and for which a state temple was built, while a sacred couch (*pulvinar*) was established at the Circus Maximus.[25]

In ancient China the question of "divine status" or condition of *shen* was everything but formalized in official terms. Dynastic clans, not unlike their Mediterranean counterparts, tended to trace their origins back to legendary sovereigns of yore, or Sages (*shengren* 聖人). The sources, however, do not describe the mythical founders of the Xia, Shang, and Zhou as the progeny of immortal gods or as gods themselves. Their accounts, rather, present models that are in a way more consistent with the contemporary scholarly categories of "culture heroes" or "paradigmatic rulers."[26] The Sages clearly embodied superior men, but they did not owe their extraordinary qualities to their closeness to a universal and absolute truth. In addition to natural gifts, self-cultivation was fundamental. Even in cases where the Sages possessed some extra-human features and powers, according to the *Classics*, they all eventually died and turned into dynastic ancestors. Unlike Olympian deities or Catholic saints, *shengren*, while paragons of virtue, were not believed to exert a direct influence on human affairs. If according to some accounts they became immortals, it meant that they were enjoying a blissful and carefree existence on some remote island and were out of this world for good.[27]

Whether no one at the Han court considered the official establishment of "religious unity" a priority, or whether political institutions were simply incapable of enforcing one (provided that it was conceivable), the Sages were never thought of as presiding over the same universe at the same time, but rather as champions of subsequent evolutionary stages. Ultimately, with the consolidations of the *ru* as intellectual elites, the authority of the Sages would be indissolubly linked to those fundamental books, the *Classics*, which described and extolled their moral virtues. In their legitimizing function, the Sages could be evoked through philological analysis rather than by sacrifice.

As for the multitude of Chinese spirits and ghosts that were worshipped locally, no ruler of the Western Han period tried to organize them systematically into an official pantheon as a means to enforce cultural uniformity across different social groups.[28] The various extra-human entities that crowd the world of the *Records* hardly embody a well-defined set of morals supposedly at basis of society. Nor do they form a polytheistic system of the Greek or Roman kind. If "[p]olytheism means that many gods are worshipped not only at the same place, but by the same community and by the same individual," and that "only the totality of the gods constitute the divine world," then certainly early Chinese *shen* do not belong to a unitary and organic "religious" whole that mirrors society's structures and hierarchies.

Before delving into the mythological narratives in the *Records*, let us address the issue of the trans-cultural usage of "divinity" again, this time in order to question its application to Han cultural and textual traditions. In early Chinese sources, the meaning of "*shen*" 神 varies in different textual and cultural contexts. When used as a noun, it is conventionally translated as "gods" or "spirits" and can also allude to the souls of the dead; when used as an adjective, it is translated as "divine," "sacred," "holy," "spiritual," or "extra-human." Michael Puett has argued that, in the Bronze Age, *shen* referred almost exclusively to non-human beings; only with the Warring States did it begin to describe "substances within humans" through the cultivation of which one could become a "god."²⁹ Although Puett's analysis is accurate, the translation of *shen* as "god" inevitably induces readers to project typically Chinese phenomena onto the wrong historical and cultural background. Before the adoption of Dong Zhongshu's interpretation of the theory of the Five Phases, there is no evidence supporting the notion that Heaven or Nature could coincide with a conscious organism or even less with a supreme *shen* comparable with anthropomorphic monotheistic deities.³⁰ The relationship of humans with Heaven did not entail an individual rapport focused on self-development. In brief, none of the various conceptions of divinity developed in the Fertile Crescent, Indo-European linguistic contexts, or the Greco-Roman world exactly corresponds to any idea found in early Chinese sources, not to mention the holistic, unitary, identitary, and in certain cases legally binding interpretations developed within Abrahamic traditions.

As for the *Records*, the range of meanings of *shen* can simultaneously apply to various notions of extra-human phenomena and faculties, without being ever defined with philosophical or theological precision. As both the *Zhong Yong* and *Chunqiu fanlu* note, *shen* can hardly be spoken about because they defy human senses.³¹ Therefore, it is arguably their ambiguity that preoccupied the authors of these ancient works. The *Records* indeed treats spirits and ghosts as the epistemological limit of human inquiries. Whether they pertain to an ontologically separate realm, or whether the "human" and the "divine" represent different stages of the same existential continuum, the author of *Records* seems mostly interested in defining the limits of human experiences and agency. Sima Qian conceived morality as a specifically human question. For him, the world of the *shen*, because of its variety and unpredictability, could hardly epitomize or legitimize unity and moral guidance; it represented a problem rather than a solution.³² The *Records*'s concern with the extra-human is mostly confined to the ways beliefs regarding spirits, ghosts, and prodigies affect human decisions and behavior.

A further element specific to discussions on a "Han religion" is that of the First Emperor of Qin's and Wu of the Han's fabled obsession with immortality.³³ In the ancient Mediterranean world, immortality was the defining condition of divinity and could be transmitted from the gods to the progeny of their occasional human sexual partners. As we have seen above, claims about divinity/immortality were customarily instrumental in reinforcing social and political hierarchies. When these claims inspired revolutionary leaders, the appeal of divinity/immortality served the propaganda about a new order that must as well be based on eternal and immutable factors and that was very often advertised as even more ancient, primeval, original, and absolute or in some way purer than the current one.

In early (and pre-Buddhist) China, however, immortality rarely coincided with those qualities included in Western definitions of "divinity." Ancient Chinese did not consider the immortality of their cultural heroes or paradigmatic figures such as the sages as an important factor per se. Nor did they believe that immortals were born as such. Their exceptional condition, in other words, was not hereditary. They were often thought as regular humans who achieved eternal life through seclusion, individualistic self-absorption, esoteric bodily practices, and particular forms of abstinence.[34] Their message, more than subversive, appeared rather as antisocial, or antipolitical. They did not wish to change society but leave it behind them. Chinese immortals usually seemed self-involved, or focused on articulating an individualistic critique of the basic values of civilization, which, especially in Han texts, was aimed against the principles celebrated by Confucius and the Classicists.

When associated with specific rulers, immortality usually served as an implicit indictment of their conduct as superstitious and immoral. According to the *Records*, the kind of immortality pursued by the First Emperor and Wu did not imply the superior ontological condition and moral prerogatives associated in the West with divine status. In fact, this text characterizes the obsession of these two rulers as a pretext to escape the duties ideally performed by a sovereign on behalf of his people, duties that the *Classics* defined in terms of filial piety.

The "Book on the Feng and Shan Sacrifices" or the "History of Make-believe"

The ritual performances carried out under Wu appeared to Sima Qian as an incoherent patchwork of badly understood practices, for they derived from different local cultural contexts and were probably conceived for finalities that were not immediately evident to the author of the *Records*. Especially in their esoteric, secret stages, their function seemed to address personal concerns of the emperor as a human being. It is telling that according to the *Records*, Emperor Wu welcomed the possibility of succeeding in the *feng* and *shan* with these words: "Alas! I sincerely wish I could be like the Yellow Emperor! Then, for me, leaving behind my wives and children would be as easy as taking my shoes off!"[35] This exclamation, as reported in the *Records*, seems to reduce Wu's quest for immortality to a way to unburden himself of his family and day's responsibilities. At the same time, it is possible that the historian reported such an unbecoming comment with intent of trivializing a more grounded stance against the familistic social vision of the Classicists that the emperor might have supported. Lastly, it cannot be excluded that Wu was purportedly using the trope of immortality to satirize the positions of the opponents to his centralizing politics.

Admittedly, Sima Qian's attitude toward immortality may have not be in keeping with the prevailing beliefs of his own time and it is impossible to ascertain if the emperor was willingly trying to confuse his closest associates and courtiers. In any case, the very structure of the chapter devoted to Wu's ceremonies suggests that Sima Qian's main goal was polemical, for he did not organize the "Book on the *Feng* and *Shan*" as a systematic description of the sacrifices. Instead, he shaped its narrative around the ruler's encounters with the *fangshi* and their individual contributions to state sacrifices, as though the historian wanted to suggest that his ruler did not have any agency.[36]

As we have seen, Sima Qian considered ritual activities under two distinct categories. The first included ceremonies, rules of conduct, and behaviors centered on filial piety (*xiao* 孝) that were ascribed to Zhou elites and textual tradition (i.e., *li* 禮). These practices did not address spirits other than ancestors and were aimed at reinforcing social connections and hierarchies. The second category included rituals and beliefs not rooted in the Zhou textual tradition. They usually involved direct contact with the extra-human and therefore could not provide unambiguous moral lessons (*si* 祀).

It is this latter kind of activity that Sima Qian researched and recorded in the "Book on the *Feng* and *Shan*."[37] Its declared topic is the history of sacrifices, from the remote origins of Chinese civilization to Emperor Wu's age. The pretext for this account is the performance of *feng* 封 and *shan* 禪 Emperor Wu embarked upon in 110 BCE, in his thirty-first year on the throne. Celebrated almost nine decades after Liu Bang had founded the empire, these ceremonies were expected to sanction the definitive legitimation of the Han Dynasty at a moment of unprecedented political stability and prosperity. However, despite the excitement for the imminent historic celebrations, there was no agreement at court about the origins, exact meaning, and proper ritual procedures of the *feng* and *shan*. The only commonly shared notion was that only rulers whose legitimacy was unquestionable could perform them successfully.[38] This is how Sima Qian weighed in on the matter in the opening of the "Book on the *Feng* and *Shan*:"[39]

Among the emperors and kings of old who received the Mandate, why are there some who did not perform the *feng* and *shan*? There have been those who did not have what was required to carry them out and those who received the positive omens but could not reach Mount Tai [for the *feng*]. Some, although they had received the Mandate, did not show sufficient merits; some could reach Mount Liangfu [for the *shan*] but lacked virtue; others had sufficient virtue but not enough time to accomplish them. And for all these reasons, the *feng* and *shan* have been so infrequent![40]

This passage implicitly states the irrelevance of the reception of the Mandate in regard to the effectiveness and success of a given reign. In other words, it seems clear enough that Sima Qian did not consider the endorsement of an individual by Heaven—and the historian does not specify how this would be manifested—sufficient to deem a sovereign worthy of the *feng* and *shan*. The virtue of his actions, in other words, had nothing to do with the intervention of external forces. Whether Sima Qian was suggesting that Heaven could favor incompetent leaders or, instead, subtly insinuating that the issue of the Mandate was altogether insignificant, the rest of his introduction clarifies that the historian considered the performance of the *feng* and *shan* unfeasible and likely useless. In citing Confucius's *Analects*, the Grand Historian promptly reminds the reader, "If for three years rites (*li* 禮) are not performed, they will fall into disuse. If for three years music is not played, it will become lost. They [the *feng* and *shan*] are therefore so rare that "the details of the ancient ceremony have been completely lost and it is now impossible to discover with any exactitude just how it was carried out."[41] He adds that the *feng* and *shan* "can yield a positive outcome when an age is at its height, and be irresponsive when it is in decline."[42]

With this last sentence, Sima Qian seems to shift the focus from the meaning of the *feng* and *shan* to the quality of governments. In a fashion that reminds us of the historian's treatment of Heaven, the references in the *Records* to these sacrifices ultimately compel readers to consider human factors instead. If we follow the logic implicit in Sima Qian's introduction to the *feng* and *shan*, we can conclude that even if Emperor Wu had received the Mandate and the right omens, showed sufficient merit, and possessed the time and the means to accomplish the sacrifices, he should not have considered such an endeavor a priority, as it would have added nothing to his rule. In addition, the *Records* laments in several instances that, after the demise of Confucius in 479 BCE, no one then living could read Heaven's signs and cosmic changes well enough to propound a model of political leadership attuned to natural rhythms.⁴³ Consequently, who could rightfully claim to have recognized the signs of the Mandate?

Thus, instead of clarifying doubts and reinforcing the legitimacy of Emperor Wu's ritual choices, Sima Qian subtly questions the very possibility of a ruler becoming involved with the extra-human sphere. He weaves a series of narratives that ultimately delegitimize Emperor Wu's ritual vision in particular, and the concern with spirits in general. In his view, the *Classics* were still invaluable,⁴⁴ not because they were a source of absolute and timeless ethical norms, but because they could contribute to the moral improvement of individuals by facilitating an emotional connection with exemplary personalities of the past.⁴⁵

In chronicling the history of China from the Yellow Emperor to the Shang, the "Book on the *Feng* and *Shan*" exhausts the topic of sacrifices in a few lines amid accounts of various exploits of each ancient ruler. Since these accounts rely on ancient sources, such as the *Book of Documents*, it seems that Sima Qian did not feel comfortable adding to or questioning materials that must have commanded deference. The text simply concentrates on ascertaining if ancient rulers were interested in giving heed to spirits and ghosts, or whether they instead relied on those human virtues (*de*) indicated in the *Classics*. Generally, the narrative singles out sovereigns who met with misfortune either because they paid too much attention to extra-human phenomena or because they ignored them altogether. For example, Kongjia 孔甲 of the Xia Dynasty, who lacked virtue, was so obsessed with spirits that one day two dragons descended from the sky and took him away.⁴⁶ Wu Yi 武乙 of the Shang (an ancestor of Confucius), notorious for taking pleasure in defying the spirits, was eventually killed by lightning.⁴⁷ Finally, the exemplary Tai Wu, 太戊 of the Shang, excelling in virtue, managed to cut down two prodigious mulberry trees that had grown to great enormity in his courtyard. Again, it seems that on these topics the *Records* aspired to alert readers to the unruliness of spirits and ghosts while affirming the importance of human qualities. As it clearly states in commenting on Tai Wu's merits, regardless of the potential meaning of the sudden appearance of the trees, "portents cannot prevail over virtue" (*yao bu sheng de* 妖不勝德)—a statement we should keep in mind in analyzing the *Records'* accounts of Emperor Wu's deeds.⁴⁸

It is with the invasion of the Zhou capital by the nomadic Rong 戎 in 771 BCE that the narration in the "Book on the *Feng* and *Shan*" becomes notably more intricate and fragmented. Without overlooking the possibility that Sima Qian presumably could access a larger and more accurate set of documents about these later ages, his stylistic and thematic choices suggest that, with the waning of the cultural legacy of the Zhou, the Central States had lost the most authoritative model of ritual behavior. According to the "Book on the *Feng* and *Shan*," as the Zhou progressively relinquished political control over China, "non-canonical" beliefs and practices proliferated. Self-proclaimed experts on spirits and ghosts, yin and yang, the Five Virtues or Phases, astrology, and alchemy began to exploit their allegedly exclusive knowledge for immediate economic and political gain.[49] Sima Qian lamented that these charlatans found in Emperor Wu an eager listener and a generous patron. For him, the ritual activities he recorded while following the Son of Heaven represented nothing more than an incoherent patchwork of misunderstood practices and beliefs, which were, in any case, incompatible with sound and effective politics. The performance of the *feng* and *shan* sacrifices in 110 BCE, according to the *Records*, epitomized the hypocrisy and moral confusion of the age.

According to the *Records*, the first ruler who showed interest in performing the *feng* and *shan* was Duke Huan 桓 of Qi (d. 643 BCE), the first feudal lord of the Spring and Autumn Period (722–453 BCE), who, as we have seen, achieved preeminence over the rivals as ruler-hegemon (*ba* 霸) after the fall of the Western Zhou.[50] This meant that Duke Huan's authority merely resulted from momentarily superior military strength and economic wealth. Hence, the house of Qi could not yet rightfully claim the moral leadership deriving from the reception of the Mandate, which was still believed to be on the side of the Eastern Zhou. Since, the historian implies, Duke Huan's virtue could not be compared to the perfect filial piety of Yao and Shun, he had to resort to the different kind of legitimization of the *feng* and *shan* sacrifices. But as the eager duke began to gather information about the appropriate procedure, Master Guan Zhong 管仲, the minister to whom Qi owed its recent successes, managed to dissuade him from the historic performance.[51] He reminded his lord that the twelve sovereigns who had succeeded in the performance of the *feng* of *shan* (the Yellow Emperor being the first) ruled in ages too remote to allow for the survival of accurate accounts. Furthermore, not only had auspicious portents not appeared, but the prodigious plants and beasts required for the sacrifices were native of distant lands beyond Duke Huan's authority.[52] In other words, according to Master Guan, Qi's domain did not include sufficient territories, nor could it claim the favor of natural and extra-human forces. In fact, the *feng* and *shan* were to be considered the exclusive prize for an empire that embraced all realms.

In order to properly assess the import of this account in the economy of the "Book on the *Feng* and *Shan*" and in the *Records*, we should consider two elements. The first is that, as we have seen in chapter 2, the *Records*, in the "Book on *Li*" identifies the commoner Guan Zhong with a form of statecraft based more on expediency than on *li* and moral exemplarity.[53] The second is that even when a ruler such as Emperor Wu announced the manifestation of the necessary omens and the acquisition of all the prodigious plants and beasts required for the ceremony, the *feng* and *shan* could still end in failure. Again, Sima Qian seems to be suggesting that morally legitimate imperial rulership has nothing to do with the direct control of the world, its creatures, and its resources.

But let us continue to follow Sima Qian's diachronic account of the sacrifices in this chapter of the *Records*. In 221 BCE, when the Qin reunified China, the question of the celebration of the *feng* and *shan* was raised once again. At this point the historian notes two facts that might well have related to the Han: Qin conquered the world not by means of virtue, but through the establishment of *fa* 法, defined as punishments and institutions;[54] its officials, mentioning the ascending power of the element of Water as one of the causes of the Qin's success, for the first time in history used the theory of the Five Phases (also attributed to Qi) to justify dynastic power.[55] This meant that, obviously, the Qin were not interested in reviving the model of the Zhou. In considering which rituals would befit the new imperial dimension of their domain, among the various regional traditions they privileged those from the state of Qi. They did so, as the *Records* emphasizes, under the sway of unreliable and dishonest *fangshi* who persuaded the First Emperor that the performance of the *feng* and *shan* represented a fundamental step toward the achievement of immortality.

As convincingly argued by Hans Van Ess, the *Records*' portrayal of the First Emperor was actually aimed at indirectly discrediting Emperor Wu.[56] In addition, we should not forget that Sima Qian's remarks about the power base of the Qin being outside the traditional ritual circuits defined by the Five Peaks could apply equally to the very legitimacy of the Han, who established their capital just a few miles south of their predecessors'. At the time, the First Emperor's *feng* and *shan* were remembered as unsuccessful. It was believed that a sudden thunderstorm had prevented the Son of Heaven from reaching the summit of Mount Tai. Sima Qian casts doubt on this piece of information by implying that it might have been nothing more than an exaggeration spread by the Classicists. As our historian suggests, this group had probably overblown the length of a momentary break taken by the sovereign under a tree, when, while on his way to the top of Mount Tai, it started to rain. And, as we have already seen in the case of Confucius dismissing the popularity of Guan Zhong, Sima Qian goes so far as to hint that the Classicists' skepticism could be archived under the category of "sour grapes," since the First Emperor had excluded them from the final phases of the ceremonies.[57] In other words, how could they question the outcome of the First Emperor's *feng* and *shan* if they were not even present? Furthermore, Sima Qian concludes his account of the sacrifices under the Qin with a short paragraph that lays out diachronic narration, causality, and ex post facto condemnation of a vanquished regime in his iconic and deliberately ambiguous style. In this way, the rhetoric surrounding the accomplishment of the *feng* and *shan* becomes an apt metaphor for Sima Qian's "historiographical disillusionment":

> Twelve years after the First Emperor celebrated the *feng* and *shan*, the Qin collapsed. Lamenting that the Qin burned the *Odes* and the *Documents* and massacred scholars, and that the people resented Qin laws until the whole world rebelled, the Classicists all declared: "When the First Emperor climbed Mount Tai, he could not complete the *feng* and *shan* because he was hit by a storm." Is this not what we call "embarking on an enterprise without having the necessary qualities?"[58]

The author of the *Records* at this point does not seem inclined to support the sacrifices carried out under Emperor Wu enthusiastically. In addition to the misgivings concerning the modalities and goals of these historic celebrations, and the fact that they were obviously not in keeping with the frugal politics of the sovereigns of old, to an astute observer such as Sima Qian it must have been evident that the lavish ceremonies and expansionistic military campaigns carried out during his time had contributed to the dramatic financial crisis that plagued the final years of Wu's tenure.

Sima Qian adds that in the early years of his reign, Emperor Wu, in an effort to counter the influence of his grandmother, Empress Dowager Dou 竇 (a Huang-Lao supporter, according to the *Records*), often promoted eminent Classicists such as Zhao Wan 趙綰, Wang Zang 王臧, and Gongsun Hong 公孫弘.[59] Complicating matters, not only did the emperor largely ignore their advice, even after his grandmother's death in 135 BCE, the emperor's ambivalent attitude did not seem to change.

We should ask whether a highly educated sovereign such as Emperor Wu could be as obsessed with his personal fixations as to become completely oblivious to the potential propagandistic import of state rituals, while passively accepting the input of magicians and charlatans. Although the Son of Heaven often acted under the sway of the families of his empresses (the Wang 王 and the Dou 竇, for example) and of cunning officials, in many instances he got rid of his closest advisers and replaced them with officials who proved equally competent. If, on one hand, in Sima Qian's narrative we can recognize the consolidation of an intellectual attitude prone to downplaying the political agency of the Son of Heaven; on the other hand we cannot exclude that a ruler such as Emperor Wu might have entertained ideas and strategies that even close observers could not immediately fathom, as they were inspired by foreign or "unorthodox" cultural and political traditions.

The Yellow Emperor as a Mortal: A Model of Unified Rulership

The *Records* does not explicitly criticize Emperor Wu. Whereas Sima Qian's skepticism about the various *fangshi* emerges clearly in his meticulous accounts of all their frauds and failures, the historian never directly recommends particular ritual corrections or behaviors, nor does he seem interested in providing alternative views. However, the acts of the remote sovereigns described in the first chapter of the *Records*, the "Basic Annals of the Five Sovereigns" ("Wudi *benji*" 五帝本紀), offers an interesting insight into Sima Qian's ideas of rulership, especially if we consider the extent to which the negative examples he reported in other chapters diverge from his declared models. The most evident of these contrasting descriptions is represented by Sima Qian's account of the accomplishments of the Yellow Emperor in the initial chapter and those attributed to the various *fangshi* in the "Book on the *Feng* and *Shan*." In the first case the culture hero dies as an ordinary human being; in the second, his major achievement consists of becoming an immortal.[60]

The historiographical works that preceded the *Records* had ignored or only briefly sketched the supposed heroics of the Yellow Emperor.[61] Sima

Qian, in his final remarks at the end of the first of the Basic Annals, states that he decided to recount the deeds of the sovereigns preceding Yao and Shun because he wanted to correct the inaccuracies that the Hundred Experts (*baijia* 百家) were spreading during his own time about those early ages in general and the Yellow Emperor in particular.[62] And the very act of writing made Sima Qian's version automatically more authoritative.[63]

Like Confucius, Sima Qian considered the mythical sovereigns Yao and Shun examples of perfect rulership. By ascribing the origins of statecraft to the Yellow Emperor, many centuries before their era, the historian was probably indirectly suggesting that the culture hero epitomized an early, less refined model of sovereignty. In other words, whereas Yao and Shun's rule embodied perfect filial piety, which they were able to transmit effortlessly to the people by example,[64] the Yellow Emperor had to cope with challenging practical tasks that necessitated direct intervention and recourse to violence.[65] In the aftermath of tyrannical rule, the elimination of dangerous foes, the pacification of the world, and the establishment of common standards represented a solid basis on which to install a rule that more closely resembled the age of the Zhou. Several pieces of evidence suggest the author fashioned such a characterization of the Yellow Emperor's activities in order to draw a comparison with the historical circumstances of the Han regime, perhaps from its origins to Sima Qian's age.[66] In 104 BCE, official propaganda was celebrating the reign of Emperor Wu as a New Beginning (*taichu* 太初), the start of a new cosmic cycle that, as the "Book on the *Feng* and *Shan*" reports, many believed to coincide with the astronomical conditions of the archaic age of the Yellow Emperor. By appropriating and re-elaborating popular tales about Emperor Wu's apparently favorite hero, the historian was probably expressing his personal judgment and advice regarding the politics of his own period. Analyzing discussions on the legacy of the Yellow Emperor in their historical context can therefore help us cast a new light on the cultural and political concerns of Emperor Wu's age.[67]

Depending on the textual contexts and theoretical approaches used to analyze the myths about the Yellow Emperor, scholars have depicted him as "the God of the Center" and the patron of medicine and exoteric practices, the embodiment of "Genealogical Ancestrality," or the expression of "Paradigmatic Emperorship."[68] In the wake of the discovery of the Mawangdui silk manuscripts in 1973, specialists have acknowledged the relevance of the Yellow Emperor during the Western Han period and interpreted his cult (in association with Laozi) as the focal point of a well-defined Huang-Lao religion or philosophy, the same one followed by Wu's influential grandmother. Such a tradition propounded a kind of universal rulership, modeled on natural rhythms that combined the physiologic and cosmological speculations of an "early Daoism" with some of the political concerns that characterized Legalist thinkers.[69] Whether or not Huang-Lao existed as a well-defined school or doctrine and regardless of how fantastic, mythological, or abstract their stories might sound, these excavated texts, together with works like the *Huainanzi*, clearly echo the political preoccupations of the phase between the struggle for the unification of China States and Emperor Wu's reign. In that tumultuous period, ministers and political advisors competed in the re-elaboration and synthesis of old ideas about rulership as well as in the creation of new models that could appeal to contemporary leaders and pretenders.

As speculations about the Five Phases (associated with five colors) attributed to Zou Yan 鄒衍 (305–240 BCE) began to spread throughout China from his hometown in the state of Qi, texts referring to mythical ancestors began to replace the character *huang* 皇, "sovereign, august," with the homophonous *huang* 黃, "yellow."[70] The earliest archeological source to mention the Yellow Emperor is an inscription on a fourth-century sacrificial bronze vase, which King Wei 威 of Qi (r. 357–320 BCE) had dedicated to his forefather Duke Wen 文 (r. 815–804 BCE). It defines the sovereign as the highest, mythical ancestor (*gaozu* 高祖) of the new royal lineage of Qi, the house of Tian 田, which, having just gained power, was in need—as often happens—of a distinct and authoritative founding father.[71] When the neighboring state of Yan attacked Qi in 286 BCE, the various experts (including the *fangshi*), who had benefited from the support of the elites in the capital, were forced to scatter throughout China and look for new patrons. It was along the routes of their diaspora that stories about the Yellow Emperor gained popularity.[72]

The *Huainanzi*, which was produced at the court of the prince Liu An 劉安 (180–122 BCE), a cousin and rival of Emperor Wu, pairs the Yellow Emperor with the (usually female) Deity of Earth, Houtu 后土, in the task of measuring and organizing the universe.[73] In his function as cosmic pivot, the Yellow Emperor is also linked to the axial Mount Kunlun 崑崙, considered a gateway to immortality and afterlife in some traditions. In astronomic texts, the Yellow Emperor appears together with the planet Saturn (Zhen Xing 鎮星 or Huangshigong 黃石公), which was, in turn, connected with the Northern Dipper (Beidou 北斗), the color yellow, the element Earth, and the yin factor.[74] The texts unearthed from Tomb 3 in Mawangdui instead depict the Yellow Emperor as the monarch who moves incessantly in order to listen to his people and who builds, autonomously, one great granary to satisfy all his subjects.[75] While all these elements recur in the tales narrated by the *fangshi* in the "Book on the *Feng* and *Shan*," they are meaningfully absent from Sima Qian's "historicized" biography of the "Basic Annals of the Five Sovereigns."[76]

This section of the *Records* introduces the Yellow Emperor as it might any other historical character, by mentioning his name, Xuan Yuan 軒轅; the name of his father, Shao Dian 少典; and his surname, Gongsun 公孫.[77] His achievements justify defining him as the typical culture hero who sanctions the passage of China to a civilized stage, or in anthropological terms, enables the shift from "nature" to "nurture." By explaining to the people the connection of Heaven and Earth, the changes between light and darkness, and the hardship of life and death, he introduces the proper ways of agriculture, animal husbandry, and the correct exploitation of all natural resources. Unlike other versions of the myth narrated in more or less contemporary texts, in this case the Yellow Emperor does not create anything, but enables humankind to better interact with the universe.[78]

The *Records* remarks that extra-human qualities (*shen ling* 神靈) were immediately evident in the Yellow Emperor at his birth. He spoke very precociously and, by the time he became an adult, had already displayed indisputable signs of superiority. He was endowed with extraordinary powers, but nothing in the texts suggests that he was in any way comparable to a traditional god of the Indo-European mold and destined to immortality. In those remote times, the *Records* reports, as the reign of the beast-like Shennong 神農/Yandi 炎帝,[79] the mythical farmer and Flame Ruler, was in decline, the feudal lords (*zhuhou* 諸侯) were striving to encroach upon each other's domains, while brutalizing and oppressing the common people.[80] To make things worse, Chi You 蚩尤, the legendary creator of metal weapons, was looming more aggressively and threateningly by the day.[81] Unable to cope with all these sources of danger, the Feudal Lords sought the help of the future Yellow Emperor. The Emperor obliged: he reorganized the armies, mastered the Five Qi (*qi* 氣),[82] planted the Five Seeds,[83] comforted the common people, inspected all the territories, and tamed various wild animals and trained them to fight on his side against Shennong/Yandi until they defeated him.[84] Then, after successfully leading the troops of the various local polities in a final battle against the unruly Chi You, he was honored as the Son of Heaven, thus replacing Shennong.[85] Whether or not the skills that allowed the Yellow Emperor to accomplish these exceptional deeds were extra-human, the *Records* clearly defines his investiture as political. It was not Heaven, which did not have any role in these foundational events, but the grateful local leaders who acknowledged the Yellow Emperor as their legitimate monarch.[86] Furthermore, the replacement of a tyrannical rule did not suffice to justify his royal authority. Once he was installed as the new ruler, he continued to engage in a series of magnanimous and groundbreaking acts, hastening to wherever his pacifying work was needed. He opened new paths, visited remote places, climbed impervious mountains, and chased away hordes of nomadic barbarians. After verifying the legitimacy of the various preexisting investitures of the nobles and their land allotments, he finally founded a capital at the foot of Mount Zhoulu 涿鹿. Even then he did not cease to go in search of further adventures.[87]

The emphasis on the Yellow Emperor's restlessness and proactive interpretation of his role is reminiscent of the campaigns Emperor Wu conducted across the country in order to fight the Xiongnu, carry out inspection travels (*xunshou*), fight private minting (and this might be echoed in the threat represented by Chi You), pursue tax evasion, and engage in various ritual activities. At the same time, this characterization also sharply contrasts with the more sedentary charismatic rulership embodied by Yao and Shun or suggested by the new official ceremonies eventually inaugurated under Emperor Cheng.

As already mentioned, the text underlines the Yellow Emperor's efforts to enforce political and cultural standards over very heterogeneous territories and peoples. However, as to the question of rituals, the Yellow Emperor portrayed at the beginning of the *Records* does not perform the *feng* and *shan* himself. After the world was again at peace, the traditional sacrifices to spirits, ghosts, mountains, and rivers, as well as the *feng* and *shan*, took place numerous times in the usual locations, as "religions uniformity or unity" did not seem to represent a priority or a concern. A further group of distinctive elements that bespeaks the ritual functions of the Yellow Emperor is represented by his usage of divination (by means of achillea stalks) for the promulgation of the calendar and the obtainment of the Precious Tripod (*bao ding* 寶鼎).[88] The *Records* narrates that following these actions, the sovereign received the auspicious omen of Earth that earned him the name of Yellow Emperor.[89] Finally, after discussing his wife and numerous descendants, the *Records* mentions the Yellow Emperor's death and place of burial on Mount Qiao 橋—he did not ascend to heaven or become an immortal.[90]

In light of the fact that Sima Qian shows the Yellow Emperor to be mortal, scholars have defined his biography of the ruler as the product of a process of historicization that is almost devoid of a symbolic, mythological function.⁹¹ Yet, if we interpret myth as "propaganda in narrative form," what we read in the "Basic Annals of the Five Sovereigns" can certainly be understood as a series of metaphors the historian employed to engage the ritual politics he describes in the second half of the "Book on the Feng and Shan." In particular, the reference to the Yellow Emperor's autonomous performance of divination and possession of the Precious Tripod, as we will see in detail below, must have resonated greatly with debates on the ritual and cosmic prerogatives of the ruler that were stirring Emperor Wu's court.⁹²

Telling Myths under Emperor Wu: Tripods, Alchemy, and Immortality as Political Metaphors

The Yellow Emperor and Emperor Wu's connection with the Precious Tripod represents the most compelling characterization of universal sovereignty expressed in the "Book on the *Feng* and *Shan*."⁹³ According to a myth reported in several textual variants, Yu the Great, founder of the Xia dynasty, had received nine tripods from the leaders of the peoples he had rescued from the flood.⁹⁴ These vessels, which symbolized dynastic legitimacy, were handed down through generation after generation, from ruler to ruler, all the way to the Zhou, until one of them supposedly disappeared in the Si 泗 River (in present-day Shandong) when the Qin destroyed the ancestral altars of the house of Shang during their ruthless advance.⁹⁵

At the time of Emperor Wu, there were expectations that the lost tripod would resurface to sanction the full restoration of imperial legitimacy, from Yu the Great to the Han. Shang bronzes were the centerpiece of aristocratic rituals involving communication with ancestral spirits. By the Han period, even though information about this dynasty was inaccurate and mainly ideological, bronze tripods still evoked the remote and hallowed origins of Chinese rulership. Simultaneously, in keeping with the cultural trends of the time, they acquired an important role within alchemic traditions, as the crucible in which the "raw" becomes "cooked" and the mixing of yin and yang can produce extraordinary transformations.⁹⁶

The first *fangshi* to entice a young Emperor Wu with fantastic tales in which the Yellow Emperor achieved immortality (by alchemic means) appeared at court around 132 BCE. According to Sima Qian, this was a certain Li Shaojun 李少君, who had no family and whose birthplace and age were unknown.⁹⁷ After being noticed in the capital for his extraordinary skills and knowledge, Li gained the attention of the Emperor by presenting himself as an expert in alimentary practices that augmented longevity.[98] In particular, the *fangshi* claimed exclusive knowledge of ritual techniques that involved the crucible of the alchemist, *zao* 竈, which, in a far-fetched fashion, he finally connected to the Yellow Emperor, a topic that apparently never ceased to delight the Son of Heaven:[99]

> Sacrifice to Zao, then the creatures[100] come. Once the creatures have arrived the powder of cinnabar can be transformed into yellow metal. With the yellow metal it is possible to make those tools to drink and eat which prolong life; once one has his life prolonged he can meet the immortals who dwell in the Penglai 蓬萊 islands in the middle of the sea. Having met them, it becomes possible to accomplish *feng* and *shan* and therefore not to die. The Yellow Emperor realized this.[101]

In order to strengthen his fabulous tale, Li Shaojun added that he had once personally encountered the immortal master An Qi 安期 in Penglai, where he had witnessed his prodigious deeds. Evidently impressed with these stories, Emperor Wu dispatched some *fangshi* to look for An Qi in Penglai. Meanwhile he dedicated himself to the use of the crucible in the way he had been instructed. Dryly, the *Records* informs the reader that after some time, Li Shaojun fell ill and died. But the Son of Heaven preferred to believe that Li had simply disappeared after becoming an immortal and continued to pursue people who could connect him with the Penglai immortals. Always without drawing explicit conclusions, the text reports that no one returned from these maritime expeditions, and that the flux of *fangshi* from Qi and Yan who came to court to tell stories about extraordinary beings (*shen*) became even more intense.

In the summer of 113 BCE, a shamaness from Fenyin 汾陰 accidentally unearthed a voluminous *ding* tripod while performing sacrifices for Houtu in the region of Wei 魏.[102] Whether it was the Yellow Emperor's Precious Tripod mentioned in the first of the Basic Annals, or the one from Yu's original set of nine that had disappeared in connection with the Qin conquest, the uncertainty of the attribution spurred an interesting discussion at court. The people in charge of rituals (probably Classicists, *ru*, as Sima Qian describes them citing the *Odes*) promptly explained the event in light of the contemporary sighting of yellow vapors and the recent capture of a deer, which in turn might have reminded everyone of the *lin* unicorn that had announced the age-changing death of Confucius.

According to the courtiers, the time was ripe to carry out grand state rituals. But the harvest had been poor that year, and the emperor, at least for once, did not seem inclined to interpret the find as an auspicious omen. Thus, the courtiers trotted out a myth in which the Yellow Emperor and the tripods became a metaphor of the purported function of monarchs in mediating between men and cosmic forces. Their story had all the elements needed to satisfy Emperor Wu's notoriously eccentric preoccupations, but they were set in a completely different context. In the courtiers' interpretation, the precious vessel did not entail extraordinary powers and immortality, but moral restraint and long life. This story obviously does not correspond to the account about the tripod in the Basic Annals. Evidently there was more at stake than the interpretation of an ancient myth:

> They say that under Taidi 泰帝 [Fuxi 伏羲][103] there flourished (*xing* 興) just one extraordinary (*shen* 神) tripod, "one" meaning "the whole": the union of Heaven, Earth, and all creatures was perfect. The Yellow Emperor made (*zuo* 作) three tripods, representing Heaven, Earth, and Man. Yu received (*shou* 收) the metal from the Nine Shepherds and cast the Nine Tripods. All used them to prepare the victims offered to the lords of high (*shangdi* 上帝),[104] spirits and ghosts. The tripods appeared in concomitance with a Sage Ruler (*sheng* 聖) and were handed down to the Xia and then to the Shang. But, as the virtue of the Zhou became perverted and the Altar of the Soil of Song was lost, the tripods fell in the water and disappeared. The temple hymn in the *Books of Odes* reads: From hall to gatehouse, from ram to bull, he moves with great cauldrons and small, neither loud nor prideful. Blesses shall he be with long life![105]

This passage introduces Taidi/Fuxi, the "culture bearer" who predated the beginning of the history in the *Records* and was associated with the union between man and woman, fishing, trapping, and the Eight Trigrams. In essence, the passage states that in that remote age, harmony reigned throughout the entire cosmos, for the realms of existence were not yet separated. Hence, humans did not need to create the tripods, which took shape as spontaneous, unprovoked phenomena. With the account about the Yellow Emperor, the text instead seems to describe a transition from a natural to a cultural phase, from primeval unity to separation. The Yellow Emperor had to "make" (*zuo* 作)—manufacture—the ritual tools that allow him to transcend his separation from the world of the spirits.[106] At this stage, because of the intervention of a new factor, perhaps human agency itself, the unity and the harmony of the universe are no longer unquestioned; they must be guaranteed and, in a sense, reestablished, through a ritual, a demiurgic process carried out with the tripods.

After this fall from primeval grace, the Yellow Emperor cast three tripods representing Heaven, Earth, and Man, so that he could connect with the three different realms. The myth justifies his sovereignty on account of his ability to create, mediate, and differentiate. His rule definitely embodies an active kind of kingship. By contrast, Yu the Great merely received (*shou* 收) the metal for his tripods from the Nine Regions of the empire. He had been the hero who saved humankind from the flood, but this act itself did not suffice to grant him the right to govern. His supreme and charismatic power and authority derived, as in the case of Yellow Emperor, from his function of connecting the three realms, but it nevertheless depended upon the acquiescence and cooperation of the leaders of the polities under his aegis—in other words, upon political sagacity and compromise.

In their mythological synthesis, the ritual experts at court described the Yellow Emperor as a worthy embodiment of a ritual conception of rulership (i.e., one characterized by its active mediating function among different existential realms), but one that was nonetheless inferior to the model embodied by the founder of the Xia. In presenting Yu as the champion of the last stage, they were implicitly propounding a form of imperial rule that was culturally and politically less active.[107] And since Emperor Wu was the intended recipient of their lesson, these ritual experts, regardless of the political interests they might have voiced, were probably also commenting on the thorny relationship between central authority and regional centers of power.

In those years, as the "Book on the Balanced Standard" ("Ping zhun shu" 平準書) attests, the imperial government was engaged in various attempts to intervene locally throughout the country in order to collect funding for the works of canalization, lavish ceremonies, and especially the numerous military campaigns against the unruly Xiongnu. These involved the expensive reconstruction of roads, bridges, and buildings, especially those which were to host public rituals.[108] Metal, which was, as seen in the passage cited above, fundamental for the production of ritual objects, weapons, and coins, constituted the focus of growing tension between center and periphery. The imperial administration was struggling to establish a uniform system of currency. Taxation remained extremely problematic, while the economic and social situation seemed even more urgent.[109] Emperor Wu had been fighting a violent and extensive war against illegal mints, producers of counterfeit coins, embezzlers, and tax evasion.¹¹⁰ According to the *Records*, the result of these efforts was that,

> [p]ractically every family of middling means or over found itself under accusation . . . The wealth confiscated from the people as a result of investigations was calculated in the billions of cash, with male and female slaves numbering in the thousands . . . All the merchants of middling or better means were ruined and the people, deciding that they had better indulge in tasty food and fine clothing while they still had the opportunity, made no effort to lay away any wealth for the future. The government officials for their part found themselves with more and more funds at their disposal, due to the salt and iron monopolies and the confiscations of wealth.¹¹¹

Of course, it is not possible to directly translate the passage about the tripods and the three ancient sovereigns into economic terms. Yet it cannot be denied that discourses on political authority, metal, spirits, and warfare were connected in the Chinese textual tradition.¹¹² In such an economic climate, the passage would have resonated deeply with Sima Qian's contemporaries. The fact that it depicted the local lords willingly and peacefully providing Yu the Great with the metal for his ritual paraphernalia, and that it represented the Yellow Emperor (to whom Emperor Wu wished to be likened) as independently creating his tripods, might have represented a powerful metaphor—especially as Sima Qian used the same character (*zhu* 鑄) for both tripod-casting in the case of Yu and coin-minting in the "Book on the Balanced Standard."

These themes appeared together in an earlier version of the story of the Nine Tripods recounted in the *Zuozhuan* 左傳 commentary of the *Spring and Autumns Annals*—a rendition that Wang Chong would attack from a "rationalistic" point of view in his *Lun Heng*. Perusing the *Zuozhuan*'s account, with which the ritual experts at Emperor Wu's court were likely familiar, allows for the assessment of the evolution of debates concerning the prerogatives of rulers in regard to the world of spirits and ghosts and the relationship between center and periphery in the period of strife preceding the unification of the Central States.¹¹³ The critique in the *Lun Heng* can on the other hand provide an interesting appraisal of how the question of *shen* could be treated at the beginning of the Eastern Han.

In the *Spring and Autumn* entry for 605 BCE (Duke Xuan 宣, Third Year, Spring), the Zhou, whose authority was largely symbolic at the time, sent an envoy to the South. They feared that the state of Chu, because of its recent victory against a barbaric tribe, might feel confident enough to challenge Zhou's waning power. The ruler of Chu expressed his ambition by doubting the actual size of the Zhou tripods, as though the vessels, by becoming smaller, were announcing the imminent shift of the Mandate. This is the elaborate rebuttal of the Zhou envoy:

> [Authority] depends on charismatic virtue (*de* 德) not on [the size of] the tripods. In the past, just when Xia possessed virtue, pictures of wondrous things (*wu* 物) were sent from afar, and the leaders of the Nine Provinces submitted metal, so that tripod cauldrons were cast with representations of wondrous things. The hundred things were therewith completely set forth, and the people thus knew the spirits and the evil things. That was why when the people entered marshes, mountains, and forests they could not meet what would harm them, nor would they encounter evil spirits. Thus they could harmonize with those above and below them and receive Heaven's favor. The last Xia king, Jie 桀, possessed dimmed virtue, and the tripods were moved to the house of Shang, to remain there for six hundred years. The last Shang king, Zhou 纣, was tyrannical and the tripods were moved to the house of Zhou. When virtue is bright and resplendent, the tripods, though small, grow weighty. When virtue is distorted, the tripods, though big, are light. . . . Although the Zhou virtue is in decline, the Mandate of Heaven has not changed. The question whether the[ir?] tripod[s] are weighty or not may not be asked yet.[114]

According to commentators of the late Warring States period, then, direct contact with the spirits characterized an earlier, remote, form of rulership. At such a stage, representations of animals still played a fundamental role (which recalls the function of totems and shamans in several civilizations) in connecting men with the realm of the invisible.[115] In subsequent and purportedly more sophisticated ages, tripods no longer served an active religious function. These metal objects merely symbolized—but did not make—the moral superiority of a given dynasty, no matter its strength. Whereas the story told at Emperor Wu's court promoted a notion of rulership that in acknowledging the investiture of local powers was less autocratic, the one outlined by the Zhou envoy seemed to state that authority must lie in moral excellence, even though the means to actually enforce it might be momentarily lacking. In sum, the Nine Tripods in the *Zuozhuan* and in the *Records* constituted a pretext to discuss the nature of imperial authority, which could be interpreted either as active and autocratic or as more receptive and collegial.

By contrast, Wang Chong's attack concentrates on the connection between supernatural qualities and charisma, between the implied sagehood of a monarch and the realm of *shen*. His critique offers evidence that, at the time, many thought that some particular paraphernalia, such as the tripods, might carry an intrinsic power by virtue of their association with the sage kings of the hallowed past:

> The tribute metal from distant places was deemed to be very beautiful, and therefore it was cast into tripods, on which all sorts of curious objects were depicted. How could this have the effect that people in forests or by lakes did not meet with specters, and could ward off the evil influence of spirits? [The tripods] cannot ward off evil influences. [. . .] There is a popular tradition that the tripods of Zhou boiled of themselves without fire,[116] and that things could be taken out of them which had not been put in. This is a popular exaggeration. The exaggerated statements preserved in the books of the Classicists (*ru* 儒), turned the ordinary emptiness of the Nine Tripods into something extra-human (*shen* 神) . . . If as a tribute from distant lands they were *shen*, why should things from distant places be more *shen*? Were they so because Yu cast them? Yu was a True Sage (*sheng* 聖) but could not do anything extra-human (*shen*). A True Sage, physically, cannot do anything extra-human (*shen*). How could the vessels he cast be extra-human?[117]

Wang Chong's tirade shows that Han popular culture appropriated myths from the classical traditions and that many believed that sovereignty not only entailed moral superiority but also extra-human powers. The thinker's attack seems directed against both trivial superstitious attitudes and more sophisticated theories, such as those associated with Dong Zhongshu.

Returning to Sima Qian's interpretation, Emperor Wu's exploitation of the aura of the tripods did not represent a way to conceptualize and legitimate a particular conception of rulership, but betrayed a specific interest in the intrinsic potential of the vessels, as if they might grant him an extraordinary journey towards immortality. Still, the Grand Historian does not, as Wang Chong might, engage in a philosophical confutation of the extraordinary powers associated with the tripods. By presenting empirical evidence—even if in his typically indirect way—the historian simply refutes all the fabulous claims about the resurfaced tripod.

Before his account of the discovery of the tripod in the "Book on the *Feng* and *Shan*," Sima Qian had already told of a certain Xinyuan Ping 新垣平, a *fangshi* who in 163 BCE had appeared at court trying to exert his influence on Emperor Wen (180–157 BCE), Emperor Wu's grandfather. Xinyuan Ping claimed that if the Son of Heaven immediately changed ritual protocols and celebrated the beginning of a new age, the lost tripod of the Zhou would resurface in Fenyin and finally sanction the Han empire's full legitimacy.[118] This was that very same Fenyin from which, fifty years later, a shamaness would come claiming to have casually "discovered" the vessel that was offered to Emperor Wu.

Sima Qian reports that Emperor Wen eventually received memorials denouncing Xinyuan's talk of *qi* vapors and *shen* as fraudulent. Hence, after having the *fangshi* swiftly executed, the *Records* reports, Emperor Wen abandoned any plans concerning new beginnings, renewal of protocols, and *shen*.[119] Thus, if Sima Qian knew of Xinyuan Ping as a notorious charlatan and trickster, he was likely insinuating that the tripod that eventually resurfaced in Fenyin might well had been buried by the same *fangshi* half a century earlier in order to manufacture a felicitous omen. Significantly, the "Book on the *Feng* and *Shan*," after a lofty citation from the *Odes*, immediately relates the failures of all the people the emperor had sent in search of the Penglai islands.[120] Again, it is clear that for Sima Qian the realm of spirits did not matter in itself, but only insofar as individuals or groups were trying to exploit it for political advantage.

Fangshi, as always, continued to come in great numbers to the capital. In the fall of 113 BCE, a certain Gongsun Qing 公孫卿 from Qi (who shared the Yellow Emperor's family name), appeared at court and garnered attention with stories about alchemy and the Yellow Emperor's tripod that seemed perfectly tailored to enthuse Emperor Wu.[121] First of all, the *fangshi* noted that in that very year in which the vessel had been found, the first day of the lunar month (*xinsi* 辛巳) corresponded with the winter solstice. This was the same cosmic conjunction that had occurred at the time of the apotheosis of Yellow Emperor. Hence, the *fangshi* announced, a new cycle was starting. To further buttress his words, Gongsun claimed to possess a document which stated that those circumstances also coincided with the period in which the Yellow Emperor had obtained the tripod and the divine calculations (*shence* 神策).¹²² After a courtier openly expressed doubt about the *fangshi*'s honesty, Gongsun Qing exploited another of the weaknesses of the Emperor and had one of his female favorites present him with a letter. Its intriguing content compelled the Son of Heaven to summon the *fangshi* and question him personally:

> I received this letter from Master Shen 申 but he is dead . . . Master Shen was a man of Qi. He met with Master Anqi 安期, who had received the oral teachings of the Yellow Emperor. He did not have any written text but only a tripod with this inscription: "The rise of the Han corresponds with the times of the Yellow Emperor. The True Sage of the Han will be either a son or a grandson or a great-grandson of Gaozu. A tripod will surface and it will be possible to meet with the *shen* and to perform the *feng* and *shan*. Of all the seventy-two rulers who attempted the *feng* and *shan*, only the Yellow Emperor was able to climb Mount Tai and perform the *feng*." The ruler of the Han who will perform this will become an immortal and ascend to Heaven!"¹²³

Gonsun Qing then told of how the Yellow Emperor traveled around the country, making sure to conquer all the lands where the Five Peaks were situated and where *shen* were worshipped. The *fangshi* defined warfare and the pursuit of immortality as the two most important activities of the Yellow Emperor. Gongsun made it clear that this ancient sovereign was always ready to behead all those who denied the existence of spirits and ghosts.¹²⁴ Then he described the Yellow Emperor's ascension to heaven while indirectly justifying the extant cult of his tomb—people were merely worshipping some items the mythical sovereign had left behind during his glorious journey:

> The Yellow Emperor collected copper from Mount Shou 首 and had it melted and cast into a cauldron at the foot of Mount Jing 荊. When the cauldron was completed, a dragon with whiskers hanging from its chin came down from the sky to fetch him. The Yellow Emperor mounted the dragon's back, followed by his ministers and palace ladies, making a company of over seventy persons . . . The lesser ministers, unable to mount the dragon

clung to its whiskers until the whiskers came out and fell to the ground, along with the bow of the Yellow Emperor. The common people gazed up into the sky until the Yellow Emperor had reached heaven and then they clasped the whiskers and the bow and began to wail.[125]

Sima Qian had already stated that these stories did not derive from the *Classics*; thus, they were untrustworthy. As the narration of the "Book on the *Feng* and *Shan*" approaches the year 110 BCE, the historic time of the celebration of the special sacrifices, the Son of Heaven is increasingly represented as being confused amid the courtiers and outsiders scrambling to gain his favor. As the Grand Historian remarks, the various recommendations made by *fangshi* and Classicists about the *feng* and *shan* sacrifices contradicted one another, and their instructions sounded absurd and impossible to follow.[126]

Conclusion: The *Feng* and *Shan* as a Grand Misunderstanding

Sightings of the prodigious phenomena that would justify the celebration of the *feng* and *shan*, the *Records* notes, were constantly reported at court for two decades during Wu's reign. In 122 BCE, after sacrificing at Yong, the emperor captured a beast that had only one horn.[127] Some courtiers persuaded him that his ritual performance had been so thorough that the Five Sovereigns were rewarding him with the auspicious omen of the *lin* 麟, a mythical unicorn-like animal. The appearance of a true *lin*, in Confucius's biography in the *Records*, had announced the imminent death of the Master and the beginning of a dark age.[128] According to the "Book on the *Feng* and *Shan*" instead, the Qi minister Guan Zhong had included the *lin* in the list of those extremely rare portents that anticipated the performance of the *feng* and *shan* during the age of the Yellow Emperor.[129]

As expected, the courtiers persuaded Emperor Wu to follow the second interpretation. Extraordinary celebrations ensued.[130] Since the performance of the *feng* and *shan* was (wrongly) judged imminent at that point, the King of Jibei 濟北 donated to the Son of Heaven Mount Tai and the surrounding commanderies he had to cross for the ritual processions. In this way, each of the Five Peaks that determined ancient China's ritual circuits finally came under the emperor's direct control. But unfortunately for him, of all the omens required for the *feng* and *shan* sacrifices that Guan Zhong had mentioned, the spontaneous appearance of spirits had not yet occurred. For this reason, the text reports, in the years following the capture of the "*lin*," the emperor continued pursuing *fangshi* who were allegedly capable of conjuring all kind of creatures. Although all the attempts failed, when the Precious Tripod was unearthed in 113 BCE—a hoax, according to Sima Qian—and Gongsun Qing hailed it as the Yellow Emperor's tripod, the Son of Heaven seemed finally persuaded of the feasibility of *feng* and *shan*.[131] Since the proper modalities and paraphernalia concerning their performance were clear to no one, Wu let courtiers and *fangshi* discuss and settle the issue. Throughout the *Records*, Sima Qian often chastises the Classicists for being needlessly fussy. As he might have expected in this circumstance, they failed to reach an agreement, for none of the actions and vessels they had considered seemed to satisfy the (hardly exhaustive) criteria laid out in the *Odes* and the *Documents*. The already impatient Emperor Wu could not wait further and decided to go forward without their advice.[132]

Before, during, and immediately after the performance the *feng* and *shan*, the *Records* reports, the emperor stopped several times along the way, either to attend cults that had been previously established by Qi or Qin or because he was confident *shen* were about to appear—to such an extent that, Sima Qian says, people began to mock the Son of Heaven by reporting the sighting of spirits, gigantic creatures, mysterious old men, and disparate evidence of extra-human presence.[133]

On May 17, 110 BCE, the emperor finally embarked upon the sacrifices. The *feng* was carried out on Mount Liangfu. As anticipated above, the Son of Heaven performed the ritual alone with a young charioteer (who died some days later under unclear circumstances).[134] The ritual consisted of raising the *feng* mound and burying in it a jade tablet that was inscribed with a secret message.[135] The *shan* was celebrated the following day, on May 18, on Mount Suran 肅然, on the northwestern foothill of Mount Tai. Whereas the *feng* had been immediately preceded by the worship of Taiyi, the *shan* was explicitly carried out by following the ritual for the cult of Houtu, which involved music, dances, and the donning of yellow clothes. Unlike the First Emperor Qin, whose performance had been allegedly hampered by a storm, Emperor Wu benefited from clement weather. Because a yellow glow was observed above the *feng* mound at dawn the following day, the sacrifices were declared a success. Through the imperial secretary, the Son of Heaven issued this edict:

I, in my humble and insignificant person, have been accorded the position of highest honor. Constantly I tremble with fear that I shall not be worthy of it, for my virtue is poor and slight and I have no understanding of ritual (*li* 禮) and music. When I performed the sacrifice to Taiyi, something that looked like a beam of light was seen faintly from afar. I was filled with awe at this strange phenomenon and would have proceeded no further, but I did not dare to halt. Thus I later ascended Mount Tai to perform the *feng* sacrifice, journeyed to Liangfu and later performed the *shan* sacrifice on Mount Suran, thus renewing myself. . . .[136]

Then, in order to celebrate the imminent announcement of a new beginning, the emperor bestowed on the common people donations of oxen and wine and granted amnesty and corvée exemptions to all the households whose lands he had passed through during the performance. A further edict was issued:

In ancient times the Son of Heaven journeyed about on an inspection tour (*xunshou* 巡狩) once every five years, and at that time he performed sacrifices to Mount Tai. The local lords who came to pay court to him constructed their lodgings there. Let an order be given to the local lords to build their own lodges at the foot of Mount Tai.[137]

Despite the humble and respectful tone, this official document seems to allude to a new model of territorial control while hinting at the tension between the center peripheries. In light of all the evidence analyzed thus far, it is likely that the inspection tours and ritual activities the emperor was carrying out all over the country might have interfered with local interests. Consequently, the decision to displace regional lords and dole out generous donations could have represented a measure to ingratiate the common people while separating them from their local leaders.

The *Records* does not provide any commentary on the imperial edicts cited above. But in covering the years following 110 BCE, its narrative style hardly conceals skepticism and sarcasm. The text describes the emperor as increasingly losing confidence that the successful performance of the *feng* and *shan* would grant the achievement of immortality. The Son of Heaven became so hopeless that he ultimately resumed his unsuccessful quest for spirits, *fangshi*, and immortals. At the peak of his desperation, the *Records* reports, he resorted to inviting shamans from the vanquished kingdom of Nanyue to live in the imperial park, as he had heard that they could conjure immortal ghosts.[138] Ironically, it is after the official promulgation of the Grand Beginning in 104 BCE that Sima Qian first directly reports an event that may have signaled Heaven's response to a human action—a swarm of locusts.[139]

Thus, while the Classicists accepted the need to confront Emperor Wu and strove to condition his vision of sovereignty by providing alternative versions of the mythological traditions on which he intended to base his sacrifices, Sima Qian, consistently with Confucius's take on spirits and ghosts, maintained high ground and laconically dismissed all discussions that ventured beyond the human realm. As for Emperor Wu, as superstitious and clueless he might have been, we cannot exclude the possibility that he actually conceived of a different model of sovereignty—one that he did not mean to advertise through erudite disquisitions about ancient texts and traditions. In the "Book on the *Feng* and *Shan*," he does not engage the Classicists' rhetorical attacks. The *Records*, instead of assessing the emperor's personal opinion, constantly depicts him as distracted by his obsessions with immortality. However, if we look at the sacrifices Wu conducted without the advice of the Classicists, and at the literature produced in his honor, his ritual vision clearly emerges as a forceful propagandistic counterpoint to his political and economic strategies.

5

Place and Ritual

From *Templum* to Text

> It was already dawn when he said, "Sire, at this point I have told you of all the cities I know." "One is left, about which you never talk." Marco hung his head. "Venice," said the Khan. Marco smiled, "What else did you want me talk about?" The Emperor did not flinch. "Still, I never heard you mention her name." And Polo replied: "Every time I describe a city, I'm saying something about Venice."
>
> —Italo Calvino, *Le città invisibili* (*Invisible Cities*)[1]

> Map is not Territory.
>
> —Jonathan Z. Smith[2]

Introduction: The Monumentality of Absence

The job of historians begins where the work of army generals ends. One of the traditional goals of the historian has been to justify post-conquest unified rule of a territory by assuring new and old aristocracies of the end of uncertainty and a return to a period of prosperity and stability. The *Records* does not fit this mold. Sima Qian suggests that Emperor Wu was uninterested in consolidating the authority of the Han dynasty by emphasizing the continuity of his tenure with exemplary models from the past. If the *Records* are to be believed, Wu wanted to get *out* of politics rather than leave his mark on it, and he entertained what could best be described as escapist delusions: he was obsessed with leaving his earthly possessions and relations behind and reaching the lands of the immortals by adhering to the instructions of the (proverbially unreliable) *fangshi*. According to the

Records, the *fangshi* took advantage of Wu's gullibility and conditioned his rule by feeding him fanciful stories about ancient sovereigns that had nothing to do with the exemplary historical precedents (i.e., the Zhou) illustrated in the *Classics*. Wu seemed tragically incapable of presenting himself as the moral center of the empire.

As I have shown, the *Records* caricaturizes Wu in part because of Sima Qian's personal animosity toward him, partly because, between the various factions of *fangshi* and Classicists at court he was feeling professionally frustrated and intellectually isolated. However, before looking at Wu's official ceremonies, it is necessary to take into account the peculiar use (from a Western point of view) by the Qin and the Han of visible signs of political and economic power. The available evidence compels us to conclude that the symbolic representation of the state's control over the land and its resources in ancient China did not take place thorough celebratory architectural projects or entail a specific conception of public space. Rather, being the rulers and the ruled, the center and the periphery separated, we see a sovereign such as Wu traveling around the capital and across the area while trying to establish a direct relationship with disparate communities and cultural traditions.

Empires from the Fertile Crescent to the Western Mediterranean left behind impressive monuments that testify to the visions, achievements, and delusions of their elites, but also to the need to make their prerogatives and claims universally acknowledged. Religious festivals and public celebrations were meant to cement consensus among different social strata. The display of wealth and status on these occasions was instrumental in celebrating the administrative and political effectiveness of the ruling groups. It also demonstrated that the elites cared for the common good, as they shared material resources and upheld traditions, interests, and values cherished by everyone. Regardless of the sincerity of such benevolence, the agency of the people, too, had to be accounted for and acknowledged. In Rome, the crowds became an important political agent rather early. Starting with the violent reaction of the public to the land reforms of the Gracchi in the second half of the second century BCE, historical sources focus increasingly on the voice of the people as an important feature of political debates and negotiations of power.[3] Political leaders would try to sway, appease, ride, heed, or defy the masses, but in any case could not ignore them. Political change, as the evolution of the Republican institutions attests, was usually the result of compromises among different constituencies of Rome.[4]

In the case of the Qin and the Han, however, the voice of the common people is somewhat harder to hear. Most of the material evidence for the early imperial period comes from aristocratic burials or mausoleums, whose contents were available to a restricted number of people, often only for a short period of time—or perhaps forever, but only to the spirits.[5] Unless future archaeological finds come along to tell us a different story, it seems safe to conclude that political power in China had vastly different ways of presenting itself, negotiating its prerogatives, and occupying shared spaces than it did in Rome.

We have seen how the *Records* considers state rituals under Emperor Wu to be aimed at fulfilling the sovereign's desire to become an immortal, a quest that did not seem to take into consideration the opinions of the public on this matter. Caesar's attempt at turning Rome into a monarchy involved the people's acknowledgment of his divine prerogatives (and his willingness to publicly accept the insignia of his superior condition). Augustus successfully re-elaborated traditional themes with the intent of advertising the new regime as a revitalization of the values of the Republican period. In doing so, he was always aware of his public persona. By contrast, the legitimization of power under Emperor Wu apparently took place mainly in the presence of select elites.[6] His autocratic rule seems not to have been backed by an extensive propagandistic plan that included monumental buildings and celebratory literature, as was the custom with Roman rulers. If the ideas about the secretive ways of effective rulership expressed in the *Han Feizi* 韓非子 (traditionally attributed to Master Han Fei, ca. 280–233 BCE), and exemplified by First Emperor of the Qin were out of fashion, loftiness, ineffability, mystery, inaccessibility, or remoteness characterized models of monarchy that envisioned the sovereign as the embodiment of eternal cosmic forces, as expressed in the cultural traditions that produced the *Huainanzi* and the *Chunqiu fanlu*.[7]

As for the actual Han court, with the exception of courtiers and high dignitaries, no one was permitted to set eyes on the Son of Heaven. Commoners who lived in the capital would never see the person of the sovereign with their own eyes. And expressions of the popular imagination in non-elite literature suggest that local spirits and ghosts were believed to be more accessible than the emperors or high-level officials—so much so that later conceptions of the afterlife were envisioned as a complex institutional system organized by different levels of administrators and functionaries: the so-called "bureaucratic metaphor."[8] Emperor Wu, reigning before the

Classicists established a "secular" notion of rulership, was not afraid to show his interest in breaking the barriers between the humans and the spirits or in participating in popular cults. Whereas the *Records* chastises the superstitious inclinations of the sovereign, Tang poetry, and "apocryphal" documents such as the *Secret History of Emperor Wu of the Han* (*Han Wudi neijzhuan* 漢武帝內傳) romanticize his fondness for extraordinary experiences. These sources expressed longing for the good old times of Emperor Wu—when, they fancied, even the Son of Heaven could establish a personal relationship with powerful and popular spirits.[9]

Rather than try to make sense of the ambiguity of Emperor Wu's relationship with the extra-human beings, I would like to suggest that his apparent ritual inconsistency is best considered either as a conscious decision that allowed him to address different publics and social groups, or as Wu's adherence to a worldview that did not conceptualize the realm of spirits and ghosts in systemic or unitary terms. We should be aware that, in formalizing his relationship with spirits and ghosts, Wu was not compelled to subsume his behavior under some unitary conception of the sacred. Such a monotheistic notion of "religion," which Abrahamic traditions considered ideal, would have been entirely foreign to him. Furthermore, while the question of coherence is generally relevant in the analysis of diachronic narratives, it is far less important at the ritual level, since ceremonial actions are customarily conceived as interruptions of linear, historical time and breaches into an a-historical foundational dimension where contradictions and conflicts are justified in cosmological terms.

The previous chapters focused on the categories of *li* and *si* as two different and coexisting attitudes toward the extra-human. They also problematized teleological assumptions about narratives of empire formation, and reconstructed literary/mythological debates on the justification of the Han empire in time and history vis-à-vis its relationship with past dynasties and political models. The present chapter focuses on space. On the one hand it concentrates on Han "non-official" literature and material evidence in order to overcome Sima Qian's dismissive attitude. On the other hand, it compares specific "rituals of place" in Rome and Han China and redefines Emperor Wu's ceremonies as a propagandistic strategy intended to validate his rulership in terms of centralized control over different territories. In other words, whereas the study of myths allowed us to explore Han ideas about the legitimacy of the dynasty in time, vis-à-vis its historical models, the analysis of rituals, and especially rituals of space, helps us understand how Emperor Wu justified the horizontal extension of his empire, and the principles according to which his authority was supposed to override that of local leaders belonging to different lineages.

In the background of Han disputes on cultural models and rituals was the tension between the central government and the marquises. Local lords had been a thorn in the emperors' side ever since the founding of the Han, and their discontent came to a boiling point with the Rebellion of the Seven Kingdoms (or States) in 154 BCE. Although past and recent historiography has tended to interpret the defeat of the anti-Han coalition as a consequence of the reestablishment of central authority, I argue that Sima Qian—as well as his sovereign—did not consider the menace presented by the local leaders to have been averted for good. After the rebellion, the *guo* were still strong enough to force Wu's father, Emperor Jing, to execute the minister who had crafted harsher centralizing policies, and to desist from exerting a more direct control on the periphery. When Emperor Wu succeeded to the throne, it was immediately clear that his government intended to reestablish the authority of the Son of Heaven as independent and uncompromising. I argue that the sovereign tried to counter interests that would be backed by the Classicists, the most vocal opponents of centralization, by promoting certain mythological models and rituals. His interest in the establishment of new official ceremonies based on "apocryphal" sources, which implied a more active role for the emperor, was an integral part of this struggle for power. Similarly, Wu's personal involvement in popular cults, either by attending them *in situ*, or by relocating or reproducing them in the imperial park (which his court poet imagined as a microcosm representing his whole reign), was consistent with his plan to seek political allies outside the court.

A cross-analysis of historical, literary, and archaeological documents allows us to reconstruct Emperor Wu's new rituals as a vehicle for promoting the idea of the Son of Heaven as the agent of cosmic order and the creator (and destroyer) of earthly boundaries. His ceremonies metaphorically justified the necessity of a tighter administrative and fiscal grip on local centers of power and production. Evidence suggests that Emperor Wu's mobility and his interest in local forms of worship were part of his plan to engage the people directly, not as an abstract multitude but as discrete groups of individuals, and that in this way he hoped to redirect the allegiance of local communities from local leaders to himself. In this light, Wu's unabashed interest in seeking out self-declared experts in alchemy, immortality, spirits, and ghosts (i.e., the *fangshi*), can be interpreted as a disguised intention to challenge the influence of the Classicists by filling the court with people who did not share Confucius's political, social, and moral vision.

Since the Classicists eventually prevailed, their historical approach would shape the way generations of scholars have interpreted the early imperial period. I believe the Classicists succeeded in making themselves indispensable by sacralizing the texts on which their authority was based as the exclusive (albeit interpretable) source of legitimacy. Following their rise to power, they promoted the role of the *Classics* to that of the "temple" in its etymological meaning of "separated, sacred space": the locus for the performance of rituals that create and validate shared values and political traditions, and by which even the Son of Heaven had to abide. Their motivations, I will argue, were political as well as cultural: Confucius's ideas about family and state expressed a specific vision of social order. Such a conception conceived legitimate political authority, literary status as deriving from landowning, was wary of the shift and unpredictable accumulation of wealth that could be produced by commercial and entrepreneurial activities and feared the creation of a national economy as a threat to traditional hierarchies.

Family, Land, and Conflict in the Early Han Empire

The tension between allegiance to the state and to one's family is a theme that runs throughout the *Records*. It tinges Sima Qian's narrative with a pessimistic outlook on the possibility of reconciling political duties and filial behavior, or in Master Han Fei's terms, the public (*gong* 公) and private (*si* 私) spheres.[10] The Han dynasty had been founded on a compromise between the efficient system of centralized bureaucratic control implemented by the Qin and the retention of a quasi-feudal quota reminiscent of the Zhou dynasty and its aristocratic system. Upon reaching the throne, Gaozu started to yield estates, titles, and relative autonomy to both members of the rebel alliance and his own family. If the Han's flexibility might have appeased potential rivals and prevented the dynasty from suffering an early collapse like the Qin, conflict between center and periphery never ceased.

In the "Chronological Table of the Feudal Lords," written after 104 BCE, Sima Qian contextualizes the evolution of power relations up to the Han:

> The Shang Dynasty and the ages before it are too far away to say much about, but we know that the Zhou Dynasty granted five degrees of noble title: duke [*gong* 公], marquise [*hou* 侯], earl [*bo* 伯], viscount [*zi* 子], and baron [*nan* 男]. When the Zhou

Dynasty enfeoffed Boqin in Lu and Kangshu in Wei it granted them each a territory of 400 square *li* (里). The size of their fiefs was unusually large because, as they were relatives of the royal family, it was proper to treat them with special deference and to reward them for their virtue . . . [T]he royal house lost its hold and the great states of the feudal lords rose to power. The Son of Heaven was too weak to be able to restore them to order. It was not that his virtue lacked purity, but that the circumstances rendered him hopeless. When the Han dynasty arose it awarded only two of the noble ranks [those of king and marquis]. In the latter years of his reign, Emperor Gaozu made an agreement with his followers that if anyone not of the Liu family should become a king, and anyone who had not distinguished himself in battle or attained high position should become a marquis, the empire should unite in punishing him.[11]

Thus, after reaffirming the point that historical continuity could not be restored, Sima Qian describes the measures taken by the Han to secure territorial unity and to simplify the hierarchical structures inherited from the previous eras. The text reports that Gaozu distributed nine of the ten states (*guo* 國) run by a king (*wang* 王) among his sons and brothers, while he enfeoffed more than one hundred of his eminent followers as marquises (*hou*).[12] The *guo* at their maximum extension occupied about two thirds of the empire's lands. They were strategically located at the northern and southern borders, as bastions against the barbarians. The lesser feudal lords were in charge of the area east of the northern mountain range:

> The largest territories consisted of as many as five or six provinces, comprising twenty or thirty cities, and their rulers set up various government offices and built palaces and towers in flagrant imitation of the Son of Heaven . . . The Han court, [In addition to the capital area,] retained possession of fifteen provinces in all, and even within this area various princesses and marquises received revenue from many of the cities. The reason for this was that, when the empire was first brought under control the emperor had few close relatives of his own clan and so set up a number of his sons by concubines in powerful positions in order that they might bring peace and order to the realm and provide aid and protection for the Son of Heaven. During the hundred

years after the founding of the Han, these various branches of the imperial family became increasingly estranged from the central court. Some among the feudal lords grew arrogant and extravagant, and were misled by the schemes of vicious ministers into evil and insubordination. The most powerful among them rebelled, while the lesser ones committed violations of the law, endangering their lives and bringing ruin among themselves and their estates. Later, the Son of Heaven, imitating the ways of antiquity, graciously allowed the feudal lords to share their blessings and to divide up their territories among their various sons and brothers.[13]

The last passage euphemistically refers to a policy attempted by Gaozu and subsequently emperors Jing and Wu (and more famously implemented by European sovereigns in the Middle Ages) of breaking down the vassals' territorial base in the hope of weakening them.

Even though the narration about the thorny relationship between the court and the vassals in the Chronological Tables continues with the Revolt of the Seven Kingdoms of 154 BCE, to have a more exhaustive insight of the author's point of view, as usual, we have to look elsewhere. In the *Records*' chapter titled "The Biography of the King of Wu [Liu] Pi" ("Wu Wang Pi liezhuan" 吳王濞列傳), we learn about the personal and political motivation that brought the king of Wu (215–154 BCE) to lead the revolt against the Han. Another chapter, "The Biographies of Yuan Ang and Chao Cuo" ("Yuan Ang Chao Cuo liezhuan" 袁盎晁錯), analyzes the careers of two important ministers who were in office under emperors Wen and Jing and who epitomized the unsolvable conundrum (lived by Sima Qian himself) of simultaneously serving the ruler with loyalty and the state with dedication and effectiveness.

Liu Pi had received the title of "King of Wu" for two reasons: as a reward for valorously fighting alongside his uncle, the Son of Heaven, against the rebellious king of Huainan in 196 BCE, and as compensation for the kingdom his father Liu Zhong 劉仲 (d. 193 BCE) had to relinquish to Emperor Gaozu, his elder brother, as punishment for fleeing in the middle of a raid of the Xiongnu.[14] As soon as Gaozu bestowed on Liu Pi the new title and estate, he realized the ambition and unruliness of his nephew. However, still feeling guilty for the demotion of his elder brother, he proceeded with the investiture. He hoped that his generosity would not cost him further losses in the future. In fact, Sima Qian reports:

> During the reign of Emperor Hui and Empress Lü, peace had just been restored to the empire and the feudal lords in the various provinces and kingdoms were busy putting their people in order. The territory of Wu possessed mountains rich in copper in the province of Yuzhang. Liu Pi set about inviting fugitives from all over the empire to come to his kingdom, minted cash from the copper ore in ever increasing quantities, and boiled the sea water to extract salt, so that he was able to dispense with the poll tax and his kingdom enjoyed great wealth and prosperity.[15]

The kingdom of Wu was subtracting resources as fundamental as copper and salt, issuing its own coinage and debasing the Han currency, extracting taxes autonomously, and sheltering fugitive criminals of all kinds in defiance of the empire's judicial authority. Yet, Sima Qian reports, Emperor Wen did not stray from his usual leniency, or more likely, did not feel confident enough to discipline such a powerful vassal. Complicating matters was an episode that occurred during the customary visit to the capital. A drunken fight between Liu Pi's son, the crown prince of Wu, and Emperor Wen's own heir, the future Emperor Jing, broke out over a chess game. The latter, enraged at his cousin's arrogance, violently hit him on the head with the heavy chessboard, killing him instantly. The victim's body was sent back to the kingdom of Wu for the proper burial. But at this point, Sima Qian reports, Liu Pi appeared more concerned with power dynamics within the imperial lineage than mourning the loss of his son. In receiving the coffin, he erupted: "The whole empire belongs to the same Liu clan! If one of our family dies in Chang'an, he should be buried in Chang'an. What reason is there to bring him here for the burial?"[16] The body was sent back to the capital and buried there, according to the father's wishes. Whether the king of Wu was unable to forgive the emperor and the prince or was already weaving treacherous plots, he stopped traveling to the court to pay homage to the Son of Heaven while continuing to run his kingdom even more autonomously. The narration continues with the Revolt of the Seven Kingdoms, but Sima Qian's stance on its causes and aftermath is more evident in the "Biography of Yuan and Chao Cuo," who served under emperors Wen and Jing, and whose careers epitomize two opposite ways of interpreting the role of officials in serving both the court and the empire.

Yuan Ang was a native of Chu.[17] Because he belonged to a powerful family that had broken Han laws, he and his relatives were relocated north of the capital, in the mausoleum town of Emperor Hui. Yuan Ang, a palace attendant, had no love of learning, but his compassionate attitude and spontaneous commitment to filial piety won him the respect of most high-ranking dignitaries, including Emperor Wen. He used his deep understanding of propriety to instruct everyone at court about how to behave according to one's position and avoid chances for friction. But he also showed flexibility. In those cases where his advice was requested after rules of etiquette had been already been breached, he helped the offender overcome his sense of guilt and limit the damage done.

Yuan Ang was extremely reliable as a courtier. In choosing his friends and allies, he especially prized filial piety and loyalty toward one's peers, so much so that he was always ready to turn a blind eye to minor faults or crimes. Above all, he strove to avert conflict. Because of these qualities, eventually the emperor appointed Yuan Ang as Prime Minister of Wu, under Liu Pi. Upon taking leave to occupy his new position, Yuan Ang's nephew informed him of irregularities in Wu's administration and rumors concerning a possible rebellion. However, instead of exposing Liu Pi's misdeeds, the nephew recommended that Yuan Ang limit himself and try and restrain the king only if he was clearly about to take action. Yuan Ang heeded the advice and succeeded in securing Liu Pi's appreciation too. After a very productive stint in Wu, the king allowed him to return to Chang'an.

When the revolt about which his nephew had warned him started, Yuan Ang, despite his closeness to Liu Pi, did not betray the Han. During the conflict Liu Pi tried to convince Yuan Ang to stand at his side as a general, but he refused. The king, furious, sent troops to imprison and kill him. Fortunately, among the soldiers guarding Yuan Ang was a man who had greatly benefited from his generosity and compassion. He recognized his savior and gratefully let him flee. Years later, Emperor Jing, who replaced his father in 157 BCE, aware of the minister's positive record, sent him back to the kingdom of Wu as master of the rites. Yuan Ang died in old age, murdered after several attempts by an assassin sent by a pretender to the throne he had opposed in the past.

Chao Cuo, whom we already encountered in chapter 2, embodies a different kind of valuable minister.[18] He eventually met disgrace for being too inflexible and outspoken, especially about the question of the independence of the *guo*.[19] The *Records* reports that Chao Cuo was proficient in the legalist teachings of Shang Yang and Shen Buhai, and courts officials held him in great esteem for his erudition. When Emperor Wen decided to recruit an expert in the *Documents*, he learned that the best was a certain Master Fu of Ji'nan, who, as an Erudite (*boshi*) at the Qin court, had managed to save a copy of this *Classic* from the notorious burning of the books ordered by the First Emperor. But Master Fu was now too old to come to the capital; when the emperor inquired about a brilliant court official who could be sent to study under Master Fu, Chao Cuo received the important recommendation of the Han official in charge of the rituals. Eventually, Chao Cuo became one of the foremost Han experts on the *Documents* and began to refer to them to propose various reforms. Early in his fast-rising career, he realized how states such as Wu were eroding the authority and the finances of the dynasty. After the death of Emperor Wen, a champion of leniency and laissez-faire, Chao Cuo convinced his successor to embark on a massive program of centralizing reforms, with the goal of enhancing productivity in all sectors and curbing the increasing power of the kingdoms. Liu Pi was the most conspicuous threat, and Chao Cuo, now Imperial Secretary, took various breaches of etiquette and misdemeanors committed by the king as a pretext to divide up and reduce the lands in his possession, then extended this treatment to all *guo*.

Chao Cuo suspected that the reason an astute man such as Yuan Ang had been silent about the possible menace of Wu, despite his knowledge of Liu Pi, must have been corruption. Hence he tried to indict and disgrace Yuan Ang, an official who was very popular and whom everyone loved. Contrary to his expectations, this attempt made Chao Cuo's position even more precarious. When it became clear that his intransigence was pushing the country into a costly civil war that the dynasty could easily lose, even his old father begged him to soften his attitude and seek compromise lest he bring ruin to the entire family.

Chao Cuo was not persuaded. His inflexibility and stubbornness had secured him the respect of all but the friendship of none. Isolated as he was, his rival Yuan Ang could approach the Son of Heaven while the revolt was in full swing and easily convince him that Chao Cuo's measures were the main cause of the disorders. Hence he recommended getting rid of him as the most efficient way to immediately appease the rebels and end the war. Emperor Jing obliged and had Chao Cuo's body severed at the waist, which was the most tragically spectacular of the ancient punishments.

Despite this sacrifice, Wu and the allied kingdoms did not retreat. Even though it is customarily held that the defeat of the rebels strengthened the authority of the central government, Sima Qian clarifies again that peace was achieved only because the dynasty had decided to not interfere in the kingdoms' affairs.[20] The *Records* further reports that, years later, another wise official confronted Emperor Jing, commenting that Chao Cuo's execution had not only failed to end the revolt, but had emboldened the kingdoms, while also making all responsible ministers wary of speaking up their minds in earnest. The Son of Heaven candidly admitted that he regretted that decision.

The historian's remarks at end of the chapter once again emphasize timeliness, as even virtue and competence at their best cannot prevail if the circumstances are not suitable. With the end of Emperor Wen's reign, Yuan Ang's outstanding social and diplomatic skills were no longer in demand. Unfortunately for Chao Cuo, he implemented his farsighted reforms when the central government was not strong enough to resist armed opposition. According to the *Records*, Yuan Ang represented an approach to politics based on personal relationships and partiality aimed at serving the common good that was, perhaps, too idealistic. Chao Cuo believed as well that his reforms would have benefited the state, but in carrying out his plans he was too inflexible and did not compromise with powerful local economic and military realities. With a note of bitterness, Sima Qian concludes the chapter on the two officials with a proverb whose implications are not too flattering for the Han dynasty: "Meddle with custom, old ways emend, and death or exile will be your end."[21]

In any case, from the stories of the Yuan Ang and Chao Cuo we acquire further interesting pieces of information that better contextualize Emperor Wu's rituals: under his father's reign, the *Classics* were not part of the indispensable curriculum of all state functionaries; officials trained in legalist doctrines were still regarded as an asset to the government; and it was conceivable to receive an eclectic education that included subjects that the Classicists would eventually condemn as unorthodox. In such a fluid cultural milieu, a Classicist approach to the state was not the most obvious choice. A further important element highlighted by these episodes is that, during the early Han, local leaders, such kings, marquises, and court officials, in addition to being customarily linked by family ties, were often close enough to share cultural, economic, and political interests, even when openly in contrast with those of the central government.

The *Records* implies that at the beginning of Emperor Wu's reign, powerful and *de facto* independent kingdoms still posed a serious threat to the court. Hence—as in the case of Chao Cuo's suspicions about Yuan Ang—it was plausible that some of the officials in the capital might have operated, directly and indirectly, on their behalf and against the imperial branch of the Liu. For this reason the central government had maintain a tighter grip on the periphery. Sima Qian indeed acknowledges that although Chao Cuo's analysis was accurate, his actions were premature. Only a generation later, Emperor Wu's government would be able, albeit momentarily, to establish state control over fundamental resources, while imposing a planned economy and fiscal centralization. As for the ritual program in which he engaged, it constituted a cultural answer to the model of laissez-faire and decentralization advocated by the Classicists.

Metaphors of Warfare and Hunting: Poetry as Propaganda

The resplendent new marble constructions in Rome, the ubiquitous statues, and the temples for the provincial cult immediately reflected the glory of Augustus and of the empire he embodied. At the same time, appealing to a more sophisticated public, Golden Age poets such as Virgil and Ovid wove complex literary and mythological allusions to the exceptionality of the Principate. Augustan-age propaganda left traces on different media. Han specialists instead have traditionally had to work with the available lacunose historical evidence.

In the case of Emperor Wu, however, we find a more explicit, direct form of apologetic literature in the poetic work of Sima Xiangru 司馬相如 (179–127 BCE, not related to Tan and Qian).[22] His biography in the *Records* has been the customary focus of studies on the literary development of the Han rhapsody (*fu* 賦), a genre that was criticized in the following ages as an opulent, overly elaborate, and often contrived intellectualistic divertissement devoid of any educational value.[23] With her latest work, Tamara Chin has revived the scholarship on this genre by studying its formal features in the context of Han discourses on expansionistic economics.[24] My approach instead analyses Sima Xiangru's *fu* in conjunction with elements of the poet's biography and administrative role under Wu. I argue that some themes and aspects of Sima Xiangru's rhapsodic production reflected and advertised specific elements of Wu's territorial and fiscal policies.[25]

Recently, Martin Kern has questioned the authenticity of some important sections of this chapter of the *Records*. He persuasively argues that the chapter's treatment of Sima Xiangru's poetic production reflects the literary and linguistic sensibilities of the post-Wu era rather than those of the Emperor's own time. However, the political and cultural aspects of Sima Xiangru's biography and oeuvre on which I concentrate, clearly attest to a phase of cultural transition that predates the period in which the Classicists became the preeminent cultural faction at court, which is to say after Wu's death. Sima Xiangru, for example, acknowledges the importance of the

Classics, but he still considers the cultural and moral paradigm they refer to—namely the Western Zhou dynasty—as secondary in importance to the autocratic conception of imperial rule championed by Wu.

The *Records* describes Sima Xiangru as a young, talented, and resourceful man from the ancient state of Shu 蜀 (present-day Sichuan). If we focus on the meaningful facts of his life and career, Sima Qian, in his usual oblique ways, seems to recount Sima Xiangru's various accomplishments in order to highlight the extravagance of Emperor Wu's cultural choices. But once we appraise the poet's biography against the major political and economic debates of the period, it provides valuable information about the model of rulership that Wu was trying to legitimize via ritual means.

Coming from a wealthy family, Sima Xiangru had the opportunity to appear at the capital and be examined for a position at court. As a child, he had shown a sincere interest in literature and impressive creative skills, but because Emperor Jing did not care about poetry, the young Sima Xiangru had no other choice but to accept, without enthusiasm, the position of mounted guard. The outlook on life of the young man from Shu changed dramatically when he became acquainted with Liu Wu 劉武, the King of Liang 梁 and younger brother of the emperor. Because of his active contribution to the war against the Seven Kingdoms, Liu Wu had been rewarded with titles and riches, which, thanks to his economic savvy, he had turned into an even larger fortune.[26] His patrimony was so impressive that it rivaled the possessions of the Son of Heaven and, according to Sima Qian's critical remarks, unduly overstepped his station.[27] Unlike his more illustrious brother, the King of Liang was very intellectually curious and enjoyed patronizing itinerant artists and literati from all over China. In one of his frequent visits to the imperial court, Liu Wu brought along a small group of his protégées, including Zou Yan, the famous thinker from Qi to whom Sima Qian attributes the first consistent elaboration of the theory of the Five Phases.[28] Sima Xiangru was so delighted with the conversation he had with these educated people that he feigned illness, took a leave from the court, and followed Liu Wu to Liang where he spent several years as a guest in the same lodge as the other scholars—an environment that surely better suited his literary aspirations.[29]

The *Records* implies that this must have been an important formative period for Sima Xiangru. His familiarity with Zou Yan could, in a way, explain the presence in his rhapsodies of cultural elements typical of Qi. In addition, it cannot be overlooked that the most influential figure in the life Sima Xiangru's generous host, the King of Liang, was the overbearing Empress Dowager Dou, wife of the late Emperor Wen, mother of the King of Liang and his brother Emperor Jing, and future Emperor Wu's grandmother. That fact that she was considered a fervent Huang-Lao follower might provide some clues about the cultural climate in which Sima Xiangru operated.[30]

Among Xiangru's compositions, the one that eventually caught Emperor Wu's attention and earned the poet an invitation to court was "The Rhapsody of Sir Vacuous" ("*Zixu fu*" 子虛賦). This poem fancifully describes Liu Wu riding through his fabulous park and performing ritualized hunts, which, as we have seen above, Sima Qian considered an excessive and inappropriate usurpation of imperial prerogatives. Once at court, Sima Xiangru admitted that his poem only befitted a feudal lord, not the Son of Heaven. Hence, he offered to compose a new rhapsody about an imperial hunt specifically for his majesty. This work, an elaboration of the *fu* already written for the King of Liang, described three imaginary characters respectively debating which one, among the hunting parks of the lords of Chu, Qi, and the Son of Heaven, was the most marvelous.[31] According to Sima Qian, Sima Xiangru's "Rhapsody of Shanglin [the imperial park]" ("Shanglin fu" 上林賦) had a satirical and moralizing purpose. In light of the materials presented so far and the Taiyi cult I will analyze below, it is evident that it addressed the political relationship between the court and the local lords.

After the first two characters have ceased arguing about the superiority of Chu and Qi, Master Not-such (Wushi Gong 無是公) speaks on behalf of the Son of Heaven and pronounces both his rivals wrong:

> Having the vassal lords present tribute is not for the articles and presents themselves, but is a means for them to report on the administration of their offices. Setting up boundaries and drawing borders are not for protection or defense, but are a means of prohibiting excessive territorial encroachment. [. . .] Moreover, in your discourses both of you gentlemen do not strive to elucidate the duties of ruler and subject or to correct the ritual behavior of the vassal lords. You merely devote yourselves to competing over the joys of excursions and sports, the size of parks and preserves, wishing to overwhelm each other with wasteful ostentation and surpass one another in wild excesses. These things cannot serve to spread fame or enhance a reputation, but are enough to defame your rulers and do injury to yourselves. Furthermore, how are the affairs of Qi and Chu worth mentioning? Have you not seen what is truly great and beautiful? Have you alone not heard of the Imperial Park of the Son of Heaven? [32]

At this point Master Not-such, in order humiliate his companions, recites the "Rhapsody of the Shanglin Park," which unfolds as a hyperbolic journey throughout the imperial possessions. In the overly elaborated description produced by Master Not-such, the Shanglin Park obviously surpasses everyone else's in beauty and is so extensive that it embraces the known world. It hosts the rarest species of plants and beasts, which the sovereign—who is the leader of the hunt, the army, and all the lands—pursues with unprecedented prowess.[33] These elements echo the search for the exotic specimens of flora and fauna required for the performance of *feng* and *shan*. In this case, though, the Son of Heaven does not wait for the most precious fruits of the land to appear spontaneously or be brought to him: he already owns them as a consequence of his military endeavors. Then, after the voluptuous description of the performances of actors, singers, and dancers who were summoned to honor the emperor, the rhapsody recovers a moralistic tone and extolls the virtue of frugality, almost as though Master Not-such suddenly regrets his celebratory foray. In touching upon themes that immediately recall the chapter on Yuan Ang and Chao Cuo, the poem becomes more explicitly political:

> Thereupon, He dissolves the feast, ends the hunt, and commands
>   His officials, saying,
> Let all land that can be reclaimed and opened up!
> Be made into farmland in order to provide for the common
>   people!
> Tear down the walls, fill in the moats,
> Allow the people of the mountains and marshes to come here!
> Restock the pools and ponds and do not ban people from them!
> Empty the palaces and lodges and do not staff them!
> Open the granaries and storehouses in order to give relief to
>   the poor and destitute!
> Supply what they lack!
> Pity widowers and widows,
> Console the orphaned and childless!
> Issue virtuous commands,
> Reduce punishments and penalties,
> Reform the institutions,
> Alter the vestment colors,
> Change the first month and day of the year,
> Make a new beginning for the empire![34]

Opening lands for cultivation and making them available to the common people meant expropriating hereditary estates or free territories to which the nobles might have felt entitled. It is not difficult to imagine how these measures could worry or enrage specific elite families, even within the Liu clan. But the rhapsody abruptly shifts subjects and reverts to hyperbolic and metaphorical description. The connection of the struggle over centralization with the question of the cultural and textual models upon which to organize the empire and society, at this point, cannot be considered casual. We find the traditional" Confucian" values and books, but placed in an unusual context:

> And then, calculating an auspicious day, he fasts and cleanses himself,
> Dons His court robes,
> And mounts the chariot of the Standard Cortege,
> Flowery banners raised on high,
> Jade simurgh bells jangling. He sports in the preserve of the *Six Classics*,
> Gallops over the road of Humaneness [*ren* 仁] and Morality [*yi* 義]
> Goes sightseeing in the forest of the *Annals*
> Shoots to the "Wildcat's Head,"
> Together with the "Zouyu."
> His corded arrows catch the "Black Crane,"
> He dances the "Shield and Axe."
> Carrying in his cart a cloud-net,
> He captures a flock of refinement.[35]
> He grieves at "Cutting Sandalwood,"
> Delights in "Rejoicing All," Cultivates His comportment in the garden of the *Rites*,
> Roams and rambles in the park of the *Documents*.
> Transmitting the doctrine of the *Changes*,
> He releases the strange beasts,
> Ascends the Luminous Hall [Mingtang 明堂],
> Sits in the Pure Temple [Qingmiao 青廟].[36]

If we analyze this last passage in light of the preceding sections cited above, the cultural foundations of the empire appear as immediately following, either chronologically or causally, the overhaul of the old territorial order. Through a series of rhetorical figures that reify, objectify, and spatialize benevolence, righteousness, and the *Classics* themselves, the rhapsody celebrates a ruler (or a government) completely in charge of the ethical and cultural landscape of China. Sima Xiangru does not describe the canonical texts as the objects of intellectual study, but as the victims and trophies of the imperial hunt. The sovereign disposes of them as his personal concrete possessions, as though they were his lands and the beasts living on them. In synthesis, the rhapsody seems to warn that Emperor Wu should embrace the *Classics* and the values they represent only as long as his autocratic power is not undermined.

The message of this rhapsody is consistent with some of Sima Xiangru's political assignments. His involvement with the government was not limited to providing conceptual tools for an important ideological battle against the Classicists. According to the *Records*, the poet from Shu was entrusted with diplomatic missions on behalf of the Son of Heaven in peripheral areas of the empire where he was called to explain to the natives the politics of the Son of Heaven. When Sima Xiangru's rhetoric skills were not successful, he had to resort to violence. As the *Records* reports, he "invaded and pacified the lands of the western barbarians," "abolished old boundaries," and "established new frontiers farther out."[37] These missions, as we shall see, reflected a specific conception of imperial authority that would also be sanctioned in Wu's ritual innovations. These were meant to stage an active, expansionistic, and autocratic view of rulership that implied the emperor's direct communication with the various peoples of China through intermediaries he appointed personally—a form of control that could prescind from the intervention of the local nobles. Such a practice would not be celebrated as exemplary after Wu's demise.

It is emblematic that the last will of Sima Xiangru before his death in 127 BCE was meant to ensure that his letter encouraging Emperor Wu to celebrate the *feng* and *shan* sacrifices would reach its addressee.[38] Had a different cultural approach prevailed after Emperor Wu's reign, Sima Xiangru would not merely be regarded as an eccentric poet mainly interested in highly elaborated (and, after all, frivolous) literary divertissements, but perhaps as the bard of a Han golden age.

Ritual, Boundaries, and Empire: The Roman and the Han Cases

Emperor Wu's imperial vision becomes more evident once we focus on the ceremonies he sponsored, participated in, or directly conducted. In order to do so, we have to integrate the fragmentary accounts provided by the *Records* with contemporary material evidence and sources that seem to belong to a cultural milieu close to Wu's background. Texts such as the *Huainanzi* or the Mawangdui silk manuscripts, which were produced under or for other members the imperial lineage of the Liu, ignored or explicitly rejected Confucius's legacy, while providing a different perspective about the themes that were capturing Wu's attention. In light of this evidence, we can reconstruct the original royal paradigm he strove to establish. Wu envisioned a conception of monarchy that directly challenged the interests of landed aristocracies and the devolutionary ideals supported by the Classicists. According to this interpretation, the ruler had an active role in regulating cosmic rhythms, relied on military strength to maintain political order, and controlled the periphery directly without intermediaries.

After Wu's death, this active interpretation of imperial sovereignty would be replaced by a Zhou-based devolutionary paradigm, which, through the centrality of the *Classics* in the curriculum of state officials, became the basis of mainstream theories on imperial sovereignty that are now closely associated with Chinese identity. As we have seen, Wu's model instead, presenting various similarities with ancient Eurasian paradigms, has prompted comparative endeavors that look at the study of the Roman Empire as a source of interpretive frameworks. My approach concentrates on the myths and rituals used to define the military role of the Princeps and the Son of Heaven in securing and expanding the boundaries of the empire. Through the historicization of debates on royal prerogatives, I explore the impact of different sociocultural contexts on official ideas about the extra-human realm, especially in regard to explaining political continuity and change. A cross-cultural analysis with Augustan Rome allows me to make the case that the eventual rejection of Wu's model hinged on his failure to achieve a compromise between local interests and the priorities of a centralized state. Whereas Roman discussions about imperial authority prioritized the centrality of collegiality, the acceptability of unified rule in Wu's China was discussed in terms of autonomy versus delegation.

By the mid-second century BCE, Rome had grown from a small city-state in the middle of Italy to the powerful ruler of the majority of the territories around the Mediterranean Sea. After decades of political turmoil and civil war, five centuries of proud Republican achievements ended with the establishment of Octavian's Principate. Roman senators had always dreaded hereditary monarchy. Kings traditionally evoked arbitrary rule and moral corruption. Their rule contradicted the bulwarks of the republican tradition (i.e., collegiality and time limits for all offices), for it was based on the claim of a privileged connection with extra-human forces and wide popular support. But while the senatorial class was particularly wary of divine rulers, it is well known that the common people tended to welcome charismatic or semi-divine leaders as saviors, especially during periods of social and political unrest. The founders of Rome's imperial tradition, Julius Caesar and his adoptive son Octavian, each succeeded, with different degrees of success, in exploiting this contradiction to their advantage.

Caesar, believed by many to be a god on earth, was eventually murdered. Octavian never officially emphasized his extra-human prerogatives, nor formalized his powers with the creation of a new office. In an extremely astute way, he succeeded in progressively establishing the notion that his exceptional position did not derive from a specific political institution but from his very person. He was ultimately able to install an imperial line despite the Senate's hostility toward hereditary monarchy.[39] In doing so, Octavian promoted a redefinition of the new cults as a reestablishment of the traditional values and customs.

In the literature produced in those years, discussions about ancient myths and rituals were clearly instrumental in redefining the relationship between the old and the new, the expanding physical limits of the empire, as well as the boundaries of the sphere of interaction between human and divine forces. In brief, the Roman authors of the early imperial period seemed focused in reconciling the diversity of the Roman Empire in one linear tradition. One emblematic marker of Octavian's revolution is his adoption of the title "Augustus" in 27 BCE. It epitomizes the transfer of fundamental prerogatives of the Roman Republic to a single individual and the overcoming of collegiality through ritual means. Octavian's new appellation had a strong relationship with the founding of Rome and the mythological account of a specific ritual that was instrumental in validating political deliberations.[40] As recounted in Livy, before choosing a location for the new city, Romulus and Remus, with the assistance of specialized priests (the *augures*), performed the *inauguratio*.[41] This ceremony consisted of the marking of a special area in the sky, the *templum*, where, after analyzing the number, kind, and trajectories of the birds flying through, the *augures* would determine whether the actions the humans were set to embark upon had divine approval.[42] Famously, after the twins received contrasting omens, a fight ensued as to which one had the mandate to found a city. Remus tried to invade the territory his brother had claimed as his own. Romulus killed him and became the first king of Rome.

If we focus on the ceremony performed by the *augures*, we learn that it was customarily carried out before important decisions of the relevant assemblies of Republican Rome. Ritually, the *inauguratio* legitimated the political decisions of the various assemblies by verifying that the gods approved of them. Thus, we can interpret the conferral of the title of "Augustus" to Octavian, four years after his victory against Mark Antony and the end of the civil wars, as a validation of the institutional and political transformations he had brought about. In other words, as "Augustus" he now symbolically appropriated the mediating function of the specialized priests and the decisional powers of the various assemblies. His person could embody the City and, therefore, its empire as legitimately conquered or negotiated the space of its expansion and prerogatives.

By contrast, Emperor Wu did not modify the appellation of "Son of Heaven," which would have indicated the will to reject (at least formally) a cultural and political bond with the rulers of Zhou. However, he did set forth a series of protocol reforms that were aimed at redefining the emperor as a more active agent of action and change. I am referring to the practice of "naming periods," *nianhao* 年號, which was introduced in the years before the celebration of the *feng* and *shan* in 110 BCE. To a certain extent the *nianhao*—especially if we think about the proclamation of the "The Grand Beginning" (*Taichu* 太初) in 104 BCE, which coincided with the publication of a new calendar and the adoption of new titles and protocols—can be considered a less hubristic or blatant version of the palingenesis envisioned by the First Emperor of Qin, who had established himself as the beginning of history. According to the *nianhao* system, the court would name specific periods of reign (of variable length) after omens or phenomena that were interpreted as announcing new cosmic phases that compelled the government to respond with appropriate politics. Of course, the cause-effect relationship could be imagined as working in the opposite way—sovereigns would justify changes of ruling strategies as necessitated by the contingent cosmic conjuncture.

Under Emperor Wu, the *nianhao* was applied retroactively to Emperor Wen's age. After Wu's death it became a convention for all dynasties.[43] This practice would be retained and read in the context of Dong Zhongshu's interpretation of the doctrine of the Mandate of Heaven. If we consider it together with Emperor Wu's other reforms, it seems to reinforce the message about a ruler who is actively in charge of all realms, cosmic, political, and human, as well as of both time and space.[44]

If the *feng* and *shan* represent extremely problematic evidence, the sacrifices to Taiyi can help reconstruct important aspects of Wu's conception of territorial authority, especially once they are appraised against historical and archeological evidence. One of Emperor Wu's official edicts explained that the *feng* and *shan* sacrifices could be carried out during the *xunshou* (imperial inspections or hunting expeditions) only after the successful performance of the sacrifices to Taiyi and Houtu. These two objects of worship feature in several texts produced between the end of the Warring States period and the early Han. In the cases in which Taiyi is mentioned alone, it usually represents the ultimate origin of the physical world. Likely for this reason, some scholars are willing to acknowledge it as evidence of a basically monotheistic tendency that would have characterized early China.[45] The accounts concerning Emperor Wu and its rituals instead mainly describe Taiyi in association with Houtu in a partnership that echoes that of yang and yin, or Heaven and Earth's duality. While the Classicists emphasized the harmonious complementarity of these two powers, Han "heterodox" texts tended to interpret Taiyi as the personification of the sky in astronomical terms, as a masculine force and origin of the martial prerogatives of the ruler,[46] and Houtu in feminine terms, as Earth representing both fertile soil to be inseminated and land to conquer.[47] In other words, while the first interpretation focused on cooperation, the second one stressed the elements of conflict and conquest. In the *Huainanzi*, a text written and compiled at the court of Liu An 劉安 (179–122 BCE), a cousin and rival of Emperor Wu, Taiyi elucidates the cosmic prerogatives of the sovereign (*di*):[48]

> The Sovereign (*di* 帝) embodies the Grand One (Taiyi); the king (*wang* 王) emulates yin and yang. The hegemon (*ba* 霸) follows the six pitch pipes. Now Taiyi encloses and contains Heaven and Earth, weighs on and crushes mountains and streams, retains or emits yin and yang, stretches out and drags along the four seasons, knots the net of the eight directional points, and weaves the web of the eight coordinates.[49]

The *Huainanzi* also attests to the fact that the cult of Taiyi epitomized a set of values that were clearly considered at odds with those embodied by the Classicists. This is the same text that harshly criticizes the *Ru* as those who "do not get to the foundations of why they have desires but instead prohibit what they desire . . . and do not attain harmony in their lives"—but praises the Perfected as those who "rest in the vast universe, roam in the country of Limitless, ascend Tai Huang [and] ride Taiyi."[50]

Conversely, Sima Qian does not seem to hold Taiyi in great consideration. He describes the establishment of its worship under Wu as the result of several ill-advised attempts to combine preexisting regional cults, which, of course, were not mentioned in the *Classics*. The *Records* informs us that in 133 BCE, in the same period in which Emperor Wu was introduced to alchemy,[51] a certain Miuji 繆忌 appeared at court, presenting a plan for the construction of an altar to Taiyi. Sima Qian notes that this *fangshi* hailed from Bo 亳, a place that the "Book on the Feng and Shan" had introduced earlier as the site of an important Qin cult—which should alert the reader about the dubious origin of the new ritual. According to the story Miuji offered the emperor, Taiyi worship was very old and had upstaged the cult of the Five Sovereigns at Yong that had been established by the Qin:

> Taiyi is the most honored of the spirits of Heaven and his helpers are the Five Sovereigns. In ancient times the Son of Heaven sacrificed to Taiyi each spring and autumn in the southern suburbs, offering one set of sacrificial animals each day for seven days. An altar (*tan* 壇) was constructed that was open on eight sides to favor the arrival of the ghosts (*gui* 鬼).[52]

We do not know if Sima Qian reported this piece of information in order to suggest that Emperor Wu was eager to see in these eight ghosts extraordinary beings that could help him achieve immortality. But the Emperor promptly ordered the Head of Sacrifices (Taizhu 太祝) to build an altar southeast of the capital, according to Miuji's instructions. The *Records* shows the Son of Heaven as irresolute and easily impressionable. After the construction of the altar, someone submitted a memorial proposing the performance of another cult (allegedly of ancient origins as well) that contradicted the story told by Miuji. The new version held that the worship of Taiyi was an element of a triad with the Heavenly Unity (Tianyi 天一) and Earthly Unity (Diyi 地一), with which the *Records* does not seem familiar. The Son of Heaven approved of this ritual, too, and commissioned the Head of Sacrifices to perform it on the same Taiyi altar built according to Miuji's plan.[53] But again, a new memorial was received. This suggested further modifications and additions that seemed even more tailored to the emperor's alleged interests and delusions. The new ritual included the

Yellow Emperor, Taiyi, the Messenger of Yin and Yang, and another set of deities that cannot be identified with certainty.[54] In this case, too, Emperor Wu obliged and had ritual officials performing these new sacrifices next to Miuji's altar.[55]

In 112 BCE, the Son of Heaven, probably not satisfied with the results of the earlier ceremonies, followed a new plan of Miuji's and commissioned the construction of a second Taiyi altar south of the Ganquan 甘泉 palace.[56] This building was organized on three tiers. The upper one, the Purple Altar (Zitan 紫壇), was dedicated to Taiyi. The one in the middle the (Wudi tan) 五帝壇, was larger, surrounded the upper one, and was dedicated to the Five Sovereigns. The Yellow Emperor, because of his association with Earth, should have occupied the central position, but in this case his altar was placed southwest of the center to give way to Taiyi.[57] The lower level was dedicated to the multitude of spirits and ghosts and to the constellation of the Northern Dipper. Five priests, whose robes matched the colors of the Five Phases, were assigned to the cult of each of the Five Sovereigns.[58] Neither altar is extant. It is not clear how the different *shen* involved in the various Taiyi cults were represented, either. We do know, however, that by Emperor Cheng's time, the performance was extravagant enough to be considered improper for a frugal ruler who wanted to follow exemplary sovereigns of the past.[59]

The Chinese scholar Li Ling has enriched the question of the possible meanings of Taiyi through the analysis of new archeological and textual finds, which he interprets in terms of astronomy, divination, and warfare. In light of specific pieces of archeological evidence, the *Records*' account of the preparation for the expedition against Nanyue 南越 is pivotal in Li's research. In 113 BCE, the year of the construction of the second Taiyi altar, the Grand Historian—in this case probably Sima Qian's father Tan—prayed to Taiyi and then raised the so-called "Taiyi Spear" (Taiyi *feng* 太一鋒) in the direction of the enemy.[60] The "Taiyi Spear" consisted of the "Numinous Flag" (*lingqi* 靈旗), which was mounted on a jujube pole and depicted the sun, the moon, the Northern Dipper, an ascending dragon, and the three stars of the Taiyi constellation.[61]

All these elements recur in the new evidence Li Ling presents and greatly help us in reconstructing the cultural context of Emperor Wu's rituals.[62] "The Book on Astronomy" in the *Records*, "Tianguan shu" 天官書, probably based on Sima Tan's work, appears to be the product of the same cultural milieu as the *Huainanzi* and the Mawangdui manuscripts.[63] Regardless of its intellectual approach, it seems focused on similar themes.

The initial entry of the "Book on Astronomy" identifies Taiyi (βUMi, Kochab) with a star in the constellation of Heaven's Culmen (*tiangjixing* 天極星), immediately above the Northern Dipper. The Northern Dipper is, in turn, associated with the emperor's chariot and patrolling expeditions (*xunshou* 巡狩), and with his function of separating and organizing yin and yang and the Five Phases.[64]

Li Ling notes that Taiyi and the Northern Dipper, represented as astronomical bodies, also featured on the pointers of Warring States divination devices, whose round and square quadrants (which were perhaps reproduced in Miuji's altar) corresponded to Heaven and Earth.[65] On the "Repel-weapons Chart" (*bibingtu* 避兵圖) depicted on a sheet of silk recovered from Tomb 3 in Mawangdui (dated 168 BCE), Taiyi instead appears as an anthropomorphic red deity *shen*, which is accompanied by other figures.[66] Li Ling identifies these by characters on the chart as warrior disciples (*wu dizi* 武弟子), the Rain Master (Yushi 雨師), the Thunder Lord (Leigong 雷公), and three dragons, one of which is holding a stove.[67] Interestingly, inside a circle under Taiyi's left arm, there is the character *she* 社, which, during the Han, could indicate the Altar of the Soil and the Millet of the Zhou or the Earth God.

The representation of an anthropomorphized Taiyi "containing" the character of the *She* altar is consistent with the ongoing struggle between the Han government and the local lords on the extent of their authority and land policies. A passage in "The Hereditary Houses of the Three Kings," ("San wang shijia" 三王世家), the last chapter of the *Records* section "The Hereditary Houses," clarifies how in this period the *She* altar, especially if we compare it with Houtu's characterization as fertile land, epitomized an old, allegedly Zhou-like, "feudal," "devoluntionary" conception of space—not as territory directly controlled by the emperor, but as the portion of land the sovereign entrusted to the authority of local leaders. This text elaborates on Emperor Wu's mistrust of family members as political collaborators and his tendency to rely more on administrative efficiency.[68] It reports that in 110 BCE, when the king of Qi, Emperor Wu's beloved son Liu Hong 劉閎, died without heirs at the age of seventeen, the Son of Heaven decided to divide up Qi into smaller administrative unities (commanderies, *jun* 郡), as he deemed it impossible to control this complex and distinctive former state by entrusting it to other members of the Liu clan. It is at this point that the *Records* seems to reveal Sima Qian's ironic intent when, in commenting on the aftermath of the Revolt of the Seven Kingdoms, "[T]he Son of Heaven, imitating the ways of antiquity, graciously allowed the feudal lords to share their blessings and to divide up their territories among their various sons and brothers."[69] At least in this case, Emperor Wu first bestowed an important kingdom on one of his direct descendants, not to any of the feudal lords, and then, after his son died, divided his estate up in administrative unities that were under the direct control of the central government.

Thus, after reporting the division of Qi in commanderies, the chapter makes the point that exemplary emperors of an undefined past (the Zhou era?) yielded control over the land to local lords, while every member of the aristocratic system was only directly in touch with nobles immediately below or above his rank. In other words, the court was not privy to, and did not interfere with, the administration of the periphery. This system of enfeoffment, the *Records* recollects, was once expressed through the "Shou ci tu 受此土" ceremony, the description of which reads like a highly idealized synthesis of old feudal concepts and late Warring States notions about the Five Phases.[70] The "Shou ci tu" revolved around the *She* Altar of the Son of Heaven, which in this case is described as a square mound of five colors. Its center was yellow, while the four sides were colored according to the four directions.[71] In the ancient ceremony of "enfeoffment," from the emperor going down, a lord would bestow on an immediately inferior nobleman a lump of dirt from his own altar, picking from the side that corresponded to the direction from which the vassal was coming. The lesser leader would go back and build a second *she* altar around the clod he had received. Then, accordingly, he would repeat the same ceremony of enfeoffment with aristocrats of lower rank.

Regardless of the historicity of the account on the "Shou ci tu" ceremony, it is beyond doubt that in this case, too, the *Records* was addressing what Emperor Wu's contemporaries felt as a contentious and highly divisive issue. At stake was the government-led cultural and political shift between two radically different conceptions of imperial power. To curb Emperor Wu's centralizing measures, his opponents were propounding a conception of indirect rulership that was modeled on filial piety and implied an articulated framework of descending hierarchical positions between the ruler and his subjects. The *Records* envisioned this system as the modular reproduction of central authority via the gradual delegation of political prerogatives to peripheral polities.

Later texts, such as the *Comprehensive Discussions in the White Tiger Hall* (the *Baihu tong* 白虎通), confirm that the "devolutionary" approach had prevailed by the reign of the Eastern Han. This work, which was probably compiled after 79 CE, consists of short questions and answers on various themes, ranging from the origins and meanings of titles and protocols to political institutions, ritual procedures, cosmological theories, music, and so on. It appears to be an attempt to consolidate contemporary practices by tracing them back, as much as possible, to authoritative texts of the Classical tradition.[72] There is not enough evidence to ascertain whether the intent of the discussions that were eventually recorded in a written form was descriptive or normative. Its cultural value doubtlessly lies in its documentation of the development of questions that were still open in Sima Qian's time and that, once settled, would condition they ways we still look at Emperor Wu's reign.

The *Baihu tong* chapter on the God of the Soil and Millet ("Sheji" 社稷) opens with a statement that seems to sanction the victory of a more sedentary kind of rulership and its divestment from local sacrifices, or, in other words, the establishment of a metonymic conception of ritual:

> Why do rulers have an Altar of the Soil and an Altar of the Millet?[73] In order to request prosperity for the realm and show gratitude when it is received. If men do not own land, they cannot sustain themselves; if they do not have grains they cannot eat. The land is so extensive and vast that it is impossible to worship it in every place. The kinds of grain are so numerous that it is not possible to worship them one by one.[74]

The descending feudal structure of the ritual becomes more evident in the explanation of the reasons why each member of the hierarchical structure worshipped two altars. According to the *Baihu tong*, the Son of Heaven and the Feudal Lords (*zhuhou* 諸侯) had two *she* altars each: the ruler, one for the realm (the *Taishe* 太社) and one for the kings/vassals (the king's *she*, *Wangshe* 王社); the Feudal Lords, one for the state (*Guoshe* 國社) and one for the marquises they controlled (*Houshe* 侯社). Officials in charge of specific areas had their own *she*, too. The *Baihu tong* validates this arrangement by referencing a passage in Confucius's *Analects* that re-reads the relations defined by filial piety in bureaucratic terms: "A Great Officer in association with the people who are under him, erects a *she* altar, which is called the "Appointed" God of the Earth (*zhishe* 置社)."[75]

According to the rhetoric of the *Baihu tong*, we can infer that, even a century after Emperor Wu's death, leaders were expected to ritually interact with colleagues who were immediately above or immediately below their ranking. Direct contact between center and periphery, as well as between the top and bottom tiers of the political system, was avoided. While Emperor Wu's ceremonies conceived the realm as an empty canvas or boundless hunting ground where the Son of Heaven was free to move and exert his pacifying and organizing powers, the official rituals that prevailed after him were aimed at replicating and reinforcing traditional political and territorial power relations.

At this point it is evident enough that some forms of worship, such as that of Taiyi or the model of Yellow Emperor popular in Huang-Lao cultural circles, better suited Emperor Wu's vision of a centralized state because of their military, cosmologic, and divinatory connotations. The kinds of foundational narratives (or myths) and ritualized performances on which he focused sought to legitimate the authority of the Son of Heaven by identifying him with the (occasionally violent) unfolding of cosmic forces. If we look at the elements involved in the Taiyi cult (e.g., the Northern Dipper, the imperial chariot, the patrolling expeditions, and so on) we can recognize a conception of authority that emanates radially from the center, while re-mapping the territory through sweeping military campaigns that indiscriminately bring every corner of the All-Under-Heaven under the imperial aegis. In such a vision, sovereign authority does not yield some of its functions though its own modular reproduction on a subordinated level, as in the case of the ceremonies connected to the *she* altar, but rather subjugates and incorporates all geographical areas of the empire.

The Problematic Legacy of Emperor Wu

In the *History of the Former Han* by Ban Gu, written in the first century CE, the "Book on the *Feng* and *Shan*" gives way to "The Treatise of the Suburban Sacrifices" ("Jiaosi zhi" 郊祀志), which consists of two sections. The first is almost a verbatim copy of the corresponding chapter in the *Records*.[76] The second resumes the narration from where Sima Qian had stopped, 109 BCE (the year after Emperor Wu completed the *feng* and *shan* sacrifices), chronicling the ritual performances of his successors year by year and ending with the "usurpation" of the power of the Western Han by Wang Mang 王莽 (45 BCE–23 CE) in 10 CE.[77] But while the thematic chapter in the *Records* opens by lamenting the impossibility of recovering the memory of the procedures, meaning, and aims of the ancient rites, Ban Gu's essay, before reproducing Sima Qian's narration, replaces his introduction by referring to the *Great Plan* (*Hong Fan*) as a source of legitimacy while stating that the sacrifices' (*si* 祀) ultimate purpose is showing filial piety (*xiao* 孝) in honoring the ancestors. The initial passage of the chapter clearly describes a process of bureaucratization of the world of the spirits that mirrors human ranks and competences.[78] It was the Sage Kings of the past who regulated the sacrifices by establishing the appropriate periods for their performance, procedures, and victims, in order to discipline the communication between the two realms. The *Records* emphasizes the dangers of disorderly intermingling between men and spirits (while hinting at the likelihood that they were the result of malicious fabrications) and the impossibility of reading their manifestations in a way that could be beneficial to society. The *Han Shu* instead affirms that regulating the interaction between men and spirits was not only possible, but one of the fundamental tasks of an effective government. In practice, according to the reformers who intended to overhaul Wu's rituals, Confucius's recommendation to avoid giving importance to extra-ordinary phenomena could be ignored as long as these phenomena were the object of discussions about textual authority, in which, of course, only select groups could engage.

Understandably, the model of sovereignty envisioned by Emperor Wu would be progressively delegitimized after his death. However, there is evidence of its popularity and resilience, as most of his successors tried to emulate it. Emperor Zhao (r. 87–74 BCE), who succeeded Wu on the throne, was too young and his reign too short to embark on any *xunshou*, the "Jiaosi zhi" remarks.[79] Emperor Xuan (r. 74–49 BCE) traveled incessantly all over China while tending to old rituals and establishing new ones.[80] Xuan was under the sway of the *fangshi* and revered Emperor Wu as the champion of a new kind of rulership. He continued to sacrifice to Taiyi, Houtu, and all the other deities in person, as he was anxious to ensure that the people received "positive influences and bumper harvests."[81] In all the states (*guo*) and commanderies (*jun*) Emperor Wu had visited during his inspection tours, Xuan built shrines with the intent of worshipping him as Supreme Ancestor (*Shizong* 世宗).[82]

If we compare Emperor Xuan's acts with the process of legitimation of hereditary monarchy in Rome, between Caesar and Octavian, the introduction of an official cult of Wu appears as a decisive step toward the establishment of an imperial cult through the "divinization" of a royal ancestor. Yet in 61 BCE, the early signs of a new surge of the Classicists became evident in a memorial Zhang Chang 張敞, an expert of the classic of the *Spring and Autumn* and newly appointed Governor of the Capital (Jingzhao Yin 京兆

尹), submitted to the throne. It solicited the emperor to follow the ways of the ancient rulers, which meant avoiding displays of extravagance and wealth and dismissing the *fangshi* and their empty words.[83] Even though the text does not report the reaction of the Son of Heaven, the episode narrated immediately after the citation of the memorial at least attests to fact that Zhang Chang did not lose favor with the sovereign.

The *Han Shu* recounts the unearthing of yet another tripod in Meiyang 美陽, roughly fifty miles west of Chang'an. When the courtiers began to debate as to whether the vessel had to be treated like the one found during Emperor Wu's reign in 113 BCE and placed in the ancestral temple of the dynasty, the same Zhang Chang asked to be consulted on account of his knowledge of ancient scripts.[84] After rehearsing the line of succession and enfeoffment from the Son of Heaven of the Zhou to the vassals of the area of the present capital, he deciphered the celebratory inscription on the tripod and offered his interpretation. Zhang Chang identified the cauldron as a ritual instrument the Zhou elites used to sacrifice to the ancestral spirits. Its presence in an area so removed from of their ancient capital did not necessitate explanations involving prodigies: the tripod represented a token of gratitude the Son of Heaven of the Zhou had bestowed upon a local lord. Then, by comparing the extraordinary (and in the context he might have meant "fraudulent") origin of Wu's vessel with the small dimensions of the one discovered in Weiyang, Zhang Chang established that such a commonplace token of political interaction was not worthy of the ancestral temple. On this matter, Emperor Xuan heeded the governor's advice, even though, the sources say, he would pursue his interest in omens and spirits until his death.

Zhang Chang's philological interpretation of the find of the bronze tripod, an object from the hallowed Zhou dynasty, epitomizes the ways in which the Classicists were using their monopoly on the past to condition the present and establish their literary expertise as the privileged source of political legitimacy. In their advance toward a preeminent political position, Emperor Yuan's 元 reign (49–33 BCE), which followed Xuan's, represents an interlocutory phase. The *Han Shu* describes Yuan as respectful of old ceremonies and fond of the Classicists, though still concerned with sacrifices to Taiyi and Houtu. But it was under Emperor Cheng 成 (33–7 BCE) that the Prime Minister Kuang Heng 匡衡 and the imperial censor Zhang Tan 張譚 could introduce radical ritual transformations that were in keeping with the views of the Classicists.[85]

As Marianne Bujard demonstrates, by purportedly interpreting to their advantage vague references in the literary canon, these two officials convinced the emperor that the most important ceremonies since the beginning of Chinese civilization were those involving the Jiao 郊 (Suburban) sacrifice. The Sage Kings of old had established that it should be addressed to Heaven and aimed at propitiating the yang principle, while sacrifices to Earth were instead to be carried out in the northern suburbs, coherently with its yin nature.[86] In memorial after memorial, Kuang Heng and Zhang Tan persuaded the emperor to observe all his ritual duties in the capital, as his travels throughout the country would have endangered him and burdened both the local functionaries and the common people. As for the cults to Taiyi and Houtu, they were first moved closer to the capital, then abolished altogether, as Kuang Heng noted that they did not correspond to the instructions in the *Classics*. According to the Prime Minister, since every aspect of society had to conform to the supreme values of sincerity (*cheng* 誠) and modesty (*zhi* 質), ceremonies that included highly elaborated objects, rare animals, singers, and dancers were to be discontinued, for they must have been introduced either by the wicked Qin or other non-exemplary feudal lords. Of all the cults in the commanderies and kingdoms that officials had entrusted to *fangshi*, 475 were to be abolished because they did not follow *li*. Of the hundreds of cults dedicated to mountains, rivers, and local deities throughout the country, only fifteen were to be maintained. Ironically, after these measures received imperial approval, Kuang Heng fell into disgrace and lost his title, estate, and position in 29 BCE.[87] When, almost at the same time, extraordinarily strong winds damaged the old sites of Emperor Wu's sacrifices, Emperor Cheng became extremely anxious and started to regret following the advice of the Prime Minister. He consulted Liu Xiang 劉向 (79–8 BCE), who was a central cultural figure during the Western Han but "with interests in the occult,"[88] and became convinced that the new restrictive policies had angered the spirits.

Hence, in 16 BCE, sixteen years after the reforms proposed by Kuang Heng, Emperor Cheng decided to reinstate the sacrifices to Houtu and Taiyi. The solemn announcement, which was pronounced by the Empress Dowager Wang, can be considered a compromise between the ideas of the Classicists and Emperor Wu's original intentions. At least officially, it defined Taiyi and Houtu more abstractly as addressed to the "Above and Below" (*shangxia* 上下), which indirectly referred to the cult of Heaven and Earth.

The "Jiaosi chapter" in the *Han Shu* treats these events only in passing, but "The Sweet Springs Palace Rhapsody" ("Ganquan fu" 甘泉賦) by Yang Xiong 楊雄, although redolent with metaphors, hyperbole, and sophisticated literary allusions, provides an interesting and detailed account of the sacrifices to Taiyi, whose performance appears as rather consistent with what might have been Emperor Wu's vision. It had been the resemblance of Yang Xiong's compositions with those by Sima Xiangru that had granted the former a stint as court poet under Emperor Cheng. Still, years later, it would be the same Yang Xiong who would contribute to the establishment of Classicist aesthetics and ideals by condemning the *fu* genre to cultural marginality with the argument that its extreme sophistication did not befit the purposes of morally inspired literature.[89]

Both Yang Xiong's "Postface" in his *Han shu* biography and the *Jiaosi zhi* report that the Son of Heaven intended to perform the Suburban *Jiao* sacrifice at the Grand Altar at Ganquan and to Houtu at Fenyin in order to propitiate the birth of a son and heir.[90] This demonstrates that despite Sima Qian's skepticism, Emperor Wu's rituals, half a century after the end of his reign, were still remembered as potentially efficacious or at least more so than the lofty, abstract ceremonies conceived by Kuang Heng. "The Sweet Springs Palace Rhapsody" seems to attests to the survival of "heterodox" practices in an era traditionally labeled as "Confucian." Even though the Classicists would eventually abrogate them again for not complying with the frugal and sober rituals of yore, the Taiyi sacrifices carried out under Emperor Wu must have represented to his successors more than the patchwork or poorly understood cults described in the *Records*.

The flowery composition by Yang Xiong mentions all the elements of the Taiyi worship reported in the *Records*, but in much more detail. Although the line between literary exaggeration and factual reality is impossible to discern, it is evident that the ceremonies in which Emperor Cheng took part were lavish and extravagant. As though openly challenging Kuang Heng's recommendations, they involved rich costumes, decorated chariots, and precious and rare goods from all over the known world, while loud music and, most likely, actors and dancers accompanied them. More importantly, Yang's rhapsody demonstrates that the military and territorial characterization of the rituals staged a century earlier had not disappeared.[91]

The rhapsody maintains the association of Taiyi with the martial elements of the Northern Dipper. It describes the emperor as a general manning his chariot, who, after mustering the troops, conducts them through a space symbolically delimited by representations of the sacred mountains—the cultural and physical boundaries of the known world. The numerous references to the past, rather than focusing on the morals of ancient kings and their ruling the world by example, emphasize the cosmic and active dimensions of sovereignty. The Son of Heaven "matches tallies with the

Three Emperors (*sanhuang* 三皇), displays merits equal to those of the Five Sovereigns (*wudi* 五帝), shows concern for his succession, bestows largesse, broadens his pathway, and inaugurates new ventures."[92] Before mounting the superbly decorated "phoenix car," he is preceded by eight warrior deities who "herald and clean the road," as was customary before a ritualized hunting and patrolling expedition (*xunshou*).[93] During the procession the Son of Heaven stops "to cleanse his mind, purify his spirit, gather his vitality, and concentrate his thoughts to solicit Heaven and Earth. Then he receives blessings from the three spirits."[94] The final sacrifice consists of burnt offering, a pyre to Taiyi, and the planting of the Numinous Flag (*lingqi*). When the ceremony is over, the emperor heads south toward the capital, and at this point the poem announces that "Heaven's threshold is agape, Earth's boundary is open, the Eight Barrens are in harmony, and the myriad states are in accord."[95] Then the emperor is finally a peer of Heaven and can receive the blessing of eternal progeny.[96]

In other words, according to the "The Sweet Spring Palace Rhapsody," the ritual was meant to reaffirm the formidable power of the emperor as the conqueror of the realm and master of the cosmos and all its creatures. In Emperor Cheng's case, though, the roaming, patrolling, conquering, and, to a certain extent, the "apotheosis" that characterized the mythical Yellow Emperor and were pursued by Emperor Wu were ritually recreated in a limited area a few miles north of Chang'an.

Chinese rulership was already adapting to an ideal that literally and metaphorically limited its sphere of action. The recovery of the cult of Taiyi in 13 BCE proved to be an exception. In the following years, an intellectual attitude prevailed that strove to limit the operations of the Son of Heaven to the practices recommended in the *Classics* and elaborated further in "metaphysical" terms by Dong Zhongshu.

Conclusions: Templum and Text: Functional Incongruity of Rituals in the Chinese Early Imperial China

Jonathan Z. Smith has noted that ancient texts that create "cosmic topographies" are customarily "the product of well organized, self-conscious scribal elites who had deep vested interests in restricting mobility and valuing place."[97] Smith argues that these kinds of elaborations likely represented the result of "a self-serving ideology, which ought not to be generalized into the universal pattern of religious experience and expression." By mainly looking at ancient Mediterranean and Middle Eastern historical realities, Smith singles out the temple as the ultimate source of cosmos-ordering literature. He writes:

> The texts are, by and large, the production of temples and royal courts and provide their raison d'être—the temple, upon which the priest's and scribe's income rested, as "Center" and microcosm; the requirements of exact repetition in ritual and the concomitant notion of ritual as a reenactment of divine activities, both of which are dependent on written texts which only the elites could read; and propaganda for their chief patron, the king as guardian of cosmic and social order.[98]

As seen at the beginning of this chapter, the *templum* of ancient Rome constituted the exceptional and sacred space of interaction in which extra-human forces manifested their approval or disapproval of human plans and actions. Specifically, what was recognized in the *templum* legitimized the deliberations of the Roman assemblies and institutions, or in other words sanctioned the gods' approval of Rome's intervention in the world. As the Principate brought back hereditary rulership, Octavian, by becoming "Augustus," could simultaneously exert the functions of the priests, the *templum*, and the dynastic ancestor. In this new role, he embodied the continuity of Roman traditions and the extension of the empire in time and space. Thanks to his appropriation of fundamental priestly functions, in a cunningly ambiguous and audience-conscious fashion, Augustus sacralized his own actions while restricting senatorial influence. The emperor's person would become the image of the empire.

By contrast, the Han dynasty was not the result of the formidable expansion of a city-state. From its very inception, rulers and courtiers struggled to compromise among the different regional traditions that constituted the realm. The person of the Son of Heaven, as the cases of the First Emperor of Qin and Wu of the Han demonstrate, could hardly embody a compromise among different interests, social groups, and cultural traditions. At least until Emperor Wu's reign, shared ideas about a common past or values had not yet been unequivocally formalized (or fabricated).

In China, pre-imperial and regional traditions concerning the extra-human realm did not become instrumental in the meta-historical justification of hereditary rule. Because of the absence of an organic conceptualization of the divine, the possible extra-human prerogatives of the emperor represented a further element of ambiguity, not an obvious symbol of unity. As far as we know, early Han sovereigns did not become the object of local, non-elite, and domestic cults as in the case of Roman emperors.[99] The denomination of spirits and ghosts (*shen* and *gui*) simply referred to the plurality of discrete local realities. It did not constitute a universal and unitary basis on which to anchor the social and political structures of a bureaucratic empire. In Confucian texts the extra-human was idiomatically associated with disorder and unrestrained force rather than with moralizing potential.

What we would call the "divine" in early China was not perceived in unitary or paradigmatic terms and did not become "the Universal" or "the Real." And it is perhaps for this reason that we find the *text* as the meta-historical locus of legitimation in early imperial China, instead of the *templum* as a sacred enclave outside ordinary time and space that defines the rules of all human interactions. The texts associated with the Zhou, Confucius, and his teachings were progressively fixed in a more or less stable corpus with their traditional sets of commentaries throughout the first two centuries of the Han Dynasty, even though debates about them never ceased. These texts were not perceived as scripture or the word of God, but they were eventually endowed with intrinsic validating power to which even rulers would submit. Through a process started under Emperor Wu of the Han, their mastery would constitute the fundamental prerequisite for coopting scholars as members of the administration. With the Sui Dynasty (581–618) such a practice became institutionalized in the system of periodic examinations, which would be abolished only in 1905.

Conclusions

The Importance of Getting Lost

> In this world there is a Mighty One
> Who dwells in the Land of the Middle
> His residence stretches ten thousand miles,
> But he is not content to stay there a moment
> Bewailing the pressure and vulgarity of the profane world,
> He departs, lightly soars, and travels far away.
>
> —Sima Xiangru, from "The Rhapsody of the Mighty One"[1]

Emperor Wu, Local Cults, and Spirit Mediums

In the pursuit of an "early Chinese religion," this book has ventured on a brief journey throughout the first centuries of the empire, using the "Book on the *Feng* and *Shan*" as a roadmap. While looking for the meaning of the sacrifices that give the name to this treatise in the *Records*, it soon became evident that celebrating Emperor Wu's rituals was not Sima Qian's main purpose. Starting with the fall of the Western Zhou in 771 BCE, the narrative of the chapter acquires layers and complexity as it approaches the Han Dynasty. In following the accounts of the historian as he accompanies his sovereign in his meandering ritual circuits, I felt compelled to extend my inquiry beyond the "Book on the *Feng* and *Shan*" to the other chapters of the *Records* as well as to other documents in the hope that the study of received and excavated texts and material evidence from the same period could assist me in painting a more complete picture. Interested in maintaining a methodologically sound route, I set as a background interpretative models deriving from the analysis of ancient Mediterranean societies with the intent to test their applicability to Chinese contexts, and eventually propose, by means of systematic historicization, original models.

Consequently, the search for "a Chinese religion" compelled me to redirect my focus to three different kinds of anachronistic projections: the Euro-American habit of seeking and recognizing familiar cultural patterns in non-Western realities; the tendency of modern and contemporary Chinese scholars to interpret the early imperial period in a way that makes it comparable—and therefore not inferior to or "other" from—Western models; the decision of Eastern Han historians to associate the promotion of the Classicists to the center of Chinese political and cultural life with the most prosperous reign of the Western Han, that of Emperor Wu. Then, in focusing on the work of his court historian, it became evident that separating the history of Wu's age from the study of Sima Qian's authorial vicissitudes was both impossible and fruitless. Inevitably, *Heaven Is Empty* tackles the subjects of a "Han religion," Wu's ritual politics, and official historiography together with the issue of ethnocentric epistemologies, as all these elements are interconnected and indissoluble.

The apparent paradox is that the inevitably fragmentary nature of the image I endeavored to reconstruct began to acquire meaning on account of its very incompleteness. While Sima Qian's approach to the "extra-human" and the political and economic tensions underlying discourses on ritual were revealing a sharper outline, the motivations of the main protagonist, Emperor Wu, became even more elusive. Throughout his reign, even when in the middle of clearly purposeful rituals, the Son of Heaven never ceased seeking ways to get as close as possible to various spirits and ghosts. His more "extravagant" interests should be the subject of an independent monograph, but here I intend to report just one very emblematic episode.[2]

According to the *Records*, ever since he stepped on the throne in 141 BCE to replace Emperor Jing, the sixteen-year-old Emperor Wu adopted a very contradictory attitude. He seemed in principle not hostile to the Classicists, but he hardly ever followed their advice. While many hoped that he would finally take charge of the overdue celebration of the dynasty and the beginning of a new era, the young Son of Heaven seemed rather focused on more immediate questions.[3] If he went out of his way to scan small towns in search of experts in the *Classics* to promote as court officials, Sima Qian remarks, it was not because he was actually interested in performing the new sacrifices in a "proper" way or rebuilding the famous Ming Tang 明堂 (Bright Hall) according to Zhou models.[4] Because his paternal grandmother was still very powerful and a Huang-Lao follower, the text suggests, his main intent was to surround himself with people with completely different backgrounds who could help him balance the authority of the overbearing relative and her palace clique.[5] Accounts in which the Emperor momentarily favors the Classicists or engages in important official missions for the state are often followed by reports about his involvement in extravagant behavior that the Classicists at court would have frowned upon.

In 133 BCE, the same year in which he travelled to Yong to perform sacrifices to the Five Sovereigns established there by the Qin,[6] the emperor began to manifest his penchant for spirits and ghosts in a rather unequivocal way. In Changling 長陵, the mausoleum town north of Chang'an where Emperor Gaozu had been buried, there lived a woman, Wangruo 宛若, who had become, according to relatives and neighbors, the channel of communication for the spirit (renamed Shenjun 神君) of her recently deceased sister-in-law. The popularity of her prognostications grew so much that soon even members of the palace aristocracy, such as the princess of Pingyuan 平原, ventured among the crowds of worshippers to see her.[7] When this story of spirit possession reached Emperor Wu, he swiftly had Wangruo sent to the capital and accommodated her in a building in the Shanglin 上林 Park ("the imperial microcosm"), where she lived for many years.

Sima Qian reports that no one was ever able to catch a glimpse of Shenjun. She very seldom spoke, and when she did, the imperial secretaries assiduously wrote down her words, which solemnly (or ironically) they called "Planning Laws" (*huafa* 畫法).[8] In this case the historian seems less hesitant than usual to manifest his skepticism. He suggests that it was Wangruo herself who spoke on behalf of Shenjun while hiding behind a curtain. Furthermore, Sima Qian writes, what she uttered was banal and uninteresting, but Emperor Wu always found great delight in it. Falling suddenly ill in 118 BCE, he requested Shenjun's prognostication. When he quickly recovered, as she had allegedly predicted, the Son of Heaven was so pleased that he bestowed on Shenjun public honors equal to those given to Taiyi.[9] Until this point, the text implies, very few people knew of Wangruo and that she resided in the imperial park.[10]

It is, of course, extremely problematic to gauge the import of Shenjun's "private" cult in its initial fifteen years. It can be inferred that the emperor's exclusive and direct access to a powerful spirit might have played a role in the power dynamics at court by eliciting the awe, hope, or fear of the palace personnel. It is also plausible that in Shenjun the emperor found solace for concerns specific to his physical and emotional wellbeing that he did not want to share. But leaving aside these conjectures, the emperor must have been aware of the political impact of making public his connection to Shenjun, who was derided by courtiers such as Sima Qian but extremely popular among the common people.[11]

Even though the text does not mention it explicitly, it cannot be overlooked that the spirit originated from an area certainly considered special because the founder of the dynasty was buried there. Commoners tended to interpret the exceptionality of the Sons of Heaven in more literal terms. After their deaths, their spirits were believed to be far more powerful than those released by ordinary people. It should not come as a surprise that the echo of the dealings of Emperor Wu with Shenjun would survive in Tang Dynasty Daoist circles, poems, and apocryphal literature and develop into popular stories about the liaison of the emperor with the goddess Xi Wang Mu 西王母, the Queen Mother of the West. These sources all more or less lament that such a wondrous encounter could have only been possible "in those fortunate times in which sovereigns were so awesome that they could consort with the gods."[12] Even today, in the area of the burial mounds north of Xi'an (the former Chang'an) it is possible to hear locals quipping, with varying degrees of irony, that over the centuries the area, although seismic, has been spared major earthquakes because numerous "sleeping dragons" (deceased emperors) lying underneath protect the center of the empire from catastrophes and destruction.

For these reasons, we cannot exclude the possibility that an otherwise shrewd emperor was actually trying to employ diverse media to cater to different social groups in an effort to defy aristocratic opposition at court. His vision might have been not dissimilar from that of Octavian Augustus's in Rome. But despite his military, political, and economic successes—at least in the first period—Emperor Wu did not even obtain the favor of the court historian, and the overtly celebratory verses of his court poet were never taken too seriously on account of their content. He lost the cultural propaganda battle, and future generations (mis)interpreted his legacy or simply read it through the point of view of his cultural enemies.

Emperor Wu was momentarily able to tilt the balance between the central state and the local lords toward the throne's side. From a cultural point of view, one strategy he employed consisted of using rituals (not a religion in an Abrahamic or polytheistic sense) for several purposes: (1) Legitimizing an active, centralizing conception of rulership for the courtiers and officials in the capitals, and perhaps even a larger public; (2) Visiting local cults, keeping local administrators and nobles in check, displaying his royal majesty, and establishing a connection with local people; and (3)

Eluding the influence and control of rival member of the imperial family and officials, as the unruliness, variety, and chaotic nature of the realm of spirits and ghosts could always represent an easy way out from cultural and procedural constrictions.

As for Sima Qian (or the *Records* with all its authors, editors, and interpolations), his accounts are fundamental to our understanding of the early Chinese Empire because they provide a unique point of view. Although a fervent admirer of Confucius, the historian was in no way a "Confucian." Since his intellectual approach did not coincide with that of most contemporary Classicists, whom he despised, it allows us to access valuable information without the filter of an apologetic re-elaboration that supported a "Confucian" conception of statecraft and society. At the same time, probably because of his tragic clash with Emperor Wu, Sima Qian could not but maintain a relatively objective analytical attitude towards his sovereign.

As for the *Records'* treatment of the extra-human world, the text does not envision spirits and ghosts as elements of an organic pantheon but of a chaotic and multifarious realm. The elusive nature of the spirits could distract elites and common people alike from more important duties concerning the state and the family. It is clear from all the evidence analyzed so far that, at least according to Sima Qian, the invocation and alleged presence of extra-human entities did not make society more moral or harmonious. On the contrary, spirits and ghosts appeared as a threat to those principles on which a stable and hierarchically organized community must be founded.

In recounting the exploits of pre-imperial monarchs, Sima Qian accepts received traditions about spirits and ghosts without directly criticizing them. However, the extent to which he emphasizes ancient rulers' fascination with the extra-human reflects Sima Qian's implicit assessment of their moral exemplarity. In chronicling the events from the Qin to his own times, he never hesitates to point out how hopes and fears concerning the invisible were exploited for economic or political gain.

Clearly the historian was not interested in spirits and ghosts *per se*. Their worship did not define the cultural identity of the elites. More than concentrating on the specific features of the cults, Sima Qian devoted his analytical skills to assessing the attention people devoted to them. As for the *Records'* historiographical approach, spirits and ghosts simply provided the epistemological boundaries, the external limits of its field of inquiry, humankind. Sima Qian did not perceive the world as a self-regulating unitary organism, nor did he believe in the presence of a conscious being that responded morally to good and bad behavior. Rather, he interpreted history and the world as the alternating of different ages and universes, each requiring recourse to specific values, skills, institutions, and timely choices. Yao and Shun, the Zhou, and Confucius of course represented Sima Qian's unequaled models. But during his times, as the central government strove to enforce administrative and economic centralization, he was adamant that the present circumstances did not for allow the establishment of an ideal, moral rulership. The establishment of the Han sanctioned a new age that was closer to the military control exercised by the ancient state of Qi after the fall of the Western Zhou than to the moral standard the Zhou had embodied. Hence Emperor Wu should have concentrated on appointing honest and capable politicians who could efficaciously respond to contingent challenges while prioritizing the establishment of a sound economic administration, as recommended by the Qi officials Guan Zhong and Yan Ying.

This decree, already cited above, shows how Emperor Wu's rulership might have worked had he stayed focused on his political duties:

> I rule by mandate. Every sovereign flourishes on different bases, there are different ways but a common goal. To act by following the people is to study customs and then make rules. Those who criticize all exalt the ancient past, but what should the common people look up to? The Han dynasty is the enterprise of just one family, if standards and rules cannot be passed down, how can we talk about posterity? Those who achieve grandiose deeds are eminent and far reaching. Those who govern in a shallow pond are petty and narrow minded. How can we not try?[13]

Finally, Sima Qian's more sincere opinion on the matters treated in the "Book on the *Feng* and *Shan*" can be summarized by the following anecdote, narrated at the end of the treatise on economics in the *Records*, just before the Grand Historian's customary final remarks. After a minor drought, the eminent official Sang Hongyang (who is the champion of centralizing policies in the *Discourses on Salt and Iron*) orders court invokers to pray for rain. But Bu Shi 卜式, one of the few court advisors Sima Qian appreciated, rebukes Sang's measures in an unequivocal way. The *Records* reports that Bu Shi was a capable and honest farmer who had always worked hard to provide for his less-skilled brother. Emperor Wu had promoted him to an official position after hearing that Bu Shi, unlike most of his wealthy contemporaries, had offered half of his fortune to defend the country against the Xiongnu. So when Sang Hongyang announced his plan, Bu Shi said, with more than a little sarcasm:

> The government officials are supposed to collect what taxes they need for food and clothing and that is all. Now Sang Hongyang has them sitting in the market stalls buying and selling goods and scrambling for profit. If Your Majesty were to boil Sang Hongyang alive, I think Heaven might send us rain![14]

Again, the issues of dedication to the state, individual profit, taxation, sacrifice, and border defense are all linked—albeit ironically—to the potential response of Heaven. Through the voice of this astute farmer-turned-official, Sima Qian was expressing his own disappointment with Han functionaries and his frustration with their hypocrisies. It is unlikely that the author of the *Records* could have known that the themes brought up by Bu Shi would be at the center of Chinese political debates for centuries to come. He had observed, however, how easily the rhetoric of Heaven could be used to buttress hyperbolic claims that could not empirically be tested. In the *Records*, Heaven is like an ancient vessel that commands awe and respect on account of its remote origins, but which is in fact empty. According to Sima Qian, capable leaders and delusional charlatans alike were free to fill the vessel as they saw fit. Only in case of success, the content would receive the same hallowed status as the vessel.

Notes

Introduction

1. All the citations from the *Records of the Grand Historian* (*Shiji* 史記), hereafter *Records* are based on: Sima Qian 司馬遷, *Shiji* 史記 (Beijing: Zhonghua shuju, 2005). For the passage above see, *Shiji*, chapter (*juan* 卷) 97, 2694 (Hereafter "*SJ*," followed by chapter and page numbers).

2. Samuel P. Huntington, *The Clash of Civilizations and the Remaking of World Order* (New York: Simon & Schuster, 1996). Francis Fukuyama, a student of Huntington's, has famously argued that the triumph of modern liberal democracy will bring about the end of ideological conflicts; see Francis Fukuyama, *The End of History and the Last Man* (New York: Free Press, 1992), and, by the same author, "Confucianism and Democracy," *Journal of Democracy* 6, no. 2 (1995): 20–33. On the debates on religion in light of today's political and ideological conflicts, see Bruce Lincoln, *Holy Terrors: Thinking about Religion after September 11* (Chicago: University of Chicago Press, 2005); Emilio Gentile, *God's Democracy: American Religion after September 11* (Westport, CT: Praeger, 2008); Reza Aslan, *How to Win a Cosmic War: God, Globalization, and the End of the War on Terror* (New York: Random House, 2009).

3. For a very popular "universalistic" reading of world monotheistic religions, see Karen Armstrong, *A History of God: The 4,000-Year Quest of Judaism, Christianity and Islam* (New York: Random House, 1993). "Non-historicizing" debates on secularism and atheism still tend to privilege philosophical and totalizing understandings of the Abrahamic traditions; see, for example, Charles Taylor, "Why We Need a Radical Redefinition of Secularism," in *The Power of Religion in the Public Sphere*, Judith Butler, Jürgen Habermas, Charles Taylor, et al., eds. (New York: Columbia University Press, 2011), 34–59. Similarly, exponents of so-called New Atheism, in attacking select aspects of the major religious traditions, implicitly reinforce essentializing or idealistic intellectual approaches to religions: see Sam Harris, *The End of Faith: Religion, Terror, and the Future of Reason* (New York: Norton, 2005);

Michel Onfray, *Atheist Manifesto: The Case against Christianity, Judaism, and Islam* (New York: Arcade Publishing, 2011). The anthropologist Talal Asad has paved the way for an approach that finally complicates and historicizes the processes whereby hegemonic discourses on religion and secularism have actually obfuscated our understanding of fundamental ritual behaviors across the so-called "public and private spheres." Although Asad's views have become essential in academic works on modernity and religion, they still do not have a noticeable impact on generalist discourses; see Talal Asad, *Formations of the Secular: Christianity, Islam, Modernity* (Stanford, CA: Stanford University Press, 2003).

4. Arguably the earliest cogent attempt at comparative sociological and quantitative analysis of Rome and China is represented by Keith Hopkins's, *Conquerors and Slaves: Urbanization in Developing Countries* (Cambridge, UK: Cambridge University Press, 1981).

5. The "Stanford Ancient Chinese and Mediterranean Empires Comparative History Project" (ACME), launched by Walter Scheidel roughly ten years ago, inaugurated a systematic approach to the Han and Roman empires based on Max Weber's (1868–1922) and Karl Wittfogel's (1896–1988) analysis of social structures and socioeconomic systems; see Walter Scheidel's (editor), *Rome and China: Comparative Perspectives on Ancient World Empires* (New York: Oxford University Press, 2009) and *State Power in Ancient China and Rome* (New York: Oxford University Press, 2015). Interestingly enough, the necessity of approaching ancient China comparatively seems to have become so ineludible that even scholars who have usually resisted forays outside a strict philological/historical approach—even if are not embracing it yet—feel compelled to manifest their endorsement to the cross analysis of ancient Rome and early China as potentially rewarding; see Michael Loewe, *Problems of Han Administration: Ancestral Rites, Weights and Measures, and the Means of Protest* (Leiden: Brill, 2016), 1–3.

6. This issue is the topic of the second half of chapter 1. For a systematic critique of anachronistic and ethnocentric usages of Abrahamic concepts of religion, see Carlin A. Barton and Daniel Boyarin, *Imagine no Religion: How Modern Abstractions Hide Ancient Realities* (New York: Fordham University Press, 2016); Brent Nongbri, *Before Religion: A History of a Modern Concept* (New Haven, CT: Yale University Press, 2013); Tomoko Masuzawa, *The Invention of World Religions: Or, How European Universalism Was Preserved in the Language of Pluralism* (Chicago: University of Chicago Press, 2005); Zvi Ben-Dor Benite, "Religions and World History," in *Oxford Handbook of World History*, Jerry Bentley, ed. (New York: Oxford University Press, 2011), 210–28; Kimberley C. Patton, Benjamin C. Ray, *A Magic still Dwells: Comparative Religion in the Postmodern Age* (Berkeley: University of California Press, 2000); Timothy Fitzgerald, *The Ideology of Religious Studies* (New York: Oxford University Press, 2000).

7. For overviews of the political, cultural and social history of the dynasties that preceded the Han, see Li Feng, *Early China: A Social and Cultural History*

(Cambridge, UK: Cambridge University Press, 2013), 228–323. For a succinct yet exhaustive overview on Qin and Han institutions, see Michael Loewe, *The Government of the Qin and Han Empires: 221 BCE–220 CE* (Indianapolis, IN: Hackett, 2006).

8. Another hindrance common to most cross-cultural approaches is represented by the different pace with which the various fields involved in interdisciplinary projects develop their theoretical outlook. As a consequence, those disciplines which are perceived as more "theoretically advanced" often constitute the model of those that are still "lagging behind," with the result that the study of early imperial China is customarily (and more or less implicitly) rooted in paradigms deriving from centuries of scholarship on the ancient Mediterranean.

9. For example, in one of the few recent cross-cultural contributions that deviate from strictly empirical themes, Michael Puett has synthesized his analysis of the cultural aspects of the establishment of hereditary monarchy in Rome and China by assuming the universality of a notion of "divine kingship," even though the semantic spheres of the Latin *divinus*, the Chinese *shen* 神, and the contemporary English *divine* overlap only tangentially; see Michael Puett, "Ghosts, Gods, and the Coming of Apocalypse: Empire and Religion in Early China and Ancient Rome," in Scheidel, ed., *State Power*, 257–59.

10. The situation is different in the field of history of religion. Because this discipline is traditionally theory-oriented, scholarship on ancient Rome and the late antique period have already been catching up with postmodern critiques of the universality of Abrahamic notions of religion. In recent works, the projection of centuries-old confessional and cultural concerns of Christian and anti-Christian historiography onto the study of "pagan" rituals and beliefs has finally come under scrutiny, while a meticulous historicization of Latin texts has been giving way to new readings that strive to recover the specificity of Roman contexts; see Clifford Ando, *The Matter of the Gods: Religion and the Roman Empire* (Berkeley: University of California Press, 2008).

11. Douglas Northrop, ed., "The Challenge of World History," in *A Companion in World History* (Hoboken, NJ: Wiley Blackwell, 2012), 4–5.

12. Reinhart Koselleck, "The Need for Theory in History," in *The Practice of Conceptual History: Timing History, Spacing Concepts* (Stanford, CA: Stanford University Press, 2002), 1–19.

13. From a theoretical and philosophical point of view, a groundbreaking effort at disambiguating comparative epistemological approaches is represented by the volumes published by David Hall and Roger Ames; see their seminal *Anticipating China: Thinking through the Narratives of Chinese and Western Culture* (Albany: SUNY Press, 1995) and *Thinking through Confucius* (Albany: SUNY Press, 1987).

14. The famous sentence "Without the Other there is no Self (*Fei bi wu wo* 非彼無我)" is in *Zhuangzi* 2, 3.

15. Arguably the most accurate and context-specific approach to "religion" in early China is the study on popular practices and individual approaches carried out

by Mu-chou Poo, *In Search of Personal Welfare: A View of Ancient Chinese Religion* (Albany: SUNY Press, 1998). As valuable and original, although seldom referenced, is Jordan Paper, *The Spirits are Drunk: Comparative Approaches to Chinese Religion* (Albany: SUNY Press, 1995), which focuses on the centrality ritual function of food and banquets. One of the earliest systematic critiques of the inadequacy of the usage of Western notions of "religion" in the study of Chinese traditions, such as Confucianism, Daoism and Buddhism, was offered by David Johnson; see David Johnson, "Remarks presented at the symposium convened in conjunction with the first annual Tanner Lectures," University of California, Berkeley, May 5, 1988.

16. Robert Ford Campany, "On the Very Idea of Religions [In the Modern West and in Early Medieval China]," *History of Religions* 42, No. 4 (May 2003): 287–319.

17. For an update reflection on the impact of Buddhism (and Buddhist studies) on our understanding of ancient China, see Robert Ford Campany, " 'Buddhism Enters China' in Early Medieval China," in *Old Society, New Belief: Religious Transformation of China and Rome, ca. 1st–6th Centuries,* Mu-chou Poo, H. A. Drake, Lisa Raphals, eds. (New York: Oxford University Press, 2017), 13–34.

18. Prior to the spread of creeds based on values that transcended local identities, the concept of "conversion" analyzed by Jerry H. Bentley is not applicable to early China; see his "Missionaries, Pilgrims, and the Spread of the World Religions," in *Old World Encounters: Cross-Cultural Contacts and Exchanges in Pre-Modern Times* (New York: Oxford University Press, 1993), 67–110.

19. Erich S. Gruen, *Rethinking the Other in Antiquity* (Princeton, NJ: Princeton University Press, 2011), 223.

20. On the usage of linguistics in the scholarship on race and ethnic and cultural identities, see Xinru Liu, "The Science of Difference: Race, Indo-European Linguistics, and Eurasian Nomads," in *A Companion in World History,* 245–57.

21. In keeping with Michael Loewe's and Michael Nylan's scholarship, I do not refer to Western Han Classicists as a homogenous philosophical or intellectual faction, nor consider the existence in this period of "Confucianism" as a coherent, organic doctrine. The study of those texts to which we refer as *Classics* constituted the background of almost all of Han educated individuals. On the formalization of the *Classics* in antiquity, see Michael Nylan, *The Five "Confucian" Classics* (New Haven, CT: Yale University Press, 2001).

22. Evidence of this tendency is the attempt to refer to Confucianism to include China in global discourses on great religious-moral traditions as well as the phenomenon of the recovery of a Confucian moral and spiritual identity as an antidote to the Western materialistic values many Chinese seem to have embraced especially as a consequence of the post-2000 economic surge; see Gan Chunsong and Zhou Yiqun, "The Religious Nature of Confucianism in Contemporary China's 'Cultural Renaissance Movement,' " *Contemporary Chinese Thought* 44, 2 (2012): 3–15; Anna Sun, *Confucianism as a World Religion: Contested Histories and Contemporary*

Realities (Princeton NJ: Princeton University Press, 2014); Sébastien Billioud and Joël Thoraval, *The Sage and the People: The Confucian Revival in China* (New York: Oxford University Press, 2015).

23. The *Records* has been partially translated in Sima Qian 司馬遷, Édouard Chavannes, trans., *Les Mémoires historiques de Sse Ma Ts'ien*, 6 vols. (Paris: E. Leroux, 1895–1904); Burton Watson, trans., *Records of the Grand Historian*, 3 vols. (New York: University of Columbia Press, 1993); and William H. Nienhauser, Jr., ed., trans., Tsai-fa Cheng et al., *The Grand Scribe's Records*, 6 vols. (Bloomington: University of Indiana Press, 1992). The most authoritative collection of commentaries on the *Records* is in Takigawa Kametaro 瀧川龜太郎, *Shiki kaichū kōshō* 史記會注考證 (Tokyo: Tōhō bunka Gakuin, 1934), Reprinted as: *Shiji huizhu kaozheng* 史記會注考證. (Taipei: Bei yue wen yi chu ban, 1998). The *Records*' historiographic approach and "religious" factors in its narratives are the subjects of chapter 2; see below for a detailed treatment and bibliography.

24. The issues regarding the authorship of the *Records* are extremely complex. The text was compiled, written, and edited by Sima Qian and his father Tan and eventually underwent several additions and interpolations. Esther Sunkyung Klein, in her "The History of a Historian: Perspectives on the Authorial Roles of Sima Qian" (PhD diss., Princeton University, 2010), has contextualized the different readings of the *Records* throughout the centuries by focusing on the ways cultural expectations modified its reception. Consistently with such an approach, Klein has aptly overcome issues about the authorship of the *Records* by focusing on the intellectual impact of the text in different periods and engaging with the notion of "author-function" (in turn borrowed from Michel Foucault). In substantial agreement with such an interpretation, in the present work, I use interchangeably "Sima Qian" and "*Records*" only for narrative purposes. For a systematic treatment of these themes, see below.

25. Michael Loewe focuses extensively on Emperor Wu (personal name Liu Che 劉徹) in the entry in his *A Bibliographical Dictionary of the Qin, Former Han & Xin Periods* (221 BC–AD 24) (Leiden: Brill, 2000), 273–82; for a monographic reconstruction of Emperor Wu's life and achievements according to the fragmentary accounts of the *Records*, see Wang Liqun 王立群, *Han Wudi: Wang Liqun du Shiji* 漢武帝: 王立群讀 "史記" (Taipei: Lianjing, 2008).

26. Richard Von Glahn, *The Economic History of China: From Antiquity to the Nineteenth Century* (Cambridge, UK: Cambridge University Press, 2016), 118. For an accurate analysis of Qin-Han fiscal policies, see Yamada Katsuyoshi 山田勝芳, *Shin Kan zaisei shûyû no kenkyû* 秦漢財政收入の研究 (Tokyo: Kyûko shoin; 1993). For a reassesment of Sima Qian's "economic" thought in relation to modern economic theories and trends, see Zhao Shanxuan 趙善軒, *Sima Qian de jingji shi yu jingji sixiang: Zhongguo de ziyoujingjizhuyizhe* 司馬遷的經濟史與經濟思想—中國的自由經濟主義者 (Taipei: Wanjuan, 2017).

27. The *Yantie lun* 鹽鐵論 is traditionally ascribed to Huan Kuan 桓寬, who lived under Xuandi 宣帝 (74–49 BCE); see Michael Loewe, "Yen t'ieh lun 鹽鐵

論," in *Early Chinese Texts*, ed., idem (Berkeley, CA: The Institute of East Asian Studies, 1993), 477–82; Michael Nylan, "The art of persuasion from 100 BCE to 100 CE," in *China's Early Empires: A Reappraisal*, M. Nylan, M. Loewe, eds. (Cambridge, UK: Cambridge University Press, 2010), 495–98; Xu Fuguan 叙复观, *Lianghan sixiangshi* 两汉思想史 (Shanghai: Huadong Shifan Daxue, 2001), 3:73–131. A partial translation of the *Yantie lun* is in Esson M. Gale, *Discourses on Salt and Iron* (Leyden: Brill, 1931).

28. Moses Finley, *The Ancient Economy* (Berkeley: University of California Press, 1973).

29. The most effective and insightful synthesis of the evolution of early Chinese imperial rituals is in Tian Tian. "The Suburban Sacrifice Reforms and the Evolution of the Imperial Sacrifices," in *Chang'an 26 BC: An Augustan Age in China*, Michael Nylan and Griet Vankeerberghen, eds. (Seattle and London: University of Washington Press, 2015), 263–91.

30. Denis Twitchett and Michael Loewe, eds., *The Cambridge History of China—Volume I, The Ch'in and the Han Empires, 221 B.C.–A.D. 220* (Cambridge, UK: Cambridge University Press, 1986), 104–06.

31. Marianne Bujard, *Le sacrifice au Ciel dans la Chine Ancienne: Théorie et pratique sous les Han Occidentaux* (Paris: Ecole francaise d'Extrême-Orient, 2000).

32. Tamara T. Chin, *Savage Exchange: Han Imperialism, Chinese Literary Style, and the Economic Imagination* (Cambridge, MA: Harvard University Press, 2014).

33. *Savage Exchange*, 69–142.

34. The doctrines and the texts conventionally associated with Huang-Lao seem to present a "more organic" integration of the political and cosmological spheres in religious terms; see John S. Major, *Heaven and Earth in Early Han Thought* (Albany: SUNY Press, 1991), Robin D. S. Yates, *Five Lost Classics: Tao, Huang-Lao, and Yin-Yang in Han China* (New York: Ballantine Books, 1997).

35. *Savage Exchange*, 188.

36. For a recent translation of this work, see Dong Zhongshu (John S. Major, Sarah A. Queen, trans.), *Luxuriant Gems of the Spring and Autumn* (New York: Columbia University Press), 2015.

37. See Michael Loewe's "'Confucian' Values and Practices in Han China," *T'oung Pao* 98, 1/3 (2012): 25–30. Liang Cai, in *Witchcraft and the Rise of the First Confucian Empire* (Albany: SUNY Press, 2013), has demonstrated the numerical "irrelevance" of Classicists at the court of Emperor Wu. This issue will be treated more extensively below throughout the whole volume. On questions concerning the interpretation and attribution of the *Luxuriant Gems*, in addition to the introductory chapters of Queen and Major's work cited above, see Fukui Shigemasa 福井重雅, "Jukyō no kangakuka o meguru teisetsu no saikento 儒教の官学化をめぐる定説の再検討," in *Kandai Jukyō no shiteki kenkyū* 漢代儒教の史的研究 (Tokyo: Kyūko Shoin, 2005), 5–104; Sarah Queen, *From Chronicle to Canon: The Hermeneutics of the Spring and Autumn according to Tung Chungshu* (Cambridge, UK: Cambridge

University Press, 2005); Marianne Bujard, "La vie de Dong Zhongshu: énigmes et hypothèses," *Journal Asiatique* 280, no. 1–2 (1992): 145–217; Gary Arbuckle, "A Note on the Authenticity of the *Chuqiu fanlu*," *T'oung Pao* 75 (1989): 226–34; and Steve Davidson, "Chunqiu fanlu," in *Early Chinese Texts*, Michael Loewe, ed. (Berkeley, CA: The Institute of East Asian Studies, 1993), 67–76.

38. See Vincent Goossaert and David A. Palmer, *The Religious Question in Modern China* (Chicago: University of Chicago Press, 2011); and See Jason Ānanda Josephson, *The Invention of Religion in Japan* (Chicago: University of Chicago Press, 2012).

39. Mu-chou Poo, *In Search*, 1–16. On transcendence and Chinese culture, see David Hall and Roger T. Ames, "Tian 天 and Dao 道 as Nontranscendent Fields: The 'Transcendence Debate' in Contemporary China," in *Thinking from the Han: Self, Truth, and Transcendence in Chinese and Western Culture* (Albany: SUNY Press, 1998), 219–52.

40. For an exhaustive introduction on the genre, see Robert F. Campany, *A Garden of Marvels, Tales of Wonder from Early Medieval China* (Honolulu: University of Hawai'i Press, 2015), xix–xli.

41. These topics will be addressed systematically in chapter 1; for a general introduction to these issues, see Jonathan Z. Smith, "Religion, Religions, Religious," in *Relating Religion: Essays in the Study of Religion* (Chicago: University of Chicago Press, 2004), 179–96; *To Take Place: Toward Theory in Ritual* (Chicago: University of Chicago Press, 1987); and Catherine Bell, "The Spectrum of Ritual Activities," in *Ritual: Perspectives and Dimensions* (Oxford: Oxford University Press, 1997), 91–169.

42. The most complete and cogent analysis of the Zhou political system (traditionally mislabeled as "feudal") is in Li Feng, *Bureaucracy and the State in Early China: Governing the Western Zhou* (Cambridge, UK: Cambridge University Press, 2008), 271–99.

43. Michael J. Puett, *The Ambivalence of Creation: Debates Concerning Innovation and Artifice in Early China* (Stanford, CA: Stanford University Press, 2001).

Chapter 1

1. See Christian P. Jones, *Between Pagan and Christian* (Cambridge, MA, Harvard University Press, 2014); Douglas R. Boin, *Coming out Christian in the Roman Empire: How the Followers of Jesus Made a Place in Caesar's Empire* (London: Bloomsbury Press, 2015).

2. Ando, *The Matter*, xvi–xvii.

3. Ando, *The Matter*, 1–18. For a more complete historical account of the meanings of *rĕligio* in ancient Rome up to Augustine's (354–430) influential analysis, see Clifford Ando, "Introduction: Religion, Law and Knowledge in Classical Rome," in *Roman Religion*, 11–22.

4. See Gregory Woolf, "Polis-Religion and its Alternatives in the Roman Provinces," in *Roman Religion*, Clifford Ando, ed. (Edinburgh: Edinburgh University Press, 2003), 39–54.

5. James B. Rives, *Religion in the Roman Empire* (Malden, MA: Blackwell, 2007), 58.

6. Peter Brown, *The Cult of the Saints: Its Rise and Function in Latin Christianity* (Chicago: University of Chicago Press, 1982).

7. A notable exception is represented by the relationship between Roman emperors and Jewish communities; see Erich Gruen, *Diaspora: Jews amidst Greeks and Romans* (Cambridge, MA: Harvard University Press, 2004), 15–53, 84–104.

8. Ando, *The Matter*, 43–58.

9. Michael Nylan, "A Problematic Model: The 'Han Orthodox Synthesis,' Then and Now," in *Imagining Boundaries: Changing Confucian Doctrines, Texts, and Hermeneutics*, Kai-Wing Chow, On-cho Ng, John B. Henderson, eds. (Albany: SUNY Press, 1999), 17–56.

10. Yang Hua 楊華, in a compelling analysis of both received and excavated sources, documented the efforts of the Qin and Han to regulate and established centralized control over ritual activities throughout China. The evidence analyzed by Yang Hua demonstrates that despite a degree of documentary uniformity achieved through a relentless process of bureaucratization, the meanings and the finality of the innumerable local ritual activities were not understandable outside their original places even decades after the foundation of the Han. See, Yang Hua 楊華, "Qinhan diguo de shenquan tongyi: chutu jianbo yu 'Fengshan shu,' 'Jiaosi zhi,' de duibi kaocha" 秦漢帝國的神權統一：出土簡帛與封禪書的對比考察, *Lishi Yanjiu* 5 (2011): 4–26.

11. See Rebecca Nedostup, *Superstitious Regimes: Religion and the Politics of Chinese Modernity* (Cambridge, MA: Harvard University Press, 2009), 27–66; Goossaert and Palmer, *The Religious Question*, 43–65.

12. Derk Bodde, *Festivals in Classical China: New Year and Other Annual Observances during the Han Dynasty (206 BC–AD 220)* (Princeton, NJ: Princeton University Press, 1975).

13. Lester J. Bilsky, *The State Religion of Ancient China* (Taipei: The Orient Cultural Service, 1975), vol. 2, 289 and passim 287–330.

14. Michael Puett, *To Become a God: Cosmology, Sacrifice, and Self-Divinization in Early China* (Cambridge, MA: Harvard University Press, 2004).

15. In this, I disagree with the view expressed by Grant Hardy, who argues that Sima Qian's idiosyncratic historiography and lack of systematic historical view is compensated by his "organicistic" approach, or, in other words, by the fact that events narrated in the *Records* are consistent once they are read against the rules of an organic cosmos. See Grant Hardy, *Worlds of Bronze and Bamboo: Sima Qian's Conquest of History* (New York: Columbia University Press: 1999), 61–113. See also chapter 2 below.

16. The Chinese expression *zongjiao* 宗教 is a loan word from the Japanese *shūkyō* 宗教, which was in turn chosen from a Buddhist Song Dynasty text (in which simply referred to an official position) in the late nineteenth century in order to translate the English "religion" or the German *religionsübung* (religious practice)–a neologism for foreign concepts; see Paper, *The Spirits*, 12–13. On the intercultural dialogue between China and Japan concerning the translation/introduction of "religion" and the mutual exchange of ideas and terms, see Antony C. Yu, *State and Religion in China, Historical and Textual Perspectives* (Chicago: Open Court, 2005), 5–25; Yu refers to Oguchi Iichi 小口偉一 and Hori Ichirō 堀一郎, eds., *Shūkyō gaku jiten* 宗教学字典 (Tokyo: Tokyo Daigaku shuppankai, 1973), 256; the introduction of *Ningen to shūkyō: kidai no nihonjin no shūkyōkan* 人間と宗教：近代日本人の宗教観, Koizumi Takashi 小泉仰 et al., ed. (Tokyo: Tokyo Bunka, 1982), 17–25; and Chen Xiyuan 陳悉遠, "Zongjiao—yige Zhongguo jindai wenhuashi shang de guanjian ci 宗教——一個中國近代文化史上的關鍵詞," *Xin shixue* 13, 4 (December 2001): 37–54 (cited in Yu, *State and Religion*, 152–53 n9–10). Also see Isomae Jun'ichi, "Deconstructing Japanese Religion—A Historical Survey," *Japanese Journal of Religious Studies* 32, 2 (2005): 235–48.

17. K. E. Brashier, *Ancestral Memory Memory in Early China*. (Cambridge, MA: Harvard University Press, 2011), 35.

18. Michael Loewe, following a strictly empirical approach categorizes imperial sacrifices as addressed to two major groups: "[P]owers that were thought to be inherent in the cosmos and capable of affecting the course of human destinies . . . memories of earlier sovereigns and to spirits of an emperor's ancestors, unseen, but still believed to exist"; see M. Loewe, *Problems*, 15.

19. A classic work on the ontological implications of the sacred-profane dichotomy is Mircea Eliade (trans. W. R. Trask), *The Sacred and the Profane: The Nature of Religion* (Orlando, FL: Harcourt, Inc., 1959).

20. See Kimberley C. Patton and Benjamin C. Ray, "Introduction," in *A Magic Still Dwells*, 1–19.

21. Jonathan Z. Smith, "On Comparison," in *Drudgery Divine: On the Comparison of Early Christianities and the Religions of Late Antiquity* (Chicago: University of Chicago Press, 1990), 51.

22. Diane L. Eck, "Dialogue and Method: Reconstructing the Study of Religion," in *A Magic Still Dwells*, 140.

23. William E. Paden, "Elements of a New Comparativism," in *A Magic Still Dwells*, 182. By the same author, see also *Religious Worlds: The Comparative Study of Religion* (Boston: Beacon Press, 1988).

24. William E. Paden, "Elements of a New Comparativism," in *A Magic Still Dwells*, 182–89.

25. Ibid., 184–86.

26. See Benjamin Caleb Ray, "Discourse about Difference: Understanding African Ritual Language," in *A Magic Still Dwells*, 101–16. As pointed out by

Wendy Doniger, later postcolonial approaches differentiated themselves from previous approaches in that they would acknowledge in the "colonized" a degree of agency or a "culture of resistance," in Edward Said's terms. See Wendy Doniger, "Post-modern and Colonial Structural Comparisons," in *A Magic Still Dwells*, 63–73.

27. Jonathan Z. Smith, "Epilogue," in *A Magic Still Dwells*, 239.

28. Wilfred Cantwell Smith, *The Meaning and End of Religion* (Minneapolis, MN: Fortress Press, 1991).

29. W. Cantwell Smith, *The Meaning and End*, 170–202. The perduring echo of Cantwell Smith's longing for unity, for example, can still be perceived in Laurie L. Patton: "The Magic in Miniature: Etymological Links in Comparative Religions," in *A Magic Still Dwells*, 193–205.

30. As for faith, for example the concepts of Greek *pístis* (πίστις) and Roman *fides* and their Christian and Abrahamic interpretations cannot be automatically translated into early Chinese contexts. And the same is true about the notion of transcendence. On faith, see Teresa Morgan, *Roman Faith and Christian Faith* (New York: Oxford University Press, 2015); Dario Sabbatucci, *La prospettiva storico-religiosa: Fede, religione e cultura* (Milano: Il Saggiatore, 1990), 1–50.

31. Fitzgerald, *The Ideology*, 7. The scholar of secularism Talal Asad instead, while acknowledging Cantwell's Smith historic contribution, in refuting an essentialist interpretation of religion, pointed out that *The Meaning and End of Religion* replaces the essentialization of the noun "religion," with the essentialization of the adjective "religious"; see Talal Asad, "Reading a Modern Classic: W. C. Smith's *The Meaning and End of Religion*," *History of Religions* 4, no. 3 (February 2001): 205–22.

32. Fitzgerald, *The Ideology*, 4; by the same author, see also "A Critique of 'Religion' as a Cross-cultural Category," *Method & Theory in the Study of Religion* 9, no. 2 (1997): 91–110 and *Discourse on Civility and Barbarity: A Critical History of Religion and Related Categories* (Oxford: Oxford University Press, 2007) in which he also analyzes the impact on contemporary discourses on identity and ideology of the traditional categories of "religion" and "secular."

33. Robert Ford Campany, "On the Very Idea of Religions (In the Modern West and in Early Medieval China)," *History of Religions* 42, no. 4 (May 2003): 287–319.

34. Campany's deft approach to the metaphorical aspects of language is indebted to the seminal work of George Lakoff and Mark Johnson. See, George Lakoff and Mark Johnson, *Metaphors We Live By* (Chicago: University of Chicago Press, 1980); George Lakoff, *Women, Fire, and Dangerous Things: What Categories Reveal about the Mind* (Chicago: University of Chicago Press, 1987).

35. Campany, "On the Very Idea," 293. As Campany notes (p. 291, footnote 11), one of the few sinologists who has addressed the problem of reification in the study of Chinese traditions has been Nathan Sivin; see his "On the Word 'Taoist' as a Source of Perplexity," *History of Religions* 17 (1978): 303–30.

36. Campany refers to the views of Geertz expressed in Clifford Geertz, "Religion as a Cultural System," in *The Interpretation of Cultures* (New York: Basic Books, 1973), 87–125. On Durkheim, also see below.

37. Campany, "On the Very Idea," 316–19. Campany refers to Ann Swidler, *Talk of Love: How Culture Matters* (Chicago: University of Chicago Press, 2001); and notes that the notion of repertoire has also been successfully applied by Robert Hymes in *Way and Byway: Taoism, Local Religion, and Models of Divinity in Sung and Modern* China (Berkeley: University of California Press, 2002), 5–12.

38. Campany, "On the Very Idea," 317.

39. A seminal inquiry on the encounter between Buddhism and Chinese traditions is Robert H. Sharf, *Coming to Terms with Chinese Buddhism: A Reading of the Treasure Store Treatise* (Honolulu: University of Hawai'i Press, 2002). See also Eric Zürcher, *The Buddhist Conquest of China: The Spread and Adaptation of Buddhism in Early Medieval China* (Leiden: Brill, 1959), 2 vols.; and Arthur F. Wright, *Buddhism in Chinese History* (Stanford, CA: Stanford University Press, 1971). On the earliest artistic evidence of Buddhism in China, see Wu Hung, "Buddhist Elements in Early Chinese Art (Second and Third Centuries AD)," *Artibus Asiae* 47 (1986): 263–376. The following reflection by R. Sharf efficaciously illustrates the complexity of the cross-cultural interaction between "foreign" and Chinese traditions: "It . . . is difficult to speak in simple terms of a Chinese dialogue of encounter with Indian Buddhism. Chinese functioned as the sole Buddhist ecclesiastical language from the inception of Buddhism in the Han down through the medieval period, and given the paucity of bilingual clerics, whatever 'dialogue' transpired took place largely among the Chinese themselves. Their encounter was with a Buddhism already sinified if only by virtue of being rendered, through a convoluted process of translation and exegesis into the native tongue . . . Besides, as philosophers of cultural incommensurability have noted, the 'other' is only recognized as such to the extent that it can be transcribed into a meaningful and thus to some extent familiar idiom"; in Sharf, *Coming to Terms*, 19.

40. The Mawangdui finds deeply impacted current scholarship on early Chinese thought. Specialists have discussed whether Huang-Lao constituted an organic doctrine, a well-defined cultural tradition, a specific subgroup of "Daoism" or instead simply loosely indicated non-*Ru* materials produced around the imperial unification of China; see Du Weiming, "The Thought of Huang-Lao: A Reflection on the Lao Tzu and Huang Ti Texts in the Silk Manuscripts of Ma-wang-tui," *Journal of Asian Studies* 39, no. 1 (1979): 95–110. Randal P. Peerenboom, *Law and Morality in Ancient China: The Silk Manuscripts of Huang-Lao* (Albany: SUNY Press, 1993); Robin D. S. Yates, *Five Lost Classics: Tao, Huang-Lao, and Yin-Yang in Han China* (New York: Ballantine Books, 1997) and Nathan Sivin, "Old and New Daoisms," *Religious Studies Review* 39, 1 (2010): 3–50.

41. On the origins of Daoism, see Isabelle Robinet (Phyllis Brooks, trans.), *Taoism: Growth of a Religion* (Stanford, CA: Stanford University Press, 1997), first

French edition in 1991. On the cultural interactions between Buddhism and Daoism, see Stephen R. Bokenkamp, *Ancestors and Anxiety: Daoism and the Birth of Rebirth in China* (Berkeley: University of California Press, 2009), 1–32; and "Imagining Community: Families Values and Morality in the Lingbao Scriptures," in *Philosophy and Religion in Early Medieval China*, Alan K. L. Chan and Yuet-Keung Lo, eds. (Albany: SUNY Press, 2010), 203–26; see also Livia Khon, "Steal Holy Food and Come Back as a Viper: Conceptions of Karma and Rebirth in Medieval China," *Early Medieval China* 4 (1998): 1–48; and Eric Zürcher, "Buddhist Influence on Taoist Scripture," *T'oung Pao* 66, nos. 1–3 (1980): 84–147. An overview of pre-imperial "non-Confucian" traditions is Donald Harper's, "Warring States Natural Philosophy and Occult Thought," in *The Cambridge History of Early China: From the Origins to 221 B.C.*, Michael Loewe and Edward L. Shaughnessy, eds. (Cambridge, UK: Cambridge University Press, 1999), 813–84.

42. *SJ* 130, 3289–290. Sima Tan in this passage cites the "Great Commentary" to the *Book of Changes* ("Yi Dachuan" 易大傳): "易大傳:「天下一致而百慮, 同歸而殊塗。」夫陰陽、儒、墨、名、法、道德, 此務為治者也, 直所從言之異路, 有省不省耳。"

43. *SJ* 130, 3290. See Kidder Smith, "Sima Tan and the Invention of Taoism, 'Legalism,' 'Et Cetera,'" *The Journal of Asian Studies* 62, no. 1 (2003): 129–56; Mark Csiksentmihalyi and Michael Nylan, "Constructing Lineages and Inventing Traditions through Exemplary Figures in Early China," *T'oung Pao* 89, 1–3 (2003), 59–99. For an insightful assessment of "Han Idea Systems," and Sima Qian's categorizations of thinkers, see Brashier, *Ancestral Memory*, 7–18.

44. Brent Nongbri has argued against the understanding of religion as a universal phenomenon and usage as an unproblematic cross-cultural category by brilliantly historicizing how it has been addressed in different contexts over time and space; see Brent Nongbri, *Before Religion: A History of a Modern Concept* (New Haven, CT: Yale University Press, 2013).

45. Smith, "Religion," 179–96.

46. John Lagerwey and Marc Kalinowski, eds., *Early Chinese Religion* (Leiden: Brill, 2009).

47. See Introduction, n. 6.

48. In the Middle Ages, theology, which was considered intrinsically superior as it dealt with the divine matter, capped the ideal pyramid represented by the sciences of the *trivium* (grammar, logic, and rhetoric) and *quadrivium* (arithmetic, geometry, music, and astronomy).

49. For the bibliography on these issues, see pp. 1–2, notes 2, 3,

50. Robert N. Bellah, *Religion in Human Evolution: From the Paleolithic to the Axial Age* (Cambridge, MA: Harvard University Press, 2011), 1; Bellah paraphrases a definition in Émile Durkheim, *The Elementary Forms of Religious Life* (New York: Free Press, 1995), 44. Durkheim's influence has been extremely relevant in Chinese studies due to the work of his student Marcel Granet (1884–1940).

51. Roy Rappaport, *Ritual and Religion in the Making of Humanity* (Cambridge, UK: Cambridge University Press, 1999).

52. Heiner Roetz, *Confucian Ethics of the Axial Age: A Reconstruction under the Aspect of the Breakthrough toward Postconventional Thinking* (Albany: SUNY Press, 1993), 19. The influence of Mircea Eliade's approach, which—in turn influenced by K. G. Jung's research—interpreted the yearning for the divine as an a priori psychological modality, still persists in contemporary scholarship. Among recent phenomenological approaches to religion, see Ninian Smart, *Dimensions of the Sacred: An Anatomy of the World's Beliefs* (Berkeley: University of California Press, 1996).

53. Georg G. Iggers, Q. Edward Wang, Supriya Mukherjee, eds., *A Global History of Modern Historiography* (London: Pearson, 2008), 48. The authors of this volume also assume cultural and functional continuity between the shamans of the Shang dynasty (1762–1122 BCE) and Sima Qian's historiographical work (pp. 46–68), whereas their treatment of later periods is less conjectural and more based on historical and textual evidence (see pp. 145–51; 213–16; 334–37).

54. On American historiographical tendencies in Chinese studies, see Paul A. Cohen, "The Problem with 'China's Response to the West,' " in *Discovering History in China: American Historical Writing on the Recent Past* (New York: Columbia University Press, 1984), 9–56. On the "invention" of China and the East as cultural entities in the nineteenth century, see the fascinating Lidia H. Liu, *The Clash of Empires: The Invention of China in Modern World Making* (Cambridge, MA: Harvard University Press, 2004).

55. See, for example, the introduction in John Lagerwey and Marc Kalinowski, eds., *Early Chinese Religion* (Leiden: Brill, 2009), 1–40.

56. Robin R. Wang, ed., *Chinese Philosophy in an Era of Globalization* (Albany: SUNY Press, 2004).

57. For example, Anthony C. Yu argues that despite several claims about China's supposed secularism or atheism, ancestral worship amounted to a religious cult in China, ever since the Shang dynasty; see Anthony C. Yu, *State and Religion in China: Historical and Textual Perspectives* (Chicago: Open Court, 2005); and Rodney L. Taylor, *The Religious Dimensions of Confucianism* (Albany: SUNY Press, 1990).

58. See Walter Scheidel, ed., *Rome and China: Comparative Perspectives on Ancient World Empires* (Oxford, UK: Oxford University Press, 2009), 3–10.

59. See Liam Matthew Brockey, *Mission to the East: The Jesuit Mission to China, 1579–1724* (Cambridge, MA: Harvard University Press, 2007); Jacques Gernet, *Chine et christianisme* (Paris: Gallimard, 1982).

60. For an example about the polemic on an "insider's vs. outsider's" perspective on Chinese civilization; see Robert Bagley's review of Wu Hung's *Monumentality* (Stanford, CA: Stanford University Press, 1995) in *the Harvard Journal of Asiatic*

Studies 51, no. 1 (June 1998): 221–56; and Wu Hung's "A Response to Robert Bagley's Review of my Book *Monumentality in Early Chinese Art and Architecture* (Stanford University Press, 1995)," *Archives of Asian Art* 51 (1998–1999): 92–102. For an analysis of the formalization of Chinese identities, see Tamara T. Chin, "Antiquarian as Ethnographer: Han Ethnicity in Early Han Studies," in *Critical Han Studies: The History, Representation, and Identity of China's Majority*, Thomas S. Mullaney, James Leibold et al., eds. (Berkeley: University of California Press, 2012), 128–46.

61. In addition to the well-known Marxist rejection of religion as "opium of the people" ("das Opium des Volkes," extrapolated from the posthumously published *Zur Kritik der Hegelschen Rechtsphilosophie*), Max Weber's legacy is still influential in the social sciences. The German scholar argued that the lack of an ethical drive toward individualism in Chinese traditional religions prevented the development of "rational bourgeois capitalism"; see Max Weber, *The Religion of China: Confucianism and Taoism* (New York: Free Press, 1964, first published in German published in 1915). Antony C. Yu (in *State and Religion*, 5 n. 2). As an example of the influence of anti-religious prejudices of Marxist scholarship on researchers outside this tradition, Yu cites the work by the Taiwanese Wang Zhixin 王志心, *Zhongguo sixiangshi dagang* 中國思想史大綱 (Taipei: Taipei Zhonghua shuju, 1977), 1–24.

62. Sébastien Billioud and Joël Thoraval, *The Sage and the People: The Confucian Revival in China* (New York: Oxford University Press, 2015).

63. See Marcel Launay, Gérard Moussay, et al., *Les missiones étrangère: Trois siècles et demi d'histoire et d'aventure en Asie* (Paris: Perrin, 2008). Matteo Ricci, *The True Meaning of the Lord of Heaven: T'ien-chu shih-I*, translated, with introduction and notes, by Douglas Lancashire and Peter Hu Kuo-chen (Taipei: Institut Ricci, 1985); Julia Ching and Willard G. Oxtoby, *Moral Enlightenment: Leibniz and Wolff on China* (Sankt Augustin: Institut Monumenta Serica, Nettetal, Steyler, 1992); Basil Guy, *The French image of China before and after Voltaire* (Geneve: Institut et Musée Voltaire, 1963); G. W. F. Hegel, *Reason in History: A General Introduction to Philosophy of History* (Upper Saddle River NJ: Prentice-Hall, 1997).

64. See, for example, Stephen F. Teiser, "The Spirits of Chinese Religions," in *Religions of China in Practice*, Donald S. Lopez, ed. (Princeton, NJ: Princeton University Press, 1996), 3–37.

65. The various processes whereby the Chinese literary canon has been arbitrarily associated to specific periods and cultural traditions for ideological purposes are analyzed by Michael Nylan, in *The 'Confucian' Classics* (New Haven, CT: Yale University Press, 2001); especially see "Claiming the Canon," 307–61.

66. For the concept of religion interpreted as a totalizing endeavor of the individual, see Paul Tillich, *Dynamics of Faith* (New York: Harper & Row, 1957).

67. Vincent Goossaert, "1898: The Beginning of the End for Chinese Religion?" *The Journal of Asian Studies* 65, no. 2 (May 2006): 320–24.

68. See Peter Brown, *Authority and the Sacred: Aspects of the Christianisation of the Roman World* (Cambridge, UK: Cambridge University Press, 1995); H. A.

Drake, *Constantine and the Bishops: The Politics of Intolerance* (Baltimore, MD: John Hopkins Press, 2002).

69. On the anachronism of the application of any concept of orthodoxy to early China, see Michael Nylan, "A Problematic Model: The Han 'Orthodox Synthesis,' Then and Now," in Imagining Boundaries, 17–56; on a comparative perspective on orthodoxy, see John B. Henderson, *The Construction of Orthodoxy and Heresy: Neo-Confucian, Jewish and Early Christian Patterns* (Albany: SUNY Press, 1998); for a historical approach to the cultural contexts of the early years of Christianity in Rome, see L. Michael White, *From Jesus to Christianity: How Four Generations of Visionaries & Storytellers Created the New Testament and Christian Faith* (San Francisco: HarperCollins, 2004), especially 1–66.

70. See, Timothy D. Barnes, "The Council of Nicaea," in *Constantine and Eusebius* (Cambridge, MA: Harvard University Press, 1981), 208–23.

71. See, David Hunt, "Christianising the Roman Empire: The Evidence of the Code," in *The Theodosian Code*, Jill Harries and Ian Wood, eds. (Ithaca, NY: Cornell University Press, 1993), 143–58; see, from Book 16, 2: "It is Our will that all the people that are ruled by the administration of Our Clemency shall practice that religion which the divine Peter the Apostle transmitted to the Romans . . . We command that those persons who follow this rule shall embrace the name of Catholic Christians. The rest, however, whom We adjudge demented and insane, shall sustain the infamy of heretical dogmas, their meeting places shall not receive the name of churches, and they shall be smitten first by divine vengeance and secondly by the retribution of Our own initiative, which We shall assume in accordance with the divine judgment"; see *The Theodosian Code*, trans. by Clyde Pharr (Princeton, NJ: Princeton University Press, 1952), 326.

72. On the complex relationship of the Roman senate with the emperor, see Richard J. A. Talbert, *The Senate of Imperial Rome* (Princeton, NJ: Princeton University Press, 1984).

73. Thomas Brady, *German Histories in the Age of Reformations, 1400–1650* (Cambridge, UK: Cambridge University Press, 2009).

74. Mu-chou Poo, *In Search of Personal Welfare: A View of Ancient Chinese Religion* (Albany: SUNY Press, 1998), 1–16.

75. Furthermore, as the Jesuit endeavored to acquire proficiency in Chinese language, culture, and customs, their missionary approach was eventually shaped by local rituals, practices, and attitudes. See Nicolas Standaert, *The Interweaving of Rituals: Funerals in the Cultural Exchange between China and Europe* (Seattle: University of Washington Press, 2008).

76. David E. Mungello, ed., *The Chinese Rites Controversy: Its History and Meaning* (Chicago: Loyola Press, 2005); George Minamiki SJ, *Chinese Rites Controversy from Its Beginning to Modern Times* (Chicago: Loyola Press, 1985).

77. See Anna Sun, *Confucianism as a World Religion: Contested Histories and Contemporary Realities* (Princeton, NJ: Princeton University Press, 2014); Huang Jinxing 黃進興, "Zuowei zongjiao de Rujiao—yige bijiao zongjiao de chubu taolun

作為宗教的儒教：一一個比較宗教的初步討論," *Yazhou yanjiu* (July 1997): 184–223. See also David L. Hall and Roger T. Ames, *The Democracy of the Dead: Dewey, Confucius, and the Hope for Democracy in China* (Chicago: Open Court, 1999).

78. Fung Yu-lan, *A History of Chinese Philosophy*, 2 vols. (Princeton, NJ: Princeton University Press, 1953).

79. Fung Yu-lan, *A Brief History of Chinese Philosophy* (New York: The Free Press, 1948), 1–15.

80. Fung, *A Brief History of Chinese Philosophy*, 16–37.

81. Correlative thinking has been often associated with primitive thinking. For a systematic treatment of the influence of such intellectual attitude on the study of Chinese thought, see the appendix of Michael Nylan, "Yin-yang, Five Phases, and Qi," in *China's Early Empires—A Re-Appraisal*, M. Nylan and M. Loewe, eds. (Cambridge, UK: Cambridge University Press, 2010), 411–13. For a compelling analysis of the applicability of Joseph Needham's "organismic thinking" to the cultural context of the Former Han, see Benjamin J. Schwartz, "Correlative Cosmology and the Realm of Religion," in *The World of Thought in Ancient China* (Cambridge, MA: Harvard University Belknap Press, 1985), 369–78. Schwartz, very interestingly, notices (on p. 375) how Emperor Wu, in conceiving and carrying out his religious activities, was not confident that "the 'system' as expounded by Dong Zhongshu" was "necessarily on his side."

82. Angus C. Graham, *Disputers of the Tao: Philosophical Argument in Ancient China* (Chicago: Open Court, 1989), ix–x; cfr., Homer H. Dubs, "The Failure of the Chinese to Produce Philosophic Systems," *T'oung Pao* 26 (1929): 96–109.

83. Karl Jaspers, *Way to Wisdom: An Introduction to Philosophy* (New Haven, CT, Yale University Press, 1951), 98. See also Karl Jaspers, *The Origin and Goal of History* (London: Routledge and Keegan, 1953).

84. Roetz, *Confucian Ethics*, 19.

85. Roetz, *Confucian Ethics*, 19, 45, 226.

86. For a "regionalist" interpretation of the cultural variety of the first Han, see Wang Baoxuan 王葆玹, "Cong Qi Qin ruxue yu Chu Lu ruxue zhi fen liu kan jinguwen jingxue de qiyuan" 从齐秦儒学与楚鲁儒学之分流看今古文经学的起源, in *Jin gu wenjingxue xinlun* 今古文经学新论 (Beijing: Zhongguo Shehui Kexue chubanshe, 1997), 19–27.

87. On the relationship between Sima Qian and his model Confucius and on the scholarly tradition on chapter 47 of the *Records* see, Stephen W. Durrant, "Sima Qian's Confucius," in *The Cloudy Mirror: Tension and Conflict in the Writings of Sima Qian* (Albany: SUNY, 1995), 29–45; Li Changzhi 李長之, "Sima Qian he Kongzi" 司馬遷和孔子, in *Sima Qian zhi renge yu fengge* 司馬遷之人格與風格 (Taibei: Li ren shuju, Minguo, 1997), 41–76.

88. A classic study on the relationship of *ru* and *fangshi* is Gu Jiegang 顧頡剛, *Qin Han de fang shi yu ru sheng* 秦汉的方士与儒生 (Shanghai: Shanghai gu ji

chubanshe, 2005). See also Kenneth J. DeWoskin (trans.), *Doctors, Diviners, and Magicians: Biographies of Fang-shi* (New York: Columbia University Press, 1983).

89. A complete survey of sacrifices under the Han is in Marianne Bujard, "Cultes d'État et cultes locaux dans la religion des Han," in *Religion et société dans la Chine ancienne et médiévale*, John Lagerwey, ed. (Paris: Les éditions du Cerf, 2009), 305–37. For a survey of Japanese scholarship on the same topic, see Meguro Kyōko 目黒杏子, "Kandai kokka saishi seido kenkyū no genjō to kadai—kōtei kenryoku to uchūron no shiten kara 漢代国家祭祀制度研究の現状と課題——皇帝権力と宇宙論の視點から," *Chūgoku Shigaku* 15 (2005): 103–19. For an analysis and interpretation see chapters 4 and 5 below.

90. In a recent publication Guolong Lai has demonstrated how a new focus on archeological evidence can greatly enrich our knowledge of early Chinese beliefs and rituals concerning the afterlife that centuries of "Confucian textual bias" had marginalized or condemned to oblivion; see Guolong Lai, *Excavating Afterlife: The Archaeology of Early Chinese Religion* (Seattle and London: University of Washington Press, 2015).

91. The relationship between ritual and economic politics in the *Records* has been explored in Yamada Katsuyoshi 山田勝芳, "Zenkan Butei dai no saishi to zaisei—Hōzensho to Heijunsho" 前漢武帝代の祭祀と財政—封禪書と平準書, *Tohoko Daigaku Kyōyobu kyō* 37 (1982): 1–20.

92. Roger T. Ames, *The Art of Rulership: A Study of Ancient Chinese Political Thought* (Albany: SUNY Press, 1994), ix.

93. This is the topic of chapter 2 below.

94. Xu Fuguan 徐復觀, *Liang Han sixiang shi* 兩漢思想史 (Taipei: Xuesheng shuju, 1980), 3: 195–97.

95. Edward Burnett Tylor (1832–1917), a "cultural evolutionist represented the most authoritative voice among those who believed that ritual derived from myth"; see his *Primitive Culture: Researches Into the Development of Mythology, Philosophy, Religion, Art, and Custom*, 2 vols. (London: John Murray, 1871). James George Frazer (1854–1941) instead famously argued that myth follows from ritual as civilizations become more complex; see his seminal *The Golden Bough: A Study in Magic and Religion*, 12 vols. (London: McMillan Press, 1906–15). Bronisław Malinowski (1884–1942) and Mircea Eliade held that myth and ritual develop independently. On Eliade, see below. As for Malinoski's influential theories see *Myth in Primitive Psychology* (London: Norton, 1926).

96. See Bruce Lincoln, *Theorizing Myth: Narrative, Ideology, and Scholarship* (Chicago: University of Chicago Press, 1999), 3–43. On discourses on oral versus literary culture, see Erick E. Havelock, *The Literate Revolution in Greece and its Cultural Consequences* (Princeton, NJ: Princeton University Press, 1981); *The Muse Learns to Write: Reflections on Orality and Literacy from Antiquity to the Present* (New Haven, CT: Yale University Press, 1986).

97. A "myth-oriented" Greece and a "ritual-oriented" Rome would become the preferred repertoire of paradigms for understanding non-European or less religiously evolved cultures.

98. Lincoln, *Theorizing Myth*, 51–21.

99. Adalbert Kuhn, *Die Herabkunft des Feuers und Göttertranks* (Gütersloh: Bertelsmann, 1886); Georges Dumézil, *Les dieux des Indo-Européens* (Paris: Presses universitaires de France, 1952); *L'idéologie tripartie des Indo-Européens* (Bruxelles: Latomus, 1958); and Scott Littleton, *The New Comparative Mythology: An Anthropological Assessment of the Theories of Georges Dumézil* (Berkeley: University of California Press, 1973). This approach was also stimulated by the development of structural linguistics by the Swiss scholar Ferdinand de Saussure (1857–1913); see Lincoln, *Theorizing Myth*, 69.

100. Lincoln, "Dumézil's German War God," in *Theorizing Myth*, 64–75. See also Erich J. Sharpe, *Comparative Religion: A History* (London: Duckworth, 1975), 27–46.

101. Lincoln, *Theorizing Myth*, 121–37. On some ideological aspects regarding the approach of the early historians of comparative religions, see Stefan Arvidsson, *Aryan Idols: The Indo-European Mythology as Science and Ideology* (Chicago: University of Chicago Press, 2006).

102. Lincoln, *Theorizing Myth*, 143. See also Robert Ellwood, *The Politics of Myth: A Study of C. G. Jung, Mircea Eliade, and Joseph Campbell* (Albany: SUNY Press, 1999). More or less explicitly, this extremely influential approach (also known as "phenomenological") has survived to this day, especially due to the monumental work and controversial legacy of Mircea Eliade (1906–1987). The Romanian polymath's multifarious influence can be exemplified by his elaboration of the notion of hierophanies, which he envisioned as breakthroughs of the Sacred into the world. According to Eliade, with these manifestations, the supernatural enables human development by providing models through mythological narratives. For him, the Sacred possessed an ontological dimension, independent from culture and historical contingency; opposed to the Profane, it was at the basis of a vision of reality that many have criticized as essentialist and aristocratic. See Lincoln, *Theorizing Myth*, 141–47; Christian K. Wedemeyer, Wendy Doniger, eds., *Hermeneutics, Politics, and the History of Religions: The Contested Legacies of Joachim Wach and Mircea Eliade* (Oxford, UK: Oxford University Press, 2010), especially 103–323; Daniel Dubuisson, *Impostures et pseudo-science: L'œvre de Mircea Eliade* (Villeneuve d'Ascq: Presses Universitaires du Septentrion, 2005).

103. Sharpe, *Comparative Religion*, 27–35.

104. Ibid., 29–30.

105. Lincoln, *Theorizing Myth*, 141–87.

106. Ibid., 207–16.

107. Ibid., 208.

108. The Chinese examination system had been inaugurated under the Sui (581–618 CE) and reached its maturity under the Northern Song (960–1127). Candidates were evaluated on the basis of their skills in citing the *Classics* in order to resolve any theoretical or practical issues concerning the state and its administration. See John W. Chaffee, *The Thorny Gates of Learning in Sung China: A Social History of Examinations* (Albany: SUNY Press, 1995); Benjamin E. Elman, *A Cultural History of Civil Examinations in Late Imperial China* (Berkeley, CA: University of California Press, 2000).

109. The ideal Zhou Dynasty extolled by the Han *ru* and that eventually shone both as political and a cultural beacon throughout imperial China does not necessarily correspond to the reconstructions of current archaeologists, historians, and textual experts. Indispensable texts for the study of the Zhou are Li Feng's *Bureaucracy and the State in Early China: Governing the Western Zhou* (Cambridge, UK: Cambridge University Press, 2008); *Landscape and Power in Early China: The Crisis and the Fall of the Western Zhou* 1045–771 BC (Cambridge, UK: Cambridge University Press, 2006); and Edward L. Shaughnessy's, *Sources of Western Zhou History: Inscribed Bronze Vessels* (Berkeley: University of California Press, 1991); and "Western Zhou History," in *The Cambridge History of Early China*, 293–351. See also Lothar von Falkenhausen, *Chinese Society in the Age of Confucius (1000–250 BC): The Archaeological Evidence (Ideas, Debates and Perspectives)* (Los Angeles: The Cotsen Institute of Archaeology Press, 2006).

110. On the cultural and political aspects of literature, see the fundamental Mark E. Lewis, *Writing and Authority in Early China* (Albany: SUNY Press, 1999).

111. James Legge, *The Chinese Classics: With a Translation, Critical and Exegetical Notes, Prolegomena, and Copious Indexes*, 5 vols. (Hong Kong: Trubner, 1861–1872). In addition to translations and commentaries, Legge also produced influential interpretive texts: *The Notions of the Chinese Concerning God and Spirits* (Hong Kong: H. K. Register Office, 1852) and *The Religions of China: Confucianism and Tàoism Described and Compared with Christianity* (London: Hodder and Stoughton, 1880) in which Legge argues that China is basically a monotheistic civilization with "some minor spirits." On the influence of Legge's contribution to the knowledge of China in the West, see Norman J. Girardot, *The Victorian Translation of China: James Legge's Oriental Pilgrimage* (Berkeley: University of California Press, 2002) and Lauren F. Pfister, *Striving for 'The Whole Duty of Man': James Legge and the Scottish Protestant Encounter with China*, 2 vols. (Mainz: The Scottish Studies Centre of the Johannes Gutenberg Universität, 2004).

112. Anne Birrell, "James Legge and the Chinese Mythological Tradition," *History of Religions* 38, no. 4 (May 1999): 331–53. For an exhaustive overview of the history of the field, see Anne Birrell, *Chinese Mythology: An Introduction* (Baltimore, MD: John Hopkins University Press, 1993), 1–22. One of the most authoritative figures in the field of Chinese mythology is Yuan Ke 袁珂 (1916–2001), one of

Birrell's teachers. Yuan Ke provided a "Marxist" legitizimation to the study of ancient myths by referring to Maxim Gorky's (1868–1936) literary theory according to which myths represented the creative effort of the common people to cope with the violence of natural forces and with the harshness of labor. See Yuan Ke, *Zhongguo gudai shenhua* 中国古代神话 (Beijing: Huaxia, 2006), 1–4. On the significance of Yang Ke's work, see also K. C. Chang, *Early Chinese Civilization: Anthropological Perspectives* (Cambridge, MA: Harvard University Press, 1976), 168–70, 174.

113. Birrell, "James Legge," 332.

114. See Birrell, *Chinese Mythology*, 13–17; Laurence A. Schneider, *Ku Chieh-kang and China's New History: Nationalism and the Quest for Alternative Traditions* (Berkeley: University of California Press, 1971); Li Xueqin 李學勤, *Zouchu Yigu shidai* 走出疑古時代 (Shenyang: Changchun chubanshe, 1997).

115. See Rebecca E. Karl et al., *Rethinking the 1898 Reform Period: Political and Cultural Change in Late Qing China* (Cambridge, MA: Harvard University Press, 2002); Min-chih Chou, *Hu Shih and Intellectual Choice in Modern China* (Ann Arbor: University of Michigan Press, 1984); Hao Chang, *Chinese Intellectuals in Crisis: Search for Order and Meaning (1890–1911)* (Berkeley: University of California Press, 1987).

116. Gu Jiegang, *Gu shi bian* 古史辯, 6 vols. (Shanghai: Shanghai Guji: 1926–41).

117. See Tze-Ki Hon, "Ethnic and Cultural Pluralism: Gu Jiegang's Vision of a New China in His Studies of Ancient History," *Modern China* 22, no. 3 (July 1996): 315–39. On Gu and his opponents, see L. A. Schneider, "From Textual Criticism to Social Criticism," in *Ku Chieh-kang*, 188–217.

118. Lincoln, *Theorizing Myth*, 146–47.

119. See Marcel Granet, *Dances et légendes de la Chine ancienne* (Paris: Musée Guimet, 1926), 2 vols. For a different view that considered popular religion just the reflection of elite culture, cf. J. J. M. De Groot (1854–1921), *Les fêtes annuellement célébrées à Émoui (Amoy): étude concernant la religion populaire des Chinois* (Paris: Leroux, 1886); *Religion in China: Universism, a Key to the Study of Taoism and Confucianism* (New York: Putnam, 1921). Influential pioneers in the study of ancient Chinese myths were the French Henri Maspéro (1883–1945), and the Swedish Bernhard Karlgren (1889–1978); through a historical approach to Chinese linguistics and by integrating literary and material analysis the former contributed to the establishment Daoist studies, the latter to that of Chinese phonetics. See Henri Maspero, "Légendes mythologiques dans le Chou King," *Journal Asiatique* 204 (1924): 11–100. Bernhard Karlgren, "Legends and cults in ancient China," *Bulletin of the Museum of Far Eastern Antiquities* 18 (1946): 199–365; for an assessment of Karlgren's impact on the study of Chinese myths see Wolfram Eberhard, "Review of Karlgren's *Legends and Cults*," *Artibus Asiae* 9 (1946): 355–64.

120. A groundbreaking approach to Chinese religion that programmatically focused on social interactions and avoided metaphysical questions was C. K. Yang,

Religion in Chinese Society: A Study of Contemporary Social Functions of Religion and Some of Their Historical Factors (Berkeley: California University Press, 1961). See also Maurice Freedman, "On the Sociological Study of Chinese Religion," in *Religion and Ritual in Chinese Society*, Arthur P. Wolf, ed. (Stanford, CA: Stanford University Press, 1974), 19–42.

121. See David Johnson, ed., *Ritual Opera, Operatic Ritual: Mu-lien Rescues His Mother in Chinese Popular Culture* (Berkeley: University of California Press, 1989).

122. See David Overmyer et al., "Chinese Religions, The State of the Field, Part II—Living Religious Traditions: Taoism, Confucianism, Buddhism, Islam and Popular Religion," *Journal of Asian Studies* 42, no. 2 (1995): 314–21; on the tripartite nature of Chinese spirits see, Arthur P. Wolf, "Gods, Ghosts, and Ancestors," in *Religion and Ritual in Chinese Society*, edited by idem (Stanford, CA: Stanford University Press, 1972), 131–82; the imperial metaphor is a concept explored in Stephan Feutchwang, *Popular Religion in China: The Imperial Metaphor* (Richmond, UK: Curzon Press, 2001); on the role of religion in interclass and intercultural communication in China see, David G. Johnson, "Communication, Class, and Consciousness in Late Imperial China," in *Popular Culture in Late Imperial China*, edited by David G. Johnson, Andrew J. Nathan, and Evelyn S. Rawski (Berkeley, University of California Press, 1985), 34–73.

123. Norman J. Girardot, for example, endeavors to go beyond Jungian meta-psychological paradigms; see his *Myth and Meaning in Early Taoism* (Berkeley: University of California Press, 1983), 6–15. Girardot assumes the existence of a unitary imperial religion based on the fusion of social, political, and cosmic order that was countered by the "myth" of Chaos (*hundun* 混沌) posited at the core of early Daoism. On page 2 he writes, "Part of the perverse genius of the early Taoists was to question the cosmological determinism of the ordinary Chinese cultural grid imposed by an Emperor's glance, Confucian Ethics, or the Chinese language. The early Taoist vision sought to return to an experience of a deeper and more primitive life-order hidden by conventional language and culture . . . The Taoists affirmed that silent, hidden, or real order of Chaos embraced both Chaos and Cosmos, non-being and being, nature and culture." Whereas this suggestive synthesis can prove extremely effective at the theoretical or philosophical level, it seems to suffer from the tendency to reification already scrutinized by Robert Campany (see above). Once appraised against historical sources, such a dualistic view, which echoes Gnosticism and Friedrich Nietzsche's (1844–1900) Apollonian and Dionysian dichotomy, gives way to a much more complicate picture in which the different textual and ritual traditions often coexisted in a seemingly incoherent fashion. A question that should always be preliminary asked is if the systemic answers we tend to glean from the sources respond to our own theoretical preoccupations or represent the voice of the very subjects of our study. Either solution is potentially valid, provided that operation of linguistic and cultural translation is carried out in an openly reflexive way. Girardot's analysis also influenced David Gordon White's

work on comparative mythology, *Myths of the Dog-Man* (Chicago: Unversity of Chicago Press, 1991), 161–79.

124. Birrell, *Chinese Mythology*, 17–18.

125. Bronisław Malinowski, *Magic, Science, and Religion, and Other Essays* (Garden City, NY: Doubleday Anchor Books, 1948); Otto Rank, *The Myth and the Birth of the Hero* (New York: Random House, 1959), first published in 1909, in German; F. R. R. S. Raglan (Lord), *The Hero: A Study in Tradition, Myth, and Drama* (New York: Oxford University Press, 1937).

126. Lewis, "The Mythology of Early China," in *Early Chinese Religion*. Vol. 1, John Lagerwey and Marc Kalinowski, eds. (Leiden: Brill, 2009), 593 n. 82.

127. Birrell, *Chinese Mythology*, 1–22.

128. For an assessment on methodological issues concerning the study of Han thought see Mark Csikszentmihalyi, *Readings in Han Chinese Thought* (Indianapolis, IN: Hackett, 2006), viii–xiii.

129. Rémi Mathieu, *Anthologie des mythes et légendes de la Chine ancienne: Textes choisis, présentés, traduits et indexés* (Paris: Gallimard, 1989).

130. Birrell, *Chinese Mythology*, 19. On typologies and structures of pantheons, see Bruce Lincoln, "Nature and Genesis of Pantheons," in *Gods and Demons, Priests and Scholars: Critical Explorations in the History of Religions* (Chicago: University of Chicago Press, 2012), 17–29. On the relationship between complex civilizations (or *civiltà superiori*) and polytheistic systems, see Angelo Brelich, *Introduzione alla storia delle religioni* (Roma: Edizioni dell'Ateneo, 1965), 151–62. A cogent analysis of centuries of negative biases against ancient polytheism is provided in Page Dubois, *A Million and One Gods: The Persistence of Polytheism* (Cambridge, MA: Harvard University Press, 2015).

131. On the applicability of the concept of monotheism to early China, see chapter 4 below. The Qin, according to Sima Qian, actually worshipped four Di (which were probably understood as dynastic ancestors) together with many others deities belonging to different local realities; see *SJ* 28, 1378.

132. For a structuralist approach, see also Sarah Allan, *The Heir and the Sage: Dynastic Legends in Early China* (San Francisco: Center for Chinese Materials, 1981).

133. Mark E. Lewis, *Sanctioned Violence in Early China* (Albany: SUNY Press, 1990); *The Flood Myths of Early China* (Albany: SUNY Press, 2006).

134. It comprises analyses of the development of the study of myths in Europe and China and five sections on specifically Chinese traditions: "myth of the early culture-hero sage kings," "myths of historical figures," "myths of figures found in tombs," "myths related to local cults," and "myths related to crafts."

135. Lewis, "The Mythology," 549. Lewis for his definition of myth, refers to the following works: Walter Burkert's *Structure and History in Greek Mythology and Ritual* (Berkeley, University of California Press, 1979), 23; Georges Dumézil (trans. Alf Hiltebeitel), *The Destiny of the Warrior* (Chicago: University of Chicago

Press, 1970), 1–2; G. S. Kirk, *Myth: Its Meaning and Functions in Ancient and Other Cultures* (Cambridge: Cambridge University Press, 1970) 31–41, 251–62.

136. Lewis, "The Mythology," 553.

137. Lewis, "The Mythology," 554.

138. Jean Levi, *Les fonctionnaires divins: Politique, despotisme et mystique en Chine ancienne* (Paris: La Librairie du XXe siecle, 1989), 203–18. Against the *ru*'s disengagement famously were the followers of Mozi 墨子 (ca. 470–ca. 391 BCE). A recent reassessment of the issue is in Roel Sterkx, "Mozi 31: Explaining Ghosts, Again," in *The Mozi as an Evolving Text: Different Voices in Early Chinese Thought*, Carine Defoort and Nicolas Standaert, eds. (Leiden: Brill, 2013), 91–141.

139. Whereas in ancient Greece immortality characterized gods as powerful entities that would constantly intervene in human affairs, generation after generation, to a certain extent safeguard the continuity of institutions and social structures, its ancient Chinese pursuer hoped to abandon civilization and social duties altogether.

140. So far, scholars who have applied structural approaches have often addressed Chinese myths as evidence of "a way of thinking that need not have any relationship to history." Sarah Allan, "Erlitou and the Formation of Chinese Civilization: Toward a New Paradigm," *Journal of Chinese Studies* 66, no. 2 (May 2007): 462. See also Wendy Doniger, *The Implied Spider: Politics and Theology in Myth* (New York, Columbia University Press, 1998), 2–3. Her work has had a deep influence on David Tracy's theological approach; see his *The Analogical Imagination: Christian Theology and the Culture of Pluralism* (New York: Crossroads, 1991).

141. See Joachim Gentz, "The Ritual Meaning of Textual Form: Evidence from Early Commentaries of the Historiographic and Ritual Traditions," in *Text and Ritual in Early China*, Martin Kern, ed. (Seattle: University of Washington Press, 2005), 125–48.

142. See Catherine Bell, "The Spectrum of Ritual Activities," in *Ritual: Perspectives and Dimensions* (Oxford, UK: Oxford University Press, 1997), 91–169.

143. Jonathan Z. Smith, *To Take Place: Toward Theory in Ritual* (Chicago: University of Chicago Press, 1987), 105.

144. J. Z. Smith, *To Take Place*, 102–06.

145. For a dualistic interpretation of rituals related to ancestors and non-canonical ones addressed to ghosts, see Richard Von Glahn, *The Sinister Way: The Divine and the Demonic in Chinese Religious Culture* (Berkeley: University of California Press, 2004).

146. In early Chinese sources the verb usually employed to refer to the worship or sacrifice of *shen* and *di*, spirits and dynastic ancestors, is *si* 祀. See Zhan Yinxin 詹鄞鑫 *Shenling yu jisi: Zhongguo chuantong zongjiao zonglun* 神靈與祭祀: 中國傳統宗教綜論 (Nanking: Jiangsu guji chubanshe, 1992).

147. On the *Liji*, see Jeffrey K. Riegel, "Li chi 禮記," in *Early Chinese Texts*, 293–97; on the *Zhouli* 周禮, William G. Boltz, "Chou li 周禮," in *Early Chinese Texts*, 24–32; on the *Yili* and 儀禮, William G. Boltz, "I li 儀禮," in *Early Chinese*

Texts, 234–43. On its periodization: Wang E 王鍔, 'Liji' chengshu kao "禮記" 成書考 (Beijing: Zhonghua, 2007); Michael Puett, "Combining the ghosts and spirits, centering the realm," in *Early Chinese Religion*, 695–720. Recent fascinating analysis of *li* are Brashier's *Ancestral Memory*, especially the chapter, "An Imaginary Yardstick for Ritual Performance," 47–101. A stimulating take on the social dynamics implied by a Confucian conception of *li* is provided in Herbert Fingarette, *Confucius: The Sacred as Secular* (Prospect Heights, Long Grove, IL: Waveland Press, 1998).

148. Yuri Pines, "Disputers of the *Li*: Breakthroughs in the Concept of Ritual in Preimperial China," *Asia Major* 13.1 (2000): 1. Pines's article provides a systematic historicization of the concepts and practices associated with *li* in pre-imperial China. A classic on Han rituals is Fujikawa Masakazu 藤川正数, *Kandai ni okeru reigaku no kenkyû* 漢代における礼学の研究 (Tokyo: Kazama Shobō, 1968).

149. See, for example, David N. Keightley, "Archaeology and Mentality: The Making of China," *Representations* 18 (Spring 1987): 191–97; Yang Qun 揚群, "Cong kaogu faxian kan li he lizhi de qiyuan yu fazhan" 從考古發現看禮和禮制的起源與發展, *Kongzi yanju* 3 (1990): 3–11 Wu, Hung, *Monumentality in Early Chinese Art and Architecture* (Stanford, CA: Stanford University Press, 1995); and Chen Shengyong 陈乘勇, "Li de qiyuan jian lun Liangzhu wenhua yu wenming qiyuan 禮的起源兼論良渚文化 與文明起源," *Hanxue yanjiu* 漢學研究 17 no. 1 (1999): 49–77.

150. See, David I. Kertzer, *Ritual, Politics and Power* (Hew Haven, CT, and London: Yale University Press, 1988), 9.

151. Loewe, "'Confucian' Values": 1–30. On Xunzi and ritual see Robert F. Campany, "Xunzi and Durkheim as Theorists of Ritual Practice," in *Discourse and Practice*, Frank Reynolds, David Tracy, eds. (Albany: SUNY Press, 1992), 197–231.

152. On the creation during the Song of a state orthodoxy, see James T. C. Liu, "How Did a Neo-Confucian School Become the State Orthodoxy?" *Philosophy East and West* 23, 4 (October 1973): 483–506.

153. The Jesuit introduced "Confucianism," to Europe as a highly sophisticated—albeit non-theistic—moral system that could favor Christian proselytism. In addition, they interpreted it in light of the preoccupation with systemic coherence characterizing Counter-Reformation Catholicism.

154. Prasenjit Duara, "Knowledge and Power in the Discourse of Modernity: The Campaigns against Popular Religion in Early Twentieth-Century China," *Journal of Asian Studies* 50, no. 1 (1991.2): 67–83.

155. See Michael Puett, "The Offering of Food and the Creation of Order: The Practice of Sacrifice in Early China," in *Of Tripod and Palate: Food, Politics and Religion in Traditional China*, Roel Sterkx, ed. (Basingstoke, UK: Palgrave MacMillan, 2005), 75–95. In this essay Puett argues against Alfred R. Radcliffe-Brown's (1881–1955) functionalist interpretation of Chinese ritual (pp. 79–80) in

A. R. Radcliffe-Brown, "Religion and Society," in *Structure and Function in Primitive Society* (New York: The Free Press, 1965).

156. Puett, "The Offering of Food," 76; in *Liji*, "Jifa," ICS 122.24.3.
157. Ibid.
158. Ibid., 82–83.
159. Ibid., 81.
160. Ibid., 93.
161. See K. E. Brashier, *Public Memory in Early China* (Cambridge, MA: Harvard University Press, 2014).
162. *Zhuangzi*, 12, 731: 夫知者不言，言者不知，故聖人行不言之教. 道不可致，德不可至. 仁可為也，義可虧也，禮相偽也. 故曰，"失道而後德，失德而後仁，失仁而後義，失義而後禮. 禮者，道之華而亂之首也。
163. On the problematic and ambiguous aspects of *li* before Sima Qian, see Michael David Kaulana Ing, *The Dysfunction of Ritual in Early Confucianism* (Oxford, UK: Oxford University Press, 2012).
164. See Adam B. Seligman and Robert P. Weller, *Rethinking Pluralism: Ritual Experience and Ambiguity* (Oxford, UK: Oxford University Press, 2012); see also Adam B. Seligman, Robert P. Weller, Michael J. Puett, and Bennet Simon, *Ritual and its Consequences: An Essay on the Limits of Sincerity* (Oxford, UK: Oxford University Press, 2008).
165. See Daniel Gardner, *Zhu Xi's Reading of the Analects: Canon, Commentary and the Classical Tradition* (New York: Columbia University Press, 2003).
166. The centrality of the issue of imperial succession is analyzed in detail by Michael Loewe's latest work; see M. Loewe, *Problems of Han Administration*, 15–62.
167. The doctrines and the texts conventionally associated with Huang-Lao seem to present a "more organic" integration of the political and cosmological spheres in religious terms; see John S. Major, *Heaven and Earth in Early Han Thought* (Albany: SUNY Press, 1991), Robin D. S. Yates, *Five Lost Classics: Tao, Huang-Lao, and Yin-Yang in Han China* (New York: Ballantine Books, 1997).

Chapter 2

1. In *SJ* 47, 1942: 天喪予! . . . 吾道窮矣! . . . 莫知我夫! 不怨天，不尤人，下學而上達，知我者其天乎!
2. In *SJ* 99, 2723: 大 直 若 詘，道固委蛇，蓋謂是乎. For the translation, see Burton Watson, *Records of the Grand Historian* (New York: Columbia University Press, 1961), 1, 246.
3. This citation (知命者不怨天，知己者不怨人) can be found both in the *Huainanzi* ("Miao Cheng Xun, 10"), which was edited and compiled under the

prince of Huainan, Liu An 劉安 (179?–122 BCE) and in Liu Xiang 劉向 (77–6 BCE), *Shuo Yuan* 說苑, "Tan cong 談叢," 16.

4. Yang Hua 楊華, "Qin Han diguo de shenquan tongyi: chutu jianbo yu 'Fengshan shu,' 'Jiaosi zhi,' de duibi kaocha" 秦漢帝國的神權統一：出土簡帛與《封禪書》、《郊祀志》的對比考察, *Lishi Yanjiu* 5 (2011): 4–26.

5. Yang Hua, "Qin Han diguo," 8.

6. Yang especially focuses on the Qin bamboo judicial texts unearthed at Shuihudi 水虎地, Hebei, in 1975. Also see A. F. P. Hulsewé, *Remnants of Ch'in Law: An Annotated Translation of the Ch'in Legal and Administrative Rules of the 3rd Century BC* (Leiden: Brill, 1985).

7. Yang Hua, "Qin Han diguo," 11.

8. It is reported that after its completion around 91 BCE, Sima Qian's copy of the *Records* was hidden by his relatives to prevent Emperor Wu from destroying it. When the book resurfaced after Wu's death, many lamented that it had suffered the loss of several sections and 10 of the original 130 chapters. In the following decades, several authors worked to fill in the gaps. The only one whose name is reported in the commentaries is Chu Shaosun 褚少孫 (32–7 BCE); his contributions seem in line with Dong Zhongshu's historiographical thought and concept of the Mandate of Heaven. According some scholars, the lost chapters of the *Records* were replaced with chapters from the *History of the Former Han* (*Han Shu*). Also see Dorothee Schaab-Hanke, "Did Chu Shaosun contribute to the tradition of the Scribe?" *Oriens Extremus* 44 (2003/04): 11–26.

9. Stephen Durrant, *The Cloudy Mirror: Tension and Conflict in the Writings of Sima* Qian (Albany: SUNY Press, 1995).

10. Michael Nylan, "Sima Qian: A True Historian?" *Early China* 23–24 (1998–1999): 203–46.

11. Michael J. Puett, *The Ambivalence of Creation: Debates Concerning Innovation and Artifice in Early China* (Stanford, CA: University of Stanford Press, 2001).

12. The *Letter to Ren An* is in *HS* 62, 2725–538. For a recent English translation, see Stephen Durrant, Wao-Yee Li, Michael Nylan, and Hans Van Ess, *The Letter to Ren An & Sima Qian's Legacy* (Seattle and London: University of Washington Press, 2016), 22–29. Sima Qian autobiography is in *SJ* 130, 3285–322.

13. See also David R. Knechtges, " 'Key Words,' Authorial Intent, and Interpretation: Sima Qian's Letter to Ren An," *Chinese Literature: Essays, Articles, Reviews* (*CLEAR*) 30 (Dec. 2008): 75–84.

14. See note 12 above.

15. For a synthesis of the debates on the letter's dating, see Hans Van Hess, "Dissent against Emperor Wu of the Han," in AA. VV. *The Letter to Ren An*, 51–53.

16. Esther Sunkyung Klein, "The History of a Historian: Perspectives on the Authorial Roles of Sima Qian" (PhD diss., Princeton University, 2010).

17. Garret Olberding has brilliantly reconstructed the sophisticated rhetorical strategies to which court historians had to resort in order to maintain the favor of

their rulers. Olberding argues that the demiurgic nature of the historian's activity of recording and organizing events could constitute a challenge on the prerogatives of the emperor: see Garret P. S. Olberding, *Dubious Facts: The Evidence of Early Chinese Historiography* (Albany: SUNY, 2012).

18. The most approachable introduction to the *Records* is still Burton Watson, *Ssu-ma Ch'ien: Grand Historian of China* (New York: Columbia University Press, 1958).

19. On the moral aspects of authorial subjectivity in the *Records*, see Martin Kern (Ke, Mading 柯馬丁), "Shiji li de 'zuozhe' gainian" 《史記》裡的「作者」概念, in *Shiji xue yu shijie hanxue lunji xubian* 史記學與世界漢學論集續編, Martin Kern and Lee Chi-hsiang 李紀祥, eds. (Taipei: Tangshan chubanshe/Tonsan Publications, 2016), 23–61.

20. This theme has been brilliantly explored in Michael J. Puett, *The Ambivalence of Creation: Debates Concerning Innovation and Artifice in Early China* (Stanford, CA: University of Stanford Press, 2001).

21. *SJ* 28, 1371.

22. The resilience in Western scholarship of the idea of the official adoption of a "Han Confucianism" under Wu is especially due to the popularity of Homer H. Dubs, "The Victory of Han Confucianism," *Journal of the American Oriental Society*, 58, no. 3 (1935): 435–49. For the text of the *History of the Former Han* by Ban Gu, I adopt the edition of the Zhonghua shuju of 1962 (Hereafter *HS*).

23. For more discussions about "Han Confucianism," see Chun-shu Chang, *The Rise of the Chinese Empire: Nation, State and Imperialism in Early China, ca 1600 B.C.–A.D. 8* (Ann Arbor: The University of Michigan Press, 2007), 1: 119–34; and Mark Edward Lewis, *Writing and Authority in Early China* (Albany: SUNY Press, 1999), 339–51.

24. A complete translation of the Gongyang commentary is in Harry Miller, *The Gongyang Commentary on The Spring and Autumn Annals: A Full Translation* (Basingstoke, UK: Palgrave Macmillan, 2015). Also see Joachim Gentz, "Language of Heaven, Exegetical Skepticism, and the Re-Insertion of Religious Concepts in the Gongyang Tradition," in *Early Chinese Religion*, 813–38.

25. On the issues of authorship and composition of the *Luxuriant Dew of the Spring and Autumn*, see Introduction, note 36.

26. Queen and Major, *Luxuriant Gems*, 17.

27. An assessment of Jia Yi's contribution in the context of early Han thought is in Michael Loewe, "Imperial Sovereignty: Dong Zhong-shu's Contribution and his Predecessors," in *Divination*, 121–40; Cai Tingji 蔡廷吉, *Jia Yi yanjiu* 賈誼研究 (Taibei: Wenshizhe Chubanshe, 1984); on the literary aspects of his production, see David Knechtges, "Jia Yi 賈誼," In *Ancient and Early Medieval Chinese Literature: A Reference Guide, Part One*, D. R. Knechtges, Taiping Chang, eds. (Leiden: Brill, 2010), 417–28; Robert Joe Cutter, "Chia I 賈誼," in *The Indiana Companion to Traditional Chinese Literature*, William Nienhauser, ed. (Bloomington: Indiana University Press, 1986), 254–55. On the attribution of the *Xinshu* to Jia Yi, see Luo Shaodan, "The

Xinshu 新書 Reexamined: An Emphasis on Usability over Authenticity," *Chinese Studies* 2, No. 1 (2013): 8–24.

28. *SJ* 6, 276–84.

29. See Allen and Major, *Luxuriant Gems*, 59–61.

30. See Cho-Yun Hsu, "The Changing Relationship between Local Society and the Central Political Power in Former Han: 206 B.C.–8 A.D.," *Comparative Studies in Society and History* 7, 4 (July 1965): 358–70.

31. A classic work on the political and social reorganization of China upon its unification is Du Zhengsheng 杜正勝, *Bianhu qimin: Chuantong zhengzhi shehui jiegou zhi xincheng* 傳統政治社會結構之形成 (Taipei: Guojia Tushuguan, 1990).

32. Loewe, *The Government*, 37–55.

33. On Shang Yang as a historical figure and on the book attributed to him, see Yuri Pines, "Dating a Pre-Imperial Text: The Case Study of the *Book of Lord Shang*," *Early China*, Available on CJO 2016 doi:10.1017/eac.2016.3.

34. On cultural aspects of the creation of the Qin and Han empires, see Puett, *The Ambivalence of Creation*, 141–76.

35. On the reduction of the kingdoms under Emperor Wu's predecessors, see Denis Twitchett and Michael Loewe, eds., *The Cambridge History of China–Volume I, The Ch'in and the Han Empires, 221 B.C.–A.D. 220* (Cambridge, UK: Cambridge University Press, 1986), 139–49.

36. See Donald B. Wagner, *The State and the Iron Industry in Han China* (Copenhagen: The Nordic Institute of Asian Studies, 2001).

37. In keeping with most of the specialists, I consider the introductions of the *shu* chapters, both for style and contents, authored by Sima Qian; see Han Zhaoqi 韩兆琦, *Shiji tiping* 史记题评 (Xi'an: Shaanxi Renmin Chubanshe, 2000), 110–14; Yang Yanqi 楊燕起, Chen Keqing 陳可青 and Lai Changchang 賴長揚, eds., *Lidai mingjia ping Shiji* 歷代名家評史記 (Peking: Beijing shifan daxue, 1986); Zhang Dake 張大可, "Shiji canque yu bucuan kaobian" 史記殘缺與補竄考辨, in *Shiji yanjiu* 史記研究 (Lanzhou: Gansu renmin, 1985), 162–87; 225–254; Li Changzhi 李長之, *Sima Qian de renge yu fengge* 司馬遷的人格與風格 (Shanghai: Kaiming shudian, 1948, reprint Hong Kong: Taiping, 1963), 151–155A. For syntheses in English of the scholarship on the *shu* chapters and the *Records* in general also see F. P. Hulsewé, "Shih chi," in *Early Chinese Texts*, 405–14.

38. *SJ* 23, 1157: 太史公曰：洋洋美德乎！宰制萬物，役使群眾，豈人力也哉？余至大行禮官，觀三代損益，乃知緣人情而制禮，依人性而作儀，其所由來尚矣。

39. On the development of concept of *de* 德 in early Chinese discourses, see Mark Csikszentmihalyi, *Material Virtue; Ethics and the Body in Early China* (Leiden: Brill, 2004), 13–57.

40. *SJ* 23, 1157–158: 人道經緯萬端，規矩無所不貫，誘進以仁義，束縛以刑罰，故德厚者位尊，祿重者寵榮，所以總一海內而整齊萬民也。

41. Wang Liqi 王利器, ed., *Yantie lun jiaozhu* 鹽鐵論校注 (Beijing: Zhonghua Shuju, 2003), 556: "刑不可任以成化，故廣德教。" Hereafter *YTLJZ*.

42. Allen and Major, *Luxuriant Gems*, 388–91.

43. Allen and Major translate the passage in the *Han Shu* (*HS* 56, 2502) in ibid., 389.

44. *Chunqiu fanlu*, "Jiyi 基義" section, 53.4: "德教之與刑罰猶此也。故聖人多其愛而少其嚴，厚其德而簡其刑." My translation is based on that on Allen and Major, in *Luxuriant Gems*, 429.

45. Cfr., *Xunzi*, 19, 417: 禮起於何也?曰：人生而有欲，欲而不得，則不能無求。求而無度量分界，則不能不爭；爭則亂，亂則窮。先王惡其亂也，故制禮義以分之，以養人之欲，給人之求。使欲必不窮於物，物必不屈於欲。兩者相持而長，是禮之所起也。"What is the origin of li? I reply: "Man is born with desires. If his desires are not satisfied, he is bound to pursue them. If in what he pursues there are no measure and limits, he is bound to contend with other men. Contention leads to disorder. Disorder leads to poverty. The ancient kings despised such disorder, and so established ritual righteousness to curb it, to nourish men's desires, and to provide them with what they pursue. They made sure that desires would not fall short of their objects, and that the objects would not be beyond what is desired. In this way, desires and their objects sustained each other over long time. This is the origin of li."

46. *SJ* 23, 1158: 人體安駕乘，為之金輿錯衡以繁其飾；目好五色，為之黼黻文章以表其能；耳樂鐘磬為之調諧八音以蕩其心；口甘五味，為之庶羞酸鹹以致其美；情好珍善，為之琢磨圭璧以通其意。故大路越席，皮弁布裳，朱弦洞越，大羹玄酒，所以防其淫侈，救其彫敝。是以君臣朝廷尊卑貴賤之序，下及黎庶車輿衣服宮室飲食嫁娶喪祭之分，事有宜適，物有節文。仲尼曰：「禘自既灌而往者，吾不欲觀之矣。」

47. *SJ* 23, 1159: 周衰，禮廢樂壞，大小相踰，管仲之家，兼備三歸. 循法守正者見侮於世，奢溢僭差者謂之顯榮。自子夏，門人之高弟也，猶云「出見紛華盛麗而說，入聞夫子之道而樂，二者心戰，未能自決」，而況中庸以下，漸漬於失教，被服於成俗乎？[. . .] 仲尼沒後，受業之徒沈湮而不舉，或適齊、楚，或入河海，豈不痛哉！

48. See, W. Allyn Rickett, *'Guanzi:' Political, Economic and Philosophical Essays from Early China—A Study and a Translation, Volume I, Revised Edition* (Boston: Cheng & Tsui. 2001), 3–46.

49. Tamara Chin has exhaustively treated the import in Han intellectual discourses of the "Qingzhong 輕重" chapters of the *Guanzi* in conceiving economic questions independently and not as an extension of disquisitions on morals; see *Savage Exchange*, 31–68; 229–94.

50. *SJ* 61, 1221–129.

51. On Guan Zhong in the *Records*, see *SJ* 62, 2131–134.

52. Recent scholarship has been clarifying the extent to which the Qin, upon vanquishing the other warring states, extended over their former territories extremely efficacious measures aimed at administrative, bureaucratic, fiscal, legal, and military centralization that would be in large part maintained under the Han. See Charles Sanft, *Communication and Cooperation in Early Imperial China: Publicizing the Qin Dynasty* (Albany: SUNY, 2014), 77–100, 123–46. Y. Pines, L. Von Falkenhausen,

G. Shelach, and R. D. S. Yates, *Birth of an Empire: The State of Qin Revisited* (Berkeley: University of California Press, 2014), 1–34.

53. *SJ* 23, 1159–160: 至秦有天下，悉內六國禮儀，采擇其善，雖不合聖制，其尊君抑臣，朝廷濟濟，依古以來。至于高祖，光有四海，叔孫通頗有所增益減損，大抵皆襲秦故。自天子稱號下至佐僚及宮室官名，少所變改。

54. *SJ* 25, 1160–1: 至秦有天下，悉內六國禮儀，采擇其善，雖不合聖制，其尊君抑臣，朝廷濟濟，依古以來。至于高祖，光有四海，叔孫通頗有所增益減損，大抵皆襲秦故。自天子稱號下至佐僚及宮室官名，少所變改。孝文即位，有司議欲定儀禮，孝文好道家之學，以為繁禮飾貌，無益於治，躬化謂何耳，[四]故罷去之。孝景時，御史大夫鼂錯明於世務刑名，數干諫孝景曰：「諸侯藩輔，臣子一例，古今之制也。今大國專治異政，不稟京師，恐不可傳後。」孝景用其計，而六國畔逆，以錯首名，天子誅錯以解難。[六]事在袁盎語中。是後官者養交安祿而已，莫敢復議。

55. Telly H. Koo, "The Constitutional Development of the Western Han Dynasty," *Journal of the American Oriental Society* 40 (1992): 170–93.

56. And one might wonder whether Sima Qian in this passage was also referring to the sensitiveness of his historical task. On Chao Cuo and his attempt to carry out centralizing reforms, also see Puett, *The Ambivalence of Creation*, 197–203.

57. Very interestingly, when Sima Qian mentions the Mandate in connection to recent rulers, he does not relate it to Heaven.

58. *SJ* 23, 1160–161: 今上即位，招致儒術之士，令共定儀，十餘年不就。或言古者太平，萬民和喜，瑞應辨至，乃采風俗，定制作。上聞之，制詔御史曰：「蓋受命而王，各有所由興，殊路而同歸，謂因民而作，追俗為制也。議者咸稱太古，百姓何望？漢亦一家之事，典法不傳，謂子孫何？化隆者閎博，治淺者褊狹，可不勉與！」乃以太初之元改正朔，易服色，封太山，定宗廟百官之儀，以為典常，垂之於後云。

59. See Introduction, note 27.

60. The close relationship between textual hermeneutics and economics is also evident in later historiography, see Nancy Lee Swann, *Food and Money in Ancient China: The Earliest Economic History of China to A.D. 25*, Hanshu 24, *with Related Texts* Han Shu 91 *and* Shih-Chih 12 (Princeton, NJ: Princeton University Press, 1950), esp. 77–305.

61. See the chapter "The Grand Inquest—81 BC," in Michael Loewe, *Crisis and Conflict in Han China* (London: Allen & Unwin, 1974), 91–112.

62. *YTLJZ* 1, 1–40.

63. *YTLJZ* 53, 551.

64. *YTLJZ* 37, 437–38.

65. *YTLJZ* 37, 637.

66. By the end of the Western Han, *li* had become a central concept in discourses about the founding values of Chinese civilization. The most widely accepted interpretation of *li* was that elaborated by Xunzi 荀子 (c. 312–230 BCE); see Robert F. Campany, "Xunzi and Durkheim as Theorists of Ritual Practice," in *Discourse and Practice*, Frank Reynolds, David Tracy, eds. (Albany: SUNY, 1992), 197–225, 227–31; Yuri Pines, "Disputers of the *Li*: Breakthroughs in the Concept

of Ritual in Pre-Imperial China," *Asia Major* (Third Series) 13, 1 (2000): 1–41; Michael David Kaulana Ing, *The Dysfunction of Ritual in Early Confucianism* (Oxford: Oxford University Press, 2014).

67. From the very mention of Dong's place of origin, it is arguable that he was not extremely popular in the first century BCE yet; on Dong Zhongshu's influence and attributed work see, Michael Loewe, *Dong Zhongshu: A "Confucian" heritage and the* Chunqiu fanlu (Leiden: Brill, 2011); see note 36 above.

68. See the chapter on natural disasters in the *YTL* (Lun zai 論菑), *YTLJZ* 54, 556: 始江都相董生推言陰陽，四時相繼，父生之，子養之，母成之，子藏之。故春生，仁；夏長，德；秋成，義；冬藏，禮。此四時之序，聖人之所則也。刑不可任以成化，故廣德教。

69. See Michael Loewe, *A Biographical Dictionary of the Qin, Former Han and Xin Periods (221 BC–AD 24)* (Leiden: Brill, 2000), 462–64; Michael Loewe, "The Fall of the House of Huo," in *Crisis and Conflict in Han China* (London: Allen & Unwin, 1974), 116–55.

70. See, Tian, "The Suburban Sacrifice," 27–78. Michael Loewe, "'Confucian' Values and Practices in Han China," *T'oung Pao*, 98, 1/3 (2012): 25–30.

71. Michael Loewe, "K'uang Heng and the Reform of Religious Practices (31 B.C.)," *Asia Major* 17, 1 part 2 (1988): 1–27.

72. On the cultural and political implication of the *xunshou* (and *Feng* and *Shan* sacrifices) throughout Chinese imperial history, see He Pingli 何平立, *Xunshou yu feng shan—Fengjian zhengzhi de wenhua guiji* 巡狩与封禅－封建政治文化轨迹 (Jinan: Qi Lu Shushe, 2003); for a brief but cogent cultural history of the *xunshou*, see Robert Campany, *Strange Writings: Anomaly Accounts in Early Medieval China* (Albany: SUNY Press, 1996), 106–13.

73. In the "Biographies of Ru Scholars," just before the episode concerning the fire at Gaozu's mortuary shrine I will analyze below, we learn that Dong's assiduous study of disasters and portents in the *Spring and Autumn* had led him to understand how to control yin and yang and determine rainfall with constant success in his brief official appointment in Jiangdu. As other works of his time, including the *Annals of Lü Buwei* 呂不韋 (*Lu Shi Chunqiu* 呂氏春秋), the *Records* treats yin and yang as meteorological aspects of reality. They do not yet constitute fundamental factors or principles of the cosmos. In fact, what Dong Zhongshu obtains by mastering them is not a superior and deeper insight into the laws of the cosmos, but merely a practical result, which, as Sima Qian reports, was not even enough to secure Dong's local political position.

74. See below.

75. For an analysis of Ban Gu's "Treatise on the Five Phases," see Aihe Wang, *Cosmology and Political Culture in Early China* (Cambridge, UK: Cambridge University Press, 2000), 130–45.

76. For an Eastern Han deconstruction of the mystique of the Sage Men, see Wang Chong, *LH* 26, 1069–85.

77. *HS* 27, 1315.
78. *HS* 27, 1316.
79. *HS* 27, 1317. For an assessment of the reliability of the accounts mentioning the episode, see Jens Østergård Petersen, "Which books did the First Emperor of Ch'in burn?—on the meaning of *Pai chia* in early Chinese sources," *Monumenta Serica* 43 (1995): 1–52.
80. See Tian Changwu 田昌五, *Wang Chong—Gudai de zhandou weiwulunzhe* 王充－古代的戰鬥唯物論者 (Beijing: Renmin, 1958); Timoteus Pokora, Michael Loewe, "*Lun heng* 論衡," in *Early Chinese Texts*, M. Loewe, ed. (Berkeley, CA: The Society For the Study of Early China, 1993), 309–12. For a partial translation, see Alfred Forke, *Lun-Hêng: Part I, Philosophical Essays of Wang Ch'ung; Part II, Miscellaneous Essays of Wang Ch'ung* (Leipzig: Harrassowitz; London: Luzac; Shanghai: Kelly and Walsh, 1907).
81. The Five Genii, *wusi* 五祀 (I follow Forke's translation) pertained to the domestic sphere and are mentioned in several received and excavated manuscripts. For their meanings and evolution see, Ding Yuanzhi 丁原植 and Yang Hua 楊華, eds., *Xin chu jianbo yu lizhi yanjiu* 新出簡帛與禮制研究 (Taipei: Taiwan Guji, 2007), 117–34.
82. See Huang Hui 黃暉, *Lun Heng jiaoshi* 論衡校釋 (Beijing: Zhonghua, 1990), 1056 (Hereafter *LHJS*): 王者祭天地，諸侯祭山川，卿、大夫祭五祀，士、庶人祭其先。宗廟、社稷之祀，自天子達於庶人。《尚書》曰：「肆類于上帝，禋于六宗，望于山川，徧于群臣。」《禮》曰：「有虞氏禘黃帝而郊嚳，祖顓頊而宗堯；夏后氏亦禘黃帝而郊鯀，祖顓頊而宗禹；殷人禘嚳而郊冥，祖契而宗湯；周人禘嚳而郊稷，祖文王而宗武王。燔柴於大壇，祭天也；瘞埋於大折，祭地也，用騂犢。埋少牢於大昭，祭時也；相近於坎壇，祭寒暑也；王宮、祭日也，夜明、祭月也，幽宗、祭星也，雩宗、祭水旱也，四坎壇、祭四方也。山林、川谷、丘陵，能出雲，為風雨，見怪物，皆曰神。有天下者祭百神。諸侯、在其地則祭，亡其地則不祭。」此皆法度之祀，禮之常制也.
83. A. Forke, *Lun-Hêng*, 516–17; *LHJS*, 1057.
84. On the relationship between Sima Qian and his model Confucius and on the scholarly tradition on chapter 47 of the *Shiji*, see Stephen W. Durrant, "Sima Qian's Confucius," in *The Cloudy Mirror*, 29–45; Li Changzhi 李長之, "Sima Qian he Kongzi 司馬遷和孔子," in *Sima Qian zhi renge yu fengge* 司馬遷之人格與風格 (Taipei: Li ren shuju, 1999), 41–76.
85. On the richness and complexity of Han intellectuals' curricula, see Michael Nylan, "The *Chin wen/Gu wen* Controversy in Han Times," *T'oung Pao* 80, 1–13 (1994): 83–145.
86. Wang Baoxuan, *Jin gu wenjingxue xinlun*, 19–27.
87. For the notion of "factionalist" struggles at the Han court, see Marianne Bujard, "Le 'Traité des sacrifices'du *Hanshu* et la mise en place de la religion d'état des Han," *Bulletin de l'Ecole Française de l'Extrême Orient* 84 (1997): 111–27. For a "regionalist" interpretation of the cultural variety of the first Han, see Wang Baoxuan 王葆玹, in *Jin gu wenjingxue xinlun*, 19–27. A classic analysis of the question is Gu

Jiegang 顾颉刚, *Qin Han de fangshi yu rusheng* 秦汉的方士与儒生 (Shanghai: Shanghai Guji Chubanshe, 1978). See also Lin Fushi 林富士, *Handai de wuzhe* 漢代的巫者 (Taibei: Taiwan Daoxiang Chubanshe, 1999). Yang Xiong 揚雄 (53 BCE–18 CE) had already noticed, together with Sima Qian's analytical acumen, the historian's penchant for the odd and extraordinary; see *Fa yan* 法言 (Shanghai: Shangwu yinshuguan, 1939), 12:2b and Michael Nylan (trans.), *Exemplary Figures—'Fa Yan'* 法言 (Seattle: University of Washington Press, 2013), 210–11.

88. *SJ* 47, 1911–912.

89. Cfr., *Lun Yu* 論語, 12, 11: 齊景公問政於孔子. 孔子對曰. 君君. 臣臣. 父父. 子子. 公 曰. 善哉. 信如君不君. 臣不臣. 父不父. 子不子. 雖有粟. 吾得而食諸。

90. See Yuri Pines, "From Teachers to Subjects: Ministers Speaking to the Rulers, from Yan Ying 晏嬰 to Li Si 李斯," in *Facing the Monarch: Modes of Advice in the Early Chinese Court*, Garret P. S. Olberding, ed. (Cambridge, MA: Harvard University Press, 2013), 69–80.

91. *SJ* 47, 1911–912. 夫儒者滑稽而不可軌法; 倨傲自順, 不可以為下; 崇喪遂哀, 破產厚葬, 不可以為俗; 游說乞貸, 不可以為國。自大賢之息, 周室既衰, 禮樂缺有閒。今孔子盛容飾, 繁登降之禮, 趨詳之節, 累世不能殫其學, 當年不能究其禮。君欲用之以移齊俗, 非所以先細民也. It was not only Sima Qian, in early Chinese cultural history, who maintained a critical attitude toward aspects of a tradition to which he was undoubtedly connected; see Michael Nylan, "Han Classicists Writing in Dialogue about Their Own Tradition," *Philosophy East and West* 47, 2 (1997): 133–88.

92. Cfr. *Mozi*, "Gong Meng 公孟" 12, 418.

93. *Yanzi Chunqiu* 8, 8. For the philological debate on the composition of the *Yanzi Chunqiu*, see Stephen W. Durrant, "Yen tzu ch'un ch'iu," in *Early Chinese Texts*, 483–89.

94. See chapter 1 above.

95. *SJ* 62, 2134–137.

96. Yan Ying's lord was the second Duke of Qi to be called Zhuang, the first one reigned from 794 to 731 BCE. They both belonged to the house of Jiang 姜.

97. *SJ* 62, 2136–137: 管仲世所謂賢臣, 然孔子小之. 豈以為周道衰微, 桓公既賢, 而不勉之至王, 乃稱霸哉?語曰「將順其美, 匡救其惡, 故上下能相親也」。豈管仲之謂乎?方晏子伏莊公尸哭之, 成禮然後去, 豈所謂「見義不為無勇」者邪?至其諫說, 犯君 之顏, 此所謂「進思盡忠, 退思補過」者哉! 假令晏子而在, 余雖為之執鞭, 所忻慕焉。

98. *SJ* 32, 1500–501.

99. *SJ* 32, 1501: 人謂崔杼:「必殺之。」崔杼曰:「民之望也, 舍之得民。」

100. *SJ* 62, 2135.

101. *SJ* 99, 2726.

102. *SJ* 97, 2699.

103. *SJ* 97, 2692: 沛公不好儒, 諸客冠儒冠來者, 沛公輒解其冠, 溲溺其中. 與人言, 常大罵. 未可以儒生說也。

104. *SJ* 99, 272: 吾迺今日知為皇帝之貴也.

105. Even though it is difficult to make such a point from the sole *Records*, Gaozu might have looked naïve and inurbane to the eyes of the more sophisticated residents of the Central Plain, also because of his relatively poor background. A self-conscious Lu Jia 陸賈 (a Chu native as well), for example, reminds the conqueror of Nan Yue 南越, Zhao Tuo 趙他, that the customs of civilization are naturally the customs of the Central States (*SJ* 97, 2697: 足下中國人，親戚昆弟墳在真定。今足下反天性，笃冠帶，欲以 區區越與天子抗衡為敵國，禍且及身矣). For a detailed hypothesis about the factors that allowed a man such as Liu Bang to become the first emperor of the Han, see chapter 3 below.

106. Cf. *SJ* 97, 2699; Gaozu, after hearing Lu Jia's explanation of the failure of the Qin, "grew embarrassed and uneasy and finally said to Master Lu: 'Try to write something for me on the reasons why Qin lost the empire and I won it, and of the success and failure of the states of ancient times.'" Watson, *Records*, I: 227.

107. *SJ* 121, 3122–124. Sima Qian considered Yuan Gu the preeminent expert on the *Odes* after Confucius himself and the forefather of the *Shijing* scholarly tradition of Qi. Under empress dowager Lü 呂, Yuan's criticism of Laozi's writings had cost him a stint in the pigpen; reinstated, he remained at court until he was ninety-nine years old, despite the envy and hostility of many of his fellow Classicists. According to the commentary on Sima Qian's biography, master Huang is the one who had introduced Sima Tan to Huang-Lao doctrines; see *SJ* 130, 3288.

108. *SJ* 121, 3122.

109. For recent analyses of the cultural and political import of omens during the Han, see Liang Cai, "The Hermeneutics of Omens: The Bankruptcy of Moral Cosmology in the Western Han China (206 BCE–8 CE)," *The Journal of the Royal Asiatic Society* 3 (April 2015): 1–21; Chen Yexin 陳葉新, *Zaihai yu liang Han shehui yanjiu* 災害與兩漢社會研究 (Shanghai: Shanghai Renmin Chubanshe, 2004); David Pankenier, "On the Reliability of Han Dynasty (206 BCE–220 CE) Solar Eclipse Records," *The Journal of Astronomical History and Heritage* 15.3 (2012): 200–212.

110. The translation is from Liang Cai, "The Hermeneutics of Omens," 3. See Dong Zhongshu, *Chunqiu fanlu zhu zi suoyin* 春秋繁露逐字索引, D. C. Lau and Chen Fangzheng, eds. (Hong Kong: Shang wu yin shu guan, 1994), 8.4, 40/26.

111. *SJ* 121, 3128.

112. Interestingly, Sima Qian and Liu Xiang remember Zhufu Yan as an official who strove to protect the court from the plots of the regional kingdoms. It was one of their rulers who would cause his fall from grace and execution by submitting in revenge documents that accused him of bribery. See Loewe, *A Biographical Dictionary*, 749–50. Zhufu Yan was also noted for attempting to disgrace eminent official by denouncing their sexual misconduct; see Paul R. Goldin, *The Culture of Sex in Ancient China* (Honolulu: Hawai'i University Press, 2002), 86. Olberding, *Dubious Facts*, 178.

113. *SJ* 121, 3128: 董仲舒弟子呂步舒不知其師書，以為下愚。於是下董仲舒吏，當死，詔赦之。於是董仲舒竟不敢復言災異。The same episode is narrated in more detail in *HS* 36, 1930 and in the *Lunheng* 84. 362, 17–20. However, considering the status of Don Zhongshu under the Eastern Han, it would not be surprising if episodes concerning his career had been embellished and used to cast a positive light on the "forefather of Han Classicists."

114. Martin Kern, "Religious Anxiety and Political Interest in Western Han Omen Interpretation: The Case of the Han Wudi Period (141–87 B.C.)," *Chûgoku shigaku* 10 (2000): 1–31.

115. Loewe, *A Biographical Dictionary*, 749–50.

116. *SJ* 47, 1942. Confucius's epistemological concerns are completely absent in the synthesis of these events reported in the *Luxuriant Gems*; see Allan and Major, *Luxuriant Gems*, 159.

117. See Wai-yee, Li, "The Capture of the *Lin* and the Birth of Historiography," in *The Readability of the Past* (Cambridge, MA, and London: Harvard University Press, 2007), 411–21. As I shall show in detail further on, Sima Qian will refer to this episode in several instances and often in a farcical context throughout *Shiji* 27, "Fengshan Shu."

118. See Michael Nylan, *The Five "Confucian" Classics* (New Haven, CT: Yale University Press, 2001), 139–42; *The Shifting Center: The Original "Great Plan" and Later Readings* (Nettetal, Germany: Steyler Verlag, 1992).

119. *SJ* 47, 1942.

120. On Dong Zhongshu's reading of the capture of the *lin* in the *Chunqiu Fanlu* (*CQFL yizheng* 義證 9), see Li, *The Readability*, 414.

121. The biography of Bo Yi and Shu Qi, opens the *Liezhuan* section in the *Shiji* (*SJ* 61, 2121–131) as though it was intended to immediately introduce the reader to the potential conflict between moral integrity and political responsibility.

122. *SJ* 47, 1943: 我則異於是，無可無不可. See also *Lun Yu* 論語, "Weizi" 微子" 18, 8.

123. *SJ* 47, 1943–944.

124. According to the "Book on Music" ("Yue shu") in the *Records*, the literary tradition and the possibility to establish and emotional connection with the men of the past were probably the elements of continuity that defined the civilization of the Central States. For a comparative assessment of the importance of hearing (and seeing) in ancient China, see Jane Geaney, *On the Epistemology of the Senses in Early Chinese Thought* (Honolulu: Hawai'i University Press, 2002), 50–83.

125. *SJ* 24, 1175–176. On the authorship of the "Yueshu," see Hans Van Ess, "Some Preliminary Notes on the Authenticity of the Treatise on Music in *Shiji* 24," *Oriens Estremus* 45 (2005–2006): 4–67; Martin Kern, "A Note on the Authenticity and ideology of Shih-chi 24, "Yueshu," *Journal of the American Oriental Society* 119, 4 (1999): 673–77. On the development and uses of music in ancient

China, see Kenneth J. DeWoskin, *A Song for One or Two: Music and the Concept of Art in Early China* (Ann Arbor: University of Michigan Press, 1982); and the more recent, Erica Fox Brindley, *Music Cosmology, and the Politics of Harmony in Early China* (Albany: SUNY Press, 2012).

126. Mark E. Lewis, *Writing and Authority in Early China* (Albany: SUNY Press, 1999), 308–17.

127. Xu Fuguan 徐復觀, *Liang Han*, 3: 196–97.

128. See Michel Foucault, *The Order of Things: An Archaeology of the Human Sciences* (New York: Random House, 1970).

129. Michael Nylan, "Towards an Archaeology of Writing: Text, Ritual and the Culture of Public Display in the Classical Period (475 B.C.E.–220 C.E.)," in *Text and Ritual in Early China*, Martin Kern, ed. (Seattle: University of Washington Press, 2005), 3–50.

130. This topic is treated in chapter 1; see above.

131. Erica Fox Brindley has argued that a notion of individual agency emerged in pre-imperial philosophical and political discourses. According to her reconstruction, this new conception developed along the universalization of ideas about the connection of man and nature. Sima Qian's stance seems to be consistent with this cultural milieu. However, his historical perspective leads him to lament the sage's impossibility to comply with the cosmic order. More or less implicitly, he blames this breach on the generations that followed the fall of the Western Zhou; cfr., Erica Fox Brindley, *Individualism in Early China: Human Agency and the Self in Thought and Politics* (Honolulu: University of Hawai'i Press, 2010), 29–53.

132. Cited in and translated from Antonio Gramsci, *Quaderni del carcere*, vol. 10 (Torino: Einaudi, 1975), 1225–226.

133. In the original text, the term *"speculativo"* refers to a kind of philosophical research that is purely theoretical and not aimed at any practical application.

134. On Gramsci and his intellectual contribution, see Walter Adamson, *Hegemony and Revolution: A Study of Antonio Gramsci's Political and Cultural Theory* (Berkeley: University of California Press, 1980).

135. Antonio Gramsci, *Quaderni del carcere*, X, 1, VIII (Torino: Einaudi, 1975), 1225–226.

136. On the relationship between "myth" and "history" in Sima Qian, see Charles LeBlanc, "A Re-examination of the Myth of Huang ti," *Journal of Chinese Religions* 13–14 (1985–86): 45–63.

137. Sima Qian, especially in the eight monographic chapters (*shu*) does provide relatively more organic views of the cosmic and the human realms—views that he connects to the almost timeless tradition of the Central States. However, the Grand Historian states that his age could not be understood by looking at the past or by applying traditional wisdom; see *SJ* 25, 1158–561; *SJ* 18, 878: 居今之世，志古之道，所以自鏡也，未必盡同。帝王者各殊禮而異務，要以成功為統紀，豈可緄乎?觀所以得尊寵及所以廢辱，亦當世得失之林也，何必舊聞?於是謹其終始，表其文，頗有所不盡本末; 著其明，疑者闕之。後有君子，欲推而列之，得以覽焉。

138. See chapter 5 below.

139. See Martin Jay, *Downcast Eyes: The Denigration of Vision in Twentieth-Century France* (Berkeley, Los Angeles, London: University of California Press, 1993), especially pp. 1–20, and the chapter "The Noblest of the Senses: Vision to Plato to Descartes," 21–82. David Chidester, *Word and Light: Seeing, Hearing, and Religious Discourse* (Urbana: University of Illinois Press: 1992).

140. See Li Wai-yee, "The Idea of Authority in the *Shih Chi* (Records of the Historian)," *Harvard Journal of Asiatic Studies* 54, 2 (Dec. 1994): 345–405.

141. Mark E. Lewis has highlighted in the how the structure of the *Records* was meant to reproduce the order of cosmos and society.

Chapter 3

1. A different version of this chapter has been already published in Filippo Marsili, "The Ghosts of Monotheism: Heaven, Fortune, and Universalism in Early Chinese and Greco-Roman Historiography," *Fragments* 3 (2013–2014): 43–77.

2. Benedict Anderson, *Imagined Communities: Reflections on the Origin and Spread of Nationalism* (New York: Verso, 1983), 204.

3. Translation in Arthur Wailey, *The Book of Songs/Shijing* (New York: Grove Press, 1996), 228 (Wen Wang 文王, Mao 毛 235).

4. Cited in and translated from Antonio Gramsci, *Quaderni del carcere*, vol. 10 (Torino: Einaudi, 1975), 1225–226.

5. Famously, the first attested explicit formalization of the connection between beliefs about the divine and identity is in Herodotus (*Histories* VIII, 144). The context of a speech about the impiety of the Persians, famously defined Greek identity in these terms: "kinship of all Greeks in blood and speech, and the shrines of gods and the sacrifices that we have in common, and the likeness of our way of life."

6. For the bibliography, see the Introduction; especially notes 5 and 6.

7. Iggers and Wang, *A Global History of Modern Historiography*, 48. On the Jesuits's attempts to find a Chinese notion or term that corresponded to that of a Christian god, see Brockey, *Journey to the East*: 85–91.

8. The prominent historian of Chinese philosophy Angus Graham identified the Zhou as the axial "time of awakening" for China, when "[t]he Chou identified their supreme authority T'ien (Heaven), a sky-god hardly distinguished from the sky itself, with Ti the high god of the Shang." See Graham, *Disputers of the Tao*, 1. On the Tian/Heaven under the Zhou, see below.

9. For the "poetic," creative function of the historian, see Hayden White, *Metahistory: The Historical Imagination in Nineteenth-Century Europe* (Baltimore, MD: John Hopkins Press, 1975), ix–xii, 5–42.

10. On the relationship between Heaven and fate in early China, see Michael Puett, "Following the Commands of Heaven: The Notion of *Ming* in Early China," in *The Magnitude of Ming*, Michael Lupke, ed. (Honolulu: University of Hawai'i

Press, 2005), 49–69. Puett shows how the tension between Heaven and fate that characterized early Chinese thought would be reconciled, also for the sake of a more organic imperial ideology, by Dong Zhongshu (ca. 179–104 BCE), whose theories became relevant with the Eastern Han (25–220 CE) and more visible in Ban Gu's (32–92 CE) *Hanshu*. On fate in Chinese culture, see also Fu Sinian, 傅斯年 "Xingming gushun bianzheng 性命古順辯證" in *Fu Mengzhen ziansheng ji* 傅孟真先生集 (Taipei: Taiwan National University, 1952). On a linguistic comparison between notions of fate in early China and ancient Greece, see Lisa Raphals, "Languages of Fate: Semantic Fields in Chinese and Greek," in *The Magnitude of* Ming, 70–106.

11. On the relationship between Fortune (*Tychê*) in Polybius and Josephus (37–100 CE) as a divine unifying force, see Eric Gruen, "Polybius and Josephus on Rome," in *Polybius & His World: Essays in Memory of F. W. Walbank*, Bruce Gibson and Thomas Harrison, eds. (Oxford: Oxford University Press, 2013), 257–58. See also Arnaldo Momigliano, "The Herodotean and Thucydidean Tradition," in *The Classical Foundations of Modern Historiography* (Berkeley: University of California Press, 1990), 29, 50.

12. See Walter Burkert, *The Orientalizing Revolution: Near Eastern Influence on Greek Culture in the Early Archaic Age* (Cambridge, MA: Harvard University Press, 1998); *Babylon, Memphis, Persepolis: Eastern Contexts of Greek Culture* (Cambridge, MA: Harvard University Press, 2007); Peregrine Horden and Nicholas Purcell, *The Corrupting Sea: A Study of Mediterranean History* (London: Blackwell, 2000).

13. On the discourse on the Other as a foil for the formalization of a given cultural identity, see Edward Said, *Orientalism* (New York: Random House, 1979); James Romm, *The Edges of the Earth in Ancient Thought: Geography, Exploration, and Fiction* (Princeton, NJ: Princeton University Press, 1992); and George Fredrickson, *The Comparative Imagination: On the History of Racism, Nationalism, and Social Movements* (Berkeley: University of California Press, 1997). For a classic formulation of ethnicity in anthropological terms, see Fredrik Barth, *Ethnic Groups and Boundaries: The Social Organization of Cultural Difference* (Boston: Little, Brown Series in Anthropology, 1969).

14. For a new analysis of Herodotus's complex attitude towards the Persians, see Gruen, *Rethinking*, 21–39; François Hartog, *The Mirror of Herodotus: The Representation of the Other in the Writing of History* (Berkeley: University of California Press, 1988). On the theme and debates on Greek identities, see; Paul Cartledge, "Herodotus and 'the Other': a meditation on empire," *EMC/CV* 9 (1990): 27–40; "'We are all Greeks?' Ancient (especially Herodotean) and Modern Contestations of Hellenism," *BICS* 2 (1995 [1996]): 75–82. On the cultural context of Greek historiography, see also Arnaldo Momigliano, "The Herodotean and Thucydidean Tradition," in *The Classical Foundation of Modern Historiography* (Berkeley: University of California Press, 1990), 29–53; also, by the same author, *Alien Wisdom: The Limit of Hellenization* (Cambridge, UK: Cambridge University Press, 1990).

15. Ray Laurence, "Territory, Ethnonyms and Geography: The Construction of Identity in Roman Italy," in *Cultural Identity in the Roman Empire*, Ray Laurence, Joanne Berry, eds. (London: Routledge, 1998), 64–78. On the complex relationship of Roman intellectual with Greek culture, see Erich S. Gruen, *Culture and National Identity in Republican Rome* (Ithaca, NY: Cornell University Press, 1992); Fabrizio Fabbrini, *Maecenas. Il collezionismo nel mondo romano dall'età degli Scipioni a Cicerone* (Arezzo: Istituto di Storia Antica, 2001).

16. On a comparative approach to the issues of the other and identity, see Mu-chou Poo, *Enemies of Civilization: Attitudes toward Foreigners in Ancient Mesopotamia, Egypt, and China* (Albany: SUNY Press, 2005).

17. Poo, *Enemies* 154–59. As an example of Chinese nationalistic attitude toward the Other, Poo cites Qian Mu, *Guoshi dagang* (Taipei: Shangwu, 1970). On the role of the *Records* in establishing a spatial and cultural conception of Chinese civilization, see Wang Mingke 王明珂, "*Shiji* wenben yu Huaxia tiguo qingjing" '史記' 文本與華夏提過情境' in *Yingxiong zuxian yu dixiong minzu—genji lishi de wenben yu qingjing* 英雄與弟兄民族—根基歷史的文本與情境 (Taipei: Yunchen Wenhua, 2006), 75–86. By the same author, on the concept of ethnic identity in historical literature, see *Huaxia bianyuan—lishi jiyi yu zuqun rentong* 華夏邊緣—歷史記憶與族群認同 (Taipei: Yunchen Wenhua, 1997).

18. Tamara Chin provides a compelling analysis of Sima Qian's attitude towardsthe Xiongnu vis-à-vis later historical works such as the *Han Shu* and the *Hou Han Shu*; see her "Defamiliarizing the Foreigner: Sima Qian's Ethnography and Han-Xiongnu Marriage Diplomacy," *Harvard Journal of Asiatic Studies* 70, 2 (Dec. 2010): 320. Chin's thesis is the basis for my analysis of the theme of ethnicity in Sima Qian. See also Zhang Dake, "Sima Qian de minzu yitong sixiang," in *Shiji yanju*, 438–53; Hyun Jin Kim, *Ethnicity and Foreigners in Ancient Greece and China* (London: Duckworth, 2009); See Nicola Di Cosmo, *Ancient China and Its Enemies: The Rise of Nomadic Power in East Asian History* (Cambridge, UK: Cambridge University Press, 2002); Sophia-Karin Psarras, "Han and Xiongnu: A Reexamination of Cultural and Political Relations," *Monumenta Serica* 51 (2003): 55–236.

19. Chin, "Defamiliarizing," 320.

20. For biographical information on Sima Qian and his father see, *SJ* 130, 3285–322; Zhang Dake 張大可, *Sima Qian pingchuan* 司馬遷評傳 (Nanjing: Nanjing Daxue, 1994).

21. Michael Loewe, "The Authority of the Emperors of Ch'in and Han," in *Divination, Mythology, and Monarchy in Han China* (Cambridge, UK: Cambridge University Press, 1994), 85–112.

22. The Zhou ruling lineage probably hailed from an area in the West, closer to the "barbarians," between Gansu and Shaanxi, even though they eventually moved towards the Central Plain; for an overview of their early history see Edward L. Shaughnessy, "Western Zhou History," in *The Cambridge History of Ancient China*, Michael; Loewe, Edward L. Shaughnessy, eds., 292–351.

23. Paul R. Goldin makes an interesting case concerning the conceptual connection between political and sexual misconduct in early China. According to Goldin, Sima Qian was punished with castration (usually reserved to sexual offenders), for his act of political insubordination was seen as endangering the social order as well as sexually promiscuous conduct would; see the chapter "Sex, Politics and Ritualization in the Early Empire" in Goldin's *The Culture of Sex*, 75–110.

24. *SJ* 110, 2879.

25. *SJ* 110, 2892. The *Records* associates the Xiongnu with the constellation of the Western Palace and with the Pleiades—the Xiongnu were ultimately part of the same universe as the Central States; see *SJ* 27, 1305.

26. *SJ* 110, 2879.

27. *SJ* 110, 2898.

28. *SJ* 1, 11: 帝顓頊高陽者，黃帝之孫而昌意之子也。靜淵以有謀，疏通而知事; 養材以任地, 載時以象天, 依鬼神以制義, 治氣以教化, 絜誠以祭祀。

29. See Gopal Sukhu, "Monkeys, Shamans, Emperors, and Poets: The *Chuci* and Images of Chu during the Han Dynasty," in *Defining Chu: Image and Reality in Ancient China*, Constance E. Cook and John Major, eds. (Honolulu: University of Hawai'i Press, 2004), 145–65.

30. Frank W. Walbank, *Polybius* (Berkeley: University of California Press, 1972), 3.

31. On the history of the Achaean League, see Frank W. Walbank, *Aratos of Sycion* (Cambridge, UK: Cambridge University Press, 1933); Robert M. Errington, *Philopoemen* (Oxford, UK: Clarendon, 1969).

32. Lycortas, as Military Commander (*hipparchos*), was selected as a member of the Achaean embassies to Rome and Alexandria in 188 BCE. In the subsequent decades, Lycortas was many times the head of the Achean League as *stratêgos*. See Craige Champion, *Cultural Politics in Polybius' 'Histories'* (Berkeley and Los Angeles: University of California Press, 2004), 16–17.

33. On Polybius in Rome, see Andrew Erskine, "Polybius among the Romans: Life in the Cyclops' Cave," in *Imperialism, Cultural Politics & Polybius*, Christopher Smith and Liv Mariah Yarrow, eds. (Oxford, UK: Oxford University Press, 2012), 17–32.

34. For an overview of Polybius's life, see Walbank, *Polybius*, 6–13; Champion, *Cultural Politics*, 15–18.

35. Walbank, *Polybius*, 7–8. On the issue of the "annexation" of Greece by Rome after the sack of Corinth, see Robert Kallet-Marx, *Hegemony to Empire: The Development of the Roman Imperium in the East from 148 to 62 B.C.* (Berkeley and Los Angeles: University of California Press, 1995), 42–57.

36. Pausanias, the Greek geographer of the second century CE, could report of monuments celebrating Polybius's activity as mediator between Greece and Rome scattered throughout the Hellenic world. See Champion, *Cultural Politics*, 18.

37. Of the forty books of the *Histories*, only the first five survive in a complete form. On the timing of the composition and publication of the *Histories*, see Walbank, *Polybius*, 13–31. On the different phases of Polybius's appraisal of Rome's military conquests and "imperialism," see Walbank, *Polybius*, 157–83; according to Walbank, Polybius's attitude toward Rome becomes less immediately intelligible in the narration of the events following the battle of Pydna in 168, as he has to account for the efforts of the Achaeans to maintain their independence and for Rome's shrewd treatment of the vanquished. On this topic, see Domenico Musti, *Polibio e l'imperialismo romano* (Napoli: Liguori Editore, 1978), 69–148.

38. See Numa Denis Fustel de Coulanges, *Polybe ou la Grèce conquise par les Romains* (PhD diss., Faculté des Lettres de Paris, 1858), 1. For the encounter of Rome and Greece, see Erich S. Gruen, *The Hellenistic World and the Coming of Rome* (Berkeley: University of California Press, 1985).

39. On the issue of Polybius's readership, I follow Champion's argument, summarized in *Cultural Politics*, 4. F. W. Walbank instead considers Polybius's intended public to have been mainly Greek, as he states in *Polybius*, 3–6; 16–19. See also Josephine Crawley Quinn, "Imagining the Imperial Mediterranean," in *Polybius & His World*, 337–52.

40. On the meanings of πραγματικὴ ἱστορία in Polybius and on his historiographical approach see Walbank, *Polybius*, 66–96; see also Paul Pédech, *Le méthode historique de Polybe* (Paris: Université de Paris, 1964), 331–54.

41. On Polybius's relationship with the Hellenic historiographical and rhetorical traditions, see Walbank, *Polybius*, 32–65; Riccardo Vattuone, "Timeo, Polibio e la storiografia greca d'occidente," in *The Shadow of Polybius: Intertextuality as a Research Tool in Greek Historiography*, Guido Schepens and Jan Bollansée, eds. (Leuven: Peeters, 2005), 73–88; Mario Attilio Levi, "La critica di Polibio a Timeo," *Studi Alessandrini* 196 (1963): 195–202.

42. Pédech (in *Le méthode historique de Polybe*, 331–354) singles out the following causal factors in the Hellenic historiography and in Polybius: influence of individuals, the character of political institutions and military expertise, geography, and fortune. Polybius (*Hist*. III, 5–7), in the analysis of the origin of war, famously expounds his theory based on the distinction among origins (ἀρχαί), causes (αἰτίαι), and alleged motives (πρόφασις).

43. This is the theme of book VI of the *Histories*. See Andrew Erskine, "How to Rule the World: Polybius Book 6 Reconsidered," in *Polybius & His World*, 231–46. See also, Clifford Ando, "Was Classical Rome a *Polis*" *Classical Antiquity* 18 (1999): 13.

44. See Champion on Book 6, 66–99; Jules Nicolet, "Polybe et les institutions romaines," *Entretiens sur l'Antiquité Classique de la Fondation Hardt* (Genève: Vandoeuvres, 1974), 209–65.

45. Champion (in *Cultural Politics*, 30–31) defines the use of the concept of "Hellenism" in Polybius and among contemporary Greek intellectuals as a cultural

strategy devised to counter Rome's power. On the development of a pan-Hellenic identity and on its different (instrumental) formulations in different historical contexts, see Champion, *Cultural Politics*, 31–40; see also C. P. Jones, "ἔθνος and γένος in Herodotus," *CQ* 46 (1996): 315–20.

46. Champion, *Cultural Politics*, 4.

47. Arnaldo Momigliano has pointed out that although Polybius was the only Greek historian to resort to the notion of cycles, he only did so with regard to the evolution of constitutions, for he did not include ordinary military and political events in this vision. See Momigliano, "Persian, Greek, and Jewish Historiography," in *The Classical Foundation of Modern Historiography*, 18.

48. *Hist.* I, 2–3.

49. Polybius acknowledges the work of Ephorus of Cumae as the first to attempt a general history; see *Hist.* V, 33, 2.

50. *Tianming* has been traditionally translated as "Mandate of Heaven." David Schaberg argued that "Heaven's Command" is more appropriate; see D. Schaberg, "Command and the Content of Tradition," in *The Magnitude of* Ming, Christopher Lupke, ed. (Honolulu: University of Hawai'i Press, 2005), 23–26. According to the theory of the Mandate of Heaven, which is expounded in its most complete form in the *Mengzi* (ca. 372–289 BCE), Heaven bestows the mandate to rule the Central States on worthy sovereigns and their lineages, while letting undeserving dynasts lose it. In *Mencius* the role of Heaven is also connected to the moral nature (*xing* 性) of men; see Robert Eno, *The Confucian Creation of Heaven: Philosophy and the Defense of Ritual Mastery* (Albany: SUNY Press, 1990), 99–130.

51. See Bujard, *Le sacrifice au Ciel*, and Watanabe Yoshihiro, "Sacrifices to Heaven in the Han and the Theory of Six Heavens," *Acta Asiatica* 98 (2010): 43–75.

52. For modern scholars looking for a metahistorical organizing principle in early Chinese civilization, Tian cannot unproblematically correspond to a monotheistic deity of the Abrahamic kind.

53. See Iggers *A Global History*, 48.

54. See Sabbatucci, *La prospettiva*, 200–34. For an original and compelling philosophical disambiguation of the concept of Heaven, see Hall and Ames, "*Tian* and *Dao* as Nontranscendent Fields," in *Thinking from the Han*, 219–252.

55. See Lillian Lan-ying Tseng's *Picturing Heaven in Early China* (Cambridge, MA: Harvard University Press, 2011).

56. The origins of the term *tian* are obscure and it is still very difficult to ascertain to what extent it was an original Zhou creation or was instead already a Shang deity. For a summary of the influential theories about *tian*'s origins and meanings by Herrlee G. Creel (who considered Tian the collectivity of the rulers of the past living in Heaven), and Shima Kunio (who interpreted *tian* as the sky, a sky-god, or the altar of that god), see Robert Eno's "Appendix A," in *The Confucian Creation of Heaven*, 181–86. See also Herrlee G. Creel, *The Origins of Statecraft in China* (Chicago: University of Chicago Press, 1970), 1: 497–504; and Shima Kunio

島邦男, *Inkyo bokuji kenkyū* 殷墟卜辞研究 (Hirosaki: Chūkokugaku Kenkyūkai, 1958), pp. 174–86. Eno (*The Confucian Creation of Heaven*, 186–89), on the basis of his philological analysis, sees *tian* also as the destination of the ashes of the sacrificial victims. Sarah Allan through a reexamination of the debates presented above, has recently interpreted Tian as both a natural phenomenon and in connection with dynastic ancestors; see Sarah Allan, "T'ien and Shang Ti in Pre-Han China," *Acta Asiatica* 98 (2010): 1–18. On the connection between Heaven and sacrifice, see Sarah Allan, "Drought, Human Sacrifice and the Mandate of Heaven in a Lost Text from the *Shangshu*," *Bulletin of the School of Oriental and African Studies* 47, no. 3 (1984): 523–39; Lewis, *Sanctioned Violence*, 205–10. On Shang ancestral cults, see Robert Eno, "Was There a High god Ti in Shang Religion?" *Early China* 15 (1990): 1–26; "Deities and Ancestors in Early Oracle Inscriptions," in *Religions of China in Practice*, Donald S. Lopez, ed. (Princeton, NJ: Princeton University Press, 1996), 41–51. James Legge, in his pioneering and still influential nineteenth-century English translation of the Chinese classics, translated Shangdi as "God"; see Birrell, "Legge": 331–53.

57. James Legge, trans., *The The Shû king*, vol. 3 of *The Sacred Books of the East*, M. Müller, ed. (Oxford, UK: Clarendon Press, 1893) 157: 己! 予惟小子, 若涉淵水, 予惟往求朕攸濟。敷賁敷前人受命, 茲不忘大功。予不敢不閉. 天降威, 用寧王遺我大寶龜, 紹天明。即命曰: "有大艱于西土, 西土人亦不靜, 越茲蠢。殷小腆誕敢紀其敘。天降威, 知我國有疵, 民不康, 曰: 予復! 反鄙我周邦。今蠢, 予翼日, 民獻有十夫予翼, 以于敉寧、武圖功。我有大事, 休?" 朕卜並吉 [...]己! 予惟小子, 不敢替上帝命。天休于寧王, 興我小邦周, 寧王惟卜用, 克綏受茲命。今天其相民, 矧亦惟卜用。嗚呼! 天明畏, 弼我丕丕基!

58. Sima Qian here echoes Confucius's lamentation that Heaven was no longer readable in his times, in the tortoise shells, the Zhou had an effective means for reading Heaven's will. See above.

59. See pp. 181–84 above.

60. Nylan, *The Five "Confucian" Classics*, 139–42.

61. See p. 156 above.

62. Legge, 3: 320–23: 我聞在昔。鯀堙洪水。汩陳其五行。帝乃震怒。不畀洪範九疇。彝倫攸斁。鯀則殛死。禹乃嗣興。天乃錫禹洪範九疇。彝倫攸敘

63. The Nine Divisions of the "Great Plan," were the "Five Phases," the "Reverent Practice of the Five Businesses," the "Earnest Devotion of the Eight Objects Government," the "Harmonious use of the Five Arrangements," the "Establishment and Use of Royal Perfection," the "Cultivation and Use of the Three Virtues," the "Intelligent use of the Examination of Doubts," the "Thoughtful Use of the Various Verifications," and the "The Hortatory Use of the Five Happinesses and the Awing Use of the Six Extremities"; see Legge, 3: 324.

64. See Nylan, *The Five "Confucian" Classics*, 127–36. Although it was based on earlier documents, the "Great Oath" was probably forged in order to please the rulers of the Western Han.

65. Translation based on Legge, *The Chinese Classics, Vol. 3*, 283–86 惟天地萬物父母，惟人萬物之靈。但聰明，作元后，元后作民父母。今商王受，弗敬上天，降災下民。沈湎冒色，敢行暴虐，罪人以族，官人以世，[...]惟受罔有悛心，乃夷居，弗事上帝神祇，遺厥先宗廟弗祀。犧牲粢盛，既于凶盜。乃曰：『吾有民有命!』罔懲其侮。天佑下民，作之君，作之師，惟其克相上帝，寵綏四方。有罪無罪，予曷敢有越厥志？

66. See Michael Carson and Michael Loewe, *"Lü shih ch'un ch'iu"* 呂氏春秋, in *Early Chinese Texts: A Bibliographical Guide*, Michael Loewe, ed. (Berkeley: University of California, Institute of East Asian Studies, 1993), 324–30. John Knoblock and Jeffrey Riegel, *The Annals of Lü Buwei: A Complete Translation and Study* (Stanford, CA: Stanford University Press, 2003); James D. Sellmann, *Timing and Rulership in Master Lü's Spring and Autumn Annals (Lüshi chunqiu)* (Albany: SUNY Press, 2002).

67. *Lüshi chunqiu* 1, 2.1: 始生之者，天也；養成之者，人也。能養天之所生而勿攖之謂天子。天子之動也，以全天為故者也。此官之所自立也。立官者以全生也；see Knoblock, Riegel, *The Annals*, 64.

68. *Lüshi chunqiu* 14, 6.1: 功名大立，天也；為是故，因不慎其人不可；[...] 夫禹遇舜，天也；禹周於天下，以求賢者，事利黔首，水潦川澤之湛滯壅塞可通者，禹盡為之，人也；see Knoblock, Riegel, *The Annals*, 323.

69. On Huang-Lao in Han historiography, see Han Van Ess, "The Meaning of Huang-Lao in *Shiji* and *Hanshu*," *Études chinoises* 12, 2 (Fall 1993): 161–177. On Sima Tan and Qian controversial relationship with Huang-Lao thought and in relation to the Mawangdui corpus, see Zheng Yuanlin 鄭圓鈴, *Shiji Huang-Lao sixiang yanjiu* 史記黃老思想研究 (Taipei: Xuehai, 1998), 111–225.

70. For the Chinese text and the translation, see Robin D. S. Yates, *Five Lost Classics*: 56–57.

71. *Xunzi*, 17, 362: 天行有常，不為堯存，不為桀亡。應之以治則吉，應之以亂則凶。

72. *Xunzi*, 17, 372: 故君子敬其在己者，而不慕其在天者；小人錯其在己者，而慕其在天者。See T. C. Kline III and Philip J. Ivanhoe, *Virtue, Nature, and Moral Agency in the Xunzi* (Indianapolis: Hackett Publishing, 2000). Some authors (for example, John Knoblock, *Xunzi: A Translation and Study of the Complete Works* (Stanford: Stanford University Press, 1988) translate Tian as Nature so that Xunzi's argument can be read in the terms if the Nature vs. Nurture opposition and as a refutation of natural determinism; see, Nicolas Zufferey, "Wang Chong et les 'ru' sous les Han: problèmes de terminologie et de méthode," *Etudes Asiatiques* 48 (1994): 1403–408.

73. Ironically the only instance in which the Mandate of Heaven (*tianming* 天命) is mentioned in connection with the Han Dynasty is in the narration of Gaozu's death, when he refuses the cures of a doctor by claiming that someone like him, anointed by Heaven, could not be healed in a traditional way. The Mandate is here evoked in a rhetorical question: "If I could conquer the world despite my humble origins and a 30-inch sword, doesn't it mean that it was because of the Mandate of Heaven?" *SJ* 8, 391: 吾以布衣提三尺劍取天下，此非天命乎？ In other

instances, around ten, the Mandate is mentioned in connection with the remote times of the Five Sovereigns and Three Dynasties.

74. It can be argued that the authors tended to treat remote events whose knowledge derived from archival materials more respectfully, whereas they were more critical or ironic in recounting facts about which they had a more direct knowledge.

75. The assumption that Emperor Wu's ceremonies were addressed univocally to Heaven is based on later historiography such as the "Jiaosi zhi" 郊祀志 (*Han Shu*, 25). For a complete translation and study of the "Jiaosi zhi," see Bujard, *Le sacrifice au Ciel*.

76. *SJ* 49, 1968. Cfr. Confucius, *Lun Yu, Weiling Gong*, 29.

77. See Nancy Lee Swann, *Pan Chao, Foremost Woman Scholar of China, First Century A. D.* (New York: Russell & Russell, 1968). Among the few scholars who engage the question of gender in early China comparatively is Yiqun Zhou; see her *Festivals, Feasts, and Gender Relations in Ancient China and Greece* (Cambridge, UK: Cambridge University Press, 2010).

78. *SJ* 49, 1968.

79. As a regent, Lü issued ordinances (*zhi* 制) stamped with her own seal, which was fashioned in jade and engraved with terms exclusively associated with the emperor. See Qin Bo 秦波, "Xi-Han huanghou yüxi he Ganlu ernian tongfanlou de faxian," 西漢皇后玉璽和甘露二年銅方爐的發現, *Wenwu* 5 (1973): 26–29.

80. *SJ* 9, 412. "Internal evidence" that Sima Qian considered Lü's rule legitimate might be elicited from the very structure and "numerology" of the *Records*. As noted by Mark Edward Lewis, the number twelve in the *benji* might symbolize cosmic completion. See M. E. Lewis, "The *Feng* and *Shan* Sacrifices," 20–50. According to some scholars, criticism of Lü's reign was expressed through a conspicuous increase in the registration of astrological phenomena. Whether such indirect attacks came from the historians or from the officers, has been the object of a heated debate between Hans Bielenstein and Wolfram Eberhard. See Hans Bielenstein, "An Interpretation of the Portents in the *Ts'ien Han Shu*," *Bulletin of the Museum of Far Eastern Antiquities* 22 (1950): 127–43; "Han Portents and Prognostications," *Bulletin of the Museum of Far Eastern Antiquities* 57 (1984): 97–112; and Wolfram Eberhard, "The Political Function of Astronomy and Astronomers in Han China." *Chinese Thought & Institution*, in J. F. Fairbank, ed. (Chicago and London: University of Chicago Press, 1957), 33–71.

81. My text offers a synthesis of *SJ* 8. 344–45. 單父人呂公善沛令，避仇從之客，因家沛焉。沛中豪桀吏聞令有重客，皆往賀。蕭何為主吏，主進，令諸大夫曰：「進不滿千錢，坐之堂下。」高祖為亭長，素易諸吏，乃紿為謁曰「賀錢萬」，實不持一錢。謁入，呂公大驚，起，迎之門。呂公者，好相人，見高祖狀貌，因重敬之，引入坐。蕭何曰：「劉季固多大言，少成事。」高祖因狎侮諸客，遂坐上坐，無所詘。酒闌，呂公因目固留高祖。高祖竟酒，後。呂公曰：「臣少好相人，相人多矣，無如季相，願季自愛。臣有息女，願為季箕帚妾。」酒罷，呂媼怒呂公曰：「公始常欲奇此女，與貴人。沛令善公，求之不與，何自妄許與劉季?」呂公曰：「此非兒女子所知也。」卒與劉季。呂公女乃呂后也，生孝惠帝、魯元公主。

82. *SJ* 8, 346: 呂后與兩子居田中耨,有一老父過請飲,呂后因餔之。老父相呂后曰:「夫人天下貴人。」令相兩子,見孝惠,曰:「夫人所以貴者,乃此男也。」相魯元,亦皆貴。老父已去,高祖適從旁舍來,呂后具言客有過,相我子母皆大貴。高祖問,曰:「未遠。」乃追及,問老父。老父曰:「鄉者夫人嬰兒皆似君,君相貴不可言。」高祖乃謝曰:「誠如父言,不敢忘德。」及高祖貴,遂不知老父處。

83. *SJ* 8, 346: 呂后與兩子居田中耨,有一老父過請飲,呂后因餔之。老父相呂后曰:「夫人天下貴人。」令相兩子,見孝惠,曰:「夫人所以貴者,乃此男也。」相魯元,亦皆貴。老父已去,高祖適從旁舍來,呂后具言客有過,相我子母皆大貴。高祖問,曰:「未遠。」乃追及,問老父。老父曰:「鄉者夫人嬰兒皆似君,君相貴不可言。」高祖乃謝曰:「誠如父言,不敢忘德。」及高祖貴,遂不知老父處。

84. *SJ* 8, 348: 秦始皇帝常曰「東南有天子氣」,於是因東游以厭之。高祖即自疑,亡匿,隱於芒、碭山澤巖石之間。呂后與人俱求,常得之。高祖怪問之。呂后曰:「季所居上常有雲氣,故從往常得季。」高祖心喜。沛中子弟或聞之,多欲附者矣。On cloud divination, see Michael Loewe, "The Oracles of the Clouds and of the Winds," in M. Loewe, *Divination, Mythology, and Monarchy in Han China* (Cambridge, UK: Cambridge University Press, 1994), 191–213. Considering the tone of the *Records* in treating Liu Bang and his family, we should wonder if the text wanted to imply that Empress Lü had means and notions other than cloud formations to find her husband.

85. *SJ* 8, 391: 病甚,呂后迎良醫,醫入見,高祖問醫,醫曰:「病可治。」於是高祖嫚罵之曰:「吾以布衣提三尺劍取天下,此非天命乎?命乃在天,雖扁鵲何益!」.

86. *SJ* 8, 391–82. For a short biography of Xiao He, see M. Loewe, *Biographical Dictionary*, 603–05.

87. *SJ* 8, 343: 好酒及色。常從王媼、武負貰酒,醉臥,武負、王媼見其上常有龍,怪之。高祖每酤留飲,酒讎數倍。及見怪,歲竟,此兩家常折券棄責。

88. *SJ* 48, 1949.

89. *SJ* 48, 1950.

90. See, Michael Loewe, "On the Terms *bao zi, yin gong, yin guan, huan*, and *shou*: Was Zhao Gao a Eunuch?" *T'oung Pao* 91, 4/5 (2005): 301–19.

91. Ibid.

92. Ibid. 乃行卜。卜者知其指意,曰:「足下事皆成,有功。然足下卜之鬼乎!」

93. *SJ* 48, 1950: 乃丹書帛曰「陳勝王」,置人所罾魚腹中。卒買魚烹食,得魚腹中書,固以怪之矣。又閒令吳廣之次所旁叢祠中,夜篝火,狐鳴呼曰「大楚興,陳勝王」。

94. Ibid.

95. Ibid.

96. *SJ* 48, 1961–965; *SJ*, see also Michael Loewe, "Imperial Sovereignty: Tung Chung-shu's contribution and his Predecessors," in M. Loewe, *Divination, Mythology, and Monarchy*, 131–33.

97. *SJ* 25, 1159–169. See chapter 1 above.

98. *SJ* 8, 347: 高祖以亭長為縣送徒酈山,徒多道亡。自度比至皆亡之,到豐西澤中,止飲,夜乃解縱所送徒。曰:「公等皆去,吾亦從此逝矣!」徒中壯士願從者十餘人。高祖被酒,夜徑澤中,令一人行前。

99. *SJ* 8, 344: 高祖常繇咸陽，縱觀，觀秦皇帝，喟然太息曰：「嗟乎，大丈夫當如此也!」. On the contrary, Liu's aristocratic rival Xiang Yu, when a boy, upon seeing Qin Shihuangdi for the first time, expressed the desire to depose and replace him; see *SJ* 7, 296.

100. On the symbolism of colors and on their association with the Han, see Michael Loewe, "Water Earth, and Fire: The Symbols of the Han Dynasty," 57–60.

101. *SJ* 8, 347.

102. *SJ* 7, 322: 漢王道逢得孝惠、魯元，乃載行。楚騎追漢王，漢王急，推墮孝惠、魯元車下，滕公常下收載之。如是者三。曰：「雖急不可以驅，奈何棄之?」於是遂得脫。

103. *SJ* 97, 2699: 陸生時時前說稱詩書。高帝罵之曰：「迺公居馬上而得之，安事詩書!」陸生曰：「居馬上得之，寧可以馬上治之乎?[. . .]秦任刑法不變，卒滅趙氏。鄉使秦已并天下，行仁義，法先聖，陛下安得而有之?」高帝不懌而有慙色，迺謂陸生曰：「試為我著秦所以失天下，吾所以得之者何，及古成敗之國。」. My translation is based on B. Watson, *Records of the Grand Historian*, 1: 226–27.

104. *SJ* 8, 381: 夫運籌策帷帳之中，決勝於千里之外，吾不如子房。鎮國家，撫百姓，給餽饟，不絕糧道，吾不如蕭何。連百萬之軍，戰必勝，攻必取，吾不如韓信。此三者，皆人傑也，吾能用之，此吾所以取天下也。項羽有一范增而不能用，此其所以為我擒也。」.

105. *SJ* 16, 760: 然王跡之興，起於閭巷，合從討伐，軼於三代，鄉秦之禁，適足以資賢者為驅除難耳。故憤發其所為天下雄，安在無土不王。此乃傳之所謂大聖乎? 豈非天哉，豈非天哉! 非大聖孰能當此受命而帝者乎?

106. *SJ* 7, 334: 吾起兵 至今八歲矣，身七十餘戰，所當者破，所擊者服，未嘗敗北，遂霸有天下。然今卒困於 此，此天之亡我，非戰之罪也。今日固決死，願為諸君快戰，必三勝之 . . . For the translation, I consulted *Records of the Grand Historian*, 1: 45–46.

107. *SJ* 7, 339: 自矜功伐，奮其私智而不師古，謂霸王之業，欲以力征經營天下，五年卒亡其國，身 死東城，尚不覺寤而不自責，過矣。乃引「天亡我，非用兵之罪也」，豈不謬哉! For the translation, see *Records of the Grand Historian*, 1: 48.

108. *SJ* 97, 2694: 臣聞知天之天者，王事可成; 不知天之天者，王事不可成。王者以民人為天，而民人以食為天。

109. See J. J. Pollitt, *Art in the Hellenistic Age* (Cambridge, UK: Cambridge University Press, 1986), 2–9.

110. See Emma Stafford, "Personification in Greek Religious Thought and Practice," in *A Companion to Greek Religion*, Daniel Ogden, ed. (Oxford, UK: Blackwell, 2007), 71–86; Liz James, "Good Luck and Good Fortune to the Queen Cities: empresses and Tyches in Byzantium," in *Personification in the Greek World: From Antiquity to Byzantium*, Emma Stafford and Judith Herrin, eds. (Aldershot: Ashgate Publishing, 2005), 293–305; Ernst H. Gombrich, "Personification," in *Classical Influences on European Culture AD 500–1500*, R. R. Bolgar, ed. (Cambridge, UK: Cambridge University Press, 1971), 247–57.

111. Tyche would be idiomatically associated with Alexander the Great and his incredible successes by Plutarch (46–120 CE) in the oration "On the Fortune

or the Virtue of Alexander." See Plutarch, *Moralia*, trans. by Harold North Fowler (Oxford, UK: Loeb Classical Library, 1936), 4: 319–77.

112. Nicole Balaiche, "Tychè et la Tychè dans le cites de la Palestine romaine," *Syria* 80 (2003): 111–38.

113. See Jacqueline Champeaux, *Fortuna: recherches sur le culte de la Fortune à Rome et dans le monde romain des origines à la mort de César*, 2 vols. (Roma: Collection de l'Ecole française de Rome, 1982); Ferdinando Castagnoli, "Il culto di Mater Matuta e della Fortuna nel Foro Boario," *Studi Romani* 27, 2 (1979): 145–52.

114. Livy I, 39, 1: While a child named Servius Tullius lay sleeping, his head burst into flames in the sight of many (see also Dionysius of Halicarnassus, 4.14, 3–4). On Augustan reforms and their connection to the Servian tradition, see M. Beard, J. North, and S. Price, *Religions of Rome: Volume 1: A History* (Cambridge, UK: Cambridge University Press, 1998), 184.

115. Livy I. 39–41 (I, 41,3; "qui sis, non unde natus sis:" Consider what you are, not whence you were born).

116. As for the rhetoric construction of Etruscan women as a foil to the modesty of Roman matrons, see Larissa Bonfante, *Etruscan Life and After Life: A Handbook of Etruscan Studies* (Detroit, MI: Wayne State University Press, 1986), 232–33.

117. Plutarch (translated by F. C. Babbitt), "On the Fortune of the Romans," in *Moralia*, Vol. IV (Cambridge, MA: Harvard University Press, Loeb Classical Library, 1933), 383.

118. *Hist.* I, 4, 1–2. Translation adapted from Polybius, *Histories*, 6 vols. trans. by W. R. Paton, revised by F. W. Walbank and C. Habicht (Cambridge, MA: Loeb Classics, Harvard University Press; Revised edition, 2010); On Tyche in Polybius, see Frank. W Walbank, *Historical Commentary on Polybius* (Oxford: Clarendon Press, 1957), 1: 16–26; Pédech, *Le méthode historique de Polybe*, 331–54.

119. On Polybius's relationship with past historiography, see Walbank's *Polybius*, 32–65.

120. The starting point of Polybius's narration is the 140th Olympiad in 220 BCE. These are in the author's opinion the fundamental events: "In Greece, what is called the Social war: the first waged by Philip, son of Demetrius and father of Perseus, in league with the Achaeans against the Aetolians, in Asia, the war for the possession of Coele-Syria which Antiochus and Ptolemy Philopator carried on against each other. In Italy, Libya, and their neighborhood, the conflict between Rome and Carthage, generally called the Hannibalian war. My work thus begins where that of Aratus of Sicyon leaves off." See *Hist.* I, 3.

121. A. Momigliano, *The Classical Foundations*, 44–53.

122. Momigliano refers in particular to Hermann Ulrici, *Charakteristik der antiken Historiographie* (Berlin, G. Reimer, 1833).

123. For this reconstruction, see, Frank. W. Walbank, "Supernatural Paraphernalia," in Walbank, *Polybius, Rome and the Hellenistic World* (Cambridge, UK: Cambridge University Press, 2003), 250–51.

124. *Hist.* XV, 20, 1–4.

125. In this passage the word choice tells us that for Polybius, Tyche could represent a hostile force, in this case almost as capricious as the gods of the Homeric tradition; see *Hist.* I, 1,2, literally "to bear the changes of Fortune with a noble composure," "τὰς τῆς τύχης μεταβολὰς γενναίως ὑποφέρειν."

126. Walbank, *Commentary on Polybius*, 16–17.

127. Walbank, *Commentary on Polybius*, 17.

128. For Walbank's critique of Polybius concept of causality, see Walbank, *Commentary on Polybius*, 1:17; and also Walbank, "Supernatural Paraphernalia," 245–57. On Polybius and causality, also see Peter S. Derow, "Historical Explanation: Polybius and his Predecessors," in *Greek Historiography*, S. Hornblower, ed. (Oxford, UK: Clarendon Press, 1994), 73–90; P. S. Derow, "Polybius, Rome and the East," *Journal of Roman Studies* 69 (1979): 1–15.

129. *Hist.* XXXVI, 17: τῶν πολλῶν δόξαις.

130. *Hist.* II 20.

131. *Hist.* VI, 56.

132. See "Libro Primo" (Book One): XI, XII, XIII, XIV, XV in *Discorsi sopra la prima deca di Tito Livio* (Torino: UTET, 1999), 507–17.

133. *Sanguo Yanyi* 三國演義 1, 1: 話說天下大勢. 分久必合, 合久必分：周末七國分爭，并入於秦。及秦滅之後，楚、漢分爭，又并入於漢。漢朝自高祖斬白蛇而起義，一統天下。 The translation is from Luo Guanzhong 羅貫中 (Moss Roberts, trans.), *Three Kingdoms* Vol. 1 (Beijing: Foreign Languages Press, 2008), 1.

134. From the Eastern Han the institutionalized interpretation of omens as fundamental elements of the official doctrine of the Mandate of Heaven will be extremely important for promotions of officials.

Chapter 4

1. *SJ* 28, 1394: 嗟乎! 吾誠得如黃帝，吾視去妻子如脫躧耳。

2. *SJ* 28, 1396.

3. Virgil, *Eclogue* 4, 4–10: "Ultima Cumaei venit iam carminis aetas; magnus ab integro saeclorum nascitur ordo: iam redit et Virgo, redeunt Saturnia regna; iam nova progenies caelo demittitur alto."

4. The study of divine kingship, as a central theme of the relationship between institutions and religion in ancient civilizations, goes back to the seminal works by Frazer and Frankfurt. See James G. Frazer, *The Golden Bough* (New York: MacMillan & Co., 1894); Henri Frankfort, *Kingship and the Gods: A Study of Ancient Near Eastern Religion as the Integration of Society and Nature* (Chicago: University of Chicago Press, 1948). For a brief synthesis of the development of the scholarship on the concept of divine kingship, see Nicole Brisch, *Religion and Power: Divine Kingship in the Ancient World and Beyond* (Chicago: University of Chicago Press, 2008), 1–11. For the application of the concept of divine kingship

to early China, see Michael Puett, "Human and Divine Kingship in Early China: Comparative Reflections," in *Divine Kingship*, Nicole Brisch, ed. (Chicago: University of Chicago Press, 2008), 207–20; Puett, *To Become a God*, 226–36; 287–315. For a "territorial" interpretation of Wudi's *feng* and *shan*, see also Mark E. Lewis, "The Feng and Shan Sacrifices of the Emperor Wu of the Han," in *State and Court Ritual in China*, Joseph McDermott, ed. (Cambridge, UK: Cambridge University Press, 1999), 20–50.

5. For a brief, but compelling, cultural history of what he defines as "Christianizing assumptions," in the study of divine rulership, see Simon R. F. Price, *Ritual and Power: The Roman Imperial Cult in Asia Minor* (Cambridge, UK: Cambridge University Press, 1985), 11–15. See also the introduction of *Rituals of Royalty: Power and Ceremonial in Traditional Societies*, David Cannadine and Simon Price, eds. (Cambridge, UK: Cambridge University Press, 1987), 1–19.

6. Giuseppe Zecchini, *Cesare e il mos maiorum* (Stuttgart: Franz Steiner Verlag, 2001).

7. In the imperial era, for example, even cults of foreign origins would be tolerated, at the condition that their worshippers also formally accepted to pay respect to the divinized emperor. Refusal to abide was understood as an active rejection of the authority of Rome and was a punishable act of political insubordination.

8. See Karl Galinsky, *Augustan Culture: An Interpretive Introduction* (Princeton, NJ: Princeton University Press, 1996), 80–224.

9. See Walter Eder (trans. K. Galinsky), "Augustus and the Power of Tradition," in *The Cambridge Companion to the Age of Augustus*, Karl Galinsky, ed. (Cambridge, UK: Cambridge University Press, 1995), 13–32. See Eric Gruen, "Augustus and the Making of the Principate," in ibid., 33–51.

10. On the visual aspects of Augustus's propaganda, see Paul Zanker, *The Power of Images in the Age of Augustus* (Ann Arbor: University of Michigan Press, 1989); John Pollini, "Man or God: Divine Assimilation and Imitation," in *Between Republic and Empire*, K. A. Raaflaub and M. Toher, eds. (Berkeley: University of California Press, 1990), 333–63; Alessandro Barchiesi, "Learned Eyes: Viewers, Image Makers," in *The Cambridge Companion*, 281–385; Rolf Michael Schneider, "Image and Empire: The Shaping of Augustan Rome," in *Conceiving the Empire: China and Rome Compared*, Fritz-Heiner Mutschler, and Achim Mittag, eds. (Oxford, UK: Oxford University Press, 2009), 269–98. On literature and propaganda, see, Diana E. E. Kleiner, "Semblance and Storytelling in Augustan Rome," in *The Cambridge Companion*, 197–233; and Jasper Griffin, "Augustan Poetry and Augustanism," in ibid., 306–39.

11. Not all contemporary poets reacted in the same way to Augustus's divinization. However, as he consolidated his authority, some complacent authors spontaneously began to retroject a fully developed the propagandistic plan onto the early phases of the Principate; see Nandini B. Pandey, "Caesar's Comet, the

Julian Star, and the Invention of Augustus," *Transactions of the American Philological Association* 143, 2 (Sept. 2013): 405–49.

12. See E. S. Ramage, "Augustus' Treatment of Julius Caesar," *Historia* 34 (1986): 223–45.

13. On the cult and religious prerogatives of Octavian Augustus, see the classic work by Lily Ross Taylor, *The Divinity of the Roman Emperor* (Oxford, UK: Oxford University Press, 1931). Also see Glen W. Bowersock, "The Pontificate of Augustus," in *Between Republic and Empire: Interpretations of Augustus and his Principate*, Kurt A. Raaflaub and Mark Toher, eds. (Berkeley: University of California Press, 1990), 380–94; On the cult of Augustus as a household deity, see Ittai Gradel, *Emperor Worship and Roman Religion* (Oxford, UK: Oxford University Press, 2002). For a historicization of the terminology related to empires in the West, see J. S. Richardson, "Imperium Romanum: Empire and the Language of Power," *The Journal of Roman Studies* 81 (1991): 1–9.

14. On the Roman emperor as a unifying symbol for the empire over the Mediterranean, see Carlos F. Noreña, *Imperial Ideals in the Roman West: Representation, Circulation, Power* (Cambridge, UK: Cambridge University Press, 2011); K. Galinsky, *Augustan Culture*, 288–331. On the imperial cult in the provinces see Steven J. Freisen, *Imperial Cults and the Apocalypse of John: Reading Revelation in the Ruins* (Oxford, UK: Oxford University Press, 2001); Clifford Ando, *Imperial Ideology and Provincial Loyalty in the Roman Empire* (Berkeley: University of California Press, 2000); Duncan Fishwick, *The Imperial Cult in the Latin West: Studies in the Ruler Cult of the Western Provinces of the Roman Empire* (Leiden: Brill, 1991); S. R. F. Price, *Rituals and Power: The Roman Imperial Cult in Asia Minor* (Cambridge, UK: Cambridge University Press, 1985).

15. See Chapter 5 below.

16. Sima Qian in his work does not chronicle Emperor Wu's reign until its end in 87 BCE. And it has been argued that the "Fengshan shu" accounts following the Grand Beginning were the result of later additions; see Zhao Zhengqun 赵生群, "*Shiji*" *wenxianxue conggao* 史记文献学丛稿 (Nanjing, Jiangsu guji chubanshe, 2000).

17. If we consider the famous letter to Ren An 任安 (in *HS* 62, 2725–238) a work of literary impersonation—as many scholars tends to do—the "Fengshan shu" represents the most telling account of Sima Qian's opinion on his age.

18. In recent times, compelling analyses of the *feng* and *shan* sacrifices have been provided by the already mentioned "The Feng and Shan Sacrifices of Emperor Wu of the Han" by Mark E. Lewis; Michael Puett's *The Ambivalence of Creation* and *To Become a God*, and Yu Hua's Yang Hua's "Qinhan diguo de shenquan tongyi." Through an analysis of historical and literary sources, Lewis interprets the sacrifices in terms of territorial, fertility, and martial rituals; Yang, by looking at historical records and various recently unearthed documents reconstructs the process of administrative and ritual rationalization carried out by the Qin and the Han, as

they tried to include all the different territories of China under one bureaucratic and cultural system.

19. For a survey about Chinese scholarship on early Chinese state-religion, see Wang Baizhong 王柏中, *Shenling shijie: zhixu de goujian yu yishi de xiangzheng* 神灵世界——秩序的构建与仪式的象征 (Beijing: Minzu chubanshe, 2005).

20. For an analysis of the symbolic connection of bronze casting and rulership in early China, see K. C. Chang, *Art, Myth, and Ritual: The Path to Political Authority in Ancient China* (Cambridge, MA: Harvard University Press, 1983), 95–106.

21. I refer to those scholarly approaches whose declared or implicit aim is the search for a distinctive and coherent structure in Chinese rituals. In the search for a rationalization of the sacred, Max Weber's influence is still noticeable. Whereas his model can still be effective in comparing the cultural role of different Christian tradition within the same cultural world, it becomes more problematic in the case of the inclusion of China, as "the divine" traditionally played a rather different function vis-à-vis political institutions.

22. Stefan Weinstock, *Divus Julius* (Oxford, UK: Clarendon Press, 1971), 80–87. Venus and Caesar appeared also on the opposite sides of Roman coins. The Greek connection might have been exploited by Caesar also in order to present his Greek education and over-refined and eccentric lifestyle under a more positive light.

23. Beard, *Religions of Rome*, 2–3. Livy, originally an admirer of Cicero and, as most educated people of his generation, an enemy of monarchy, wrote during the period of appeasement that followed the triumph of Octavian, and eventually accepted his rule as inevitable and legitimate; on Livy's political evolution and relationship with the *Princeps*, see Ronald Syme, "Livy and Augustus," *Harvard Studies in Classical Philology* 64 (1959): 27–87.

24. On the various legends concerning either Romulus's apotheosis or murder by the senators (given in Livy, I.16–2.8a), see Beard, *Religions of Rome*, 4–6. Not surprisingly the cult of a divinized Romulus appears in the Roman sources starting with the first century BCE. See Duncan Fishwick's *The Imperial Cult in the Latin West* (Leiden: Brill, 1993), 53. On the ambiguous state (between gods and ancestors) of heroes, see Angelo Brelich, *Heros: Il culto greco degli eroi e il problema degli esseri semi-divini* (Roma: Edizioni dell'Ateneo, 1966).

25. Gradel, "Caesar's Divine Honors," in *Emperor Worship*, 4–72. Gradel also argues that, to an extent, the attributes of divinity associated to Caesar have to be interpreted in a relative way, as they were meant to emphasize Caesar's godlike (and not yet absolutely divine) exceptionality.

26. Dynastic ancestors were worshipped in China as immortal deities in popular cults, but as "gods" they did figure in discourses about imperial legitimation. See Allan, *The Heir and the Sage*.

27. For example, the cult of Hou Ji, the "god" of the Soil and patron the grains, as founder of the Zhou exclusively regarded the living heirs of lineage he had originated. In other words, he never became a Han god; see *SJ* 28, 1357.

28. See Ramsay MacMullen, *Paganism in the Roman Empire* (New Haven, CT: Yale University Press, 1981). The "melting pot" of Roman popular religion actually resembles the situation of popular cults in early China. The difference was in the way political power relied on religion for legitimation.

29. Puett, *To Become a God*, 21; 31–79; 80–121. The *Chunqiu fanlu* (in chapter 19 "Li yuan shen 立元神, 156–62) offers a definition *shen* that is associated to the superior powers, prerogatives, and responsibilities of a ruler as a True Sage (*sheng* 聖) who maintains the harmony between Nature (*tiandi* 天地) and Man. See also Queen, *From Chronicle to Canon*, 89. Queen therein comments on the meaning of *shen* as an innate human component in the famous account on the "Daoist" practices and beliefs attributed to Sima Tan (in *SJ* 130, 3289). On *gui* and *shen* in Han thought, also see Csikszentmihalyi, *Readings*, 116–39.

30. After creating the universe ex nihilo, these continue to keep a watchful eye on human beings and judge whether they abide by revealed divine laws, which are customarily recorded in sacred texts. As synthesized by Csikszentmihalyi, Mozi 墨子 (479–438 BCE) and his followers were considered "staunch advocates of the retributive power of demons and spirits that delivered an automatic reward for acts that had positive social utility and punishment for those that did not"; see Csikszentmihalyi, *Readings in Han Chinese Thought*, 118–19; and chapter 31 of the *Mozi*, "Explaining Demons" ("Minggui" 明鬼), in *Mozi xiangu*, 8. 153. However, Mozi's views were often challenged and never became mainstream.

31. In the famous passage in the *Zhong Yong* Confucius was certainly referring to ancestral spirits: "The Master said, 'How abundantly do spiritual beings display the powers that belong to them! We look for them, but do not see them; we listen to, but do not hear them; yet they enter into all things, and there is nothing without them. They cause all the people in the kingdom to fast and purify themselves, and array themselves in their richest dresses, in order to attend at their sacrifices'"; this classic translation is in *The Four Books: Confucian Analects, The Great Learning, The Doctrine of the Mean, and The Works of Mencius. With English notes and translation by James Legge* (Boston: The Riverside Press, 1882), 35–36; in *Zhong Yong*, 16: 1–2: 子曰。鬼神之為德。其盛矣乎。視之而弗見。聽之而弗聞。體物而不可遺。使天下之人齊明盛服，以承祭祀，洋洋乎如在其上，如在其左右。

32. David Hall and Roger Ames argue that since *shen* 神 probably derives from *shen* 伸, "to extend," which in most of the cases indicates the awesome or fearsome extraordinary faculties and capabilities of things or living beings, it could not imply transcendence; see Hall and Ames, *Thinking from the Han*, 236–37. M. Puett holds instead that attempts at redefining the boundaries between the human and the divine (whether the two realms where continuous or not) presented important cultural and political implications; see M. Puett, *To Become a God*, 21. A further inquiry on *shen* and its possible interpretations is in Willard J. Peterson, "Making Connections: 'Commentary on the Attached Verbalization' of the *Book of Changes*," *Harvard Journal of Asiatic Studies* 42, 1 (June 1982): 104. For the Aristotelian

derivation and analytical inadequacy of the divine/human dichotomy, see Gebhard J. Selz, "The Divine Prototypes," in N. Brisch, *Religion and Power*, 13–32.

33. Michael Puett, in *Becoming a God*, especially on the basis of his analysis of the *Chunqiu fanlu*, interprets the latter's pursuit as an attempt at self-divinization.

34. A fundamental work on the subject of early developments concepts of hedonistic life, longevity, and immortality is Yü Ying-shih, "Life and Immortality in the Mind of Han China," *Harvard Journal of Asiatic Studies* 25 (1964–1965): 80–122. For a bibliographical survey of later works on the same subject, see also Livia Kohn, "Eternal Life in Taoist Mysticism," *Journal of the American Oriental Society* 110, no. 4 (Oct.–Dec. 1990): 622–40. On the pervasiveness of the theme of immortality on Han art, see, Susan N. Erickson, "Boshanlu: Mountain Censers of Western Han Period: A Typological and Iconological Analysis," *Archives of Asian Art* 45 (1992): 6–28. On immortality in early Chinese poetry see, Stephen Owen, "Immortals," in *The Making of Early Chinese Classical Poetry* (Cambridge, MA, Harvard University Press, 2006), 139–177. In the ancient Near East, mythical sovereigns such as Gilgamesh would reject immortality in order to stress their connection with their mortal subjects. See V. A. B. Hurowitz, "Finding New Life in Old Words: World Play in the *Gilgames* Epic," in *Gilgames and the World of Assyria: Proceedings of the Conference Held at Mandelbaum House, The University of Sidney, 21–23 July 2004*, J. J. Azize and N. K. Weeks, eds. (Leuven: Peeters, 2007), 67–78.

35. *SJ* 28, 1394: 嗟乎！吾誠得如黃帝，吾視去妻子如脫躧耳。

36. Sima Qian shows Emperor Wu as inclined to associate himself with particular individuals or groups for immediate strategic reasons rather than carrying out coherent and far-reaching plans. For example, in *SJ* 121, 3115, we read of a young Wu promoting a group of influential Classicists with the intent of limiting the influence of his grandmother Dowager Empress Dou 竇, who was known for her Huang-Lao sympathies. In the "Book on the Balanced Standard," Sima Qian presents Wu's economic policies as influenced by officials he would enthusiastically appoint and frequently, for various reasons, dismiss.

37. Itano Chôhachi already argued that Emperor Wu's religious activities represented an attempt to promote his autocratic conception rulership over the models propounded in the *Classics*: see, Itano Chôhachi 板野長八, *Chūgoku kodai ni okeru ningenkan no tenkai* 中国古代における人間観の展開 (Tokyo: Iwanami Shoten, Shōwa, 1972).

38. Interestingly enough, the *Records* reports elsewhere that the *feng* and *shan* were also celebrated by Huo Qubing (the father of the young charioteer who suddenly dies after having accompanied Emperor Wu during the performance of the *shan* in 110 BCE). This famous general engaged in the sacrifices after repeated victories had greatly inflated his pride. See *SJ* 111, 2936.

39. *SJ* 28, 1355.

40. Ibid.

41. *SJ* 28, 1355; *Analects* 17: 21.

42. *SJ* 28, 1355: 每世之隆，則封禪答焉，及衰而息.

43. The Grand Historian does mention Dong Zhongshu, whom the *Han Shu* would eventually credit with the elaboration of the official ideology of the Han dynasty. However, Sima Qian simply describes him as an underachieving classicist whose alleged ability to predict rainfall could not even ensure him a decent political career. See chapter 2 above.

44. Sima Qian in the "Book on the *Feng* and *Shan*" explicitly mentions the *Odes* and the *Documents*.

45. See *SJ* 24, 1175–176; the ideas expressed in the "Book on Music" ("Yue shu" 樂書) seem the inspiration of the author of the "Letter to Ren An," in which Sima Qian (or his impersonator) seems to show a particular affinity with those moral paragons who lived in ungrateful times, under irresponsive political leaders, and who fought against adverse circumstances. See Nylan, "Sima Qian: A True Historian?" *Early China* 24 (1998): 1–44.

46. *SJ* 28, 1356.

47. Ibid.

48. Ibid.: 妖不勝德. Cfr. *Huainanzi* "Mou Cheng" 繆稱," 10, 100: 國有妖祥，不勝善政。

49. Only the *Records* chapter on astronomy mentions the Five Phases, *wu xing* 五行 (twice, in *SJ* 27, 1293 and 1342), whereas the "Book on the *Feng* and *Shan*" mentions the Five Virtues, *wu de* 五德 (once, in *SJ* 28, 1368). Sima Qian's never describes yin and yang, the Five Phases, and alchemy as the bases of distinct philosophical systems or schools that were active at his time, although it is clear that the number five (*wu* 五) was associated with sets of things or systems perceived as complete. Note the recurrence of *wu* in the Huangdi's founding acts (*SJ* 1, 1–4). For a discussion on the cultural relevance of these concepts in early China, see Nathan Sivin, "The Myth of the Naturalists," in *Medicine, Religion, and Philosophy in Ancient China*, Nathan Sivin (Aldershot, UK: Variorum, 1995), 1–33. For an overview on recent studies about ideas conventionally (and often wrongly) attributed to Daoist thought, see Nathan Sivin, "Old and New Daoisms," *Religious Studies Review* 39, 1 (2010): 31–50.

50. *SJ* 28, 1361.

51. Ibid.

52. These were the millet from Huoshang, grain from Beili, a special kind of reed growing between the Huai and the Yangtze rivers, a couple of fish from the Eastern Sea that shared one eye, birds from the Western Sea whose wings grew together, the spontaneous appearance of fifteen strange animals, the phoenix, the *lin* unicorn, and the "auspicious grain"; see *SJ* 28, 1361.

53. See chapter 2 above.

54. *SJ* 28, 1371.

55. See Michael Loewe, "Water, Earth, and Fire: The Symbols of the Han Dynasty," in *Divination, Mythology and Monarchy in Han China*, Idem (Cambridge, UK: Cambridge University Press, 1994), 55–60.

56. Hans Van Ess, "Emperor Wu of the Han and the First August Emperor of the Qin in Sima Qian's *Shiji*," in Yuri Pines et al., *Birth of an Empire: The State of Qin Revisited* (Berkeley: University of California Press, 2014), 239–57.

57. *SJ* 28, 1367: 始皇之上泰山，中阪遇暴風雨，休於大樹下。諸儒生既絀，不得與用於封事之禮，聞始皇遇風雨，則譏之。

58. 1371: 始皇封禪之後十二歲，秦亡。諸儒生疾秦焚詩書，誅僇文學，百姓怨其法，天下畔之，皆曰：「始皇上泰山，為暴風雨所擊，不得封禪。」此豈所謂無其德而用事者邪？

59. See *SJ* 121, 3115.

60. In *SJ* 28, 1396. When Emperor Wu wondered how it was possible that the Yellow Emperor became an immortal if his burial place was well known, someone replied that the mound only contained the Yellow Emperor's hat and clothes, which he had dropped upon ascending to Heaven.

61. See Charles LeBlanc, "A Re-interpretation of the Myth of Huang-ti," *Journal of Chinese Religions* 13–14 (1985–86): 45–63. As pointed out by LeBlanc in his systematic survey on all the literary references to Yellow Emperor, the date of compilation of most of the texts mentioning him (e.g., *Guanzi*, *Zhuangzi*, *Han Feizi*, *Shan Hai jing*, and so on) is very problematic. The *Records* represents one of the few sources whose mythological narrations can be connected more directly to specific historical events and social conditions. The Yellow Emperor does not feature at all in the *Book of Documents*, whereas the *Book of Changes* (Zhou Yi 周易), the *Book of Rites* (Liji 禮記), and the *Zuozhuan* commentary on the *Spring and Autumn Annals* (Zuozhuan Chunqiu 左傳春秋) mention him only in passing. The bibliographical chapter of the *Han Shu* mentions the existence during the Western Han of a work named *The Ordinances of the Yellow Emperor* (Huangdi ming 黃帝命). Although it is not extant, Mark Csikszentmihalyi has argued that some fragments survive in other texts, see his "Reimagining the Yellow Emperor's Four Faces," *Text and Ritual in Early China*, M. Kern, ed., 226–48.

62. *SJ* 1, 46.

63. On the role of writing in the formation of Chinese civilization see Lewis, *Writing*, 99–146.

64. *SJ* 28, 1355–356; *SJ* 1, 14–24.

65. *SJ* 1, 1–4.

66. This is evident especially if we consider that the Yellow Emperor is portrayed in the act of establishing unified rule and common standards over diverse territories that had just experienced tyranny.

67. *SJ* 28, 1359, 1361, 1364, 1366, 1385–386, 1392–304, 1396–397, 1400–003.

68. See LeBlanc, "A Re-interpretation of the Myth of Huang-ti," 45–48. His reconstruction of the etymology of Huangdi's name is based on Gu Jiegang, *Shilin zashi chubian* 史林雜識初編 (Beijing: Zhinghua shuju, 1963), 184.

69. For the bibliography on the Mawangdui manuscripts and their cultural import, see Chapter 1, note 40.

70. See, Robert Yates, *Five Lost Classics: Tao, Huang-Lao and Yin-Yang in Han China* (New York: Ballantine, 1997), 19. In *SJ* 74, 2344, Zou Yan is depicted as a very skilled expert of yin and yang, natural sciences, and geography, who, by studying minor phenomena, aimed at larger truths. He recounted a history of the Central States that started with the Yellow Emperor. His speeches were lofty but were never written down. According to Sima Qian, Zou Yan speculations about the natural were rooted on moral qualities and human relations. See also Sivin, *Medicine, Religion, and Philosophy*, 7–13.

71. Yates, *Five Lost Classics*, 19.

72. On cultural patronage and transmission in early China, see Sivin, "The Myth of the Naturalists," 19–29.

73. *Huainanzi* 3:6a. p. 71. On ancient cults of Houtu, see Birrell, *Chinese Mythology*, 161–62. On contemporary cults, see L. Yang, D. An, and J. Anderson Turner, *Handbook of Chinese Religions* (Santa Barbara, CA: ABC-CLIO, 2005), 135–37. On the cultural and political context of the compilation of the *Huainanzi*, see Griet Vankeerberghen, *The* Huainanzi *and Liu An's Claim to Moral Authority* (Albany, SUNY Press, 2001).

74. *SJ* 27, 1290. See also Isaia Iannacone, *Misurare il cielo: l'antica astronomia cinese* (Napoli: L'Orientale, 1986), 144–47.

75. Translated in Yates, *The Five Lost Classics*, 106–11.

76. See LeBlanc, "A Re-interpretation," 50–51; *Zhuangzi*, 6:2, 41, and in the *Huangdi Sijing*, 2, 82b, 93a; 121a.

77. *SJ* 1, 1.

78. These aspects of the Yellow Emperor are analyzed in M. Puett, *The Ambivalence of Creation*, 131–140.

79. The conflation of Shennong with Yandi—originally two distinct legendary rulers—seems a Han Dynasty common misunderstanding. Chapter 1 of the *Records* uses both names to refer to the same being. See Birrell, *Chinese Mythology*, 131–32. On Shennong as the rival of the Yellow Emperor in the *Huainanzi*, see Major, *Heaven and Earth in Early Han Thought: Chapters Three, Four and Five of* Huainanzi (Albany: SUNY Press, 1993), 8–14.

80. This chapter describes Shennong's reign only in negative terms, as it presents it already in a descending phase. Sima Qian's choice to focus on the Yellow Emperor can be explained by the popularity achieved by this legendary figure during the Han.

81. See also Birrell, *Chinese Mythology*, 50–51. On the theme of the paradigmatic violence/complementarity of the relationship of the Yellow Emperor

and Chi You in received and excavated texts, see M. Lewis, *Sanctioned Violence*, 174–85.

82. This may be an early reference to those speculations that would be eventually formalized in the Five Phases (Wuxing 五行). See Sivin, *Medicine, Philosophy, and Religion*, 2–7. Very interestingly, Shun (in *SJ* 28, 1356) mastered the Five Li (*wu li* 五禮).

83. The Five Seeds were exactly what immortals abstained from. See Yu, "Life and Immortality," 51.

84. *SJ* 1, 3: 軒轅之時，神農氏世衰。諸侯相侵伐，暴虐百姓，而神農氏弗能征。於是軒轅乃習用干戈，以征不享，諸侯咸來賓從。而蚩尤最為暴，莫能伐。炎帝欲侵陵諸侯，諸侯咸歸軒轅。軒轅乃修德振兵，治五氣，蓺五種，撫萬民，度四方，教熊羆貔貅貙虎，以與炎帝戰於阪泉之野。

85. *SJ* 1, 5. On whether Sima Qian believed in the Mandate of Heaven, see chapter 3 above.

86. *SJ* 1, 5: 而諸侯咸尊軒轅為天子，代神農氏，是為黃帝。

87. *SJ* 1, 6: 東至于海，登丸山，及岱宗。西至于空桐，登雞頭。南至于江，登熊、湘。北逐葷粥，合符釜山，而邑于涿鹿之阿。

88. *SJ* 1, 6: 置左右大監，監于萬國。萬國和，而鬼神山川封禪與為多焉。獲寶鼎，迎日推筴。

89. *SJ* 1, 6: 有土德之瑞，故號黃帝. On divination in early China, see Michael Loewe, "Divination by Shells, Bones and Stalks in the Han Period," and "The Oracles of the Clouds and the Winds," in *Divination, Mythology, and Monarchy in Han China*, Michael Loewe (Cambridge, UK: Cambridge University Press, 1994), 160–213; and Dario Sabbatucci, *Divinazione e cosmologia* (Milano: Il Saggiatore, 1989), 5–89.

90. *SJ* 1, 10.

91. LeBlanc, "A Re-examination," 56.

92. Chang, *Art, Myth, and Ritual*, 95–106.

93. For Wu Hung, the Nine Tripods epitomize the Chinese concept of monumentality, as they embodied "permanence, grandiosity, and stillness" and "not only commemorated a past event but also legitimated and consolidated the consequence of the event." See Wu Hung, *Monumentality in Early Chinese Art and Architecture* (Stanford, CA: Stanford University Press, 1995), 1, 5.

94. On the same topic, see Puett, *To Become a God*, 63.

95. It is not clear what was known of the actual Yu tripods at the time of Sima Qian. According to what he writes, some believed that the Qin had obtained all of them from the Zhou; see *SJ* 28, 1365: 其後百二十歲而秦滅周，周之九鼎入于秦。或曰宋太丘社亡，而鼎沒於泗水彭城下。

96. See Yang Xiong, *The Canon of Supreme Mystery*, trans. M. Nylan (Albany: SUNY Press, 1995), 280–86.

97. *SJ* 28, 1385–386.

98. In a banquet held by the Marquis of Wu'an 武安, Tian Fen 田蚡, Li impressed everyone by showing precise knowledge of past circumstances regarding guests. He was also able to guess that a particular ritual bronze vessel had belonged to Duke Huan of Qi. Sima Qian perhaps expected his readers to suspect independently that Li could have obtained those pieces of information by means of a previous inquiry. See *SJ* 28, 1385.

99. *Zao* in this case can refer either to the crucible itself or to the Stove God, whose cult is still popular today throughout China; see Robert L. Chard, "Rituals and Scriptures of the Stove Cult," in *Ritual and Scripture in Chinese Popular Religion: Five Studies*, David Johnson, ed. (Berkeley, CA: Chinese Popular Culture Project, 1995), 3–54.

100. *Wu* 物, in the text, is usually translated as "things" or "creatures." According to a passage in Wang Chong (*Lunheng*, 26, 2), *wu* can refer to anything capable of transformation without external intervention. On this topic, see below in this chapter.

101. *SJ* 28, 1385: 少君言上曰：「祠竃則致物，致物而丹沙可化為黃金，黃金成以為飲食器則益壽，益壽而海中蓬萊僊者乃可見，見之以封禪則不死，黃帝是也。臣嘗游海上，見安期生，安期生食巨棗，大如瓜。安期生僊者，通蓬萊中，合則見人，不合則隱。」於是天子始親祠竃，遣方士入海求蓬萊安期生之屬，而事化丹沙諸藥齊為黃金矣。

102. *SJ* 28, 1392.

103. On Fuxi, see Birrell, *Chinese Mythology*, 44–47.

104. On the debate on the possible meanings of *shangdi*, see chapter 3 above.

105. *SJ* 28, 1392: 聞昔泰帝興神鼎一，一者壹統，天地萬物所繫終也。黃帝作寶鼎三，象天地人。禹收九牧之金，鑄九鼎。皆嘗亨鬺上帝鬼神。遭聖則興，鼎遷于夏商。周德衰，宋之社亡，鼎乃淪沒，伏而不見。頌云『自堂徂基，自羊徂牛；鼐鼎及鼒，不吳不驁，胡考之休』。

106. The import of the term *zuo* and its meanings in Chinese narratives about the origins of civilizations has received the most thorough analysis by Michael Puett, in *The Ambivalence of Creation*. In agreement with his interpretation, in this passage it undoubtedly refers to the action of making, manufacturing (as in the case of the Greek ποιέω) as it represent the evolution of a phase that does not require active, autocratic rulership, while anticipating the stage of collegial power. Puett provides a further examination of the philological question in the appendix of his monograph, "The Semantic of Creation," in *The Ambivalence of Creation*, 217–24. His argument engages these influential essays: Gen-Ichiro Yoshioka, *A Semantic Study of the Verbs of Doing and Making in the Indo-European Languages* (Tokyo: Tokyo Tsukiji Type Foundry, 1908); and Zeng Xiantong 曾憲通, "'Zuo' zi tanyuan—jian tan 'lei' zi de liubian" 作字探源－兼談耒字的流變, *Guwenzi Yanjiu* 19 (1992): 408–21.

107. Sima Qian, in *SJ* 30, 1438, reports that it was in 114 BCE (a year before the tripod surfaced) that the Son of Heaven had begun to carry out inspection

travels throughout the commanderies (*jun* 郡) and kingdoms (*guo* 國) of the empire.

108. See "Ping zhun shu" *SJ* 30, 1438. In 115 BCE the Yellow River had flooded the northeastern territories, famine had ensued and "the distress was so great that people were reduced at times to cannibalism." See *SJ* 30, 1437.

109. See *SJ* 30, 1433–434: "(In 114 BCE) an order was issued forbidding any further minting of coins in the provinces and kingdoms. All minting was to be done by three offices set by the Shanglin 上林 Park (in the capital Chang'an). Since there were already a number of coins in circulation, it was ordered that no cash other than those minted by the three offices should be accepted as a legal tender anywhere in the empire. All copper coins previously minted in the provinces and kingdoms were withdrawn from circulation and melted down, the copper being turned over to the three offices. After this there were fewer and fewer people who attempted to mint their own cash, since the cost of making a passable imitation did not repay the effort." For the translation see, B. Watson, *Records*, 2: 77.

110. See Donald B. Wagner, *The State and the Iron Industry in Han China* (Copenhagen: The Nordic Institute of Asian Studies, 2001).

111. *SJ* 30, 1435: 中家以上大抵皆遇告。... 得民財物以億計, 奴婢以千萬數, ... 於是商賈中家以上大率破, 民偷甘食好衣, 不事畜藏之產業, 而縣官有鹽鐵緡錢之故, 用益饒矣。

112. Chang *Art, Myth, and Ritual*, 95–106.

113. On the problematic dating of the *Zuozhuan*, which is probably later than conventionally held, see Nylan, *The Five 'Confucian' Classics*, 253–89.

114. The translation of the passage, which I have slightly modified to address the present topic, was very kindly provided by Li Wai-yee. Duke Xuan, 3rd Year, Spring: 在德不在鼎。昔夏之方有德也。遠方圖物。貢金九牧。鑄鼎象物。百物而為之備。使民知神姦。故民入川澤山林。不逢不若。螭魅罔兩。莫能逢之。用能協于上下。以承天休。桀有昏德。鼎遷于商。載祀六百。商紂暴虐。鼎遷于周。德之休明。雖小。重也。其姦回昏亂。雖大。輕也。... 周德雖衰。天命未改。鼎之輕重。未可問也。

115. The interpretation provided by the Zhou envoy, Wangsun Man 王孫滿, might represent a Warring States period attempt at understanding the meaning of the zoomorphic designs on the extant bronzes from previous ages, which, evidently, was no longer obvious. For the debate on the meanings of the motifs on Chinese bronzes, see Sarah Allan, "Art and Meaning," in *The Problem of Meaning in Early Chinese Ritual Bronzes*, Roderick Whitfield, ed. (London: School of Oriental Studies, 1993), 9–34; see also in the same work, Robert Bagley, "Meaning and Explanation," 35–13. For a classic "phenomenological" analysis of shamanism, see Mircea Eliade, *Shamanism: Archaic Techniques of Ecstasy* (London: Arcana, 1989). On the concept of totem in Chinese culture, see Sarah Allan, "Sons of Suns: Myth and Totemism in Early China," *Bulletin of the School of Oriental and African Studies* 44 (1981): 290–326.

116. This statement about the intrinsically extraordinary faculties of the *ding* tripods is found in the "Gengzhu 耕柱" chapter of the *Mozi*. See Sun Yinrang 孫詒讓, *Mozi xian gu* 墨子閒詁 (Beijing: Zhinghua shuju, 1986), 388.

117. *Lun Heng*, 26, 376–77: 夫金之性, 物也, 用遠方貢之為美, 鑄以為鼎, 用象百物之奇, 安能入山澤不逢惡物, 辟除神姦乎... 世俗《傳》言:「周鼎不爨自沸, 不投物, 物自出。」此則世俗增其言也, 儒書增其文也, 是使九鼎以無怪空為神也。且夫謂周之鼎神者, 何用審之?周鼎之金, 遠方所貢, 禹得鑄以為鼎也。其為鼎也, 有百物之象。如為遠方貢之為神乎?遠方之物安能神?如以為禹鑄之為神乎?禹聖, 不能神。聖人身不能神, 鑄器安能神?如以金之物為神乎?則夫金者、石之類也, 石不能神, 金安能神?以有百物之象為神乎?夫百物之象, 猶雷鐏也, 雷鐏刻畫雲雷之形, 雲雷在天, 神於百物, 雲雷之象不能神, 百物之象安能神也?

118. *SJ* 28, 1383.

119. *SJ* 28, 1384.

120. *SJ* 28, 1393.

121. Ibid.

122. A circumstance that recalls the Yellow Emperor receiving the tripod and promulgating a new calendar after divining with achillea stalks in the first chapter of the *Basic Annals*.

123. *SJ* 28, 1393: 受此書申公, 申公已死。... 申公, 齊人。與安期生通, 受黃帝言, 無書, 獨有此鼎書。曰:『漢興復當黃帝之時』。曰『漢之聖者在高祖之孫且曾孫也。寶鼎出而與神通, 封禪。封禪七十二王, 唯黃帝得上泰山封』漢主亦當上封, 上封能僊登天矣。...

124. Ibid.

125. *SJ* 28, 1393–394: 黃帝采首山銅, 鑄鼎於荊山下。鼎既成, 有龍垂胡顏下迎黃帝。黃帝上騎, 羣臣後宮從上者七十餘人, 龍乃上去。餘小臣不得上, 乃悉持龍顏, 龍顏拔, 墮, 墮黃帝之弓。百姓仰望黃帝既上天, 乃抱其弓與胡顏號, 故後世因名其處曰鼎湖, 其弓曰烏號。

126. *SJ* 28, 1397.

127. *SJ* 28, 1387.

128. *SJ* 47, 1942. On the meaning of this passage, which in turn cites a *Chunqiu* entry (Duke Ai, fourteenth year, Spring), see also chapter 2 above.

129. *SJ* 28, 1361.

130. *SJ* 28, 1387.

131. *SJ* 28, 1397.

132. *SJ* 28, 1398.

133. Ibid.

134. *SJ* 28, 1398.

135. Ibid.

136. Ibid.: 朕以眇眇之身承至尊, 兢兢焉懼不任。維德菲薄, 不明于禮樂。脩祠太一, 若有象景光, 屑如有望, 震於怪物, 欲止不敢, 遂登封太山, 至于梁父, 而後禪肅然。自新。...

137. *SJ* 28, 1398: 古者天子五載一巡狩，用事泰山，諸侯有朝宿地。其令諸侯各治邸泰山下。

138. *SJ* 28, 1399.

139. *SJ* 28, 1402. See also, Michael Loewe, "The Grand Beginning—104 BC," in *Crisis and Conflict in Han China*, M. Loewe (London: Allen & Unwin, 1974), 17–36.

Chapter 5

1. Italo Calvino, *Le città invisibili* (Torino: Einaudi, 1972), 39–40; the translation is by the author.

2. This is the title of a collection of essays by Jonathan Z. Smith, *Map is not Territory: Studies in the History of Religions* (Chicago: University of Chicago Press, 1993).

3. P. A. Brunt, "The Roman Mob," *Past & Present* 35 (Dec. 1966): 3–27; Fergus Millar, *The Crowd in Rome in the Late Republic* (Ann Arbor: University of Michigan Press, 1998).

4. Adam Ziolkoski, "Civic Rituals and Political Spaces in Republican and Imperial Rome," in *The Cambridge Companion to Ancient Rome*, Paul Erdkamp, ed. (Cambridge, UK: Cambridge University Press, 2013), 380–409; Gregory Smith and Jan Gadeyne, eds., *Perspectives on Public Space in Rome: From Antiquity to the Present Day* (New York: Ashgate, 2013).

5. Starting in the seventeenth century, Qing scholars have argued that coherent conceptions of the afterlife were entirely absent in China before Buddhism. See Gu Yanwu 顧炎武 (1613–1682), *Rizhilü jishi* 日知錄 集釋 (Changsha: Yuelu shushe, 1994). For a cogent survey of the development of views of the afterlife in Western and Chinese scholarship, see Jue Guo, "Concepts of Death and the Afterlife Reflected in Newly Discovered Tomb Objects and Texts from Han China," in *Mortality in Traditional Chinese Thought*, Amy Olberding and Philip J. Ivanhoe, eds. (Albany: SUNY Press, 2011), 85–115. In the same edited volume, Poo Mu-chou notes that although prior to the Eastern Han and the introduction of Buddhism there existed different conception of the afterlife in China, they did not constitute organic systems of ideas nor did they have a role in defining religious systems. See Poo Mu-chou, "Preparation for the Afterlife in Ancient China," in *Mortality in Traditional Chinese Thought*, 13–33. On the material, representational aspects of funerary culture in China, see Wu Hung's compelling *The Art of the Yellow Springs: Understanding Chinese Tombs* (Honolulu: Hawai'i University Press, 2010).

6. Historians have long debated whether Caesar was following a previous plan or whether his decision to rule as a monarch was a consequence of the extraordinary honors he received from the senate and the common people. For an

exhaustive survey, see Zwi Yawetz, "Caesar and Caesarism in the Historical Writing of the Nineteenth and Twentieth Centuries," in *Julius Caesar and his Public Image* (Ithaca, NY: Cornell University Press, 1983), 10–57.

7. See Yuri Pines, "Submerged by Absolute Power: The Rulers Predicament," in *Dao Companion to the Philosophy of Han Fei*, Paul R. Goldin, ed. (New York: Springer, 2013), 67–86; Albert Galvany, "Beyond the Rule of Rules: The Foundations of Sovereign Power in the *Hanfei zi*," in *Dao Companion to the Philosophy of Han Fei*, 87–106.

8. See pp. 96–97 above.

9. Originally attributed to Ban Gu, the *Han Wudi neizhuan* is now believed to have been compiled between the fourth and sixth centuries CE. An analysis with a translation of the text is available in Kristofer Marinus Schipper, *L'Empereur Wou des Han dan la legend taoiste* (Paris: École française d'Extrême-Orient, 1965). In the introduction, Schipper mentions Emperor Wu's popularity among Tang dynasty poets. The most interesting quote is in Li Bai's 李白 (701–762) poem "Zhou Mu bahuang yi" 周穆八荒意, in which Wu is compared to King Mu of Zhou (ca. 976–922 BCE) in his unrestrained search for pleasure, fondness for visiting remote places, and consorting with female deities; in Idem, 1–2.

10. For an analysis of the public/private opposition and references, see Paul R. Goldin, "Introduction Han Fei and the *Hanfei zi*," in *Dao Companion to the Philosophy of Han Fei*, 3–5.

11. *SJ* 17, 801; Translation based on Burton Watson, *Records*, II, 423–24: 殷以前尚矣。周封五等：公，侯，伯，子，男。然封伯禽、康叔於魯、衞，地各四百里，親親之義，襃有德也；. . .王室缺，侯伯彊國興焉，天子微，弗能正。非德不純，形勢弱也。漢興，序二等。高祖末年，非劉氏而王者，若無功上所不置而侯者，天下共誅之。高祖子弟同姓為王者九國，唯獨長沙異姓，而功臣侯者百有餘人。

12. The only sovereign who did not belong to the Liu lineage was Wu Rui 吳芮 (d. 202 BCE), the King of Changsha. A magistrate under the Qin, he joined Liu Bang during the rebellion, therefore the first emperor of Han rewarded him with an estate and a title.

13. *SJ* 17, 802: 而內地北距山以東盡諸侯地，大者或五六郡，連城數十，置百官宮觀，僭於天子。. . .凡十五郡，而公主列侯頗食邑其中。何者？天下初定，骨肉同姓少，故廣彊庶孽，以鎮撫四海，用承衞天子也。漢定百年之間，親屬益疏，諸侯或驕奢，忕邪臣計謀為淫亂，大者叛逆，小者不軌於法，以危其命，殞身亡國。天子觀於上古，然後加惠，使諸侯得推恩分子弟；translation based on B. Watson, *The Records*, II, 424–25.

14. *SJ* 106, 2821.

15. *SJ* 106, 2822. Trans. B. Watson, *Records*, I, 404: 會孝惠、高后時，天下初定，郡國諸侯各務自拊循其民。吳有豫章郡銅山，濞則招致天下亡命者〔益〕〔盜〕鑄錢，煮海水為鹽，以故無賦，國用富饒。

16. *SJ* 106, 2823:「天下同宗，死長安即葬長安，何必來葬為！」

17. Yuan Ang's biography is in *SJ* 101, 2737–3742.
18. His biography in the *Records* is in *SJ* 101, 2742–749.
19. See also Sadao Nishijima, "The Economic and Social History of Former Han," in *The Cambridge History of China: Volume I: the Ch'in and Han Empires, 221 B.C.–A.D. 220*, Denis Twitchett and Michael Loewe, eds. (Cambridge, UK: Cambridge University Press, 1986), 545–607.
20. This point is clearly stated also in the "Book on *Li*," in the *Records*; see Chapter 2 above.
21. *SJ* 101, 2748: 語曰「變古亂常，不死則亡」，豈錯等謂邪.
22. David Knechtges considers Wu the first emperor to be seriously interested in literature. Although Wu is remembered for having expanded the scope of the Music Bureau (*Yuefu* 樂府), the role of Chinese emperors during the Qin and the Western Han in patronizing the arts, establishing literary standards and collecting popular songs is the object of several controversies, see David R Knechtges, "The Emperor and Literature: Emperor Wu of the Han," in *Imperial Rulership and Cultural Change in Traditional China*, Frederick P. Brandauer and Chün-chieh Huang, eds. (Seattle: University of Washington Press, 1994), 51–76; Anne Birrell, "Mythmaking and *Yüeh-fu*: Popular Songs and Ballads in Early Imperial China," *JAOS* 109, 2 (1989): 223–35; Yao Daye 姚大業, *Han Yuefu xiaolun* 漢樂府小論 (Tianjin: Baihua Wenyi Chubanshe, 1984; Hellmut Wilhelm, "The Bureau of Music of Western Han," in *Society and History: Essays in Honor of Karl August Wittfogel*, Gary L. Ulmen, ed. (The Hague: Mouton Publishers, 1978), 123–35. On Sima Xiangru's poetry, see David R. Knechtges, *The Han Rhapsody: The Study of the* Fu *of Yang Hsiung (53 B.C.–A.D. 18)* (Cambridge, UK: Cambridge University Press, 1976), 44–58.
23. Sima Xiangru biography is in *SJ* 117, 2999–3074. In addition to his poetic skills, the text emphasizes Sima Xiangru's passionate temperament, which sets him aside from the model of the ideal Confucian official. Famously, the young man from Shu fell in love at first sight and eloped with the woman who would become his spouse without the approval of his father-in-law. The poet and intellectual Yang Xiong 楊雄 (53 BCE–18 CE), who authored *fu* rhapsodies in his youth, eventually dismissed the genre as not befitting grown men; See Yang Xiong (Michael Nylan, trans. and intr.), *Exemplary Figures "Fayan* 法言*"* (Seattle: University of Washington Press, 2013), 22–23 (*Fayan* 2.1); see also Martin Kern, "Western Han Aesthetics and the Genesis of the *Fu*," *Harvard Journal of Asiatic Studies* 63 (2003): 383–437.
24. See the chapter "Quantification: Poetic Expenditure in the Epideictic *Fu*," in T. Chin, *Savage Exchange*, 69–152.
25. Mark E. Lewis is one of the few scholars who has engaged Sima Xiangru's works beyond a philological perspective, as a valuable expression of Han culture. In addition to the article on the *feng* and *shan* cited above, for an anthropological analysis of imperial hunts and symbolic violence, see *Sanctioned Violence*, 150–157; for Sima Xiangru as an erudite and lexicographer intent on creating a literary representation of the Han empire, see *Writing and Authority*, 317–25.

26. Liu Wu was the youngest and favorite son of Emperor Wen. Because of the special attentions he received since his childhood, his biography suggests, he expected to legitimately sit on the throne of the Son of Heaven sooner or later, despite his position in the succession order. His biography is in *SJ* 58, 2081–090.

27. *SJ* 58, 2089.

28. On Zou Yan, see Chapter 4, note 70.

29. Among the scholars mentioned by the *Records*, there were Mei Sheng 枚乘 of Huaiyin 懷陰, and Master Zhuang Ji 莊忌 of Wu 吳. These authors of *fu* were both at the service of Liu Pi the king of Wu. When they failed to stop him from raising his army against the emperor in 154 BCE, they left him (together with Zou Yan) and eventually found protection as support under Liu Wu. To Mei Sheng, barely mentioned in the *Records* the *Han Shu* devotes a full chapter; see Loewe, *A Biographical Dictionary*, 435–36. Not too much is known about Zhuang Ji; see Ibid., 745.

30. Interestingly, Empress Dowager Dou tried to compromise Emperor Wu's fate, her grandchild, even before he could access the throne. In order to advance her other—and favorite—son, she almost succeeded in persuading Emperor Jing to breach the etiquette rules of succession and replace the legitimate heir apparent, his direct descendent, with his own brother Liu Wu. When Yuan Ang finally convinced the sovereign that this was inopportune, Liu Wu and his mother became enraged at the adviser and sent some retainers to kill him. The plot was discovered before it could be successful and the King of Liang was banished from the court. See *SJ* 58, 2083–085.

31. For the dating of this rhapsody, see David R. Knechtges and Tong Xiao, *Wen Xuan or Selections of Refined Literature, Volume II :Rhapsodies on Sacrifices, Hunting, Travel, Sightseeing, Palaces and Halls, Rivers and Seas* (Princeton, NJ: Princeton University Press, 1987), 73–74.

32. For a translation of this passage with detailed annotations, see Knechtges and Xiao *Wen Xuan II*, 73–75. *SJ* 117, 3016: 夫使諸侯納貢者，非為財幣，所以述職也；封疆畫界者，非為守禦，所以禁淫也。今齊列為東藩，而外私肅慎，捐國踰限，越海而田，其於義故未可也。且二君之論，不務明君臣之義而正諸侯之禮，徒事爭游獵之樂，苑囿之大，欲以奢侈相勝，荒淫相越，此不可以揚名發響，而適足以貶君自損也。且夫齊楚之事又焉足道邪！君未睹夫巨麗也，獨不聞天子之上林乎？

33. Elaborated royal or aristocratic hunts were (and in certain cases still are) carried out throughout the ancient and early-modern world. For a survey of the study of their cultural and political meanings in different contexts, see Thomas T. Allsen, *The Royal Hunt in Eurasian History* (Philadelphia: University of Pennsylvania Press, 2006).

34. For a detailed commentary on the translation, see Knechtges and Xiao *Wen Xuan II*, 111–13; *SJ* 117, 3041: 於是乃解酒罷獵，而命有司曰：『地可以墾辟，悉為農郊，以贍萌隸；隤牆填塹，使山澤之民得至焉。實陂池而勿禁，虛宮觀而勿仞。發倉廩以振貧窮，補不足，恤鰥寡，存孤獨。出德號，省刑罰，改制度，易服色，更正朔，與天下為始。』

35. Considering the context redolent with literary references to famous poems and songs, the line "捃摭雅" could be read as "[he] captures the *Odes*"; see the commentary on *SJ* 117, 3041.

36. Knechtges and Xiao *Wen Xuan II,* 111–13; *SJ* 117, 3041–042:「於是歷吉日以齊戒，襲朝衣，乘法駕，建華旗，鳴玉鸞，游乎六藝之囿，騖乎仁義之塗，覽觀春秋之林，射貍首，兼騶虞，弋玄鶴，建干戚，載雲罕，揜羣雅，悲伐檀，樂樂胥，修容乎禮園，翱翔乎書圃，述易道，放怪獸，登明堂，坐清廟....

37. *SJ* 117, 3048: 司馬長卿便略定西夷，邛、筰、冄、駹、斯榆之君皆請為內臣。除邊關，關益斥，西至沫、若水，南至牂柯為徼，通零　關道，橋孫水以通邛都。還報天子，天子大說。

38. *SJ* 117, 3063–074.

39. On the Augustus's political strategies see, Erich Gruen, "Augustus," 33–51.

40. Beard, *Religions of Rome* I, 20–24; 181–84. See also Gerzy Linderski, "The Augural Law," *Aufstieg und Niedergang der römischen Welt* II.16.3 (1986): 2146–312.

41. Livy I. 7–9.

42. An interesting analysis of the study of etymology of "*Templum*" as separate, cut-off space, across cultures is in L. Patton, "The Magic in Miniature," 193–205. She focuses on the Mark Taylor's critique of Jacques Derrida's "negative theology." See, Mark C. Taylor, *Nots (Religion and Postmodernism)* (Chicago: University of Chicago Press, 1993), 50, 54; and Jacques Derrida, "How to Avoid Speaking: Denials," in *Languages of the Unsayable: The Play of Negativity in Literature and Literary Theory,* Sanford Budick and Wolfgang Iser, eds. (New York: Columbia University Press, 1989), 50, 52, 66.

43. With the Ming and Qing, each Son of Heaven only maintained one Nian Hao throughout his tenure, so that era years became interchangeable with the posthumous names customarily given to the deceased emperors.

44. We could say that the tradition of the *nianhao* still survives today in the adoption of slogans for particular political phases of the P.R.C., such as "Harmony" (*Hexie* 和諧) under Hu Jintao 胡锦涛 (1940–), or the "Chinese Dream" (*Zhongguo meng* 中國夢) under Xi Jinping 习近平 (1953–).

45. See, for example, David W. Pankanier, "Looking to the Supernal Lord," in *Astrology and Cosmology in Early China: Conforming Earth to Heaven* (Cambridge, UK: Cambridge University Press, 2013), 83–117.

46. *SJ* 27, 1290. See Iannacone, *Misurare,* 144–47. In the *Huainanzi* 淮南子, which was produced at the court of the prince Liu An 劉安 (180–122 BCE), a cousin and rival of Emperor Wu, the Yellow Emperor is associated with the (usually female) Deity of Earth, Houtu 后土 in the task of measuring and dividing the universe. In his regulating function, the Yellow Emperor was also linked to the axial Mount Kunlun 崑崙 (in turn associated with immortality and afterlife). Astronomic texts mentioned him in association with the planet Saturn (Zhen Xing 鎮星 or Huangshigong 黃石公), which was in turn connected with the Northern Dipper (Beidou 北斗), the color yellow, earth, and the yin factor. The earliest lit-

erary sources that mention Taiyi are the *Zhuangzi*, the *Xunzi*, the *Lüshi chunqiu*, the *Heguanzi*, and the *Huainanzi*. See Li Ling, "An Archaeological Study of Taiyi 太一 (Grand One) Worship," *Early Medieval China* 2 (1995–1996): 1–8. The first comprehensive study of Taiyi (carried out with Gu Jiegang's advice) is Qian Baocong 錢寶琮, "Taiyi kao" 太一考, *Yanjing Xuebao* 12 (1932): 2449–478. See also, Gu Jiegang 顧頡剛 et al., "Sanhuang kao" 三皇考, in *Gushi bian* 7 no. 2 (1982): 20. A set of fifth and forth-century bamboo texts unearthed in 1993, in Guodian, Hubei (former State of Chu) has provided the earliest Chinese cosmogonic myth featuring Taiyi conceived in "Daoistic" terms as the creative force at the origin of the universe; see Li Xueqin 李學勤, "Taiyi sheng shui de shushu jieshi" 太一生水的數術解釋, *Daojia wenhua yanjiu* 17 (1999): 297–300; Sarah Allan, "The Great One, Water, and the Laozi: New Light from Guodian," *T'oung Pao* Second Series 89, no. 4/5 (2003): 237–85; Scott Cook, "*Taiyi Sheng Shui*' 太一生水 The Great Unity Gives Birth to Water (a.k.a. 'Laozi C,' Part Two)," in *The Bamboo Texts of Guodian: A Study & Complete Translation* (Ithaca, NY: Cornell University East Asia Program, 2012), 323–54. Roger T. Ames has interpreted the myth of Taiyi in the Guodian as an example of the typically Chinese concept of "creation in *situ*," which characterizes both Daoist and Confucian traditions. For Ames, the notion of in "creation *in situ*," unlike that of "creation *ex nihilo*," does not include any a-historical void, but "a fecund receptivity," and entails "particularity, temporality, collateral rationality, and productive indeterminacy"; See Roger T. Ames, "Collaterality in Early Chinese Cosmology: An Argument for Confucian Harmony (He) as *Creatio in Situ*," *Early China* 37 (2014): 1–26.

47. The scarcity of the available information on specific characteristics of Houtu has spurred several scholarly debates about its gender as a deity and its relation with the *she* and the Millet (or Lord Millet) altars (see, Birrell, *Chinese Mythology*, 160–63). Yet the *Records* undoubtedly defines Houtu in terms of land fertility and as a cult that was particularly meaningful to the common people (*SJ* 28, 1392). Emperor Wu resorted to worshipping it in specific circumstances: when he feared that the offerings to the Five Sovereigns, a dynastic cult, were not yielding any results (*SJ* 28, 1389); in the wake of a natural disaster; or when he needed to invoke a bumper harvest on behalf of the starving populace (*SJ* 28, 1392). Finally, when after the victorious campaign against Nanyue in 113 BCE Emperor Wu honored both Taiyi and Houtu, he was simultaneously sanctioning his control over the land in a way that could be broadly understood in military, economic, and agricultural terms. On contemporary cults of Houtu, see Yang, *Handbook of Chinese Mythology*, 135–37.

48. On the cultural and political context of the compilation of the *Huainanzi*, see the introduction of John S. Major et al., *The Huainanzi, A Guide to the Theory and Practice of Government in Early Han China* (New York: Columbia University Press, 2010), 1–39. Aihe Wang has analyzed the clash between as Liu An and Emperor Wu as determined by two contrasting visions of empire. Her research

argues that the *Huainanzi* propounded the model of the ruler as a military leader and as a conqueror whereas Emperor Wu was trying to establish a moralizing view indebted to Dong Zhongshu's theories; see Wang, *Cosmology*, 173–209.

49. *Huainanzi*, 8.7: "帝者體太一，王者法陰陽，霸者則四時，君者用六律。乘太一者，牢籠天地，彈壓山川，含吐陰陽，伸曳四時，紀綱八極" For the translation see, J. S. Major, et al., *The Huainanzi*, 277.

50. *Huainanzi* 7,15, in Major, *The Huainanzi*, 258–59. On the *Huainanzi* and its polemic stance against the authority of the textual tradition, see Sarah A. Queen, "Representations of Confucius in the *Huainanzi*," in *The* Huainanzi *and Textual Production in Early China*, Sarah Queen amd Michael Puett, eds. (Leiden: Brill, 2014), 83–123.

51. See Chapter 4 above.

52. *SJ* 28, 1386.

53. Ibid.

54. Ibid.

55. Ibid.

56. *SJ* 28, 1394.

57. As mentioned by Li in his "An Archaeological Study of Taiyi," 4. See also the *Liji* ("Yueling," 16:7b) associated Earth with the third month of the summer, which corresponds, spatially, to southwest.

58. For a reconstruction of the Taiyi altar, see Li, "An Archaeological Study of Taiyi," 2–5: also *SJ* 28, 1394; *HS* 25, 1230, 1256.

59. For an accurate reconstruction and analysis of this ceremony, see Martin Kern, "Tropes of Music and Poetry: From Wudi (r. 141–87 BCE) to ca. 100 CE," in *China's Early Empires: A Re-Appraisal*, 480–91.

60. *SJ* 28, 1395. This ritual is interestingly similar to the ceremony that, according to classic Roman historiography, the Fetiales would carry out ever since the archaic period to ensure that the war Rome was about to engage would be a "just" one; see Beard, *Religions of Rome I*, 26–27; Alan Watson, *International Law in Archaic Rome: War and Religion* (Baltimore, MD: John Hopkins University Press, 1993), 1–9.

61. *SJ* 28, 1395.

62. Li, "An Archaeological Study of Taiyi," 12–26.

63. See David W. Pankenier, "The *Huainanzi*'s 'Heavenly Patterns' and the *Shiji*'s "Treatise on the Celestial Offices": What's the Difference? in *The* Huainanzi *and Textual Production*, 199–224.

64. *SJ* 27, 1289–293.

65. Li Ling, in particular, refers to the *shi* 式, but in early China, divination devices, board games, and objects of daily use with a cosmological meaning were several; for a synthesis of the literature on the topic, see Mark E. Lewis, *The Construction of Space in Early China* (Albany: SUNY Press, 2006), 273–305.

66. The colors used in the chart were yellow, red, azure, black, and white, the same as the Five Phases.

67. Li Ling in his essay corrects previous readings of the chart by comparing it with the decorations on a dagger-axe excavated in 1960 from a Warring State tomb in Hubei. For an early analysis of the chart, see Zhou Shirong 周世榮, "Mawangdui Han mu de 'Shenqi' tu bohua," 馬王堆漢墓的神祇圖帛畫 *Kaogu* 10 (1990): 925–28. For the dagger-axe, see Wang Yutong 王毓彤, "Jingmen chutu yijian tongge" 荊門出土一件銅戈, *Wenwu* 1 (1963): 64–65.

68. *SJ* 60, 2115.

69. *SJ* 25, 1159–169; see p. 145 above.

70. *SJ* 60, 2115–116.

71. A very similar description is provided in the *Baihutong*, which in turn attributes it to the *Chunqiu wenyi* 春秋文義, a non-extant text that seems to represent re-reading of earlier traditions in terms of Five Phases theory.

72. A full translation of the *Baihutong* is in Tjan Tjoe Som, *'Po hu t'ung': The Comprehensive Discussions in the White Tiger Hall*. 2 Vols. (Leiden: Brill, 1949–1952).

73. Interestingly enough here *ji* is not referred to Houji, Lord Millet, worshipped by the Zhou, but to the grain itself.

74. *BHT* 2, 1 王者所以有社稷何？為天下求福報功。人非土不立，非穀不食。土地廣博，不可遍敬也；五穀眾多，不可一一祭也。

75. Som, *White Tiger Hall*, 383; cfr. *BHT*, 2, 1. IA, 21 a–b; cfr *Lun Yu* XI, 24.

76. *HS* 25, 1189–239.

77. *HS* 25, 1241–272. The most complete and accurate analysis (with translation) of the second part of the "Jiaosi zhi" is Marianne Bujard, *Le sacrifice au Ciel dans la Chine ancienne: Théorie et pratique dans les Han Occidentaux* (Paris: École française d'Extrême-Orient, 2000). As is well-known, Wang Mang tried to overhaul the Han's system of land tenure through reallotments that angered powerful and influential members of the political aristocracy; his biography is in *HS* 99, 4039–196.

78. *HS* 25, 1189: 洪範八政，三曰祀。 祀者，所以昭孝事祖，通神明也。旁及四夷，莫不修之；下至禽獸，豺獺有祭。 是以聖王為之典禮。民之精爽不貳，齊肅聰明者，神或降之，在男曰覡，在女曰巫，使制神之處位，為之牲器。使先聖之後，能知山川，敬於禮儀，明神之事者，以為祝；能知四時犧牲，壇場上下，氏姓所出者，以為宗。 故有神民之官，各司其序，不相亂也。民神異業，敬而不黷，故神降之嘉生，民以物序，災禍不至，所求不匱。

79. *HS* 25, 1248.

80. Ibid.

81. *HS* 25, 1248: 朕親飭躬齊戒，親奉祀，為百姓蒙嘉氣，獲豐年焉。

82. Ibid.

83. *HS* 25, 1251: 願明主時忘車馬之好，斥遠方士之虛語，游心帝王之術，太平庶幾可興。 It seems that a "modernist" attitude prevailed at court as long as the powerful Huo Guang 霍光, who had been appointed by Emperor Wu, was alive. After his death in 68 BCE, the influence of the Classicists is clearly on the rise. Zhang Chang is one of the politicians/scholars who emerged in this phase. His biography is in *HS* 76, 3217–240. See also M. Loewe, *Biographical Dictionary*, 676–77.

84. On the tripod unearthed in Fenyin in 113 BCE and the discussion it elicited, see Chapter 4 above.

85. Between the two officials, Kuang Heng was undoubtedly the most relevant. Despite his humble background, he succeeded in obtaining an outstanding education in the *Classics*, the most important political offices. For his merits Emperor Yuan enfeoffed Kuang Heng as Marquise of Le'An (Le'an hou 樂安侯), which comprised 600 households. See *HS* 81, 3341.

86. See M. Bujard, *Le sacrifice au Ciel*, 165–70.

87. *HS* 86, 3345.

88. M. Loewe, *Biographical Dictionary*, 372.

89. *HS* 87, 3522.

90. Ibid.

91. Interestingly enough, of the nine officials who opposed the abolition of Taiyi and Houtu, the text only mentions the Minister of War, Xu Jia 許嘉, by name. This element seems to confirm the military connotations of Wu's sacrifices, which might have been aimed at establishing a particular connections with the army and its officials; see *HS* 25, 1254.

92. *HS* 87, 3523. On Yang Xiong as an author of rhapsodies and the annotated translation of the "The Sweet Springs Palace Rhapsody," see David R. Knechtges (trans. and annot.), *Wen Xuan or Selections of Refined Literature*, Vol. I (Princeton, NJ: Princeton University Press, 1987), 1–39.

93. These eight spirits (*ba shen* 八神) may be related to the eight ghosts (*ba gui* 八鬼) mentioned in Sima Qian's description of the first Taiyi Altar; see above, pp. 357–59.

94. *HS* 87, 3530: 惟夫所以澄心清魂，儲精垂思，感動天地，逆釐三神者。

95. D. Knechtges, *Wen Xuan*, 37. *HS* 87, 3533: 天閫決兮地垠開，八荒協兮萬國諧。

96. D. Knechtges, *Wen Xuan*, 39.

97. Jonathan Z. Smith, "Map is not Territory," in *Map is not Territory: Studies in the History of Religions* (Chicago: University of Chicago Press, 1993), 293.

98. Ibid.

99. See I. Gradel, *Emperor Worship*, 198–233.

Conclusions

1. The Mighty One (*Da ren* 大人) is Emperor Wu. *SJ* 117, 3056: 世有大人兮，在于中州。宅彌萬里兮，曾不足以少留。悲世俗之迫隘兮，揭輕舉而遠遊。

2. Either under the influence of the *fangshi* as usual, or due to his notorious infatuation with spirits and ghosts, the Son of Heaven had also sponsored rituals such as the cult of the Jewel of Chen (Chenbao 陳寶), in Baoji, a few miles west of the capital and also the site of the burial of the Flaming Emperor, Yandi 炎帝,

brother and rival of the Yellow Emperor. The cult of the Jewel of Chen (still extant today in Baoji, Shaanxi) had also received official sponsorship under the Qin. See Marianne Bujard, "Le Joyau De Chen: Culte Historique, Culte Vivant," *Cahiers d'Extreme-Asie* 10 (1998): 131–81.

3. *SJ* 28, 1384.

4. *SJ* 28, 1401. Emperor Wu's Mingtang, to the chagrin of the court Classicists, did not correspond to the one described in the *Classics*. See Piero Corradini, "Ancient China's Ming Tang between Reality and Legend," *Rivista di Studi Orientali* 69, 1–2 (1995): 173–206; Henri Maspéro, "Le Ming-T'ang et la crise religeuse chinoise avant les Han," *Mélanges Chinois et Bouddhiques* 9 (1951): 1–71; Yang Hongxun 楊鴻勳, "Mingtang de kaoguxue yanjiu" 明堂的考古學研究, *Tōhō Gakuhō* 70 (March 1998): 2–94.

5. *SJ* 28, 1384.

6. These sacrifices were in turn based on Warring States local cults. The Qin initially worshipped only four sovereigns. It was Gaozu who added a fifth altar dedicated to Heidi 黑帝, the Black Sovereign; see *SJ* 28, 1378.

7. *SJ* 28, 1384:「是時上求神君，舍之上林中蹄氏觀。神君者，長陵女子，以子死，見神於先後宛若。宛若祠之其室，民多往祠。平原君往祠，其後子孫以尊顯。及今上即位，則厚禮置祠之內中。聞其言，不見其人云。」

8. *SJ* 28, 1388.

9. Ibid.:「壽宮神君最貴者太一，其佐曰大禁、司命之屬，皆從之。」

10. Ibid.:「非可得見，聞其言，言與人音等。時去時來，來則風肅然。居室帷中。時晝言，然常以夜。天子祓，然后入。因巫為主人，關飲食。所以言，行下。又置壽宮、北宮，張羽旗，設供具，以禮神君。神君所言，上使人受書其言，命之曰「畫法」。」

11. In Tang popular culture in the *Han Wudi neizhuan*, and in the "Rhapsody of the Mighty One" by Sima Xiangru, Shenjun is replaced by Xiwangmu.

12. See p. 323, n. 419.

13. *SJ* 23, 1160–61:「蓋受命而王，各有所由興，殊路而同歸，謂因民而作，追俗為制也。議者咸稱太古，百姓何望?漢亦一家之事，典法不傳，謂子孫何?化隆者閎博，治淺者褊狹，可不勉與！」

14. *SJ* 30, 1442:「縣官當食租衣稅而已，今弘羊令吏坐市列肆，販物求利。亨弘羊，天乃雨。」

Bibliography

Adamson, Walter. *Hegemony and Revolution: A Study of Antonio Gramsci's Political and Cultural Theory.* Berkeley: University of California Press, 1980.

Allan, Sarah. "Sons of Suns: Myth and Totemism in Early China." *Bulletin of the School of Oriental and African Studies* 44 (1981): 290–326.

———. *The Heir and the Sage: Dynastic Legends in Early China.* San Francisco: Center for Chinese Materials, 1981.

———. "Drought, Human Sacrifice and the Mandate of Heaven in a Lost Text from the *Shangshu*," *Bulletin of the School of Oriental and African Studies* 47, no. 3 (1984): 523–39.

———. "Art and Meaning." In *The Problem of Meaning in Early Chinese Ritual Bronzes*, edited by Roderick Whitfield, 9–34. London: School of Oriental Studies, 1993.

———. "The Great One, Water, and the Laozi: New Light from Guodian." *T'oung Pao* Second Series 89, no. 4/5 (2003): 237–85.

———. "Erlitou and the Formation of Chinese Civilization: Toward a New Paradigm." *Journal of Chinese Studies* 66, no. 2 (May 2007): 461–96.

———. "T'ien and Shang Ti in Pre-Han China." *Acta Asiatica* 98 (2010): 1–18.

Allsen, Thomas T. *The Royal Hunt in Eurasian History.* Philadelphia: University of Pennsylvania Press, 2006.

———. "Collaterality in Early Chinese Cosmology: An Argument for Confucian Harmony (He) as *Creatio in Situ.*" *Early China* 37 (2014): 1–26.

Ames, Roger T. *The Art of Rulership: A Study of Ancient Chinese Political Thought.* Albany: SUNY Press, 1994.

———. "Collaterality in Early Chinese Cosmology: An Argument for Confucian Harmony (He) as *Creatio in Situ.*" *Early China* 37 (2014): 1–26.

Anderson, Benedict. *Imagined Communities: Reflections on the Origin and Spread of Nationalism.* New York: Verso, 1983.

Ando, Clifford, ed. "Was Classical Rome a *Polis?*" *Classical Antiquity* 18 (1999): 13.

———. *Imperial Ideology and Provincial Loyalty in the Roman Empire.* Berkeley: University of California Press, 2000.

———. *Roman Religion.* Edinburgh: Edinburgh University Press, 2003.

———. *The Matter of the Gods: Religion and the Roman Empire.* Berkeley: University of California Press, 2008.

Arbuckle, Gary. "A Note on the Authenticity of the *Chuqiu fanlu.*" *T'oung Pao* 75 (1989): 226–34.

Armstrong, Karen. *A History of God: The 4,000-Year Quest of Judaism, Christianity and Islam.* New York: Random House, 1993.

Arvidsson, Stefan. *Aryan Idols: The Indo-European Mythology as Science and Ideology.* Chicago: University of Chicago Press, 2006.

Asad, Talal. "Reading a Modern Classic: W. C. Smith's *The Meaning and End of Religion.*" *History of Religions* 4, no. 3 (Feb. 2001): 205–22.

———. *Formations of the Secular: Christianity, Islam, Modernity.* Stanford, CA: Stanford University Press, 2003.

Aslan, Reza. *How to Win a Cosmic War: God, Globalization, and the End of the War on Terror.* New York: Random House, 2009.

Bagley, Robert. "Meaning and Explanation." In *The Problem of Meaning in Early Chinese Ritual Bronzes.* Edited by Roderick Whitfield, 35–13. London: School of Oriental Studies, 1993.

———. "Review of Wu Hung's *Monumentality.*" *Harvard Journal of Asiatic Studies* 51, no. 1 (June 1998): 221–56.

Balaiche, Nicole. "Tychè et la Tychè dans le cites de la Palestine romaine." *Syria* 80 (2003): 111–38.

Ban, Gu 班固. *Hanshu* 漢書. Beijing: Zhonghua Shuju, 1962.

Barchiesi, Alessandro. "Learned Eyes: Viewers, Image Makers." In *The Cambridge Companion to the Age of Augustus*, edited by K. Galinsky, 281–385. Berkeley: University of California Press, 1990.

Barnes, Timothy D. *Constantine and Eusebius.* Cambridge, MA: Harvard University Press: 1981.

Barth, Fredrik. *Ethnic Groups and Boundaries: The Social Organization of Cultural Difference.* Boston: Little, Brown Series in Anthropology, 1969.

Barton, Carlin A., and Daniel Boyarin. *Imagine no Religion: How Modern Abstractions Hide Ancient Realities.* New York: Fordham University Press, 2016.

Beard, Mary, John North, and Simon Price. *Religions of Rome: Volume 1: A History.* Cambridge, UK: Cambridge University Press, 1998.

Bell, Catherine. "The Spectrum of Ritual Activities." In *Ritual: Perspectives and Dimensions.* C. Bell, 91–169. Oxford, UK: Oxford University Press, 1997.

———. *Ritual: Perspectives and Dimensions.* Oxford: Oxford University Press, 1997.

Bellah, Robert N. *Religion in Human Evolution: From the Paleolithic to the Axial Age.* Cambridge, MA: Harvard University Press, 2011.

Ben-Dor Benite, Zvi. "Religions and World History." In *Oxford Handbook of World History*, edited by Jerry Bentley, 210–28. New York: Oxford University Press, 2011.

Bentley, Jerry H. "Missionaries, Pilgrims, and the Spread of the World Religions." In *Old World Encounters: Cross-Cultural Contacts and Exchanges in Pre-Modern Times*, edited by J. H. Bentley, 67–110. New York: Oxford University Press, 1993.

Bielenstein, Hans. "An Interpretation of the Portents in the *Ts'ien Han Shu*." *Bulletin of the Museum of Far Eastern Antiquities* 22 (1950): 127–43.

———. "Han Portents and Prognostications." *Bulletin of the Museum of Far Eastern Antiquities* 57 (1984): 97–112.

Billioud, Sébastien, and Joël Thoraval. *The Sage and the People: The Confucian Revival in China*. New York: Oxford University Press, 2015.

Bilsky, Lester J. *The State Religion of Ancient China*, 2 vols. Taipei: The Orient Cultural Service, 1975.

Birrell, Anne. "Mythmaking and *Yüeh-fu*: Popular Songs and Ballads in Early Imperial China." *JAOS* 109, no. 2 (1989): 223–35.

———. *Chinese Mythology: An Introduction*. Baltimore, MD: John Hopkins University Press, 1993.

———. "James Legge and the Chinese Mythological Tradition." *History of Religions* 38, no. 4 (May 1999): 331–53.

Bodde, Derk. *Festivals in Classical China: New Year and Other Annual Observances during the Han Dynasty* (206 BC–AD 220). Princeton, NJ: Princeton University Press, 1975.

Boin, Douglas R. *Coming out Christian in the Roman Empire: How the Followers of Jesus Made a Place in Caesar's Empire*. London: Bloomsbury Press, 2015.

Bokenkamp, Stephen R. *Ancestors and Anxiety: Daoism and the Birth of Rebirth in China*. Berkeley: University of California Press, 2009.

———. "Imagining Community: Families Values and Morality in the Lingbao Scriptures." In *Philosophy and Religion in Early Medieval China*, edited by Alan K. L. Chan and Yuet-Keung Lo, 203–26. Albany: SUNY Press, 2010.

Boltz, William G. "Chou li 周禮." In *Early Chinese Texts*, edited by M. Loewe, 24–32. Berkeley: The Institute of East Asian Studies, 1993.

———. "I li 儀禮." In *Early Chinese Texts*, edited by M. Loewe, 234–43. Berkeley: The Institute of East Asian Studies, 1993.

Bonfante, Larissa. *Etruscan Life and After Life: A Handbook of Etruscan Studies*. Detroit, MI: Wayne State University Press, 1986.

Bowersock, Glen W. "The Pontificate of Augustus." In *Between Republic and Empire: Interpretations of Augustus and his Principate*, edited by Kurt A. Raaflaub and Mark Toher, 380–94. Berkeley: University of California Press, 1990.

Brady, Thomas. *German Histories in the Age of Reformations, 1400–1650*. Cambridge, UK: Cambridge University Press, 2009.

Brashier, K. E. *Ancestral Memory in Early China*. Cambridge, MA: Harvard University Press, 2011.

———. *Public Memory in Early China*. Cambridge, MA: Harvard University Press, 2014).
Brelich, Angelo. *Introduzione alla storia delle religioni*. Roma: Edizioni dell'Ateneo, 1965.
———. *Heros: Il culto greco degli eroi e il problema degli esseri semi-divini*. Roma: Edizioni dell'Ateneo, 1966.
Brisch, Nicole. *Religion and Power: Divine Kingship in the Ancient World and Beyond*. Chicago: University of Chicago Press, 2008.
Brockey, Liam Matthew. *Mission to the East: The Jesuit Mission to China, 1579–1724*. Cambridge, MA: Harvard University Press, 2007.
Brown, Peter. *The Cult of the Saints: Its Rise and Function in Latin Christianity*. Chicago: University of Chicago Press, 1982.
———. *Authority and the Sacred: Aspects of the Christianisation of the Roman World*. Cambridge, UK: Cambridge University Press, 1995.
Brunt, P. A. "The Roman Mob." *Past & Present* 35 (Dec., 1966): 3–27.
Bujard, Marianne, "La vie de Dong Zhongshu: énigmes et hypothèses." *Journal Asiatique* 280, 1–2 (1992): 145–217.
———. "Le 'Traité des sacrifices'du *Hanshu* et la mise en place de la religion d'état des Han." *Bulletin de l'Ecole Française de l'Extrême Orient* 84 (1997): 111–27.
———. "Le Joyau De Chen: Culte Historique, Culte Vivant." *Cahiers d'Extreme-Asie* 10 (1998): 131–81.
———. *Le Sacrifice Au Ciel Dans La Chine Ancienne: Théorie et pratique sous les Han Occidentaux*. Paris: Ecole francaise d'Extrême-Orient, 2000.
Burkert, Walter. *Structure and History in Greek Mythology and Ritual*. Berkeley, University of California Press, 1979.
———. *The Orientalizing Revolution: Near Eastern Influence on Greek Culture in the Early Archaic Age*. Cambridge, MA: Harvard University Press, 1998.
———. *Babylon, Memphis, Persepolis: Eastern Contexts of Greek Culture*. Cambridge, MA: Harvard University Press, 2007.
Cai, Tingji 蔡廷吉. *Jia Yi yanjiu* 賈誼研究. Taibei: Wenshizhe Chubanshe, 1984.
Calvino, Italo. *Le città invisibili*. Torino: Einaudi, 1972.
Campany, Robert Ford. "Xunzi and Durkheim as Theorists of Ritual Practice." In *Discourse and Practice*, edited by Frank Reynolds, David Tracy, 197–231. Albany: SUNY Press, 1992.
———. *Strange Writings: Anomaly Accounts in Early Medieval China*. Albany: SUNY, 1996.
———. "On the Very Idea of Religions [In the Modern West and in Early Medieval China]." *History of Religions* 42, no. 4 (May 2003): 287–19.
———. *A Garden of Marvels, Tales of Wonder from Early Medieval China*. Honolulu: University of Hawai'i Press, 2015.
———. "'Buddhism Enters China' in Early Medieval China." In *Old Society, New Belief: Religious transformation of China and Rome, ca. 1st–6th Centuries*, edited

by Mu-chou Poo, H. A. Drake, and Lisa Raphals, 13–34. New York: Oxford University Press, 2017.

Cannadine, David, and Simon Price, eds. *Rituals of Royalty: Power and Ceremonial in Traditional Societies*. Cambridge, UK: Cambridge University Press, 1987.

Cantwell Smith, Wilfred. *The Meaning and End of Religion*. Minneapolis, MN: Fortress Press, 1991.

Carson, Michael, and Michael Loewe. "*Lü shih ch'un ch'iu*" 呂氏春秋. In *Early Chinese Texts: A Bibliographical Guide*, edited by Michael Loewe, 324–30. Berkeley, CA: Institute of East Asian Studies, 1993.

Cartledge, Paul. "Herodotus and 'the Other': a meditation on empire," *EMC/CV* 9 (1990): 27–40.

———. "'We are all Greeks?' Ancient (especially Herodotean) and Modern Contestations of Hellenism," *BICS* 2 (1995 [1996]): 75–82.

Castagnoli, Ferdinando. "Il culto di Mater Matuta e della Fortuna nel Foro Boario." *Studi Romani* 27, 2 (1979): 145–52.

Chaffee, John W. *The Thorny Gates of Learning in Sung China: A Social History of Examinations*. Albany: SUNY Press, 1995.

Champeaux, Jacqueline, *Fortuna: recherches sur le culte de la Fortune à Rome et dans le monde romain des origines à la mort de César*, 2 vols. Roma: Collection de l'Ecole française de Rome, 1982.

Champion, Craige. *Cultural Politics in Polybius' 'Histories.'* Berkeley and Los Angeles: University of California Press, 2004.

Chang, Chun-shu. *The Rise of the Chinese Empire: Nation, State and Imperialism in Early China, ca. 1600 B.C.–A.D. 8*, 2 vols. Ann Arbor: University of Michigan Press, 2007, 119–34.

Chang, K. C. *Art, Myth, and Ritual: The Path to Political Authority in Ancient China*. Cambridge, MA: Harvard University Press, 1983.

Chang, K. C., ed. *Early Chinese Civilization: Anthropological Perspectives*. Cambridge, MA. Harvard University Press, 1976.

Chard Robert L. "Rituals and Scriptures of the Stove Cult." In *Ritual and Scripture in Chinese Popular Religion: Five Studies*, edited by David Johnson, 3–54. Berkeley, CA: Chinese Popular Culture Project, 1995.

Chavannes Édouard, trans. *Les Mémoires historiques de Sse Ma Ts'ien*, 6 vols. Paris: E. Leroux, 1895–1904.

Chen Shengyong 陈乘勇. "Li de qiyuan jian lun Liangzhu wenhua yu wenming qiyuan" 禮的起源兼論良渚文化 與文明起源. *Hanxue yanjiu* 漢學研究 17 no. 1 (1999): 49–77.

Chen, Xiyuan 陳悉遠. "Zongjiao—yige Zhongguo jindai wenhuashi shang de guanjian ci" 宗教——一個中國近代文化史上的關鍵詞. *Xin shixue* 13, no. 4 (December 2001): 37–54.

Chen, Yexin 陳葉新. *Zaihai yu liang Han shehui yanjiu* 災害與兩漢社會研究. Shanghai: Shanghai Renmin Chubanshe, 2004.

Chidester, David. *Word and Light: Seeing, Hearing, and Religious Discourse.* Urbana: University of Illinois Press: 1992.

Chin, Tamara T. "Defamiliarizing the Foreigner: Sima Qian's Ethnography and Han-Xiongnu Marriage Diplomacy." *Harvard Journal of Asiatic Studies* 70, 2 (Dec. 2010): 311–54.

———. "Antiquarian as Ethnographer: Han Ethnicity in Early Han Studies." In *Critical Han Studies: The History, Representation, and Identity of China's Majority*, edited by Thomas S. Mullaney and James Leibold et al., 128–46. Berkeley: University of California Press, 2012.

———. *Savage Exchange: Han Imperialism, Chinese Literary Style, and the Economic Imagination.* Cambridge, MA: Harvard University Press, 2014.

Ching, Julia, and Willard G. Oxtoby. *Moral Enlightenment: Leibniz and Wolff on China.* Sankt Augustin: Institut Monumenta Serica, Nettetal, Steyler, 1992.

Chou, Min-chih. *Hu Shih and Intellectual Choice in Modern China.* Ann Arbor: University of Michigan Press, 1984.

Cohen, Paul A. *Discovering History in China: American Historical Writing on the Recent Past.* New York: Columbia University Press, 1984.

Cook, Constance E., and John Major, eds. *Defining Chu: Image and Reality in Ancient China.* Honolulu: University of Hawai'i Press, 2004.

Cook, Scott. "*Taiyi Sheng Shui*' 太一生水 The Great Unity Gives Birth to Water (a.k.a. 'Laozi C,' Part Two)." In *The Bamboo Texts of Guodian: A Study & Complete Translation*, by idem, 323–54. Ithaca, NY: Cornell University East Asia Program, 2012.

Corradini, Piero. "Ancient China's Ming Tang between Reality and Legend." *Rivista di Studi Orientali* 69, 1–2 (1995): 173–206.

Crawley Quinn, Josephine. "Imagining the Imperial Mediterranean." In *Polybius & His World: Essays in Memory of F. W. Walbank*, edited by Bruce Gibson and Thomas Harrison, 337–52. Oxford, UK: Oxford University Press, 2013.

Creel, Herrlee G. *The Origins of Statecraft in China.* Chicago: University of Chicago Press, 1970.

Csiksentmihalyi, Mark, and Michael Nylan. "Constructing Lineages and Inventing Traditions through Exemplary Figures in Early China." *T'oung Pao* 89, 1–3 (2003), 59–99.

Csiksentmihalyi, Mark. *Material Virtue; Ethics and the Body in Early China.* Leiden: Brill, 2004.

———. "Reimagining the Yellow Emperor's Four Faces." *Text and Ritual in Early China*, edited by Martin Kern, 226–48. Seattle: University of Washington Press, 2005.

———. *Readings in Han Chinese Thought.* Indianapolis, IN: Hackett, 2006.

Cutter, Robert Joe. "Chia I 賈誼." In *The Indiana Companion to Traditional Chinese Literature,* edited by William Nienhauser, 254–55. Bloomington: Indiana University Press, 1986.
Davidson, Steve. "Chunqiu fanlu." In *Early Chinese Texts,* edited by Michael Loewe, 67–76. Berkeley, CA: The Institute of East Asian Studies, 1993.
De Groot, J. J. M. *Les fêtes annuellement célébrées à Émoui (Amoy): étude concernant la religion populaire des Chinois.* Paris: Leroux, 1886.
———. *Religion in China: Universism, a Key to the Study of Taoism and Confucianism.* New York: Putnam, 1921.
Derow, Peter S. "Polybius, Rome and the East," *Journal of Roman Studies* 69 (1979): 1–15.
———. "Historical Explanation: Polybius and his Predecessors." In *Greek Historiography,* edited by S. Hornblower. Oxford, UK: Clarendon Press, 1994.
Derrida, Jacques. "How to Avoid Speaking: Denials." In *Languages of the Unsayable: The Play of Negativity in Literature and Literary Theory,* edited by. Sanford Budick and Wolfgang Iser, 50, 52, 66. New York: Columbia University Press, 1989.
DeWoskin, Kenneth J. *A Song for One or Two: Music and the Concept of Art in Early China* (Ann Arbor: University of Michigan Press, 1982).
———. (translator). *Doctors, Diviners, and Magicians: Biographies of Fang-shi.* New York: Columbia University Press, 1983.
Di Cosmo, Nicola. *Ancient China and Its Enemies: The Rise of Nomadic Power in East Asian History.* Cambridge, UK: Cambridge University Press, 2002.
Ding, Yuanzhi 丁原植, and Yang Hua 楊華, eds. *Xin chu jianbo yu lizhi yanjiu* 新出簡帛與禮制研究. Taipei: Taiwan Guji, 2007.
Dong, Zhongshu (attributed to). *Luxuriant Gems of the Spring and Autumn,* translated by Major John S. and Sarah A. Queen. New York: Columbia University Press, 2015.
Dong, Zhongshu. *Chunqiu fanlu zhu zi suoyin* 春秋繁露逐字索引, edited by D. C. Lau and Chen Fangzheng. Hong Kong: Shang wu yin shu guan, 1994.
Doniger, Wendy. *The Implied Spider: Politics and Theology in Myth.* New York, Columbia University Press, 1998.
———. "Post-modern and Colonial Structural Comparisons." In *A Magic Still Dwells,* edited by K. C. Patton and B. C. Ray, 63–76. Berkeley: University of California Press, 2000.
Drake, H. A. *Constantine and the Bishops: The Politics of Intolerance.* Baltimore, MD: John Hopkins Press, 2002.
Du, Weiming. "The Thought of Huang-Lao: A Reflection on the Lao Tzu and Huang Ti Texts in the Silk Manuscripts of Ma-wang-tui." *Journal of Asian Studies* 39, no. 1 (1979): 95–110.

Du, Zhengsheng 杜正勝. *Bianhu qimin: Chuantong zhengzhi shehui jiegou zhi xincheng* 傳統政治社會結構之形成. Taipei: Guojia Tushuguan, 1990.

Duara, Prasenjit. "Knowledge and Power in the Discourse of Modernity: The Campaigns against Popular Religion in Early Twentieth-Century China." *Journal of Asian Studies* 50, no. 1 (1991.2): 67–83.

Dubois, Page. *A Million and One Gods: The Persistence of Polytheism*. Cambridge, MA: Harvard University Press, 2015.

Dubs, Homer H. "The Failure of the Chinese to Produce Philosophic Systems." *T'oung Pao* 26 (1929): 96–109.

———. "The Victory of Han Confucianism." *Journal of the American Oriental Society*, 58, no. 3 (1935): 435–49.

Dubuisson, Daniel. *The Western Construction of Religion: Myths, Knowledge, and Ideology*. Translated by William Sayers. Baltimore, MD: John Hopkins University Press, 2003. (French edition published in 1998.)

———. *Impostures et pseudo-science: L'œvre de Mircea Eliade*. Villeneuve d'Ascq: Presses Universitaires du Septentrion, 2005.

Dumézil, Georges. *Les dieux des Indo-Européens*. Paris: Presses universitaires de France, 1952.

———. *L'idéologie tripartie des Indo-Européens*. Bruxelles: Latomus, 1958.

———. *The Destiny of the Warrior*. Translated by Alf Hiltebeitel. Chicago: University of Chicago Press, 1970.

Durkheim Émile. *The Elementary Forms of Religious Life*. New York: Free Press, 1995.

Durrant, Stephen W. *The Cloudy Mirror: Tension and Conflict in the Writings of Sima Qian*. Albany: SUNY Press, 1995.

Durrant, Stephen, Wao-Yee Li, Michael Nylan, and Hans Van Ess. *The Letter to Ren An & Sima Qian's Legacy*. Seattle and London: University of Washington Press, 2016.

Eberhard, Wolfram. "Review of Karlgren, *Legends and Cults*." *Artibus Asiae* 9 (1946): 355–64.

———. "The Political Function of Astronomy and Astronomers in Han China." In *Chinese Thought & Institution*, edited by J. F. Fairbank, 33–71. Chicago and London: University of Chicago Press, 1957.

Eck, Diane L. "Dialogue and Method: Reconstructing the Study of Religion." In *A Magic Still Dwells*, edited by K. C. Patton and B. C. Ray, 131–52. Berkeley: University of California Press, 2000.

Eder, Walter. "Augustus and the Power of Tradition." Translated by K. Galinsky. In *The Cambridge Companion to the Age of Augustus*, edited by Karl Galinsky. 13–32. Cambridge, UK: Cambridge University Press, 1995.

Eliade, Mircea. *The Sacred and the Profane: The Nature of Religion*. Translated by W. R. Trask. Orlando, FL: Harcourt, Inc., 1959.

———. *Shamanism: Archaic Techniques of Ecstasy*. London: Arcana, 1989.

Ellwood, Robert. *The Politics of Myth: A Study of C. G. Jung, Mircea Eliade, and Joseph Campbell*. Albany: SUNY Press, 1999.

Elman, Benjamin E. *A Cultural History of Civil Examinations in Late Imperial China.* Berkeley: University of California Press, 2000.

Eno, Robert. "Was There a High god Ti in Shang Religion?" *Early China* 15 (1990): 1–26.

———. *The Confucian Creation of Heaven: Philosophy and the Defense of Ritual Mastery.* Albany: SUNY Press, 1990.

———. "Deities and Ancestors in Early Oracle Inscriptions." In *Religions of China in Practice*, edited by. Donald S. Lopez, 41–51 (Princeton, NJ: Princeton University Press, 1996.

Erickson, Susan N. "Boshanlu: Mountain Censers of Western Han Period: A Typological and Iconological Analysis." *Archives of Asian Art* 45 (1992): 6–28.

Errington, Robert M. *Philopoemen.* Oxford, UK: Clarendon, 1969.

Ersking, Andrew. "Polybius among the Romans: Life in the Cyclops' Cave." In *Imperialism, Cultural Politics & Polybius*, edited by Christopher Smith and Liv Mariah Yarrow, 17–32. Oxford, UK: Oxford University Press, 2012,

———. "How to Rule the World: Polybius Book 6 Reconsidered." In *Polybius & His World: Essays in Memory of F. W. Walbank*, edited by Bruce Gibson and Thomas Harrison, 231–46. Oxford, UK: Oxford University Press, 2013.

Fabbrini, Fabrizio. *Maecenas. Il collezionismo nel mondo romano dall'età degli Scipioni a Cicerone.* Arezzo: Istituto di Storia Antica, 2001.

Feutchwang, Stephan. *Popular Religion in China: The Imperial Metaphor.* Richmond, UK: Curzon Press, 2001.

Fingarette, Herbert. *Confucius: The Sacred as Secular.* Prospect Heights, Illinois: Waveland Press, 1998.

Finley, Moses. *The Ancient Economy.* Berkeley: University of California Press, 1973.

Fishwick, Duncan. *The Imperial Cult in the Latin West: Studies in the Ruler Cult of the Western Provinces of the Roman Empire.* Leiden: Brill, 1991.

Fitzgerald, Timothy. "A Critique of 'Religion' as a Cross-cultural Category." *Method & Theory in the Study of Religion* 9, no. 2 (1997): 91–110.

———. *The Ideology of Religious Studies.* New York; Oxford, UK: Oxford University Press, 2000.

———. *Discourse on Civility and Barbarity: A Critical History of Religion and Related Categories.* Oxford, UK: Oxford University Press, 2007.

Forke, Alfred. *Lun-Hêng: Part I, Philosophical Essays of Wang Ch'ung; Part II, Miscellaneous Essays of Wang Ch'ung.* Leipzig: Harrassowitz; London: Luzac; Shanghai: Kelly and Walsh, 1907.

Foucault, Michel. *The Order of Things: An Archaeology of the Human Sciences.* Random House: New York, 1970.

Fox Brindley, Erica. *Individualism in Early China: Human Agency and the Self in Thought and Politics.* Honolulu: University of Hawai'i Press, 2010.

———. *Music Cosmology, and the Politics of Harmony in Early China.* Albany: SUNY Press, 2012.

Frankfort, Henri. *Kingship and the Gods: A Study of Ancient Near Eastern Religion as the Integration of Society and Nature.* Chicago: University of Chicago Press, 1948.

Frazer, James George. *The Golden Bough: A Study in Magic and Religion*, 12 vols. London: McMillan Press, 1906–15.

Fredrickson, George. *The Comparative Imagination: On the History of Racism, Nationalism, and Social Movements.* Berkeley: University of California Press, 1997.

Freedman, Maurice. "On the Sociological Study of Chinese Religion." In *Religion and Ritual in Chinese Society*, edited by Arthur P. Wolf, 19–42. Stanford, CA: Stanford University Press, 1974.

Freisen, Steven J. *Imperial Cults and the Apocalypse of John: Reading Revelation in the Ruins.* Oxford, UK: Oxford University Press, 2001.

Fu, Sinian, 傅斯年. *Mengzhen ziansheng ji* 傅孟真先生集. Taipei: Taiwan National University, 1952.

Fujikawa, Masakazu 藤川正數. *Kandai ni okeru reigaku no kenkyû* 漢代における礼学の研究. Tokyo: Kazama Shobō, 1968.

Fukui, Shigemasa 福井重雅. *Kandai Jukyō no shiteki kenkyū* 漢代儒教の史的研究. Tokyo: Kyūko Shoin, 2005.

———. "Tō Chūjo no kenkyū" 董仲舒の研究, in *Kandai Jukyō no shiteki kenkyū: Jukyō no kangakuka o meguru teisetsu no saikentō* 漢代儒教の史的研究: 儒教の官學化をめぐる定說の再檢討. Tokyo: Kyūko Shoin, 2005, 361–86.

Fukuyama, Francis. *The End of History and the Last Man.* New York: Free Press, 1992.

———. "Confucianism and Democracy." *Journal of Democracy* 6, no. 2 (1995): 20–33.

Fung, Yu-lan. *A Brief History of Chinese Philosophy.* New York: The Free Press, 1948, 1–15.

———. *A History of Chinese Philosophy*, 2 vols. Princeton, NJ: Princeton University Press, 1953.

Fustel de Coulanges, Numa Denis. *Polybe ou la Grèce conquise par les Romains.* PhD diss., Faculté des Lettres de Paris, 1858.

Galinsky, Karl. *Augustan Culture: An Interpretive Introduction.* Princeton, NJ: Princeton University Press, 1996.

Galvany Albert. "Beyond the Rule of Rules: The Foundations of Sovereign Power in the *Hanfei zi*." In *Dao Companion to the Philosophy of Han Fei*, edited by Paul R. Goldin, 87–106. New York: Springer, 2013.

Gan, Chunsong, and Yichun Zhou. "The Religious Nature of Confucianism in Contemporary China's 'Cultural Renaissance Movement.'" *Contemporary Chinese Thought* 44, 2 (2012): 3–15.

Gardner, Daniel. *Zhu Xi's Reading of the Analects: Canon, Commentary and the Classical Tradition.* New York: Columbia University Press, 2003.

Geaney, Jane. *On the Epistemology of the Senses in Early Chinese Thought.* Honolulu: Hawai'i University Press, 2002.

Geertz, Clifford. "Religion as a Cultural System." In *The Interpretation of Cultures*. Idem, 87–125. New York: Basic Books, 1973.

Gentile, Emilio. *God's Democracy: American Religion after September 11*. Westport, CT: Praeger, 2008.

Gentz, Joachim. "The Ritual Meaning of Textual Form: Evidence from Early Commentaries of the Historiographic and Ritual Traditions." In *Text and Ritual in Early China*, edited by Martin Kern, 125–48. Seattle: University of Washington Press, 2005.

———. "Language of Heaven, Exegetical Skepticism, and the Re-Insertion of Religious Concepts in the Gongyang Tradition." In *Early Chinese Religion*, 2, edited by John Lagerwey and Mark Kalinowski, 813–38. Leiden: Brill, 2009.

Gernet Jacques. *Chine et christianisme*. Paris: Gallimard, 1982.

Girardot Norman J. *Myth and Meaning in Early Taoism*. Berkeley: University of California Press, 1983.

———. *The Victorian Translation of China: James Legge's Oriental Pilgrimage*. Berkeley: University of California Press, 2002.

Goldin, Paul R., ed. *The Culture of Sex in Ancient China*. Honolulu: Hawai'i University Press, 2002.

———. *Dao Companion to the Philosophy of Han Fei*. New York: Springer, 2013.

Gombrich, Ernst H. "Personification." In *Classical Influences on European Culture AD 500–1500*, edited by R. R. Bolgar, 247–57. Cambridge, UK: Cambridge University Press, 1971.

Goossaert, Vincent. "1898: The Beginning of the End for Chinese Religion?" *The Journal of Asian Studies* 65, no. 2 (May 2006): 320–24.

Goossaert, Vincent, and David A. Palmer. *The Religious Question in Modern China*. Chicago: University of Chicago Press, 2011.

Gordon White, David. *Myths of the Dog-Man*. Chicago: University of Chicago Press, 1991.

Gradel, Ittai. *Emperor Worship and Roman Religion*, Oxford, UK: Oxford University Press, 2002.

Graham, Angus C. *Disputers of the Tao: Philosophical Argument in Ancient China*. Chicago: Open Court, 1989.

Gramsci, Antonio. *Quaderni del carcere*, 4 vols. Torino: Einaudi, 1975.

Granet, Marcel. *Dances et légendes de la Chine ancienne*, 2 vols. Paris: Musée Guimet, 1926.

Griffin, Jasper. "Augustan Poetry and Augustanism." In *The Cambridge Companion to the Age of Augustus*, edited by K. Galinsky, 306–39. Berkeley: University of California Press, 1990.

Gruen, Eric S. *Culture and National Identity in Republican Rome*. Ithaca, NY: Cornell University Press, 1992.

———. "Augustus and the Making of the Principate." In *The Cambridge Companion to the Age of Augustus*, edited by K. Galinsky 33–51. Cambridge, UK: Cambridge University Press, 1995.

———. *Diaspora: Jews amidst Greeks and Romans*. Cambridge, MA: Harvard University Press, 2004.

———. *Rethinking the Other in Antiquity*. Princeton, NJ: Princeton University Press, 2011.

———. "Polybius and Josephus on Rome." In *Polybius & His World: Essays in Memory of F. W. Walbank*, edited by Bruce Gibson and Thomas Harrison, 255–65. Oxford, UK: Oxford University Press, 2013.

Gu, Jiegang 顾颉刚. *Gu shi bian* 古史辩, 6 vols. Shanghai: Shanghai Guji: 1926–41.

———. *Shilin zashi chubian* 史林雜識初编. Beijing: Zhinghua shuju, 1963.

———. *Qin Han de fangshi yu rusheng* 秦汉的方士与儒生. Shanghai: Shanghai Guji Chubanshe, 1978.

Gu, Yanwu 顧炎武. *Rizhilü jishi* 日知録 集釋. Changsha: Yuelu shushe, 1994.

Guo, Jue. "Concepts of Death and the Afterlife Reflected in Newly Discovered Tomb Objects and Texts from Han China." In *Mortality in Traditional Chinese Thought*, edited by Amy Olberding and Philip J. Ivanhoe, 85–115. Albany: SUNY Press, 2011.

Guy, Basil. *The French image of China before and after Voltaire*. (Geneve: Institut et Musée Voltaire, 1963.

Hall, David L. and Roger T. Ames. *Thinking through Confucius*. Albany: SUNY Press, 1987.

———. *Anticipating China: Thinking through the Narratives of Chinese and Western Culture*. Albany: SUNY Press, 1995.

———. *Thinking from the Han: Self, Truth, and Transcendence in Chinese and Western Culture*. Albany: SUNY Press, 1998.

———. "*Tian* and *Dao* as Nontranscendent Fields." in *Thinking from the Han: Self, Truth, and Transcendence in Chinese and Western Culture*, 219–253. Albany: SUNY Press, 1998.

———. *The Democracy of the Dead: Dewey, Confucius, and the Hope for Democracy in China*. Chicago: Open Court, 1999.

Han, Zhaoqi 韩兆琦. *Shiji tiping* 史记题评. Xi'an: Shaanxi Renmin Chubanshe, 2000.

Hao, Chang. *Chinese Intellectuals in Crisis: Search for Order and Meaning (1890–1911)*. Berkeley: University of California Press, 1987.

Hardy, Grant. *Worlds of Bronze and Bamboo: Sima Qian's Conquest of History*. New York: Columbia University Press: 1999.

Harper, Donald. "Warring States Natural Philosophy and Occult Thought." In *The Cambridge History of Early China: From the Origins to 221 B.C.*, edited by Michael Loewe and Edward L. Shaughnessy, 813–84. Cambridge, UK: Cambridge University Press, 1999.

Harris, Sam. *The End of Faith: Religion, Terror, and the Future of Reason*. New York: Norton, 2005.
Hartog, François. *The Hellenistic World and the Coming of Rome*. Berkeley: University of California Press, 1985.
———. *The Mirror of Herodotus: The Representation of the Other in the Writing of History*. Berkeley: University of California Press, 1988.
Havelock, Erick E. *The Literate Revolution in Greece and its Cultural Consequences* Princeton, NJ: Princeton University Press, 1981.
———. *The Muse Learns to Write: Reflections on Orality and Literacy from Antiquity to the Present*. New Haven, CT: Yale University Press, 1986.
He, Pingli 何平立. *Xunshou yu feng shan—Fengjian zhengzhi de wenhua guiji* 巡狩与封禅—封建政治文化轨迹. Jinan: Qi Lu Shushe, 2003.
Henderson, John B. *The Construction of Orthodoxy and Heresy: Neo-Confucian, Jewish and Early Christian Patterns*. Albany: SUNY Press, 1998.
Hon, Tze-Ki. "Ethnic and Cultural Pluralism: Gu Jiegang's Vision of a New China in His Studies of Ancient History." *Modern China* 22, no. 3 (July 1996): 315–39.
Hopkins, Keith. *Conquerors and Slaves: Urbanization in Developing Countries*. Cambridge, UK: Cambridge University Press, 1981.
Horden, Peregrine, and Nicholas Purcell. *The Corrupting Sea: A Study of Mediterranean History*. London: Blackwell, 2000.
Hsu, Cho-Yun. "The Changing Relationship between Local Society and the Central Political Power in Former Han: 206 B.C.–8 A.D." *Comparative Studies in Society and History*, 7 no. 4 (Jul. 1965): 358–70.
Huang, Hui 黃暉. *Lun Heng jiaoshi* 論衡校釋. Beijing: Zhonghua shuju, 1990.
Huang, Jinxing 黃進興. "Zuowei zongjiao de Rujiao—yige bijiao zongjiao de chubu taolun" 作為宗教的儒教：一個比較宗教的初步討論, *Yazhou yanjiu* (July 1997): 184–223.
Hulsewé, Paul. *Remnants of Ch'in Law: An Annotated Translation of the Ch'in Legal and Administrative Rules of the 3rd Century BC*. Leiden: Brill, 1985.
———. "Shih chi." In *Early Chinese Texts*, edited by Michael Loewe, 405–14. Berkeley, CA: The Institute of East Asian Studies, 1993.
Hunt, David. "Christianising the Roman Empire: The Evidence of the Code." In *The Theodosian Code*, edited by Jill Harries and Ian Wood, 143–58. Ithaca, NY: Cornell University Press, 1993),
Huntington, Samuel P. *The Clash of Civilizations and the Remaking of World* Order. New York: Simon & Schuster, 1996.
Hurowitz, V. A. B. "Finding New Life in Old Words: World Play in the *Gilgames* Epic." In *Gilgames and the World of Assyria: Proceedings of the Conference Held at Mandelbaum House, The University of Sidney, 21–23 July 2004*, edited by J. J. Azize and N. K. Weeks, 67–78. Leuven: Peeters, 2007.
Hymes, Robert. *Way and Byway: Taoism, Local Religion, and Models of Divinity in Sung and Modern China*. Berkeley: University of California Press, 2002.

Iggers, Georg G., Q. Edward Wang, and Supriya Mukherjee, editors. *A Global History of Modern Historiography*. London: Pearson, 2008.

Ing, Michael David Kaulana, *The Dysfunction of Ritual in Early Confucianism*. Oxford, UK: Oxford University Press, 2012.

Isomae, Jun'ichi. "Deconstructing Japanese Religion—A Historical Survey." *Japanese Journal of Religious Studies* 32, no. 2 (2005): 235–48.

Itano, Chôhachi 板野長八. *Chūgoku kodai ni okeru ningenkan no tenkai* 中国古代における人間観の展開. Tokyo: Iwanami Shoten, Shōwa, 1972.

James, Liz. "Good Luck and Good Fortune to the Queen Cities: Empresses and Tyches in Byzantium." In *Personification in the Greek World: From Antiquity to Byzantium*, edited by Emma Stafford and Judith Herrin. 293–305. Aldershot, UK: Ashgate Publishing, 2005.

Jaspers, Karl. *Way to Wisdom: An Introduction to Philosophy*. New Haven, CT, Yale University Press, 1951.

———. *The Origin and Goal of History*. London: Routledge and Keegan, 1953.

Jay, Martin. *Downcast Eyes: The Denigration of Vision in Twentieth-Century France*. Berkeley: University of California Press, 1993.

Johnson, David. "Remarks presented at the symposium convened in conjunction with the first annual Tanner Lectures." University of California, Berkeley, May 5, 1988.

———. "Communication, Class, and Consciousness in Late Imperial China." In *Popular Culture in Late Imperial China*, edited by David G. Johnson, Andrew J. Nathan, and Evelyn S. Rawski, 34–73. Berkeley, University of California Press, 1985.

———, ed. *Ritual Opera, Operatic Ritual: Mu-lien Rescues His Mother in Chinese Popular Culture*. Berkeley: University of California Press, 1989.

Jones, Christian P. "ἔθνος and γένος in Herodotus." *CQ* 46 (1996): 315–20.

———. *Between Pagan and Christian*. Cambridge, MA: Harvard University Press, 2014).

Josephson, Jason Ānanda. *The Invention of Religion in Japan*. Chicago: University of Chicago Press, 2012.

Kallet-Marx, Robert. *Hegemony to Empire: The Development of the Roman Imperium in the East from 148 to 62 B.C.* Berkeley: University of California Press, 1995.

Karl, Rebecca E. et al. *Rethinking the 1898 Reform Period: Political and Cultural Change in Late Qing China*. Cambridge, MA: Harvard University Press, 2002.

Karlgren, Bernhard. "Legends and cults in ancient China." *Bulletin of the Museum of Far Eastern Antiquities* 18 (1946): 199–365.

Keightley, David N. "Archaeology and Mentality: The Making of China." *Representations* 18 (Spring 1987): 191–97.

Kern, Martin (Ke, Mading 柯馬丁). "Shiji li de 'zuozhe' gainian" 《史記》裡的「作者」概念, in *Shiji xue yu shijie hanxue lunji xubian* 史記學與世界漢學論集續, edited by Martin Kern and Lee Chi-hsiang 李紀祥, 23–61. Taipei: Tangshan chubanshe/Tonsan Publications, 2016.

Kern, Martin. "A Note on the Authenticity and ideology of Shih-chi 24, 'Yueshu.'" *Journal of the American Oriental Society* 119, 4 (1999): 673–77.

———. "Religious Anxiety and Political Interest in Western Han Omen Interpretation: The Case of the Han Wudi Period (141–87 BC)." *Chûgoku shigaku* 10 (2000): 1–31.

———. "Western Han Aesthetics and the Genesis of the *Fu*." *Harvard Journal of Asiatic Studies* 63 (2003): 383–437.

———, ed. *Text and Ritual in Early China*. Seattle: University of Washington Press, 2005.

———. "Tropes of Music and Poetry: From Wudi (r. 141–87 BCE) to ca. 100 CE." In *China's Early Empires: China's Early Empires—A Re-Appraisal*, edited by M. Nylan and M. Loewe, 480–91. Cambridge, UK: Cambridge University Press, 2010.

Kertzer, David I. *Ritual, Politics and Power*. New Haven, CT, and London: Yale University Press, 1988.

Kim, Hyun Jin. *Ethnicity and Foreigners in Ancient Greece and China*. London: Duckworth, 2009.

Kirk, G. S. *Myth: Its Meaning and Functions in Ancient and Other Cultures*. Cambridge, UK: Cambridge University Press, 1970.

Klein, Esther Sunkyung. "The History of a Historian: Perspectives on the Authorial Roles of Sima Qian." PhD diss., Princeton University, 2010.

Kleiner, Diana E. E. "Semblance and Storytelling in Augustan Rome." In *The Cambridge Companion to the Age of Augustus*, edited by K. Galinsky, 197–233. Berkeley: University of California Press, 1990.

Kline, T. C. III, and Philip J. Ivanhoe. *Virtue, Nature, and Moral Agency in the Xunzi*. Indianapolis, IN: Hackett Publishing, 2000.

Knechtges, David R., and Tong Xiao. *Wen Xuan or Selections of Refined Literature, Volume II: Rhapsodies on Sacrifices, Hunting, Travel, Sightseeing, Palaces and Halls, Rivers and Seas*. Princeton, NJ: Princeton University Press, 1987.

Knechtges, David R. *The Han Rhapsody: The Study of the* Fu *of Yang Hsiung (53 B.C.–A. D. 18)*. Cambridge, UK: Cambridge University Press, 1976.

———, (translation. and annotation). Wen Xuan *or Selections of Refined Literature*, Vol. I. Princeton, NJ: Princeton University Press, 1987.

———. "The Emperor and Literature: Emperor Wu of the Han." In *Imperial Rulership and Cultural Change in Traditional China*, edited by Frederick P. Brandauer and Chün-chieh Huang, 51–76. Seattle: University of Washington Press, 1994.

———. "'Key Words,' Authorial Intent, and Interpretation: Sima Qian's Letter to Ren An." *Chinese Literature: Essays, Articles, Reviews (CLEAR)* 30 (Dec. 2008): 75–84.

———. "Jia Yi 賈誼." In *Ancient and Early Medieval Chinese Literature: A Reference Guide, Part One*, edited by D. R. Knechtges, Taiping Chang, 417–28. Leiden: Brill, 2010.

Knoblock, John, and Jeffrey Riegel, trans. and eds. *The Annals of Lü Buwei: A Complete Translation and Study*. Stanford, CA: Stanford University Press, 2003.

Knoblock, John, trans. and ed. *Xunzi: A Translation and Study of the Complete Works*. Stanford, CA: Stanford University Press, 1988.

Kohn Livia. "Eternal Life in Taoist Mysticism." *Journal of the American Oriental Society* 110, no. 4 (Oct.–Dec. 1990): 622–40.

———. "Steal Holy Food and Come Back as a Viper: Conceptions of Karma and Rebirth in Medieval China." *Early Medieval China* 4 (1998): 1–48.

Koizumi, Takashi 小泉 仰 et al., eds. *Ningen to shūkyō: kidai no nihonjin no shūkyōkan* 人間と宗教: 近代日本人の宗教観. Tokyo: Tokyo Bunka, 1982.

Koo, Telly H. "The Constitutional Development of the Western Han Dynasty." *Journal of the American Oriental Society* 40 (1992): 170–93.

Koselleck, Reinhart. "The Need for Theory in History." In *The Practice of Conceptual History: Timing History, Spacing Concepts*, R. Koselleck, 1–19. Stanford, CA: Stanford University Press, 2002.

Kuhn, Adalbert. *Die Herabkunft des Feuers und Göttertranks*. Gütersloh: Bertelsmann, 1886.

Lagerwey, John, and Marc Kalinowski, editors. *Early Chinese Religion*. 2 vols. Leiden: Brill, 2009.

Lai, Guolong. *Excavating Afterlife: The Archaeology of Early Chinese Religion*. Seattle and London: University of Washington Press, 2015.

Lakoff, George, and Mark Johnson. *Metaphors We Live By*. Chicago: University of Chicago Press, 1980.

Lakoff, George. *Women, Fire, and Dangerous Things: What Categories Reveal about the Mind*. Chicago: University of Chicago Press, 1987.

Launay, Marcel, and Gérard Moussay et al. *Les missiones étrangère: Trois siècles et demi d'histoire et d'aventure en Asie*. Paris: Perrin, 2008.

Laurence, Ray. "Territory, Ethnonyms and Geography: The Construction of Identity in Roman Italy." In *Cultural Identity in the Roman Empire*, edited by Ray Laurence and Joanne Berry, 64–78. London: Routledge, 1998.

LeBlanc, Charles. "A Re-examination of the Myth of Huang ti." *Journal of Chinese Religions* 13–14 (1985–86): 45–63.

Legge, James, trans. *The Chinese Classics: with a Translation, Critical and Exegetical Notes, Prolegomena, and Copious Indexes*, 5 vols. Hong Kong: Trubner, 1861–1872.

———. trans. *The The Shû king*, vol. 3 of *The Sacred Books of the East*, edited by F. Max Müller. Oxford, UK: Clarendon Press, 1893.

Legge, James. *The Religions of China: Confucianism and Tâoism Described and Compared with Christianity*. London: Hodder and Stoughton, 1880.

———. *The Notions of the Chinese Concerning God and Spirits*. Hong Kong: H. K. Register Office, 1852.

Levi, Jean. *Les fonctionnaires divins: politique, despotisme et mystique en Chine ancienne*. Paris: La Librairie du XXe siecle, 1989.

Levi, Mario Attilio. "La critica di Polibio a Timeo." *Studi Alessandrini* 196 (1963): 195–202.
Lewis, Mark Edward. *Sanctioned Violence in Early China*. Albany: SUNY Press, 1990.
———. *Writing and Authority in Early China*. Albany: SUNY Press, 1999.
———. "The Feng and Shan Sacrifices of the Emperor Wu of the Han." In *State and Court Ritual in China*, edited by Joseph McDermott, 20–50. Cambridge, UK: University of Cambridge Press, 1999.
———. *The Construction of Space in Early China*. Albany: SUNY Press, 2006.
———. *The Flood Myths of Early China*. Albany: SUNY Press, 2006.
———. "The Mythology of Early China." In *Early Chinese Religion*, 2 vols., edited by John Lagerwey and Marc Kalinowski, 543–94. Leiden: Brill, 2009.
Li, Changzhi 李長之. *Sima Qian de renge yu fengge* 司馬遷的人格與風格. Shanghai: Kaiming shudian, 1948, reprint Hong Kong: Taiping, 1963.
Li Feng. *Landscape and Power in Early China: The Crisis and the Fall of the Western Zhou 1045–771 BC*. Cambridge, UK, Cambridge University Press, 2006.
———. *Bureaucracy and the State in Early China: Governing the Western Zhou*. Cambridge, UK: Cambridge University Press, 2008.
———. *Early China: A Social and Cultural History*. Cambridge, UK: Cambridge University Press, 2013.
Li, Ling. "An Archaeological Study of Taiyi 太一 (Grand One) Worship." *Early Medieval China* 2 (1995–1996): 1–8.
Li, Wai-yee. "The Idea of Authority in the *Shih Chi* (Records of the Historian)." *Harvard Journal of Asiatic Studies* 54, 2 (Dec. 1994): 345–405.
———. *The Readability of the Past in Early Chinese Historiography*. Cambridge and London: Harvard University Press, 2007.
Li, Xueqin 李學勤. *Zouchu Yigu shidai* 走出疑古時代. Shenyang: Changchun chubanshe, 1997.
———. "Taiyi sheng shui de shushu jieshi" 太一生水的數術解釋, *Daojia wenhua yanjiu* 17 (1999): 297–300.
Liang, Cai. *Witchcraft and the Rise of the First Confucian Empire*. Albany: SUNY Press, 2013.
———. "The Hermeneutics of Omens: The Bankruptcy of Moral Cosmology in the Western Han China (206 BCE–8 CE)." *The Journal of the Royal Asiatic Society* 3 (April 2015): 1–21.
Lin, Fushi 林富士. *Handai de wuzhe* 漢代的巫者. Taibei: Taiwan Daoxiang Chubanshe, 1999.
Lincoln, Bruce. *Theorizing Myth: Narrative, Ideology, and Scholarship*. Chicago: University of Chicago Press, 1999.
———. *Holy Terrors: Thinking about Religion after September 11*. Chicago: University of Chicago Press, 2005.

———. *Gods and Demons, Priests and Scholars: Critical Explorations in the History of Religions*. Chicago: University of Chicago Press, 2012.

Linderski, Gerzy. "The Augural Law." *Aufstieg und Niedergang der römischen Welt* II.16.3 (1986): 2146–312.

Littleton, Scott. *The New Comparative Mythology: An Anthropological Assessment of the Theories of Georges Dumézil*. Berkeley: University of California Press, 1973.

Liu, James T. C. "How Did a Neo-Confucian School Become the State Orthodoxy?" *Philosophy East and West* 23, 4 (October 1973): 483–506.

Liu, Lidia H. *The Clash of Empires: The Invention of China in Modern World Making*. Cambridge, MA: Harvard University Press, 2004.

Liu, Xinru. "The Science of Difference: Race, Indo-European Linguistics, and Eurasian Nomads." In *A Companion in World History*, edited by D. Northrop, 245–57. Hoboken, NJ: Wiley Blackwell, 2012.

Loewe, Michael. "The Fall of the House of Huo." In *Crisis and Conflict in Han China*, idem, 116–55. London: Allen & Unwin, 1974.

———. "K'uang Heng and the Reform of Religious Practices (31 B.C.)." *Asia Major* 17, no. 1 part 2 (1988): 1–27.

———. "Imperial Sovereignty: Tung Chung-shu's Contribution and His Predecessors." In *Divination, Mythology, and Monarchy Han China*, idem, 131–33. Cambridge, UK: University of Cambridge Press, 1994.

———. "The Authority of the Emperors of Ch'in and Han." In *Divination, Mythology, and Monarchy in Han China*, idem, 85–112. Cambridge, UK: University of Cambridge Press, 1994.

———. *Divination, Mythology, and Monarchy in Han China*. Cambridge, UK: University of Cambridge Press, 1994.

———, ed. "The Grand Beginning—104 BC." In *Crisis and Conflict in Han China*, idem, 17–36. London: Allen & Unwin, 1974.

———. *Early Chinese Texts*. Berkeley, CA: The Institute of East Asian Studies, 1993.

———. "Yen t'ieh lun 鹽鐵論." In *Early Chinese Texts*, edited by M. Loewe, 477–82. Berkeley: The Institute of East Asian Studies, 1993.

———. "The Oracles of the Clouds and of the Winds." *Divination, Mythology, and Monarchy in Han China*, idem, 191–213. Cambridge, UK: Cambridge University Press, 1994.

———. "Water Earth, and Fire: The Symbols of the Han Dynasty." In *Divination, Mythology, and Monarchy in Han China*, idem, 57–60. Cambridge, UK: Cambridge University Press, 1994.

———. *A Bibliographical Dictionary of the Qin, Former Han & Xin Periods (221 BC–AD 24)*. Leiden: Brill, 2000.

———. "On the Terms *bao zi, yin gong, yin guan, huan*, and *shou*: Was Zhao Gao a Eunuch?" *T'oung Pao* 91, 4/5 (2005): 301–19.

———. *The Government of the Qin and Han Empires, 221 BCE–220 CE*. Indianapolis, IN: Hackett, 2006.

———. "'Confucian' Values and Practices in Han China." *T'oung Pao*, 98, 1/3 (2012): 25–30.

———. *Dong Zhongshu: A "Confucian" Heritage and the* Chunqiu fanlu. Leiden: Brill, 2011.

———. *Problems of Han Administration: Ancestral Rites, Weights and Measures, and the Means of Protest*. Leiden: Brill, 2016.

Luo, Guanzhong 羅貫中. *Three Kingdoms*, 3 vols., translated by Moss Roberts. Beijing: Foreign Languages Press, 2008.

Luo, Shaodan. "The *Xinshu* 新書 Reexamined: An Emphasis on Usability over Authenticity." *Chinese Studies* 2, no. 1 (2013): 8–24.

Machiavelli, Niccolò. *Discorsi sopra la prima deca di Tito Livio*. Torino: UTET, 1999.

MacMullen, Ramsay. *Paganism in the Roman Empire*. New Haven, CT: Yale University Press, 1981.

Major, John S. *Heaven and Earth in Early Han Thought*. Albany: SUNY Press, 1991.

Malinowski, Bronisław. *Myth in Primitive Psychology*. London: Norton, 1926.

———. *Magic, Science, and Religion, and Other Essays*. Garden City: Doubleday Anchor Books, 1948.

Marsili, Filippo. "The Ghosts of Monotheism: Heaven, Fortune, and Universalism in Early Chinese and Greco-Roman Historiography." *Fragments* 3 (2013–2014): 43–77.

Maspéro, Henri. "Légendes mythologiques dans le Chou King." *Journal Asiatique* 204 (1924): 11–100.

———. "Le Ming-T'ang et la crise religeuse chinoise avant les Han." *Mélanges Chinois et Bouddhiques* 9 (1951): 1–71.

Masuzawa, Tomoko. *The Invention of World Religions: Or, How European Universalism Was Preserved in the Language of Pluralism*. Chicago: University of Chicago Press, 2005.

Mathieu, Rémi. *Anthologie des mythes et légendes de la Chine ancienne: Textes choisis, présentés, traduits et indexés*. Paris: Gallimard, 1989.

Meguro, Kyōko 目黒杏子. "Kandai kokka saishi seido kenkyū no genjō to kadai—kōtei kenryoku to uchūron no shiten kara 漢代国家祭祀制度研究の現状と課題——皇帝権力と宇宙論の視點から." *Chūgoku Shigaku* 15 (2005): 103–19.

Millar, Fergus. *The Crowd in Rome in the Late Republic*. Ann Arbor: University of Michigan Press, 1998.

Miller, Harry. *The Gongyang Commentary on The Spring and Autumn Annals: A Full Translation*. Basingstoke, UK: Palgrave Macmillan; 2015.

Minamiki, George, SJ. *Chinese Rites Controversy from Its Beginning to Modern Times*. Chicago: Loyola Press, 1985.

Momigliano, Arnaldo. "Persian, Greek, and Jewish Historiography." In *The Classical Foundation of Modern Historiography*, idem, 5–28. Berkeley: University of California Press, 1990.

———. "The Herodotean and Thucydidean Tradition." In *The Classical Foundation of Modern Historiography*, idem, 29–53. Berkeley: University of California Press, 1990.

———. *Alien Wisdom: The Limit of Hellenization*. Cambridge, UK: Cambridge University Press, 1990.

Morgan, Teresa. *Roman Faith and Christian Faith*. New York: Oxford University Press, 2015.

Mungello, David E., ed. *The Chinese Rites Controversy: Its History and Meaning*. Chicago: Loyola Press, 2005.

Musti, Domenico. *Polibio e l'imperialismo romano*. Napoli: Liguori Editore, 1978.

Mutschler, Fritz-Heiner, and Achim Mittag. *Conceiving the Empire: China and Rome Compared*. Oxford, UK: Oxford University Press, 2009.

Nedostup, Rebecca. *Superstitious Regimes: Religion and the Politics of Chinese Modernity*. Cambridge, MA: Harvard University Press, 2009.

Nicolet, Jules. "Polybe et les institutions romaines." In *Entretiens sur l'Antiquité Classique de la Fondation Hardt*, idem, 209–65. Genève: Vandoeuvres, 1974.

Nienhauser, William H. Jr., ed. and trans., Tsai-fa Cheng et al., trans. *The Grand Scribe's Records*, 6 vols. Bloomington: University of Indiana Press, 1992.

Nishijima, Sadao. "The Economic and Social History of Former Han." In *The Cambridge History of China: Volume I: the Ch'in and Han Empires, 221 B.C.–A.D. 220*, edited by Denis Twitchett and Michael Loewe, 545–607. Cambridge, UK: Cambridge University Press, 1986.

Nongbri, Brent. *Before Religion: A History of a Modern Concept*. New Haven, CT: Yale University Press, 2013.

Noreña, Carlos F. *Imperial Ideals in the Roman West: Representation, Circulation, Power*. Cambridge, UK: Cambridge University Press, 2011.

Northrop, Douglas. "The Challenge of World History." in *A Companion in World History*, edited by D. Northrop, 4–5. Hoboken, NJ: Wiley Blackwell, 2012.

Nylan, Michael, and Griet Vankeerberghen, eds. *Chang'an 26 BC: An Augustan Age in China*. Seattle and London: Washington University Press, 2015.

Nylan, Michael. *The Shifting Center: The Original "Great Plan" and Later Readings*. Nettetal, Germany: Steyler Verlag, 1992.

———. "Sima Qian: A True Historian?" *Early China* 23–24 (1998–1999): 203–46.

———. "A Problematic Model: The 'Han Orthodox Synthesis,' Then and Now." In *Imagining Boundaries: Changing Confucian Doctrines, Texts, and Hermeneutics*, edited by Kai-Wing Chow, On-cho Ng, and John B. Henderson, 17–56. Albany: SUNY Press, 1999.

———. "Towards an Archaeology of Writing: Text, Ritual and the Culture of Public Display in the Classical Period (475 BCE–220 CE)." In *Text and Ritual in Early China*, edited by Martin Kern, 3–50. Seattle: University of Washington Press, 2005.

———. "The art of persuasion from 100 BCE to 100 CE." In *China's Early Empires: A Reappraisal*, edited by M. Nylan, M. Loewe, 492–504. Cambridge, UK: Cambridge University Press, 2010.

———. "Yin-yang, Five Phases, and Qi." In *China's Early Empires—A Re-Appraisal*, edited by M. Nylan and M. Loewe, 411–13. Cambridge, UK: Cambridge University Press, 2010.

———. *Exemplary Figures—'Fa Yan'* 法言. Seattle: University of Washington Press, 2013.

———, trans. "The *Chin wen/Gu wen* Controversy in Han Times." *T'oung Pao* 80, 1–13 (1994): 83–145.

———. *The Five "Confucian" Classics*. New Haven, CT: Yale University Press, 2001.

Olberding, Garret P. S. *Dubious Facts: The Evidence of Early Chinese Historiography*. Albany: SUNY, 2012.

———, ed. *Facing the Monarch: Modes of Advice in the Early Chinese Court*. Cambridge, MA: Harvard University Press, 2013.

Oguchi, Iichi 小口 偉一 and Hori Ichirō 堀 一郎, eds. *Shūkyō gaku jiten* 宗教学字典. Tokyo: Tokyo Daigaku shuppankai, 1973.

Onfray, Michel. *Atheist Manifesto: The Case against Christianity, Judaism, and Islam*. New York: Arcade Publishing, 2011.

Overmyer, David et al. "Chinese Religions, The State of the Field, Part II—Living Religious Traditions: Taoism, Confucianism, Buddhism, Islam and Popular Religion." *Journal of Asian Studies* 42, no. 2 (1995): 314–21.

Overmyer, David, and David N. Keightley, et al., "Chinese Religions: The State of the Field, Part I. Early Religious Traditions: The Neolithic Period through the Han Dynasty." *The Journal of Asian Studies* 54, no. 1 (Feb. 1995): 124–60.

Owen, Stephen. *The Making of Early Chinese Classical Poetry*. Cambridge, MA, Harvard University Press, 2006.

Paden, William E. *Religious Worlds: The Comparative Study of Religion*. Boston: Beacon Press, 1988.

———. "Elements of a New Comparativism." in *A Magic Still Dwells*, edited by K. C. Patton and B. C. Ray, 82–92. Berkeley: University of California Press, 2000.

Pandey, Nandini B. "Caesar's Comet, the Julian Star, and the Invention of Augustus." *Transactions of the American Philological Association* 143, 2 (September 2013): 405–49.

Pankanier, David W. "On the Reliability of Han Dynasty (206 BCE–220 CE) Solar Eclipse Records." *The Journal of Astronomical History and Heritage* 15.3 (2012): 200–12.

———. *Astrology and Cosmology in Early China: Conforming Earth to Heaven*. Cambridge, UK: Cambridge University Press, 2013.

———. "The *Huainanzi*'s 'Heavenly Patterns' and the *Shiji*'s 'Treatise on the Celestial Offices': What's the Difference?" In *The* Huainanzi *and Textual Production in*

Early China, edited by Sarah H Queen and Michael Puett, 199–224. Leiden: Brill, 2014.

Paper Jordan. *The Spirits are Drunk: Comparative Approaches to Chinese Religion.* Albany: SUNY Press, 1995.

Patton, Kimberley C., and Benjamin C. Ray, eds. *A Magic still Dwells: Comparative Religion in the Postmodern Age.* Berkeley: University of California Press, 2000.

Patton, Laurie L. "The Magic in Miniature: Etymological Links in Comparative Religions." In *A Magic Still Dwells*, edited by K. C. Patton and B. C. Ray, 193–205. Berkeley: University of California Press, 2000.

Pédech, Paul. *Le méthode historique de Polybe.* Paris: Université de Paris, 1964.

Peerenboom, Randal P. *Law and Morality in Ancient China: The Silk Manuscripts of Huang-Lao.* Albany: SUNY Press, 1993.

Petersen, Jens Østergård. "Which books did the First Emperor of Ch'in burn?—on the meaning of *Pai chia* in early Chinese sources." *Monumenta Serica* 43 (1995): 1–52.

Peterson, Willard J. "Making Connections: 'Commentary on the Attached Verbalization' of the *Book of Changes.*" *Harvard Journal of Asiatic Studies* 42, 1 (June 1982): 67–116.

Pfister, Lauren F. *Striving for 'The Whole Duty of Man': James Legge and the Scottish Protestant Encounter with China*, 2 vols. Mainz: The Scottish Studies Centre of the Johannes Gutenberg Universität, 2004.

Pharr, Clyde, translator. *The Theodosian Code.* Princeton, NJ: Princeton University Press, 1952.

Pines, Y. L. Von Falkenhausen, G. Shelach, and R. D. S. Yates, eds. *Birth of an Empire: The State of Qin Revisited.* Berkeley: University of California Press, 2014.

Pines, Yuri L. "Disputers of the *Li*: Breakthroughs in the Concept of Ritual in Preimperial China." *Asia Major* 13 no. 1 (2000): 1–41.

———. "From Teachers to Subjects: 'Ministers Speaking to the Rulers, from Yan Ying 晏嬰 to Li Si 李斯.'" In *Facing the Monarch: Modes of Advice in the Early Chinese.* Cambridge, MA: Harvard University Press, 2013, edited by Garret P. S. Olberlding. 69–80.

———. "Submerged by Absolute Power: The Rulers Predicament." In *Dao Companion to the Philosophy of Han Fei*, edited by Paul R. Goldin, 67–86. New York: Springer, 2013.

———. "Dating a Pre-Imperial Text: The Case Study of the *Book of Lord Shang*," *Early China*, Available on CJO 2016 doi:10.1017/eac.2016.3.

Plutarch. *Moralia*, Vol. 5. Translated by Harold North Fowler. Oxford, UK: Loeb Classical Library, 1936.

Pokora Timoteus, and Michael Loewe. "*Lun heng* 論衡." In *Early Chinese Texts*, edited by M. Loewe, 309–12. Berkeley, CA: The Society for the Study of Early China, 1993.

Pollini, John. "Man or God: Divine Assimilation and Imitation." In *Between Republic and Empire*, edited by K. A. Raaflaub and M. Toher, 333–63. Berkeley: University of California Press, 1990.
Pollitt, J. J. *Art in the Hellenistic Age*. Cambridge, UK: Cambridge University Press, 1986.
Polybius. *Histories*, 6 vols. Translated by W. R. Paton, revised by F. W. Walbank and C. Habicht. Cambridge, MA: Loeb Classics, Harvard University Press; Revised edition, 2010.
Poo, Mu-chou. *In Search of Personal Welfare: A View of Ancient Chinese Religion*. Albany: SUNY Press, 1998.
———. *Enemies of Civilization: Attitudes toward Foreigners in Ancient Mesopotamia, Egypt, and China*. Albany: SUNY Press, 2005.
Price, Simon R. F. *Ritual and Power: The Roman Imperial Cult in Asia Minor*. Cambridge, UK: Cambridge University Press, 1985.
Psarras, Sophia-Karin. "Han and Xiongnu: A Reexamination of Cultural and Political Relations." *Monumenta Serica* 51 (2003): 55–236.
Puett, Michael J. *The Ambivalence of Creation: Debates Concerning Innovation and Artifice in Early China*. Stanford, CA: Stanford University Press, 2001.
———. *To Become a God: Cosmology, Sacrifice, and Self-Divinization in Early China*. Cambridge, MA: Harvard University Press, 2004.
———. "Following the Commands of Heaven: The Notion of *Ming* in Early China." In *The Magnitude of* Ming, edited by Michael Lupke, 46–69. Honolulu: University of Hawai'i Press, 2005.
———. "The Offering of Food and the Creation of Order: The Practice of Sacrifice in Early China." In *Of Tripod and Palate: Food, Politics and Religion in Traditional China*, edited by Roel Sterkx, 75–95. Basingstoke, UK: Palgrave MacMillan, 2005.
———. "Human and Divine Kingship in Early China: Comparative Reflections." In *Divine Kingship*, edited by Nicole Brisch, 207–20. Chicago: University of Chicago Press, 2008.
———. "Combining the Ghosts and Spirits, Centering the Realm." In *Early Chinese Religion*, edited by John Lagerwey and Marc Kalinowski, 695–720. Leiden: Brill, 2009.
———. "Ghosts, Gods, and the Coming of Apocalypse: Empire and Religion in Early China and Ancient Rome." In *State Power in Ancient China and Rome*, edited by W. Scheidel, 230–95. New York: Oxford University Press, 2015.
Qian, Baocong 錢寶琮. "Taiyi kao" 太一考. *Yanjing Xuebao* 12 (1932): 2449–478.
Qin, Bo 秦波, "Xi-Han huanghou yüxi he Ganlu ernian tongfanlou de faxian," 西漢皇后玉璽和甘露二年銅方爐的發現. *Wenwu* 5 (1973): 26–29.
Queen, Sarah A., and John S. Major, eds. and trans. *Luxuriant Gems of the Spring and Autumn (Attributed to Dong Zhongshu)*. New York: Columbia University Press, 2016.

Queen, Sarah A. *From Chronicle to Canon: The Hermeneutics of the Spring and Autumn according to Tung Chungshu*. Cambridge, UK: Cambridge University Press, 2005.

———. "Representations of Confucius in the *Huainanzi*." In *The* Huainanzi *and Textual Production in Early China*, edited by Sarah H Queen and Michael Puett, 83–123. Leiden: Brill, 2014.

Radcliffe-Brown, Alfred R. *Structure and Function in Primitive Society*. New York: The Free Press, 1965.

Raglan (Lord), F. R. R. S. *The Hero: A Study in Tradition, Myth, and Drama*. New York: Oxford University Press, 1937.

Ramage, E. S. "Augustus' Treatment of Julius Caesar." *Historia* 34 (1986): 223–45.

Rank, Otto. *The Myth and the Birth of the Hero*. New York: Random House, 1959 (first published in 1909 in German).

Raphals, Lisa. "Languages of Fate: Semantic Fields in Chinese and Greek." In *The Magnitude of* Ming, edited by Michael Lupke, 70–106. Honolulu: University of Hawai'i Press, 2005.

Rappaport, Roy. *Ritual and Religion in the Making of Humanity*. Cambridge, UK: Cambridge University Press, 1999.

Ray, Benjamin Caleb. "Discourse about Difference: Understanding African Ritual Language." In *A Magic Still Dwells*, edited by K. C. Patton and B. C. Ray, 101–16. Berkeley: University of California Press, 2000.

Ricci, Matteo. *The True Meaning of the Lord of Heaven: T'ien-chu shih-I*, translated, with introduction and notes, by Douglas Lancashire and Peter Hu Kuo-chen. Taipei: Institut Ricci, 1985.

Richardson, J. S. "Imperium Romanum: Empire and the Language of Power." *The Journal of Roman Studies* 81 (1991): 1–9.

Rickett, W. Allyn. *'Guanzi:' Political, Economic and Philosophical Essays from Early China—A Study and a Translation, Volume I, Revised Edition*. 3 vols. Boston: Cheng & Tsui. 2001.

Riegel, Jeffrey K. "Li chi 禮記." In *Early Chinese Texts*, edited by M. Loewe, 293–97. Berkeley, CA: The Institute of East Asian Studies, 1993.

Rives, James B. *Religion in the Roman Empire*. Malden, MA: Blackwell, 2007.

Robinet, Isabelle. *Taoism: Growth of a Religion*. Phyllis Brooks, translator. Stanford, CA: Stanford University Press, 1997 (first French edition in 1991).

Roetz, Heiner. *Confucian Ethics of the Axial Age: A Reconstruction under the Aspect of the Breakthrough toward Postconventional Thinking*. Albany: SUNY Press, 1993.

Romm, James. *The Edges of the Earth in Ancient Thought: Geography, Exploration, and Fiction*. Princeton, NJ: Princeton University Press, 1992.

Sabbatucci, Dario. *Divinazione e cosmologia*. Milano: Il Saggiatore, 1989.

———. *La prospettiva storico-religiosa: Fede, religione e cultura*. Milano: Il Saggiatore, 1990.

Said, Edward. *Orientalism*. New York: Random House, 1979.
Sanft, Charles. *Communication and Cooperation in Early Imperial China: Publicizing the Qin Dynasty*. Albany: SUNY, 2014.
Schaab-Hanke, Dorothee. "Did Chu Shaosun contribute to the tradition of the Scribe?" *Oriens Extremus* 44 (2003/04): 11–26.
Schaberg, David. "Command and the Content of Tradition." In *The Magnitude of Ming*, edited by C. Lupke, 23–26. Honolulu: University of Hawai'i Press, 2005.
Scheidel, Walter, ed. *Rome and China: Comparative Perspectives on Ancient World Empires*. New York: Oxford University Press, 2009.
———. *State Power in Ancient China and Rome*. New York: Oxford University Press, 2015.
Schipper, Kristofer Marinus. *L'Empereur Wou des Han dan la legend taoiste*. Paris: École française d'Extrême-Orient, 1965.
Schneider, Laurence A. *Ku Chieh-kang and China's New History: Nationalism and the Quest for Alternative Traditions*. Berkeley: University of California Press, 1971.
Schneider, Rolf Michael. "Image and Empire: The Shaping of Augustan Rome." In *Conceiving the Empire: China and Rome Compared*, edited by Fritz-Heiner Mutschler, and Achim Mittag, 269–98. Oxford, UK: Oxford University Press, 2009.
Schwartz, Benjamin J. *The World of Thought in Ancient China*. Cambridge MA: Belknap Press, 1985.
Seligman Adam B., Robert P. Weller, Michael J. Puett, and Simon Bennett. *Ritual and its Consequences: An Essay on the Limits of Sincerity*. Oxford, UK: Oxford University Press, 2008.
Seligman Adam B., and Robert P. Weller. *Rethinking Pluralism: Ritual Experience and Ambiguity*. Oxford, UK: Oxford University Press, 2012.
Sellmann, James D. *Timing and Rulership in Master Lü's Spring and Autumn Annals (Lüshi chunqiu)*. Albany: SUNY Press, 2002.
Selz, Gebhard J. "The Divine Prototypes." In *Religion and Power: Divine Kingship in the Ancient World and Beyond*, edited by N. Brisch, 13–32. Chicago: University of Chicago Press, 2008.
Sharf, Robert H. *Coming to Terms with Chinese Buddhism: A Reading of the Treasure Store Treatise*. Honolulu: University of Hawaii Press, 2002.
Sharpe, Erich J. *Comparative Religion: A History*. London: Duckworth, 1975.
Shaughnessy, Edward L. *Sources of Western Zhou History: Inscribed Bronze Vessels*. Berkeley: University of California Press, 1991.
———. "Western Zhou History." In *The Cambridge History of Early China: From the Origins to 221 B.C.*, edited by Michael Loewe and Edward L. Shaughnessy, 293–351. Cambridge, UK: Cambridge University Press, 1999.
Shima, Kunio 島邦男. *Inkyo bokuji kenkyū* 殷墟卜辞研究. Hirosaki: Chūkokugaku Kenkyūkai, 1958.
Sima, Qian 司馬遷. *Shiji* 史記. Beijing: Zhonghua shuju, 2005.

Sivin, Nathan. "On the Word 'Taoist' as a Source of Perplexity." *History of Religions* 17 (1978): 303–30.

———. "The Myth of the Naturalists." in *Medicine, Religion, and Philosophy in Ancient China*, Idem, 1–33. Aldershot, UK: Variorum, 1995.

———. "Old and New Daoisms." *Religious Studies Review* 39, 1 (2010): 31–50.

Smart, Ninian. *Dimensions of the Sacred: An Anatomy of the World's Beliefs*. Berkeley: University of California Press, 1996.

Smith, Gregory, and Jan Gadeyne, eds. *Perspectives on Public Space in Rome: From Antiquity to the Present Day.* New York: Ashgate, 2013.

Smith, Jonathan Z. *To Take Place: Toward Theory in Ritual*. Chicago: University of Chicago Press, 1987.

———. *Drudgery Divine: On the Comparison of Early Christianities and the Religions of Late Antiquity*. Chicago: University of Chicago Press, 1990.

———. *Map is not Territory: Studies in the History of Religions*. Chicago: University of Chicago Press, 1993.

———. "Religion, Religions, Religious." In *Relating Religion: Essays in the Study of Religion,* idem, 179–96. Chicago: University of Chicago Press, 2004.

———. *Relating Religion: Essays in the Study of Religion*. Chicago: University of Chicago Press, 2004.

Smith, Kidder. "Sima Tan and the Invention of Taoism, 'Legalism,' 'Et Cetera.'" *The Journal of Asian Studies* 62, no. 1 (2003): 129–56.

Som, Tjan Tjoe, trans. *'Po hu t'ung': The Comprehensive Discussions in the White Tiger Hall*. 2 vols. Leiden: Brill, 1949–1952.

Stafford, Emma. "Personification in Greek Religious Thought and Practice." In *A Companion to Greek Religion*, edited by Daniel Ogden, 71–86. Oxford, UK: Blackwell, 2007.

Standaert, Nicolas. *The Interweaving of Rituals: Funerals in the Cultural Exchange between China and Europe*. Seattle: University of Washington Press, 2008.

Sterkx, Roel. "Mozi 31: Explaining Ghosts, Again." In *The Mozi as an Evolving Text: Different Voices in Early Chinese Thought*, edited by Carine Defoort and Nicolas Standaert, 91–141. Leiden: Brill, 2013.

———, ed. *Of Tripod and Palate: Food, Politics and Religion in Traditional China*. Basingstoke, UK: Palgrave MacMillan, 2005.

Sukhu, Gopal. "Monkeys, Shamans, Emperors, and Poets: The *Chuci* and Images of Chu during the Han Dynasty." In *Defining Chu: Image and Reality in Ancient China*, edited by Constance E. Cook and John Major, 145–65. Honolulu: University of Hawai'i Press, 2004.

Sun, Anna. *Confucianism as a World Religion: Contested Histories and Contemporary Realities*. Princeton, NJ: Princeton University Press, 2014.

Sun, Yinrang 孫詒讓. *Mozi xian gu* 墨子閒詁. Beijing: Zhonghua shuju, 1986.

Swann, Nancy Lee. *Food and Money in Ancient China: The Earliest Economic History of China to A. D. 25, Hanshu 24, with Related Texts Han Shu 91 and Shih-Chih 12*. Princeton, NJ: Princeton University Press, 1950.

———. *Pan Chao, Foremost Woman Scholar of China, First Century A. D.* New York: Russell & Russell, 1968.

Swidler, Ann. *Talk of Love: How Culture Matters.* Chicago: University of Chicago Press, 2001.

Syme Ronald. "Livy and Augustus." *Harvard Studies in Classical Philology* 64 (1959): 27–87.

Takigawa, Kametaro 瀧川龜太郎. *Shiki kaichū kōshō* 史記會注考證. Tokyo: Tōhō bunka Gakuin, 1934. Reprinted as: *Shiji huizhu kaozheng* 史記會注考證. Taipei: Beiyue wenyi, 1998.

Talbert, Richard J. A. *The Senate of Imperial Rome.* Princeton, NJ: Princeton University Press, 1984.

Taylor, Charles. "Why We Need a Radical Redefinition of Secularism." In *The Power of Religion in the Public Sphere*, edited by Judith Butler, Jürgen Habermas, Charles Taylor, et al., 34–59. New York: Columbia University Press, 2011.

Taylor, Lily Ross. *The Divinity of the Roman Emperor.* Oxford, UK: Oxford University Press, 1931.

Taylor, Mark C. *Nots (Religion and Postmodernism).* Chicago: University of Chicago Press, 1993.

Taylor, Rodney L. *The Religious Dimensions of Confucianism.* Albany: SUNY Press, 1990.

Teiser, Stephen F. "The Spirits of Chinese Religions." In *Religions of China in Practice*, edited by Donald S. Lopez, 3–37. Princeton, NJ: Princeton University Press, 1996.

Tian, Changwu 田昌五. *Wang Chong—Gudai de zhandou weiwulunzhe* 王充一古代的戰鬥唯物論者. Beijing: Renmin, 1958.

Tian, Tian. "The Suburban Sacrifice Reforms and the Evolution of the Imperial Sacrifices." In *Chang'an 26 BC: An Augustan Age in China.* Seattle and London: Washington University Press, 2015, edited by Michael Nylan and Griet Vankeerberghen with the kind assistance of Michael Loewe, 263–91.

Tillich, Paul. *Dynamics of Faith.* New York: Harper & Row, 1957.

Tracy, David. *The Analogical Imagination: Christian Theology and the Culture of Pluralism.* New York: Crossroads, 1991.

Tseng, Lillian Lan-ying. *Picturing Heaven in Early China.* Cambridge, MA: Harvard University Press, 2011.

Twitchett, Denis, and Michael Loewe, eds. *The Cambridge History of China–Volume I, The Ch'in and the Han Empires, 221 B.C.–A.D. 220.* Cambridge, UK: Cambridge University Press, 1986).

Tylor, Edward Burnett. *Primitive Culture: Researches Into the Development of Mythology, Philosophy, Religion, Art, and Custom*, 2 vols. London: John Murray, 1871.

Ulrici, Hermann. *Charakteristik der antiken Historiographie.* Berlin, G. Reimer, 1833.

Van Ess, Hans. "The Meaning of Huang-Lao in *Shiji* and *Hanshu.*" *Études chinoises* 12, no. 2 (Fall 1993): 161–77.

———. "Some Preliminary Notes on the Authenticity of the Treatise on Music in *Shiji* 24." *Oriens Estremus* 45 (2005–2006): 48–67.

———. "Emperor Wu of the Han and the First August Emperor of the Qin in Sima Qian's *Shiji*." In *Birth of an Empire: The State of Qin Revisited*, edited by Yuri Pines et al., 239–57. Berkeley: University of California Press, 2014.

———. "Dissent against Emperor Wu of the Han." In *The Letter to Ren An*, Stephen Durrant, Wao-Yee Li, Michael Nylan, and Hans Van Ess, 51–53. Seattle and London: University of Washington Press, 2016.

Vattuone, Riccardo. "Timeo, Polibio e la storiografia greca d'occidente." In *The Shadow of Polybius: Intertextuality as a Research Tool in Greek Historiography*, edited by Guido Schepens and Jan Bollansée, 73–88. Leuven: Peeters, 2005.

von Falkenhausen, Lothar. *Chinese Society in the Age of Confucius (1000–250 BC): The Archaeological Evidence (Ideas, Debates and Perspectives)*. Los Angeles: The Cotsen Institute of Archaeology Press, 2006.

Von Glahn, Richard. *The Economic History of China: From Antiquity to the Nineteenth Century*. Cambridge, UK: Cambridge University Press, 2016.

———. *The Sinister Way: The Divine and the Demonic in Chinese Religious Culture*. Berkeley: University of California Press, 2004.

Wagner, Donald B. *The State and the Iron Industry in Han China*. Copenhagen: The Nordic Institute of Asian Studies, 2001.

Wailey, Arthur. *The Book of Songs/Shijing*. New York: Grove Press, 1996.

Walbank, Frank W. *Aratos of Sycion*. Cambridge, UK: Cambridge University Press, 1933.

———. *Historical Commentary on Polybius*. Oxford, UK: Clarendon Press, 1957.

———. *Polybius*. Berkeley: University of California Press, 1972.

———. *Polybius, Rome and the Hellenistic World: Essays and Reflections*. Cambridge, UK: Cambridge University Press, 2002.

Wang, Aihe. *Cosmology and Political Culture in Early China*. Cambridge, UK: Cambridge University Press, 2000.

Wang, Baizhong 王柏中. *Shenling shijie: zhixu de goujian yu yishi de xiangzheng* 神灵世界—秩序的构建与仪式的象征. Beijing: Minzu chubanshe, 2005.

Wang, Baoxuan 王葆玹. *Jin gu wenjingxue xinlun* 今古文经学新论. Beijing: Zhongguo Shehui Kexue chubanshe, 1997.

Wang, E 王鍔. "'Liji' chengshu kao" 禮記成書考. Beijing: Zhonghua, 2007.

Wang, Liqi 王利器, ed. *Yantie lun jiaozhu* 鹽鐵論校注. Beijing: Zhonghua Shuju, 2003.

Wang, Liqun 王立群. *Han Wudi: Wang Liqun du* Shiji 漢武帝：王立群讀"史記." Taipei: Lianjing, 2008.

Wang, Mingke 王明珂. *Huaxia bianyuan—lishi jiyi yu zuqun rentong* 華夏邊緣一歷史記憶與族群認同. Taipei: Yunchen Wenhua, 1997.

———. "*Shiji* wenben yu Huaxia tiguo qingjing" '史記' 文本與華夏提過情境. In *Yingxiong zuxian yu dixiong minzu—genji lishi de wenben yu qingjing* 英雄與弟兄民族—根基歷史的文本與情境. Idem, 75–86. Taipei: Yunchen Wenhua, 2006.

Wang, Robin R., ed. *Chinese Philosophy in an Era of Globalization*. Albany: SUNY Press, 2004.
Wang, Yutong 王毓彤. "Jingmen chutu yijian tongge" 荊門出土一件銅戈. *Wenwu* 1 (1963): 64.
Wang, Zhixin 王志心. *Zhongguo sixiangshi dagang* 中國思想史大綱. Taipei: Taipei Zhonghua shuju, 1977.
Watanabe, Yoshihiro. "Sacrifices to Heaven in the Han and the Theory of Six Heavens." *Acta Asiatica* 98 (2010): 43–75.
Watson, Alan. *International Law in Archaic Rome: War and Religion*. Baltimore, MD: John Hopkins University Press, 1993.
Watson, Burton, trans. *Records of the Grand Historian*, 3 vols. New York: University of Columbia Press, 1993.
Weber, Max. *The Religion of China: Confucianism and Taoism*. New York: Free Press, 1964 (first edition in German published in 1915).
Wedemeyer Christian K., and Wendy Doniger, eds. *Hermeneutics, Politics, and the History of Religions: The Contested Legacies of Joachim Wach and Mircea Eliade*. Oxford, UK: Oxford University Press, 2010.
Weinstock, Stefan. *Divus Julius*. Oxford, UK: Clarendon Press, 1971.
White, Hayden. *Metahistory: The Historical Imagination in Nineteenth-Century Europe*. Baltimore, MD: John Hopkins Press, 1975.
White, Michael L. *From Jesus to Christianity: How Four Generations of Visionaries & Storytellers Created the New Testament and Christian Faith*. San Francisco: HarperCollins, 2004.
Wilhelm, Hellmut. "The Bureau of Music of Western Han." In *Society and History: Essays in Honor of Karl August Wittfogel*, edited by Gary L. Ulmen, 123–35. The Hague: Mouton Publishers, 1978.
Wolf, Arthur P. "Gods, Ghosts, and Ancestors." In *Religion and Ritual in Chinese Society*, edited by idem, 131–82. Stanford, CA: Stanford University Press, 1974.
Woolf, Gregory. "Polis-Religion and its Alternatives in the Roman Provinces." In, *Roman Religion*, edited by C. Ando, 39–54. Edinburgh: Edinburgh University Press, 2003.
Wright, Arthur F. *Buddhism in Chinese History*. Stanford, CA: Stanford University Press, 1971.
Wu, Hung. "Buddhist Elements in Early Chinese Art (second and third centuries AD)." *Artibus Asiae* 47 (1986): 263–376.
———. *Monumentality in Early Chinese Art and Architecture*. Stanford, CA: Stanford University Press, 1995.
———. "A Response to Robert Bagley's Review of my Book *Monumentality in Early Chinese Art and Architecture* (Stanford University Press, 1995)." *Archives of Asian Art* 51 (1998–1999): 92–102.
———. *The Art of the Yellow Springs: Understanding Chinese Tombs*. Honolulu: Hawai'i University Press, 2010.

Xu, Fuguan 徐復觀, *Liang Han sixiang shi* 兩漢思想史, 3 vols. Taipei: Xuesheng shuju, 1980.

Yamada, Katsuyoshi 山田勝芳. "Zenkan Butei dai no saishi to zaisei—Hōzensho to Heijunsho" 前漢武帝代の祭祀と財政―封禪書と平準書. *Tohoku Daigaku Kyōyobu kyō* 37 (1982): 1–20.

———. *Shin Kan zaisei shûyû no kenkyû* 秦漢財政収入の研究. Tokyo: Kyûko shoin; 1993.

Yang Xiong, *The Canon of Supreme Mystery*, translated by M. Nylan. Albany: SUNY Press, 1995.

Yang, C. K. *Religion in Chinese Society: A Study of Contemporary Social Functions of Religion and Some of Their Historical Factors*. Berkeley: University of California Press, 1961.

Yang, Hongxun 楊鴻勳. "Mingtang de kaoguxue yanjiu" 明堂的考古學研究. *Tôhô Gakuhô* 70 (March 1998): 2–94.

Yang, Hua 楊華. "Qinhan diguo de shenquan tongyi: chutu jianbo yu 'Fengshan shu,' 'Jiaosi zhi,' de duibi kaocha" 秦漢帝國的神權統一：出土簡帛與封禪書的對比考察. *Lishi Yanjiu* 5 (2011): 4–26.

Yang, L., D. An, and J. Anderson Turner, *Handbook of Chinese Religions*. Santa Barbara, CA: ABC-CLIO, 2005.

Yang, Qun 揚群. "Cong kaogu faxian kan li he lizhi de qiyuan yu fazhan" 從考古發現看禮和禮制的起源與發展. *Kongzi yanju* 3 (1990): 3–11.

Yang, Xiong 揚雄. *Fa yan* 法言. Shanghai: Shangwu yinshuguan, 1939.

Yang, Xiong. *Exemplary Figures "Fayan* 法言*,"* translated by Michael Nylan. Seattle: University of Washington Press, 2013.

Yang, Yanqi 楊燕起, Chen Keqing 陳可青, and Lai Changchang 賴長揚, eds. *Lidai mingjia ping Shiji* 歷代名家評史記. Peking: Beijing shifan daxue, 1986.

Yao, Daye 姚大業. *Han Yuefu xiaolun* 漢樂府小論. Tianjin: Baihua Wenyi Chubanshe, 1984.

Yates, Robin D. S. *Five Lost Classics: Tao, Huang-Lao, and Yin-Yang in Han China*. New York: Ballantine Books, 1997.

Yawetz, Zwi. *Julius Caesar and his Public Image*. Ithaca, NY: Cornell University Press, 1983.

Yoshioka, Gen-Ichiro. *A Semantic Study of the Verbs of Doing and Making in the Indo-European Languages*. Tokyo: Tokyo Tsukiji Type Foundry, 1908.

Yu, Antony C. *State and Religion in China, Historical and Textual Perspectives*. Chicago: Open Court, 2005.

Yü, Ying-shih. "Life and Immortality in the Mind of Han China." *Harvard Journal of Asiatic Studies* 25 (1964–1965): 80–122.

Yuan, Ke 袁珂. *Zhongguo gudai shenhua* 中国古代神话. Beijing: Huaxia, 2006.

Zanker, Paul. *The Power of Images in the Age of Augustus*. Ann Arbor: University of Michigan Press, 1989.

Zecchini, Giuseppe. *Cesare e il mos maiorum*. Stuttgart: Franz Steiner Verlag, 2001.

Zeng, Xiantong 曾憲通. "'Zuo' zi tanyuan—jian tan 'lei' zi de liubian" 作字探源—兼談耒字的流變. *Guwenzi Yanjiu* 19 (1992): 408–21.

Zhan, Yinxin 詹鄞鑫. *Shenling yu jisi: Zhongguo chuantong zongjiao zonglun* 神靈與祭祀: 中國傳統宗教綜論. Nanking: Jiangsu guji chubanshe, 1992.

Zhang, Dake 張大可. *Shiji yanjiu* 史記研究. Lanzhou: Gansu renmin, 1985.

———. *Sima Qian pingchuan* 司馬遷評傳. Nanjing: Nanjing Daxue, 1994.

Zhao, Shanxuan 趙善軒. *Sima Qian de jingji shi yu jingji sixiang: Zhongguo de ziyoujingjizhuyizhe* 司馬遷的經濟史與經濟思想—中國的自由經濟主義者. Taipei: Wanjuan, 2017.

Zhao, Zhengqun 赵生群. *"Shiji" wenxianxue conggao* 史记文献学丛稿. Nanjing, Jiangsu guji chubanshe, 2000.

Zheng, Yuanlin 鄭圓鈴. *Shiji Huang-Lao sixiang yanjiu* 史記黃老思想研究. Taipei: Xuehai, 1998.

Zhou, Shirong 周世榮. "Mawangdui Han mu de 'Shenqi' tu bohua" 馬王堆漢墓的神祇圖帛畫. *Kaogu* 10 (1990): 925–28.

Zhou, Yiqun. *Festivals, Feasts, and Gender Relations in Ancient China and Greece*. Cambridge, UK: Cambridge University Press, 2010.

Ziolkoski, Adam. "Civic Rituals and Political Spaces in Republican and Imperial Rome." In *The Cambridge Companion to Ancient Rome*, edited by Paul Erdkamp, 380–409. Cambridge, UK: Cambridge University Press, 2013.

Zufferey, Nicolas. "Wang Chong et les 'ru' sous les Han: problèmes de terminologie et de méthode." *Etudes Asiatiques* 48 (1994): 1403–408.

———. *To the Origins of Confucianism: The 'Ru' in Pre-Qin Times and During the Early Han Dynasty*. Bern: Peter Lang, 2003.

Zürcher, Eric. *The Buddhist Conquest of China: The Spread and Adaptation of Buddhism in Early Medieval China*, 2 vols. Leiden: Brill, 1959.

———. "Buddhist Influence on Taoist Scripture." *T'oung Pao* 66, nos. 1–3 (1980): 84–147.

Index

Achaean League, 107–109, 256nn31–32
Aeneas, 144
Ai 哀, Duke of Lu 魯, 94
Alchemists. See *fangshi* 方士
Alchemy, 140, 151, 166, 177, 195, 271n49
Alexander the Great, 107, 263–64n111
Allan, Sarah, 72, 238n30, 239n140, 258–59n56, 276n115
Ames, Roger, 42, 219n13, 269–70n32, 282–83n46
ancestors, cult of, 54–56, 106, 138, 144–48, 156, 201, 206
An Qi 安期, 160
Ando, Clifford, 23–24, 219n10, 223nn3–4
Annals of Master Lü. See *Lüshi Chunqiu* 呂氏春秋
Antiochus III of Syria, 129, 264n120
Aristotle, 43, 269–70n32
Asad, Talal, 218n3
Astronomy: 5–6, 27, 64, 115, 155–57, 194, 196–97; "Book on" ("Tian guan shu" 天官書), 197–98
augures, 192–94
Augustus, Octavian, 19–20, 25, 137–40, 175, 185, 192–93, 201, 205–206; as an honorific title, 192–95, 206
Axial Age, 38–43

Baihu tong 白虎通 (*Comprehensive Discussions in the White Tiger Hall*), 198–89
"Balanced Standard" ("Book on the"). See "Ping zhun shu" 平準書
Ban, Gu 班固, 6, 66–67, 81–84, 184
Ban, Zhao 班昭, 116
bawang 霸王 (hegemon king), 20, 74, 85
Beidou 北斗 (Northern Dipper), 156, 196–97, 200, 204
Bell, Catherine, 53–54
Bellah, Robert, 33–34
bibingtu 避兵圖 (Repel-weapons chart), 197
Bilsky, Lester, 26
Birrell, Anne, 47, 49–50
Bo 亳, location, 195
Bo Yi 伯夷 (and Shu Qi 叔齊), 74, 94
Bodde, Derk, 25–26
Brashier, K. E., 26–27
Bright Hall. See Ming Tang 明堂
Bu, Shi 卜式, 214–15
Buddhism, 4, 13, 30–32, 40, 57, 102, 227n39
Bujard, Marianne, 8, 202
"bureaucratic metaphor," 175

Cai, Liang, 222n37
Campany, Robert Ford, 4, 30–31
Cantwell Smith, Wilfred, 29–30

Catholic Church. *See under* Christianity
Catholicism. *See under* Christianity
Champion, Craige, 109
Chang, K. C., 268n20
Chang'an, 21, 66, 81, 84, 104, 141, 181–82, 205, 211–12
Changes (Book of). See *Yijing* 易經
Changling 長陵, 211
Chao, Cuo 晁錯, 76, 180–88
Chen, She 陳涉, 120–23
Chenbao 陳寶 (Jewel of Chen, the), 286–87n2
Cheng 成, *see* Liu Ao, Emperor of the Western Han, 80, 83, 158, 202–204
Chi You 蚩尤, 50, 157–58
Chin, Tamara T., 8–9, 104, 185
Christianity: Catholic Church, 14, 24–25, 37–38, 136, 139; Christianity in late antiquity, 24–25, 373; Christianity and teleology, 3–5, 23–24, 34, 43, 61, 102–103, 110, 128, 136; Christianity and universalism, 40, 101–104, 136; Jesuits, 35–36, 38, 46; Protestantism, 47, 53, 44–46, 136; Reformation, 38, 44–46, 136
Chu 楚 (ancient Chinese state), 62, 66, 74, 94, 105–107, 120–21, 124, 132, 164, 181, 187
Chu, Shaosun 褚少孫, 242n8
Chunqiu 春秋 (*Spring and Autumn Annals*), 9, 62, 67, 80, 82, 93–95, 163–64, 201–202
Chunqiu fanlu 春秋繁露 (*Luxuriant Gems of the Spring and Autumn*), 9, 67–68, 72, 91, 115, 175
Classicists/ "Confucians." See *ru* 儒
Cold War, 1
commanderies and counties. See *junxian* 郡縣

comparative approaches: to Chinese religions, 2–15, 27–32, 41–48, 101–107, 133–34, 136–32, 139, 142–47, 157, 191, 201–202; to empire formation, 2–3, 31, 59–62, 109, 143; to religions, 33–36, 38–49, 44–45
Comprehensive Discussions in the White Tiger Hall. See *Baihu tong* 白虎通
Confucianism. See also under "*ru*": according to western observers, 5–6, 13, 27, 34–58, 213, 217n2; contemporary revival of, 36, 220–21n22; during the Han, 6, 8–12, 15–20, 26, 32, 67–72, 77, 81–84, 90–93, 106, 123, 140–43, 147, 189, 191, 199, 204, 213–14; "Han Confucianism," 9–11, 26, 67, 93, 95, 140, 243nn22–23
Confucius (Kongzi 孔子), 14, 23, 66–67, 72–78, 84–90, 93–95, 114–15, 149–50, 153, 160, 168, 170, 177–78, 201, 207, 214
Constantine, Roman emperor, 230–31n68, 70
correlative thinking, 39–40, 232n81
Croce, Benedetto, 96–97, 101
Csikszentmihalyi, Mike, 71, 269nn29–30
Cui, Zhu 崔杼, 88–89

"Dagao" 大誥 ("Great Announcement"), 110–11
dao 道 (the Way) 3, 56, 59, 82
Daoism, 4, 13, 16, 30–32, 114, 156, 212
Darwin, Charles, 45
de 德 (Virtue, virtues), 71, 80, 150, 164
delegatory kin-ordered settlement state (concept developed by Li Feng), 16

Demetrius of Phalerum, 129
deus ex machina, 130
Dewey, John, 39
Discourses on Salt and Iron. See *Yantielun* 鹽鐵論
"Discussion of the Faults of the Qin." See "Guo Qin lun" 過秦論
divinity: of Chinese emperors, 10, 24–25, 27, 46, 51–54, 60, 97–98, 106, 121, 144–47, 192, 207; divine cult of the Roman emperor, 136–40, 143–45; theoretical discussion on the notion of, 2–4, 10, 12–19, 24, 37, 130–33, 135–44, 175, 192
Divus Iulius, 144
dominate, 37
Documents (Book of / Classic of). See *Shujing* 書經
Dong, Zhongshu 董仲舒, 9–10, 67, 72, 80–82, 92–93, 112, 115, 146, 165, 193, 205
Doniger, Wendy, 52
Dou 竇, Empress, 153–54, 186, 270n36, 281n30
Dubuisson, Daniel, 33
Dubs, Homer H., 243n22
Dumézil, George, 44
Durkheim, Émile, 30, 34, 45, 48
Durrant, Stephen, 63

Eck, Diana L., 28
Eliade Mircea, 229n52, 233n95
empire. See *under* comparative approaches
Eno, Robert, 258n50, 259n56
ethnocentrism, 17, 35
Etiquette and Rites. See *Yili* 儀禮

fa 法, 152
fa 罰, 25
Fa yan 法言, 248–49n87

Fan, Ye 范曄, 104
fangshi 方士. See also under alchemy, 6–8, 19, 41, 67, 85, 98, 148, 152, 154, 156–57, 160–61, 166–71, 173–75, 195, 201–203
feng 封 and *shan* 禪: "Book on the," 70, 76, 78, 142, 147–54, 155, 157–60, 166, 168, 171, 200, 209, 214; sacrifices, 77, 105, 142, 147–54, 158–60, 167–71, 188, 190, 193, 194–96, 200
filial piety. See *xiao* 孝
First Emperor of Qin (Qin Shihuangdi 秦始皇帝), 66, 68–70, 113, 118, 120, 122–23, 140, 146–47, 152, 153, 169, 175, 183, 193, 206
Fitzgerald, Timothy, 29–30
Five Peaks (Wuyue 五嶽), 66, 153, 168
Five Phases. See Wuxing 五行
Five Qi. See Wu Qi 五氣
Five Relations. See Wu Lun 五倫
Five Sovereigns. See wudi 五帝
Fortuna. See Fortune
Fortune, Mediterranean deity (Fortuna in Latin, Tyche in Greek), 16–19, 101–103, 109, 127–33
Foucault, Michel, 30, 64
Fox Brindley, Erica, 251–52n125, 252n31
fu 賦 (rhapsody), 8, 185–90, 203–204
Fu, Su 扶蘇, 120
Fukui, Shigemasa 福井重雅, 222–23n37
Fung, Yu-lan, 39–40
Fuxi 伏羲 (also known as Taidi 泰帝), 82, 161

Ganquan 甘泉, 196, 204
"Ganquan fu" 甘泉賦 (Sweet Springs Palace Rhapsody), 203–204
gaozu 高祖 (one of the attributes of the Yellow Emperor), 156

Gaozu 高祖, Han emperor. *See* Liu Bang 劉邦
Geertz, Clifford, 30
globalization, 1
gong 公 (public), 178
Gongsun 公孫 (family name of the Yellow Emperor), 157
Gongsun, Hong 公孫弘, 154
Gongsun, Qing 公孫卿, 135, 166–69
Gongyang 公羊 philological tradition, 67, 90
Goossaert, Vincent, 10
Graham, Angus C., 39–40
Gramsci, Antonio, 97
Granet, Marcel, 48
"Great Announcement." *See* "Dagao" 大誥
Grand Beginning. *See Taichu* 太初
"Great Oath." *See* "Taishi" 泰誓
Gruen, Eric, 4
Gu, Jiegang 顧頡剛, 47–48
Guan Zhong 管仲, 74, 86–88, 151–53, 169, 214
Guanzi 管子, 56, 245n48, 49
gui 鬼 (ghosts). *See also shen* 神, 8–16, 22–23, 27, 32, 48, 51, 53, 55, 62, 65–66, 80, 97–98, 106, 119–20, 139, 142, 145–46, 150–51, 160, 163, 167, 171, 175–77, 195–96, 207, 210–11, 213
Gun 鯀, 111–12
guo 國, 62, 69, 93, 177, 179, 182–83, 199, 201
"Guo Qin lun" 過秦論 ("Discussion of the Faults of the Qin"), 68

Hall, David, 42
Han Feizi, 韓非子, 175
Han Wudi neizhuan 漢武帝內傳, 176, 279n9
Han, Xin 韓信, 124

Han Shu 漢書 (*History of the Former Han*), 6, 66–67, 72, 81, 201–202
Heaven (Chinese concepts of *Tian* 天), 5, 9–10, 15, 18–19, 22, 34, 59, 66–67, 81–84, 91–94, 98–99, 101–102, 106, 109–26, 133, 146, 149–50, 153, 157–58, 161–62, 167, 194–97, 203, 205, 215
Hegel, G. W. F. (and Hegelianism), 3, 40, 96–97
hegemon king. *See bawang* 霸王
"Hereditary House of Duke Tai of Qi." *See* "Qi Tai Gong Shijia" 齊太公世家
"Hereditary Houses of the Three Kings." *See* "San wang shijia" 三王世家
Herodotus, 49, 129
historicism, 96–97
History of the Former Han. See Han Shu 漢書
History of the Later Han. See Hou Han Shu 後漢書
Hong Fan 洪範 (Great Plan), 82, 93, 201
Hou Han Shu 後漢書, 104
Houji 后稷 (Lord Millet), 283
Houtu 后土, 21, 41, 81, 156, 160, 169, 194, 197, 201–204, 273n73
Hu, Shih 胡適, 47
Huainanzi 淮南子, Prince of Huainan 淮南. *See* Liu An 劉安
Huainanzi 淮南子, text, 7, 56, 59, 156, 175, 191, 194, 196
Huan 桓, Duke of Qi, 74, 87, 151–52
Huan Kuan 桓寬, 221–22n27
Huang, Sheng 黃生, 90
Huangdi 黃帝. *See* Yellow Emperor)
Huang-Lao 黃老, 8, 16, 31, 90, 114, 153, 155–56, 187, 210, 227n40, 250n107

Huangshigong 黃石公, 156, 282n46
Huhai 胡亥 (Second Emperor of Qin), 120
Hui 惠, Emperor of the Western Han, 116–17, 181
hujian fa 互見法 ("mutual illumination"), 64
Hundred Days Movement, 37, 47
Hung, Wu, 227n39, 274n93, 278n5
Huntington, Samuel P., 217n2
Huo, Guang 霍光, 285–86n83
Huo, Qubing 霍去病, 278n38

Iggers, Georg, 34
immortality, 8, 19–20, 24, 41, 49, 53, 135, 140, 142–48, 154, 156–61, 166–67, 170–71, 173, 175, 177, 195
inauguration, 192–93
Instructions for Women. See *Nüjie* 女誡
instrumentum regni, 20, 58, 103, 131–32
interpretatio romana, 25

Jaspers, Karl, 40–41
Jesuits. See under Christianity
Jia Yi 賈誼, 68, 75, 121–22
Jiao 郊 (Suburban) sacrifice, 203–204
"*Jiaosi zhi*" 郊祀志, 200–204
Jibei 濟北, King of, 168–69
Jie 桀, 114, 164
Jin 晉 (ancient state of China), 88
Jing 景, Emperor of the Western Han, 75–76, 90, 177, 180–83, 187, 210
Jing 景, Duke of Qi, 85
Jing 荊, Mount, 167–68
Jiu ding 九鼎. See Nine Tripods
Jizi 箕子 (or Master Ji), 82, 111
Johnson, David, 220–21n15, 237n121
Julius Caesar, 137, 143, 192

Jung, Carl G., 234n102
junxian 郡縣 (commanderies and counties), 12, 68–69, 168, 197–98, 201, 203

Kang, Youwei 康有為, 47
Kern, Martin, 92, 185
Kertzer, David, 54
Kim, Esther, 64
Knechtges, David, 280n22
Kongjia 孔甲, 150
Kongzi 孔子. See Confucius
Koselleck, Reinhart, 3
Kuang, Heng 匡衡, 80–81, 202–204
Kuhn, Adalbert, 44

LeBlanc, Charles, 271n18
Legge, James, 47
Lévi-Strauss, Claude, 45
Lewis, Mark Edward, 50–52, 95, 253n141
li 禮, 18, 46, 53–58, 65, 68, 70–81, 83, 89, 95, 106–107, 115, 148–49, 152, 170, 176, 203
li 禮, "Book on." See "*Li shu*" 禮書
Li Sheng 酈生 (Master Li), 126
Li, Feng, 16
Li, Ling 李零 (contemporary Chinese scholar), 196–97
Li, Ling 李陵 (Chinese general under the Han dynasty), 105
Li, Shaojun 李少君, 159–60
"*Li shu*" 禮書, 70
Li, Si 李斯, 69, 120
Liji 禮記 (*Records of Rites*), 53–56, 83
lin 麟, 93, 160, 168–69
Lincoln, Bruce, 45
lingqi 靈旗 (Numinous Flag), 196, 205
Liu, An 劉安 (Prince of Huainan 淮南), 156, 194
Liu, Ao 劉驁. See Cheng 成, Emperor

Liu, Bang 劉邦 (Emperor Gaozu 高祖, founder of the Western Han), 12, 52, 69, 75, 89–90, 92, 105, 107, 115–26, 132, 148, 167, 178–80, 211

Liu, Bingyi 劉病已 (Emperor Xuan 宣 of the Western Han), 80, 201–202

Liu, Che 劉徹. *See* Wu, Emperor Wu of the Western Han

Liu, Fuling 劉弗陵 (Emperor Zhao 昭 of the Western Han), 79

Liu Heng 劉恆 (Emperor Wen 文 of the Western Han), 75–76, 166, 181–86, 193

Liu, Hong 劉閎 (son of Emperor Wu), 197

Liu, Pi 劉濞, King of Wu 吳, 180–83

Liu Qi 劉啓 (Emperor Jing 景 of the Western Han), 75–76, 90, 177, 180–83, 187, 210

Liu, Shi 劉奭 (Emperor Yuan 元 of the Western Han), 80, 202

Liu, Ying 劉盈 (Emperor Hui 惠 of the Western Han), 116, 117, 181

Liu, Wu 劉武, King of Liang 梁, 186–87

Liu, Xiang 劉向, 59, 203

Liu, Zhong 劉仲, younger brother of Liu Bang 劉邦, 180

Livy, 18, 103, 131–32, 144, 192

Loewe, Michael, 6–7, 80, 140–41

Lord Millet. *See* Houji 后稷

Lu 魯, ancient Chinese State, 93–94, 179

Lu, Jia 陸賈, 123–24, 126

Lü 呂 (Empress), 115–19, 181

Lü, Bushu 呂步舒, 92–93

Lü, Buwei 呂不韋, 113

Lü, Yuan, 117

Lucius Tarquinius Superbus, 127–28

Lun Heng 論衡 (*Disquisitions*), 83, 163

Luo 雒, River, 82, 93

Lüshi Chunqiu 呂氏春秋 (*Annals of Master Lü*), 113

Luxuriant Gems of the Spring and Autum. *See Chunqiu fanlu* 春秋繁露

Machiavelli, Niccolò, 103, 131

Major, John, 67, 72

Malinowski, Bronisław, 49

Mandate of Heaven. *See tianming* 天命

Mark Antony, 193

Marx, Karl, 3, 14, 35–36, 40, 46, 97

Masuzawa, Tomoko, 33

Mathieu, Rémi, 49–50

Mauss, Marcel, 48

Max Müller, Friedrich, 47

Meiji Japan, 10, 37

miaochan xingxue 廟產興學, 37

Ming Tang 明堂 (Bright Hall), 210

Miuji 繆忌, 195–97

mixin 迷信, 37

Modernists (historical category introduced by Michael Loewe), 7–8, 11, 69–70, 81, 141

Momigliano, Arnaldo, 129

monopolies (on salt and iron), 7, 11, 20, 69–70, 79, 141, 163

monotheism, hegemony of, 1–5, 13, 18, 23–27, 29, 35, 37, 43, 51, 60, 102–103, 110, 146, 176, 194

mos maiorum, 20, 137

Mozi 墨子, 32

Mozi 墨子 (the text), 86

Munda, battle of, 144

Music (Book on). *See* "Yue shu" 樂書

Music, Bureau (*Yuefu* 樂府), 280n22

"mutual illumination." *See hujian fa* 互見法

myth (theoretical discussions on), 7–8, 12, 16–17, 20–21, 43–52

Nanyue 南越, 171, 196
nianhao 年號, 78, 193
Nicaea (Council of, Nicaean Christianity), 61, 231n70
Northern Dipper. See Beidou 北斗
Northrop, Douglas, 3
Nüjie 女誡, 77
Nylan, Michael, 63

Octavian Augustus, 20, 25, 137–40, 192–93, 201, 206, 212
Odes (Book of Odes/Book of Songs). See Shijing 詩經
Opium Wars, 10
orthodoxy, 37, 41, 43, 61, 142
orthopraxy, 23, 61
Other (otherness), 3–4, 27, 33, 52, 57, 95, 104–106, 129

Paden, William E., 29
Palmer, David, 10
patria potestas, 27
pax deorum, 58
Pédech, Paul, 257n42
Penglai 蓬萊 (islands), 160, 166
Perseus of Macedon, 107, 129
Philip V of Macedon, 129
Philopoemen, 108
pietas, 27
Pines, Yuri, 54
"Ping zhun shu" 平準書 ("Book on the Balanced Standard"), 162, 163, 270n36
Pingyuan 平原, Princess of, 211
Plato, 43–44
Plutarch, 128
Polybius, 18–19, 103, 107–109, 127–33
polytheism, 2, 24, 43
Poo, Mu-chou, 13, 38
postcolonialism, 2, 27, 29, 45, 51
postmodernism, 2, 27–29, 34, 45, 51
pragmatism (philosophical current), 39

primus inter pares, 138
Princeps, 191
Principate, 21, 185
Protestantism. See under Christianity
Ptolemy V of Egypt, 129
Puett, Michael, 18, 54–56, 63, 145–46, 219n9
Pydna, battle of, 107, 129

qi 氣, 3, 13, 55, 118, 157, 166
Qi 齊 (ancient Chinese state), 6, 9, 20, 74, 85–88, 90, 142, 151–52, 156, 160, 166–69, 186–87, 197–98, 214
"Qi Tai Gong Shijia" 齊太公世家 ("The Hereditary House of Duke Tai of Qi"), 88
Qiao 橋 Mount, 158
Qin 秦 (ancient Chinese state and dynasty), 2, 5, 9, 11–12, 22, 49–50, 56, 60–63, 66–72, 75–76, 79–80, 82–83, 90, 102, 105, 112–13, 115, 118–25, 132, 136–37, 139–40, 142, 152–53, 159–60, 169, 174–75, 178, 182, 193, 195, 203, 206, 211, 213
Qin Shihuangdi 秦始皇帝. See First Emperor of Qin
Qing 清 Dynasty, 10–11, 25, 36–37, 78
Queen Mother of the West. See Xi Wang Mu 西王母
Queen, Sarah, 67

Raglan, F. R. R. S., Lord, 49
Rank, Otto, 49
Rappaport, Roy, 34
Records of Rites. See Liji 禮記
Red Emperor (Chidi 赤帝), 122
Reformation. See under Christianity
Reformists (historical category introduced by Michael Loewe), 7–8, 81, 141

religio, 24, 137
religion: Abrahamic religions (influence on Chinese studies), 5, 13, 17–19, 23–58 (passim), 60, 101–104, 143, 146, 176, 212; comparative approaches to, 12–16, 27–43, 47–52; early Chinese religion, 3, 27, 32, 142, 209–10
Ren An 任安, letter to, 63–64
Repel-Weapons Chart. See *bibingtu* 避兵圖
Rhapsody. See *fu* 賦
"Rhapsody of Sir Vacuous." See "Zixu fu" 子虛賦
Rites of Zhou. See *Zhouli* 周禮
ritual: in early China, 52–57, 65–84; in the Qin/Han period, 149–54, 158, 160–71, 185–215; theoretical discussions on, 4–5, 12–18, 25–27, 43–46, 49–58, 65–70, 173–78, 205–207
Rives, James, 24
Roetz, Heiner, 41
Romulus, 137, 144, 192
Ru 儒 (Classicists/"Confucians"). *See also under* Confucianism, 6–18, 21, 41, 52, 54, 65, 67–68, 74, 76–93, 116, 139–40, 143, 147–48, 153–54, 160, 165, 168–69, 171, 174, 176–78, 185, 190–91, 194, 201–203, 210–13

sacer, 13, 53
salt and iron (and alcohol) monopolies of, 11, 20, 69, 141, 163, 181
"San wang shijia" 三王世家 ("The Hereditary Houses of the Three Kings"), 197
Sang, Hongyang 桑弘羊, 7, 80, 140–41, 215
sanjiao 三教 (Three Traditions), 13–14

Second Emperor of Qin. *See* Huhai 胡亥
Schaberg, David, 258n50
Scheidel Walter, 218n5
Scipio, Cornelius Aemilianus, 108
Secret History of Emperor Wu of the Han. *See Han Wudi neijzhuan* 漢武帝內傳
secularism, 1–6, 18–19, 26, 32, 35–36, 38–39, 45–46, 54, 70, 106, 114, 176, 217–18n3
Seligman, Adam, 57
Servius Tullius, 127–28
Seven Kingdoms, revolt of, 76, 132, 177, 180–81, 186
shan 禪 (sacrifice), 142, 147–54, 158, 160, 167–71, 188, 190, 193–94
Shang 商 Dynasty, 36, 66, 74, 82, 94–95, 105, 111–12, 124–25, 144, 150, 159, 161, 164, 178
Shang, Yang 商鞅 (Lord od Shang), 69, 182
Shanglin 上林 Park, 211, 276n109
"Shanglin *fu*" 上林賦 ("Rhapsody of the Shanglin Park"), 187–88
Shangshu 尚書 (*Shijing/Book of Documents/Documents*), 110–12, 123, 150, 153, 169, 182–83, 189
Shao Dian 少典, 157
Sharf, Robert, 227n39
She 社, Altar, 197–98
shen 神, 13, 55, 65, 84–83, 106, 144–46, 160–61, 163, 165–67, 196–97, 207, 219n9
shence 神策, 167
shengren 聖人, 81–82, 144–45
Shenjun 神君, 211–12
Shennong 神農, 157–58, 273n79
shenquan 神權, 37
shenquan tongyi 神權統一, 60
Shijing 詩經 (*Odes/Book of Poems*), 89, 123, 153, 160, 161, 166, 169

Shima, Kunio 島邦男, 258–59n56
Shimonoseki (treaty of), 37
"Shou ci tu" 受此土, 198–99
Shou 首, Mount, 167
Shu 蜀, Ancient Chinese State, 186, 190
Shu Qi 叔齊. See Bo Yi 伯夷 (and Shu Qi 叔齊)
Shujing 書經. See *Shangshu* 尚書
Shun 舜, 113, 151, 155, 158, 214
Shusun, Tong 叔孫通, 75–76, 89–90
Si 泗, River, 159
si 祀, 18, 61, 65, 83, 148, 176, 201
si 私, 178
Sima, Qian 司馬遷, 5–8, 19–20, 32, 51–52, 63–66, 74–78, 85–109, 114–15, 119–26, 131, 140, 143, 146–47, 149–55, 160, 163, 166, 168–71, 177–78, 181, 183, 186–87, 195, 211–15
Sima, Tan 司馬譚, 6, 66, 82, 105
Sima, Xiangru 司馬相如, 185–87, 190, 204, 209
Smith, Jonathan Z., 28, 32, 53, 205–206
space (ritual/sacred space), 16, 20, 52, 57, 176–78, 193, 197, 204–207
Spring and Autumn Annals. See *Chunqiu* 春秋
structuralism, 17, 48–51
Suburban sacrifice. See Jiao 郊
"Suburban Sacrifices," "Treatise of." See "Jiaosi zhi" 郊祀志
Suran 肅然, Mount, 169–70
"Sweet Springs Palace Rhapsody." See "Ganquan fu" 甘泉賦
Swidler, Ann, 30–31

Tacitus, 18
Tai Wu 太戊, 150
Tai 泰, Mount, 61, 77, 149, 153, 168–70
Taichu 太初 (Grand Beginning), 77, 78, 155, 171, 193

Taidi 泰帝. See Fuxi 伏羲
Taiping Rebellion, 10
"Taishi" 泰誓 ("Great Oath"), 112, 259n64
Taiyi 太一, 21, 41, 81, 169–70, 187, 194–97, 200–205, 211
Taiyi feng 太一鋒 (Taiyi spear), 196
Tanaquil, Queen, 127–28
Tarquinius Priscus, 127–28
templum, 52, 192–93, 205–207
Thapsus, battle of, 144
Theodosius I, 37
Three Religions (or traditions). See *sanjiao* 三教
Thucydides, 129
Thyche. See Fortune
Tian 天. See Heaven
Tian 田 (aristocratic house from Qi), 156
"Tianguan shu" 天官書 ("Book on Astronomy"), 197–97
tianming 天命 (Mandate of Heaven), 9, 67, 90–91, 109–11, 115, 117, 119, 149, 150–51, 164, 193, 242n8, 246n58, 258n50
tripods (*ding* 鼎), 158, 159–69, 202

universalism, 18, 40–41, 101–109, 136

Venus Genitrix, 144
von Glahn, Richard, 7

Walbank, Frank W., 107, 130
Wang, Chong 王充, 83, 163, 165–66
Wang, Edward, 34
Wang 王, Empress, 154, 203
Wang, Mang 王莽
Wang, Zang 王臧, 153–54
Wangruo 宛若, 211
Weber, Max, 35
Wei 魏, ancient Chinese state, 160, 79
Wei 威, King of Qi 齊, 156

weiyan 微言, 64
Weller, Robert, 57
Wen 文, Duke of Qi 齊, 156
Wen 文, Emperor of the Western Han, 75–76, 166, 181–86, 193
Wen, King of Zhou, 82
Western Zhou Dynasty. *See* Zhou 周 Dynasty
White Emperor (Baidi 白帝), 122
world history, 140
Wu 武, Emperor of the Western Han, 1–22 (passim), 26, 41, 50, 57–58, 60–62, 66–68, 70, 72, 74, 77–82, 86, 91–92, 105, 115, 122, 135, 137–43, 147–71, 173, 175–77, 184–87, 190–91, 193–207, 209–15
Wu, Guang 吳廣, 120–21
Wu, King of Zhou, 82
wudi 五帝 (Five Sovereigns), 66, 154, 168, 195–96, 205, 211, 260–61n73, 283n47
Wu Yi 武乙, 150
Wuyue 五嶽. *See* Five Peaks

Xi Wang Mu 西王母 (Queen Mother of the West), 212
Xia 夏 Dynasty, 66, 82, 104–106, 111–12, 125, 144, 150, 159, 161, 162, 164
Xiang Yan 項燕, 120
Xiang, Yu 項羽, 120, 123, 125–26
Xianyang 咸陽, 66
xiao 孝 (filial piety), 90–91, 106, 115, 121, 123, 144, 147–48, 151, 155, 178, 182, 198–99, 201
Xiao, He 蕭何, 118, 124
ximin 細民, 86
xing 刑, 71
Xinyuan, Ping 新垣平, 166
Xiongnu 匈奴, 106, 120, 158, 162, 180, 214

Xu, Fuguan 徐復觀, 42, 96
Xuan 宣, Emperor of the Western Han, 80, 201–202
Xuan Yuan 軒轅, 157
xunshou 巡狩, 158, 170, 194, 197, 201, 205
Xunzi 荀子, 70–72

Yan 燕 (ancient Chinese state), 156, 160
Yan, Hui 顏回, 93
Yan, Ying 晏嬰, 85–88, 90, 214
Yandi 炎帝, 157, 273n79
yang 陽. *See* yin and yang
Yang, Hua 楊華, 60–61, 224n10
Yang, Xiong 揚雄, 203–204
Yantielun 鹽鐵論 (*Discourses on Salt and Iron*), 7, 71, 79–81, 141, 214
Yanzi Chunqiu 晏子春秋, 86
Yao 堯, 114, 151, 155, 158, 214
Yates, Robert, 222n34
Yellow Emperor (Huangdi 黃帝), 50, 106, 135, 142–43, 147, 150–51, 154–68
yi 義, 56, 71, 80, 106, 189
yi 儀, 71
Yijing 易經 (*The Book of Changes*), 82, 189
Yili 儀禮 (*Etiquette and Rites*), 53
yin 陰 and yang 陽, 3, 9, 32, 39, 67, 72, 80, 82, 90–91, 114, 115–19, 151, 156, 159, 194, 196–97, 203
Ying, Zheng 贏政. *See* First Emperor of Qin
Yu the Great (Da Yu 大禹), 19–20, 48, 82, 111–13, 159, 161–65
Yuan, Ang 袁盎, 180–85, 188, 281n30
Yuan 元, Emperor of the Western Han, 80, 202
Yuan, Gu 轅固, 90
"Yueshu" 樂書 ("Book on Music"), 95–96

zao 竈 (the crucible), 160
Zhang, Chang 張敞, 201–202, 285n83
Zhang, Liang 張良, 124
Zhang, Tan 張譚, 202–203
Zhao, Gao 趙高, 120
Zhao 昭, Emperor of the Western Han, 79
Zhao, Wan 趙綰, 153–54
zhiguai 志怪, 14
Zhou 周 Dynasty, 8, 14, 16, 20, 21, 36, 42, 46, 53, 56, 64–66, 68, 73, 75, 77–78, 80, 82–87, 90, 94–95, 105, 110–12, 125, 132, 139, 144, 148, 151, 155, 159, 161, 164–66, 174, 178–79, 186, 191, 193, 197–98, 202, 207, 209–10, 214
Zhou 紂, Shang king, 111
Zhouli 周禮 (*Rites of Zhou*), 53
Zhoulu 涿鹿, Mount, 158
Zhu, Xi 朱熹, 57
Zhuan Xu 顓頊, 106
Zhuang 莊, Duke of Qi 齊, 87–88
Zhuangzi 莊子 (the thinker and the text *Zhuangzi*) 3, 56, 96
Zhufu, Yan 主父偃, 92–93, 250n112
"Zixu fu" 子虛賦 ("Rhapsody of Sir Vacuous"), 187
Zongjiao 宗教, 37, 60–61, 225n16
Zou, Yan 鄒衍, 156, 186, 273n70, 281n29

www.ingramcontent.com/pod-product-compliance
Lightning Source LLC
Chambersburg PA
CBHW030008240426
43672CB00007B/873